Industrial Labor on the Margins of Capitalism

Max Planck Studies in Anthropology and Economy
Series editors:
Stephen Gudeman, University of Minnesota
Chris Hann, Max Planck Institute for Social Anthropology

Definitions of economy and society, and their proper relationship to each other, have been the perennial concerns of social philosophers. In the early decades of the twenty-first century these became and remain matters of urgent political debate. At the forefront of this series are the approaches to these connections by anthropologists, whose explorations of the local ideas and institutions underpinning social and economic relations illuminate large fields ignored in other disciplines.

Industrial Labor on the Margins of Capitalism

Precarity, Class, and the
Neoliberal Subject

Edited by

CHRIS HANN AND JONATHAN PARRY

berghahn
NEW YORK • OXFORD
www.berghahnbooks.com

First published in 2018 by
Berghahn Books
www.berghahnbooks.com

© 2018, 2022 Chris Hann and Jonathan Parry
First paperback edition published in 2022

Library of Congress Cataloging-in-Publication Data
A C.I.P. cataloging record is available from the Library of Congress

British Library Cataloguing in Publication Data
A catalogue record for this book is available from the British Library

ISBN 978-1-78533-678-2 hardback
ISBN 978-1-80073-199-8 paperback
ISBN 978-1-78533-679-9 ebook

Contents

◆ Illustrations

Figures

Tables

▼ Preface

CHRIS HANN

Industrial methods of production have transformed the planet in the last two centuries and continue to do so. But is the social theory produced in those world regions where the transformations began sufficient to grasp the global industrialization of the twenty-first century? The concept of class, as exemplified by the urban proletariat, has always been contested. Is the Marxist definition still analytically helpful? If not, can the concept be constructively reformulated? Does the concept of *precariat* (Standing 2011) usefully supplement Marx's proletariat? Does it denote a separate social class? Can class express a powerful subjective identity? If not, what other factors shape the collective identities and personhood of industrial workers? These are just a few of the questions explored in this book.

The "second world" of socialism was a monumental effort to organize industrial society along lines radically different from those of the prototype in the capitalist West. The realities seldom lived up to the ideals of Marxist-Leninist-Maoist ideology. From Lenin's enthusiastic espousal of Taylorist managerial philosophy to more subtle patterns of mutual influence during the decades of the Cold War, East converged with West in certain respects (Bockman 2011). But factory organization and incentive structures for both managers and workers continued to diverge from capitalist prototypes in significant ways. In Eastern Europe, for example, a high proportion of factory workers commuted throughout their working lives from villages, where they continued to cultivate small plots. Thus they participated simultaneously in agricultural and industrial divisions of labor. This was less common in the Soviet Union and East Germany, but here too evidence shows that no matter how alienating the factory work process, industrial relations and workers' social life outside the factory differed significantly from what sociologists documented for the West. It is unsurprising that researchers have recently identified a sense of loss and even nostalgia about the era in which jobs were secure and membership in a socialist brigade brought emotional satisfaction that is hard to find today (Müller 2007).

By the end of the twentieth century this experiment was at an end—even in a few large states in East Asia that still claimed to be socialist. Instead of comparing the second world to the first, social scientists realized that many postsocialist states had much in common with the states of the

"Global South" (a label that is beginning to look as inadequate as the earlier notion of a "third world"). Now, in the era of neoliberalism, some observers argue that the logic of capitalist class struggle results in global processes of dispossession and the polarization of societies (Harvey 2005). Others, however, detect more positive trends: for the first time since the original industrial revolution, massive regional shifts and the rise of new "middle classes" may be contributing to a reduction in global social inequality (Milanovic 2015). The statistical calculations supporting these analyses are controversial; scholarly positions tend to correlate with political and ideological standpoints, most notably concerning "the market".

In order to move beyond ideologies and develop better theories of where human society is headed, it is necessary to have empirical data. This volume presents the results of field research, primarily ethnography. No other method gives comparable insight into lifeworlds—in this case, the worlds of industrial workers at their workplaces, but also in their domestic settings (which occasionally coincide with the locus of production), and with careful attention to their age and gender, to rural backgrounds and migration histories, to ethnicity and caste, and so forth. When persons whose incomes and degrees of job security vary greatly are found to be living alongside each other, and even within the same household, their patterns of interaction have implications that are unlikely to emerge from published statistics or from formal interviews with individual employees.

Industrial work remains relatively unfamiliar territory for social anthropologists. In the years 2012–2015 it was my privilege at the Max Planck Institute for Social Anthropology to share the leadership of a postdoctoral research group with Catherine Alexander and Jonathan Parry. In recruiting the team for the project "Industry and Inequality in Eurasia," we chose to expand the postsocialist framework elaborated by previous groups of this kind at the institute. The members of the core group, who all carried out fresh field research during their fellowships, were Michael Hoffmann, Eeva Kesküla, Dimitra Kofti, Dina Makram-Ebeid, Andrew Sanchez and Tommaso Trevisani. During the three years of the project, I-Chieh Fang and Christian Strümpell collaborated closely with us as associates. Jonathan Parry visited most researchers at their field sites. Our enquiries were enhanced by several internal workshops. We thank James Carrier, Geert De Neve, Don Kalb, and Massimiliano Mollona for augmenting the critical feedback to individual presenters at these sessions, which helped greatly in the clarification of collective goals.

All members of the core group contributed to the organization of a final meeting in May 2015, "Regular and Precarious Forms of Labour in Modern Industrial Settings," which expanded the geographical frame to include several regions outside Eurasia. Thanks are due to Michael Burawoy not only for his stimulating keynote but for participating throughout and delivering a comprehensive digest at the end of the meeting. Preliminary versions of the chapters of this volume were presented at this workshop, where they benefited from the comments of a distinguished crew of discussants: Sarah Ashwin, Jan Breman, James Carrier, Don Kalb, Sharryn Kasmir, Jens Lerche, Massimiliano Mollona, Frances Pine and Gavin Smith.

Final editorial responsibilities were shared between myself and Jonathan Parry. Johnny's Introduction reviews the case studies presented in the chapters that follow and places them in the broader empirical and theoretical context of other writings on labor in our globalized world. We both extend our warm thanks to Anke Meyer for all her assistance in preparing the manuscript.

Chris Hann is a Founding Director of the Max Planck Institute for Social Anthropology in Halle. He has published extensively on Eastern Europe, especially Hungary and Poland, both before and after the collapse of socialism. He is co-author of *Economic Anthropology: History, Ethnography, Critique* (with Keith Hart, 2011), and co-editor of *Economy and Ritual: Studies of Postsocialist Transformations* and *Oikos and Market: Explorations in Self-Sufficiency after Socialism* (both with Stephen Gudeman, 2015).

References

Bockman, Johanna. 2011. *Markets in the Name of Socialism: The Left-Wing Origins of Neoliberalism*. Stanford, CA: Stanford University Press.

Harvey, David. 2005. *A Short History of Neoliberalism*. Oxford: Oxford University Press.

Milanovic, Branko. 2015. *Global Inequality: A New Approach for the Age of Globalization*. Cambridge, MA: Harvard University Press.

Müller, Birgit. 2007. *Disenchantment With Market Economics: East Germans and Western Capitalism*. New York: Berghahn Books.

Standing, Guy. 2011. *The Precariat: The New Dangerous Class*. London: Bloomsbury.

Introduction

Precarity, Class, and the Neoliberal Subject

Jonathan Parry

Industrial Labor on the Margins of Capitalism: the title of our volume requires explanation. It is not our intention to imply that the multinational mega-corporations that employ some of the workforces it describes are peripheral. By "margins," we aim to conjure settings geographically removed from the *historical* epicenter of industrial capitalism. Rather than Western Europe and North America, our case studies come from Eastern Europe, Africa, Asia, and the Caribbean. Five are from the postsocialist world; that is, they deal with contexts where the whole basis of the social order has profoundly changed within the last generation.

Many of the chapters deal with workforces that are divided between a core of regular company workers and a penumbra of insecure casual and temporary labor. With globalization and economic liberalization, the relative size of these two kinds of workforce has in most cases changed significantly, as have the relationships between them. The first section of this Introduction discusses this division in general terms. The second asks if the two types of workers should be seen as belonging to separate social classes. The final section addresses the issue of personhood. The neoliberal order, we are often told, instills a new kind of subjectivity, an idea of the entrepreneurial individual engaged in a constant process of self-fashioning. What does our ethnography tell us about the success of that project?

The Decline of the Regular Worker?

In *The Great Transformation*, his most powerful and passionate work, Karl Polanyi (1957 [1944]) told the story of an institutional revolution that occurred in England in the first half of the nineteenth century and eventually transformed the world economy. Its most profound consequence was that the "factors of production"—land (which is to say, nature), labor (the human person), and money—became commodities ("fictitious" commodities, Polanyi insisted) that could be freely transacted on the market and were regulated by it. Formerly restricted in its scope, the market principle now dominated both the natural environment and human society for the first time in history. Otherwise stated, this institutional revolution was a precondition for the emergence of an integrated, full-fledged market system based on laissez-faire doctrines that presupposed as complete a separation as possible between the economic and political spheres. The invisible hand of the market can result in the greatest good of the greatest number only if the market is liberated from the meddlesome interference of the state and allowed to develop as an autonomous domain, supposedly governed by its own distinctive rules and principles, and free from the requirements of ordinary morality (Dumont 1977). As Adam Smith famously taught: "It is not from the benevolence of the butcher, the brewer, or the baker that we expect our dinner, but from their regard to their own self-interest" (quoted in ibid.: 63). As Polanyi saw clearly, however, the state had never in reality renounced its role in the direction of the economy. It was midwife and nursemaid to the "free market." "Laissez-faire was planned. Planning was not." There was "nothing natural about laissez-faire ... [it] was enforced by the state" (Polanyi 1957: 144). What was in fact largely spontaneous was the collectivist reaction against it—the inevitable result of the suffering caused by commodification. To mitigate its human costs, society was forced to bring the economy back under social control by 're-embedding' it in its social matrix.

This counter-movement involved (albeit limited) steps to de-commodify labor and provide it with some protection against the vagaries of the market. Under pressure from organized labor and its political allies, the state established a social safety net and legislated on the terms of the employment contract. By the mid-twentieth century, what became known as the "standard employment relationship/contract" was the norm in the wealthier capitalist countries of the West. It was premised on stable, full-time jobs. Maximum working hours were regulated; workers were paid not only for days worked but also for periods of recuperation, and were somewhat shielded from arbitrary dismissal. That enabled them to organize in support of their demands.

What Polanyi did not foresee was that the market would not remain caged, that there would be a reaction against the reaction to it that would include concerted attempts to remove what were now billed as "rigidities in the labor market" and dismantle the social safety net. He did not predict that the more frictionless flow of capital across national boundaries, buttressed by neoliberal policies and dogma, would move things back toward the re-commodification of labor. Even where once it was dominant, the standard employment relationship is, according to some (e.g., Castells 1996), a form that is now superseded.

That may be an exaggeration. According to European Commission statistics, in 2003, permanent full-time jobs were still "the predominant employment relationship" (Bosch 2006: 47), though the issue is complicated by problems of comparability. What that relationship means in different parts of the European Union is variable. In terms of working hours and pay, the gap between full and part-time workers is wider in the United Kingdom than elsewhere, though in terms of statutory protection against dismissal it is narrower. Those in full-time employment may be no more secure because Britain, like the United States, has done more to deregulate labor conditions and gone further in weakening the influence of unions (ibid.: 48–50). Throughout most of Europe over the past three decades, however, a growing proportion of the workforce has been hired on a casual or part-time basis. This is correlated with growth in female employment and of the service economy, and the trend has been toward an erosion of the standard employment relationship in terms of both the proportion of workers it covers and the protections it affords. Moreover, greater precarity affects a broader range of positions on the hierarchy of labor. While vulnerability to unemployment was once seen as the hallmark of the proletarian condition (e.g., Lockwood 1958: 55), today managers and white-collar workers are often equally exposed.

Setting aside the "second world" of Marxist-Leninist-Maoist socialism, the "standard employment contract" was only ever of major significance in the most affluent Western countries and possibly Japan, and only at a specific historical juncture. As Breman (2013) has emphasized, it was never standard for most workers in most parts of the world. In India, for example, it is almost exclusively organized/formal–sector workers (never more than about 8 percent of the total workforce, the majority of them employees of the state) who have been the (at least theoretical) beneficiaries of most of the labor legislation that guarantees enforceable minimum wages, regulates hours and conditions of work, requires employers to heed health and safety rules, gives workers the right to join unions, and provides them with a considerable measure of job security. Unorganized/informal–sector labor, the overwhelming majority of the manual workforce, is (in practice) unprotected. Further, Fernandes (2000) has shown how a large segment of the "new middle class" who work in Mumbai offices now experiences employment conditions that differ little from those of contract workers in industry: jobs are insecure and allow them little autonomy, they are subject to strict surveillance and subject to periodic layoffs, and wages are well below those of regular employees and lack the fringe benefits that the latter receive.

Several of the chapters in this volume document cases in which the regular workforce has historically enjoyed significant job security. What most of them stress is workers' growing precarity and the deteriorating conditions of their employment. Hoffmann's chapter is an outlier here. The power of the recently installed Maoist union has made workers in the Nepali food-processing factory he studied—or at least, those of the "right" ethnicity—*more*, rather than less, secure. In instances in which there was formerly a large regular workforce, its strength has been radically reduced and its labor replaced by that of much cheaper and more flexible contract workers.

But there is again an exception. In the coal mines and coal-washing plant that Kesküla studied in Kazakhstan, there is no subcontracting. Instead the entire workforce is made up of regulars who overwhelmingly come from Russian-speaking backgrounds and are of non-Kazakh ethnicity. Mining communities, concentrated in separated townships scattered across the steppe, have a strong sense of solidarity and of their distinctive identity. There is no contract labor, Kesküla suggests, because the owner—the steel magnate Lakshmi Mittal—acquired these mines almost by default when he took over the nearby Temirtau steel plant (see Trevisani's chapter). Lacking previous mining experience, Mittal delegated their operation to local managers, who considered it impossible to run them with low-skilled casual labor—a judgment colored by two recent major accidents that resulted in serious labor unrest and adverse publicity. Also significant is the preferential recruitment of the children of existing workers, a long established policy that led to the formation of much valorized "labor dynasties." Of these management often positively approves. They are seen as an instrument of control (recalcitrant workers jeopardize not only their own jobs but those of their kin), and as a way of economizing on training (recruits learn the ropes from family members). In this case, moreover, many managers themselves come from mining backgrounds. Thus both sides of industry have a stake in ensuring that only regular workers are employed, and that those recruited are qualified by kinship. It is a form of "opportunity hoarding" that keeps outsiders out—perhaps especially those of Kazakh ethnicity (who now monopolize government jobs).

Even in this case, however, a shrinking of the permanent workforce has given rise to a problem that several other contributors stress—that of reproduction. Earlier, the child of a regular worker could expect to succeed to a parent's job as a matter of customary right, but that is no longer so. Members of the younger generation are now generally condemned to work on casual or temporary contracts, eke out a living in the informal economy, emigrate, or face unemployment.

Whereas the strength of the permanent workforce has everywhere declined, the degree to which those who still hold regular posts in these large industries are now more precarious, and have experienced any marked deterioration in their terms of employment, is variable. The comparison between our five steel plant examples is suggestive. In the cases of Bulgaria (Kofti) and Kazakhstan (Trevisani), many workers with notionally permanent positions have been made redundant, wages have been cut and benefits curtailed, and those who manage to cling to their jobs are now required to work with greater intensity in worse conditions. Casualization has hit women harder than men, with knock-on effects on gender relations and domestic power. Though formerly public-sector units, both of these plants (which notably are the ones located in postsocialist settings) have been privatized, and only since privatization have these changes occurred. The other three plants (in Indonesia described by Rudnyckyj, in Egypt described by Makram-Ebeid, and in India described by Strümpell) remain in the public sector. Though in these the subjective sense of precarity may have grown—partly because of the threat of privatization and partly because everybody is aware that alternative jobs in the local economy are much less secure— the objective conditions of the regular workforce do not appear to have deteriorated greatly. Its size has been radically cut, but that has been accomplished largely through voluntary retirement schemes, natural attrition, and a moratorium on recruitment, rather than through enforced redundancies. Wages and benefits have not been significantly reduced, and there is little evidence of any significant intensification of labor. Many of the most unpleasant, arduous, and dangerous tasks are now performed by insecure, poorly paid contract laborers, often under the supervision of regular workers.

In the Tata Motors plant that Sanchez studied in Jamshedpur (India), the situation is similar. The core workforce continues to be extremely well remunerated by all local standards, to enjoy considerable job security, and to work at a rather relaxed pace. Though Tata is a private-sector conglomerate, a significant stake in it is owned by the state (Sanchez 2016: 94), and historically pay and conditions in its companies come as close as the Indian private sector gets to those in public-sector units. In his present contribution, Sanchez is mainly concerned with the contrast in political outlook between these workers and workers in a small, unorganized sector scrapyard. What his ethnography sharply brings out is a characteristic of the workforce we encounter elsewhere: regular and temporary workers are often close kin (compare the chapters by Makram-Ebeid, Kofti, and Trevisani).

The plant's management is predominantly Bengali; its workforce, predominantly Bihari and almost exclusively male. Managers and workers are distinguished by regional ethnicity and language. Tata has always prided itself on providing its workers with lifetime employment, decent wages, and generous welfare provision, and has long operated a policy that gives each worker the right to nominate a "ward" (usually a son), who on the worker's retirement will in principle be appointed to a regular post in the plant. Under the pressures of economic liberalization and globalization, however, this paternalistic regime has been undermined. The permanent workforce is dwindling, and their labor is being replaced by non-unionized, impermanent workers who are paid much less and have no claim on company welfare. Most of the latter are the often highly educated wards of regular workers. Many are notionally appointed as "apprentices" and "trainees" who do not even have to be paid the legal minimum wage, and though they do exactly the same jobs as the permanent workforce, most remain low-paid casual workers indefinitely. They consequently burn with resentment and a sense of betrayal—not least of betrayal by their union, which has been complicit in this informalization. Thus permanent and impermanent workers often belong to the same households or at least share the same regional origins, though by now most have been settled in Jamshedpur so long that they no longer have meaningful ties with their ancestral villages and no rural base to fall back on.

What 'manufactures consent' in this context? Why does this younger generation of workers work? A large part of the answer is their dream that a secure Tata job might eventually materialize. As Sanchez shows in his recent monograph (2016: chapter 6), in the performance of their duties regular employees can get away with a good deal of truculence and foot-dragging that would never be tolerated from temporary workers (who are now more than three-quarters of the total labor force [ibid.: 8]). So why does Tata retain a regular workforce at all? The obvious explanations are that the company is constrained by labor laws, by the legal difficulty of laying them off, and by the legacy of its carefully nurtured tradition of paternalism. But Sanchez himself comes to the more intriguing conclusion that the existence of permanent workers is what allows management to count on the compliance of the rest. Temporary workers put up with their lot only because they believe in the possibility of being eventually regularized. A core workforce, however small, is needed less for its own contribution to production than for the effort that others can be induced to make in the increasingly forlorn hope of one day joining its ranks.[1]

It has, of course, always been the case that even when companies run their core operations with a regularly employed full-time workforce, it makes business sense for them to hire temporary labor to cope with spikes in demand and do unskilled ancillary jobs that are only intermittently required. Indeed, it would often seem that a high degree of job security for the regular workforce is contingent on a pool of flexible labor that can be taken on when needed and dumped when not. Through much of the second half of the twentieth century, the Japanese "salaryman" working for a big corporation could expect lifetime employment with pay and conditions markedly superior to those of the much larger number of workers in small-scale factories (Dore 1973; Roberson 1998). Both were again sharply differentiated from casual labor hired through the *yoseba* (day labor market). These "men of uncertainty"—mostly rootless and (by the time of Gill's fieldwork) aging single men cut off from their kin and employed on short-term contracts—represent the antithesis of the salaryman in that they live apart from the two main institutions of Japanese society, the company and the family (Gill 1999, 2001). When recession hits the big corporations, the *yoseba* degenerates into a species of skid row. The two poles of the hierarchy are inseparably linked: the lifetime employment of the salaryman could only be sustained while there were flexible workers to meet employers' fluctuating demand for labor. As Parry (2009, 2013a) has also suggested for the central Indian steel town of Bhilai, the security of some is dependent on the precarity of others.

It seems obvious that the ratio of casual to regular workers will vary from one to another industry, and depend among other things on the sophistication of its technology and the need for specialist skills to operate it, and on the volatility of the market for its products. Construction is clearly an industry that needs flexible labor, as sites turn over rapidly, there is no fixed place of employment, and labor requirements fluctuate day by day—and indeed, a high proportion of its workers are temporary the world over. In the service sector, the tourist industry stands out. At the other end of the spectrum, large-scale integrated steel plants would be hard to operate without a reliable nucleus of regular workers. If production is disrupted at a critical point in the cycle, the whole plant grinds to a halt and crucial items representing enormous capital investments, such as blast furnaces and coke oven batteries, are at serious risk of long-term damage. It is different in their ancillary mines: while a blast furnace that is subject to an unscheduled stoppage of even short duration might take months to repair and re-fire, coal and ore can be stockpiled and what is left in the ground today can be dug up tomorrow. That makes steel plants peculiarly vulnerable to lightning wildcat strikes, which gives labor considerable bargaining power and management every incentive to create at least a core of "loyal" workers who can be counted on to keep the plant running in return for high wages, good benefits, and the promise of secure jobs.

Though now privatized in Pernik (Bulgaria) and Temirtau (Kazakhstan), all five of the steel plants discussed here began by providing housing for workers, and three of them built company townships. That says something about the political aspirations of the state at the time of their construction—aspirations that included the creation of a modern industrial working class that would carry the torch of history for a resurgent nation, fashioning a new kind of worker in a new kind of society. More prosaically, this investment in housing also tells us that those who planned these mega-industrial projects envisaged a settled labor force with considerable security and commitment to their jobs.

These plants are now technologically quite antiquated and the replacement of many machines is long overdue. As Trevisani describes in his chapter and as Makram-Ebeid (2013) shows elsewhere, it is experienced workers, not managers, who know how to keep this increasingly unreliable machinery running. Such workers are not easy to replace.

It may also be significant that steel is a capital-intensive industry with high energy and raw material costs. As a proportion of total production costs, the cost of labor is characteristically quite low. Relatively high rates of remuneration for the core workforce do not greatly add to the price of saleable steel, and it is plausible that public-sector management has been historically predisposed to regard them as a price worth paying for industrial peace. In the current era of globalized competition, however, that concession tends to look less appealing. In India, labor costs per tonne have recently been up to seven times higher in state-run plants than in some large private-sector units.[2] And self-evidently, management complacency about the cost of regular labor does not square with the fact that all the plants discussed in this volume have taken steps to reduce their wage bills by substantially cutting their core workforce and replacing it with contract labor.

It is, however, doubtful that this has been solely driven by the desire to cheapen labor. Often it would seem that its casualization is as much about discipline and control as it is about cost. Being easier to fire, temporary workers are generally easier to sweat—even if, for reasons we come to later, in Trevisani's case it is regular workers who feel most compelled to intensify their labor. But certainly, private industrialists in India—although seldom slow to take advantage of the lower price of contract labor—commonly claim that their main reason for favoring it is that while temporary workers work, regular workers malinger. And more generally, the subjugation of labor is as important a consideration as its price—even if that subjugation is ultimately also directed at the extraction of greater surplus value.

The two chapters in this volume that deal with the clothing industry suggest it is significantly less reliant on a stable regular workforce. Garment production, especially when heavily exposed to a fickle export market, is plainly vulnerable to volatility. Fashions change rapidly, and much demand is seasonal. Flexible labor is what employers want. The chapter by Carswell and De Neve deals with the booming urban and peri-urban agglomeration surrounding the south Indian garment-producing town of Tirupur, which now manufactures for export on a very large scale. Workers work long hours at high intensity to fill orders with tight turnaround times for a market that brooks no delay. Labor turnover is high, and few workers remain with the same employer for more than two or three years. Almost all are hired through a contractor, whom they often follow from factory to factory, though others strike out on their own in search of more skilled employment and better pay and conditions. All of these jobs are flexible—which is to say that in this industry, there is no division between regular company and irregular contract labor.

In the Trinidadian case discussed by Prentice, garment production began as a home-based cottage industry organized on a "putting-out" basis, though it was subsequently centralized in factories. Her story is of a widespread return to a putting-out system, and of the implications for labor of this reversal of the old teleological narrative in which cottage industry is permanently superseded by factory production. Globalization and economic liberalization inexorably fostered competition between garment-producing countries. Caribbean manufacturers found it hard to survive, resulting in factory closures and widespread layoffs amongst the predominantly female labor force. Those quickest on their feet responded by shifting production from the formal to the informal sector. Workers were sent home with industrial-grade sewing machines to become self-employed "micro-entrepreneurs", who are, for the most part indistinguishable from disguised wage laborers. They produce on piece-rates and have no guaranteed hours, and their employers are no longer obliged to pay them the minimum wage and can cut their costs on electricity and the provision of work space. The risks of production and of market fluctuations are devolved onto the workers themselves, and unionization has declined as formal wage employment is replaced by insecure home-based work. The state has actively promoted this trend by deciding—as neoliberal orthodoxy teaches—that the salvation of the national economy depends on removing the fetters that once stifled the entrepreneurial capacities of the individual. In the state rhetoric of empowerment, Prentice writes, "insecurity becomes recast as freedom, self-exploitation reframed as 'being your own boss.'" The reality is that most of these workers are now more precarious and materially worse off.

However, it would be too simple to put this kind of "regression" down to recent neoliberal trends alone. They have certainly given new impetus to putting-out, but periodic reversion to the practice has probably been a recurrent, long-standing feature of capitalist production. Based on research conducted in 1980, Harriss (1984) has documented for a very different industry a similar trend: owners of medium-sized engineering companies were laying off regular workers, and encouraging some to set up small workshops, to which they supplied secondhand machinery and gave orders. For them the advantages were manifold, but the most prominent was that of alleviating their problem of labor control.

Though in a less pronounced form, the textile industry (which produces cloth rather than clothing) often has has similar characteristics to garment production. Chandavarkar's (1994) study of the Bombay mills during the first four decades of the twentieth century privileges the constraints that confronted the owners, preeminently the difficulty of mobilizing capital, which required them to pay attractive dividends to investors; and market volatility. In response, they tailored production to short-term demand. That required flexible labor. About one-third of the workforce was taken on casually at the factory gates, and even "permanent" workers were subject to layoffs and redundancy. By comparison with the Japanese textile industry over that period, however, both the productivity and the turnover of labor were low (Wolcott 1994). Japanese mill workers were mainly girls aged fifteen to eighteen who typically remained in the industry for no more than a couple of years, and who consequently saw little benefit in striking. Indian mill hands, by contrast, were predominantly male, aspired to permanent employment, and were prepared to strike for long-term goals and to make it both costly and risky for their employers to force through productivity deals that would result in job losses. The moral seems simple: the social profile of the workforce, and its willingness to assert itself, may explain a great deal about the degree of precarity to which it is subject.

Where workers are highly skilled and companies invest heavily in training, it is a priori probable that they will try to retain them in regular jobs. But though Tirupur's tailors and cutters are extremely skilled, their skills are generally acquired on the job and are not in short supply; and labor turnover is high. As Carswell and De Neve emphasize, skill is a necessary condition for getting and retaining employment but is by no means sufficient. Its deployment is structurally constrained—by gender and caste in particular. Many married women cannot get jobs commensurate with their skills because they are hamstrung by their domestic responsibilities; many Dalits (ex-"Untouchables") from outlying settlements cannot move into better ones in town, or upgrade their skills, because they are bonded to dominant-caste power loom owners in their villages. To keep their families afloat, they have taken advances they cannot repay. That they would otherwise prefer work in town is due less to the difference in pay than to a wish to escape rural caste oppression through urban employment. Partly for that reason, the wage gap between the skilled and the unskilled is surprisingly low. Caste oppression deflates the price of skill because many low-caste people are prepared to accept low wages in order to free themselves from it. The general message, however, is that by itself skill is no guarantee of regular or even of more rewarding employment because structural inequalities determine who can acquire and deploy it. In Prentice's chapter, what enables Victoria to succeed as a micro-entrepreneur while Lana cannot is not differential skill, but social capital. In the very different setting of the Stomana steel plant (Kofti), it is not competence that gets you a job or protects you from redundancy, but real or fictive kin relations with people higher in the factory hierarchy.

If skill alone is not much protection against precarity, the want of it certainly makes workers vulnerable, because they are readily substitutable (Beynon 1984). Taylorist management methods break production down into the simplest, most mindless steps (Braverman 1974). A labor regime of this sort underlies the alienation, the high turnover, and the easy disposability of workers in the German-owned car factory in Russia described in the chapter by Morris and Hinz. But as the history of Ford shows, even where labor is unskilled and easy to replace, excessive workforce churning can be prohibitively costly to the company, which is why Henry Ford took the dramatic step of simultaneously cutting working hours and more than doubling the wage by introducing the five-dollar day (Miller 1992: 65f). High labor force turnover has elsewhere been seen as a problem for reasons that are not simply economic. The regularization of labor in the Mombasa docks in colonial Kenya was driven by political and ideological considerations. Casual labor was associated with indiscipline and political subversion, and challenged the colonialists' conception of what a modern industrial labor force should be. Decasualization was above all about producing predictable, tractable workers (Cooper 1992).

Plainly, globalization has shifted the balance of power between capital and labor. Confronted by labor conditions not to their liking, companies can realistically threaten to shift production to other national jurisdictions where regulation is laxer, and labor is cheaper and more compliant. Schober's chapter deals with a large South Korean shipbuilding concern that has relocated a substantial part of its operations to the Subic Bay Freeport Zone in the Philippines. One major objective of this move was to neutralize the power of the assertive unions at its yards in Korea. In Subic, nearly all labor is hired through subcontractors. As this case and others in this volume remind us, these globalized capital flows are not simply another instance of the economic imperialism of the usual suspect Western powers. One of the three mining companies on the Zambian Copperbelt on which Lee focuses is Chinese-owned, while a second is owned by a UK-registered Indian company. The Temirtau steel plant (Trevisani) and the Karaganda mines (Keskülä) in Kazakhstan were acquired by a London-based Indian steel magnate. The Nepali food-processing units of which Hoffmann writes were set up by a Marwari[3] industrialist of Indian origin. One of the factories in mainland China on which Fang reports is Taiwanese-owned, and the Bulgarian steel plant that Kofti studied belongs to a Greek multinational.

Capital flight is constrained by the costs of relocation and by the ownership structure of the company. Of the five steel plants examined in this book, two have been privatized. At these there is a real possibility that the company will run down its operations, sell, or even close the plant. Should bottom-line calculations dictate, it will switch its investments elsewhere, and the company may have a clear interest in ensuring that this bottom line is illegible to outsiders (see Trevisani's chapter). Keeping workers guessing about the company's intentions and in suspense about the security of their jobs predisposes them to acquiesce to the deterioration of their employment conditions. Meanwhile, the three public-sector plants are differently placed. The Steel Authority of India, for example, would stir up a political storm if it closed its plant in Odisha in order to release funds for investment in another Indian state, and there is no question of relocating to Kazakhstan. Capital flight is a much smaller threat. That is of a piece with our earlier observation that in none of these public-sector instances have the labor conditions of the regular workforce degenerated to the extent that they have in the privatized cases.

The threat of capital *flight* to labor in countries from which it might exit is well understood. Equally important is the impact that the obverse process of capital *incursion* has on labor conditions in the places to which it flees. It is often accompanied by a dilution or even a wholesale suspension of workers' rights as governments vie with each other to attract inward investment, thereby creating the "race to the bottom" that Cross (2014: 35) identifies in his discussion of Special Economic Zones in India. Investors are offered significant tax breaks, as well as exemptions from many government controls and labor laws, including the obligation to recognize unions. Following the liberalization of the Indian economy, state governments were given more autonomy to set their own economic strategies and drum up inward investment. Initially these zones remained under tight state control, but liberalization created inexorable pressure to deregulate further. It was not only state governments that competed with each other to attract outside capital, but also different national economies (ibid.: chapter 2). The cheaper and more submissive the workforce they could offer, the greater their chances of success. Assuring the "right" labor conditions may involve stamping on nascent labor movements.

A case in point, drawn from central India, is the brutal suppression to which a group of unions united under the banner of the Chhattisgarh Mukti Morcha (CMM) were subjected in the early 1990s. The movement specifically championed the rights of contract workers in the iron ore mines attached to the Bhilai Steel Plant and in Bhilai's private-sector industry—an unusual phenomenon in that most such labor is in India non-unionized. Other notable features of the CMM included its militancy, its attempts to make common cause between workers and peasants, and the comparative modesty of its immediate demand that existing government legislation on contract labor should be actually implemented (Parry 2009 and forthcoming). This last notwithstanding (it aimed to uphold the law, after all), the state hounded it with ruthless determination, acting in collusion with local industrial interests (which had a notorious record of flouting its laws). Though we cannot elaborate here on what is an extremely complex story, one headline conclusion is that a major part of the explanation for its nakedly partisan role was the timing. In Bhilai itself, CMM militancy was reaching a crescendo on the private-sector industrial estate just as the central government was embarking on serious measures to liberalize the economy. That offered unprecedented opportunities for attracting inward investment—provided that the region could offer a cheap, flexible, docile labor force. As the state government and local industrialists saw it, it was imperative that the new labor movement should be speedily crushed. It was.

In this volume, Schober reports allegations that unions were unofficially banned from Subic as a sop to potential investors; and the Philippine state certainly adopted a relaxed interpretation of its own laws to make subcontracting easier. The resulting fragmentation of the labor force makes it even harder to organize strong unions. Of the three Copperbelt mining companies Lee studied, the Chinese-owned one has had the most effective union because it hires labor through a single contractor. The others recruit through a number.

We cannot, of course, assume that capital incursions are unwelcome to the local populations they most directly affect. There are generally both winners and losers. Though the jobs created may pay only a fraction of the wage they attract in the country from which the capital has fled, they are frequently far better rewarded than any other work that is locally available. Often, however, it is not the locals who get them. Outsiders are easier to discipline (e.g., Cross 2014: 85–86). Though employment in start-ups on green field sites may offer an escape from local structures of domination, the dominant are commonly less sanguine, though some will be consoled by the boom in real estate prices that new factories may bring. Jobs in them provide new opportunities for self-fashioning. "It is important," Wolf (1992: 135) writes in her study of "factory daughters" in Java, "to understand that workers find factory employment preferable to arduous agricultural labor, to highly controlled and poorly paid positions in domestic service, and to being under the eyes and constant control of parents and other relatives in the village. ... Although it is undeniable that factory work is exploitative, it is equally undeniable that young village women prefer it to other meager choices." It gives them a new sense of self-worth.

The impact of capital incursion on the local labor regime may critically depend on the objectives of the investors. What fundamentally distinguishes the Chinese-owned company from the other two multinational mining corporations in Lee's chapter is that its strategy was geared to obtaining the ore the Chinese economy requires, whereas the other two companies set their sights on short-term shareholder profits. From that the rest follows. In the interests of fulfilling its target output, the Chinese company ran its operations through a single contractor; its workforce was consequently less fragmented and its union was able to leverage significant gains in terms of job security (if not wages). In the interests of maximizing shareholder returns, both other companies ran their operations through multiple contractors, between whom they fostered competition and from whom they squeezed the cheapest possible deals. The workforce was parceled between them, the unions were weaker, and the workers, though paid somewhat better, were more likely to be laid off at short notice.

To draw together the main strands in our discussion so far, we can say that in most industrial settings at most times and places, the standard employment relationship was never the predominant form. Even where it formerly existed, the protections it once afforded have now been significantly dismantled. The global trend has been toward increasing precarity, and a weakening of the power of organized labor brought about by the threat of capital flight and incursions, the casualization of jobs, and increased subcontracting. The more casualized the workforce, the harder it is to organize strikes. Those who lead and actively participate in them are more easily fired; workers who are anyway unlikely to remain in the job for long have little incentive to make immediate sacrifices for future gains, and casualization and high labor turnover are conducive to the atomization of the workforce and inimical to the development of strong workplace solidarities. Job insecurity inhibits not only collective action but also rational planning (Bourdieu 1998), and in the absence of adequate state welfare provision it encourages reliance on familial networks of support, and on patrons and brokers. That in turn promotes dependency and an unwillingness to challenge the status quo (Wood 2003). Skill by itself is scant protection against precarity, but to be unskilled is to be highly vulnerable to it. The uncertainty bred by job insecurity affects those who currently have jobs as well as the unemployed, and rapidly becomes a widely diffused state of mind that gnaws at the collective consciousness. Though the precariat has been called "the new dangerous class" (Standing 2011), it is neither new nor dangerous. It is too difficult to organize, too fragmented, and often too demoralized to be that.

This pessimistic conclusion admittedly runs counter to a recent literature that stresses the success of informal labor organizations in various parts of the world. Take Agarwala's (2013) argument that in India the "informal" cannot be equated with the "unorganized," that informal labor organizations have managed to extract significant gains for their members, and that neoliberal policy agendas have in fact strengthened their hand in launching a "Polanyian" countermovement against the commodification of labor. These gains have been won by making welfare claims on the *state* as *citizens* rather than by wringing concessions from their *employers* as *workers*. According to Agarwala, the differential success of this strategy in different Indian states is explained by two key variables: the intensity of competition between political parties (irrespective of their ideological orientation) for the electoral support of the poor;[4] and the extent to which they have espoused a neoliberal policy agenda. Electoral competition persuades parties to champion worker demands because informal labor organizations offer them vote banks. Neoliberal development strategies push the latter into a Faustian bargain: in exchange for welfare benefits, they promise the compliant and flexible workforce on which those strategies are premised. The case is cogently made but not quite conclusive. Even in Agarwala's privileged examples, only a small fraction of informal labor appears to be effectually organized, and she offers no hard evidence on whether they vote as a block on the basis of class interests or on how that vote is mobilized (supposedly through neighborhood organizations). The compulsion to "buy" workers' consent to current labor conditions is surely diminished by the capacity of the state and the employers to coerce consent, and by the fact that workers have no alternative but to submit to them. Many of the most basic rights of citizenship often have no real meaning for the truly disadvantaged. Most relevant here, however, is that none of the chapters in this volume suggest that informal-sector labor is effectively organized.

Our discussion further suggests that there may be limits to casualization, and particular circumstances in which the existence of casual labor sustains the security of a regular workforce. These limits vary significantly between industries. Maintenance of a core labor force of regular workers may be the employers' best strategy, encouraged by the high costs of training, the need for predictability, and their investment objectives. Casualization of the workforce may be limited by its commitment to industrial jobs and its willingness to defend them, which in turn depends on its sociological makeup and historical experiences. In our steel plant examples, workers in public-sector units have proved less vulnerable than those in privately owned plants, largely because they are shielded by the political imperatives of the state.

Unquestionably, casualization is driven by capital's quest to cheapen labor, though its objectives are commonly equally aimed at making it more tractable and subservient. In the end this second objective may serve the first, but it is not safe to assume that the two are always in harmony. *De*-casualization may also be seen as an instrument of control—a means of producing a less unruly and unpredictable workforce—even if this strategy proves more costly in financial terms. Under neoliberal conditions, the role of the state has proved equally crucial in shaping the landscape of labor, almost always in the direction of making it more flexible. Political considerations may be as consequential as economic ones. As Mirowski (2014: 40) observes, "mature neo-liberalism is not at all enamored of the minimalist night watchman state of the classical liberal tradition." The "neo" in neoliberalism signals the role that the doctrine accords the state in molding subjectivities, social relations, and collective representations (ibid.: 54). The neoliberal order is a product of "political will," "a mode of domination" (Bourdieu 1998: 84–85). In many of our case studies, it was the development policies and the legislation of the postcolonial state that created and entrenched a sharp divide within the manual workforce between a privileged enclave of regular company workers with secure jobs and the rest of the labor force; and it is the state—often under pressure from international financial institutions—that later led the assault on the "rigidities in the labor market" that it had itself created. In so doing, what it had also fostered was the development of a huge gap in the conditions of the two kinds of worker.

That raises the question of whether—and under what circumstances— this differentiation has given rise to a distinction of *class* between them, and it is to this issue that now we turn.

A Distinction of Class?

In the past, regular jobs in many of the workplaces dealt with in this collection were, by the standards of the manual labor force as a whole, privileged. Some still are. Compared to informal-sector workers, permanent employees in India's formal sector are highly remunerated. Their jobs are often so secure that they constitute something like a property right (which is how

Makram-Ebeid's Egyptian steel plant workers describe them). They are often, in effect, heritable. As in Sanchez's case, the right of workers to nominate their own successors has been widely conceded. Quasi-hereditary succession to industrial jobs has been common elsewhere. The "labor dynasties" of Soviet industry were valorized and remain so in much of the postsocialist world (as Kofti, Kesküla, and Trevisani testify).[5] The literature on Indian industry reports many instances in which jobs have been seen as a legitimate source of what amounts to a rental income: a worker hives off all or part of his (or very rarely her) duties to a substitute who receives some fraction of the wage while he collects the rest. Sometimes he was able to surreptitiously sell the position (or his nomination of a successor to it).[6] The crux is that such jobs provide a degree of security that may constitute "a partial alternative to ownership" (Lockwood 1958: 204) in that they provide shelter from the uncertainties of the labor market.

In a country like India, the significance of such security can hardly be overstated. Sengupta, Kannan, and Ravendran (2008) estimated that in 2004/05 more than one-fifth of the total population had incomes below the official poverty line (i.e., insufficient for their minimum nutritional needs). More than another half teetered on the brink of that condition or were vulnerable to it, meaning that their households were "only one illness away from chronic poverty" (Krishna 2011: 157). A regular job in a state-run enterprise or one of the big private factories is an effective shield against that kind of vulnerability. The distinction between those whose employment has meaningful legal protection and those whose livelihoods depend on the immediate requirements of their current employer marks one of the deepest rifts in the Indian social order. Job security is at least as important a determinant of class positioning as ownership of the means of production. For many workers, a regular job is often far more significant than the possession of land.

Standing's (2011) discussion of "the precariat" highlights this divide. The precariat, he proposes, constitutes a "class-in-the-making" that is separate from both "the salariat" with stable full-time employment, and the shrinking proletariat. Breman (2013), however, calls it a "bogus concept" that sets up artificial distinctions between different fractions of labor that share the same fundamental predicaments. Several of our contributors are also skeptical—Strümpell because different forms of precarity may be cumulative, whereas Standing privileges work and employment and has little to say about the precarity of habitation; and Kofti because company and contract workers in Stomana are now both precarious, and because they often belong to the same households. That makes it unrealistic to see them as separate classes. Sanchez (on whose analysis we comment later) makes a similar case; and further argues that there is no divide between regular and temporary Tata workers in terms of values and political attitudes, though between the latter and informal-sector workers there is a big gap. The precariat cannot therefore be understood as a unitary class. All that notwithstanding, Standing's class scheme underscores the stark division within the manual labor force that several of our case studies suggest. Several but not all—and the crucial question concerns the conditions under which that division gets crystallized.

As already suggested, the state has often played a critical role. In mixed economies with important state sectors—like Turkey, Mexico, India and Egypt—government-run enterprises developed generic similarities, including workforces that enjoyed high wages and considerable job security, and that were increasingly separated from unorganized sector labor (Waterbury 1993). From the Communists' coming to power until at least the early 1980s, the Chinese industrial workforce was differentiated between those employed in modern, large-scale state-owned factories and those working in cooperative and more small-scale local government units, in addition to which there were temporary workers in state enterprises and workers in rural industries (Walder 1986; Lee 2007: 36). In terms of pay, perks and security, a large gap separated these fractions of labor, and mobility between them was limited. For more recent times, Pun (2005) has emphasized the division between *gongren*, the old "proletariat" with secure jobs in state-run factories and rights of permanent urban residence, and the *dagongzai* and *dagongmei* (the "boys" and "younger sisters" who "work for a boss" in Special Economic Zones), who are overwhelmingly flexible rural labor with only temporary residence rights—rights that are a major determinant of life chances. In this volume Fang discusses the divide between the old working class (*gongren jieji*) and peasant workers (*nongmingong*), as well as the difference in one of the factories she studied between "staff workers" (*zigong*), who are nearly all locals with residence rights, and "basic workers" (*yuangong*) who are overwhelmingly rural migrants without such rights. In terms of pay and security they are sharply differentiated.

For sub-Saharan Africa, Arrighi and Saul (1973) once argued that security and high wages encourage the "labor aristocracy" to sever ties with their rural roots, and that politically they are aligned with the "elite" and "sub-elite" as "junior partners" in "the dominant power bloc." This thesis was hotly contested, perhaps most compellingly by case studies of labor disputes in West Africa (Peace 1975; Jeffries 1975). These seemed to show that these workers were capable of radically challenging the political elite, and that in doing so they had the support of other sections of the working population, for whom they were spokesmen and from whom they did not see themselves as distinct. Cooper (1996: 462) subsequently dismissed the argument as "misplaced from the start" because it was based on the false premise that such workers are indeed deracinated. Ferguson's (1999) account of Copperbelt miners, however, presented evidence that they frequently are cut off from their rural kin; indeed, Cooper's (1992) own study of the decasualization of labor on the Mombasa docks had showed that colonial policy had created a separate enclave of secure, highly paid workers. Later, Saul (1975) conceded that there may be instances in which the most privileged workers identify "downward" rather than "upward" and suggested that the analytical challenge is to specify the conditions that favor one or another of those outcomes. The discussion of "structuration" that follows is intended to bear on that agenda.

Though Standing sees the precariat as a distinct social class, he is not explicit about the concept of class that informs his analysis. The one adopted here owes more to Weber than Marx. Weber gives the state greater scope for autonomous action independent of class interests, and his concept of class allows for distinctions (based on their market capacities) between those separated from the means of production—between, for example, white- and blue-collar workers, or between manual workers of different kinds. The focus is on life chances, which members of the same class share and which differentiate them from others. The approach (like Marx's) is relational, and it encourages us to look at the way in which the privileges of some come at the cost of others and are reproduced through processes of exclusion and opportunity hoarding that restrict outsiders' access to positions of advantage. Class is at bottom an economic phenomenon, and a *social* class is made up of the totality of economic positions "between which mobility either within the lifetime of the individual or over successive generations is a readily possible and typically observable occurrence" (Weber 1978: 57). Unlike social stratification theory, which portrays the social order as a gradation with multiple rungs, the idea of "class society" is premised on its division into a small number of distinct groups defined by their unequal economic positions. For classes to have any social reality, there must be significant breaks between them, marked by differences in the lifestyles and life experiences typical of their members. Classes must have some sense of themselves as identifiable groups if they are to pursue their own interests.

Giddens's notion of "structuration" addresses how that sense of identity comes about—how economic classes become *social* classes that are no longer merely a matter of economic differentiation but are freighted with wider social meaning and salience (Giddens 1975; Kingston 2000). Economic inequalities do not of themselves produce that result, nor is it necessarily the case that the steeper the inequality, the more crystallized social classes will be. Economic inequality is a necessary but not a sufficient condition for class structuration. Among the variables that determine its degree, mobility between classes—both within the lifetime of the individual and across generations—is critical. The more mobility there is, the less likely people are to identify with a stable class identity. A working environment that minimizes contact between members of different classes is important, as is residential segregation, which partly sets patterns of socialization outside the workplace. Structuration plainly depends on the degree to which social interactions are confined to people of the same class, on the frequency with which marriage ties and the bonds of kinship and friendship cross class boundaries, and on whether individuals of different classes join in associations that bring them together or set them apart. Common consumption patterns and lifestyles, along with shared tastes, attitudes, and beliefs, also have a self-evident bearing on whether people think of themselves as being of the same kind and as having a distinctive culture. Where classes are highly structured, they are likely to be characterized by common political orientations and sympathies. Classes may be more strongly structured on some of these parameters than others, and structuration is always matter of degree and is never complete. The tighter their structuration, however, the more sharply classes emerge as identifiable groups, though their boundaries can never "be drawn like lines on a map" (Giddens 1975: 273).

The manual workforce of the central Indian steel town of Bhilai, as Parry (2009, 2013a, 2013b, forthcoming) has argued, is bifurcated into two distinct classes that are strongly structured in the ways described. In the mid 1980s, the public-sector Bhilai Steel Plant (BSP) had 65,000 workers on its direct payroll—a total since cut by more than half, despite expansion of output. This was achieved without forced redundancies, and those who have regular posts continue to enjoy high wages and secure jobs. It is the deployment of cheap, "flexible" contract labor that makes this possible. At the same time, private-sector industry in the area has boomed, though only a minority of the sector's workers are company employees. To evade the labor laws, most are hired through contractors. Apart from the division between the workforces of public- and private-sector companies, and between regular and contract workers within each sector, there is also a vast army of largely unskilled temporary labor that works for daily wages in both the formal and informal economies. Materially and socially, however, the real rift is between those with regular jobs in the organized sector on the one hand, and on the other those who work in it as contract labor, or outside it in the unorganized/informal sector. The distinction is entrenched in local categories. The first kind of worker "has *naukri*" (a "service" position seen as a kind of "office" and spoken of as something one possesses).[7] The second "does *kam*" (insecure untenured "work," paradigmatically for daily wages). Those who have *naukri* refer to those who do *kam* as the "labor class," which is certainly not how they think of themselves or are thought of by others—which is unhesitatingly as "middle class." As everybody sees it, these are distinct kinds of people, unequal in dignity and resources, and different in outlook and values.

Only the baldest summary of the evidence that supports this analysis is possible here, but amongst the most salient findings is that over time the BSP workforce has become a largely self-reproducing stratum into which mobility from below is highly restricted. Given today's minimal recruitment, BSP sons can now no longer count on following in their fathers' footsteps, but they have a significantly better chance of landing some form of middle-class employment than the son of a contract or construction worker has of obtaining a regular BSP position. Rather, "labor-class" people move readily and frequently between typically labor-class jobs: contract work in the plant, construction work outside it, loading and unloading jobs, and various forms of self-employment. In earlier times it was not uncommon for one member of the household to hold a BSP post while his sibling(s) worked in the informal sector; but as households have partitioned and the generations have succeeded each other over the years, "the axiom of kinship amity" (Fortes 1969) has often buckled under the pressures of class differentiation as the BSP branch of the family distances itself from the embarrassing encumbrance of its poor relations. Residentially, the two strata are also increasingly segregated (for much the same reasons explored by Strümpell). In terms of the "size of the purse," BSP workers comfortably qualify as middle-class, and on top of their wage they get valuable benefits and easy access to soft company credit that enables them to invest in urban property and/or agricultural land. Furthermore, their undemanding work schedules allow them to run lucrative moonlighting businesses. Meanwhile, the monthly incomes of many contract workers in the plant fall below the poverty line. BSP workers can sustain life styles and afford consumer durables of which contract workers can only dream.

Though company workers and contract labor often rub shoulders on the BSP shop floor, they do not fraternize. In the mid 1990s the plant was greatly overmanned; for regular workers time discipline was lax and the pace of work leisurely (Parry 1999). Ten years later time discipline was tighter, but BSP workers were doing less of the work themselves, having increasingly become a supervisory workforce overseeing the labor of the contract workers who were assigned the most arduous and unpleasant tasks, often toiling continuously throughout two back-to-back shifts. It seems reasonable to infer that BSP employees can only be paid so well and work so little because the contract labor that is progressively replacing them is paid so little and must work so hard—in short, that the relationship between them is one of exploitation. Certainly they do not always share the same interests, and union politics both reflect and exacerbate the division. The regular BSP workforce is represented by a "recognized" union that has generally cooperated closely with management. Most contract labor is un-unionized, and whenever it has tried to organize, the official union, contractors, and management have colluded to suppress their lèse-majesté. In the late 1970s and the 1980s, there was a prolonged period of strife in BSP's iron ore mines and a series of violent confrontations between a new union championing the cause of the contract workers in the manual mines[8] and the officially "recognized" union that represented regular workers in the mechanized mines. The main bone of contention was a mechanization program that threatened jobs in the manual mines. When the trouble subsequently spread to Bhilai's private-sector industrial estate, contract labor went on strike while company workers either stayed out of the fray or took the company's side. Meanwhile, the official union from the mines supplied the bosses with blackleg labor.

The two kinds of workers are also set apart in numerous ways outside the world of work: their children have very different kinds of upbringing; the conjugal bond and the stability of marriage are valued differently; and the two groups have markedly different propensities for suicide, ideas about the costs and benefits of industrial modernity, and orientations to time (Parry 2001, 2005, 2007, 2012). In short, we are dealing here with two distinct social classes that are highly structured on the axes Giddens identified: low rates of mobility across the divide, a high degree of residential segregation, attenuated kinship ties, contrasting lifestyles and consumption patterns, and a distance maintained between them on the BSP shop floor, where their interactions are hierarchically structured. Their interests are not always the same and sometimes conflict, and their relationship may involve a significant element of exploitation.

Given their institutional links (both are managed by the same public-sector holding company), their common history (both were part of Nehru's modernizing vision and began production in 1959), and their geographical proximity, it is unsurprising that the pattern of differentiation that Strümpell reports for contemporary Rourkela is close to that outlined for Bhilai. What he shows, however, is that until recently the divide between organized and unorganized labor was masked by ethnicity, and that greater residential segregation has played a crucial role in restricting mobility and hardening the class boundaries between them. The Rourkela Steel Plant (RSP) was built in the highlands of western Odisha in an area dominated by Adivasis (supposedly autochthonous "Tribals") who, as part of the compensation package for their requisitioned land, were promised one compensatory plant job per household. The many cases of failure to fulfill this commitment have been a running sore ever since.

Though many of the pioneer workers were migrants from distant parts of the country, a clamor soon arose for preference to be given to recruits from coastal Odisha. The plant belonged to "their" state, even if the local Adivasis regarded them as "foreigners." Their demands were difficult to resist because the state government's survival hinged on electoral support from the eastern coastal belt. In those early years, ethnic politics became explosive and Rourkela experienced horrific communal violence (Parry and Strümpell 2008). Its ethnic divisions were reflected in its spatial organization: the company town was the preserve of nonlocal RSP workers, both coastal Odias and those from outside Odisha. The displaced Adivasis were relocated in resettlement colonies on its periphery or lived in *bastis* (slum-like settlements) on encroached land, where they were joined by rural kin who came in search of employment. These settlements were thus a mix of RSP workers who had been given jobs in lieu of their fields, and informal-sector workers. Union politics in Rourkela broadly reflected its ethnic divisions, and RSP workers from the resettlement colonies supported the campaigns for compensatory RSP employment for the so far neglected locals. Ethnic loyalties overrode the incipient class division between them.

That has since changed. Nowadays out-of-state migrants are rarely recruited, the RSP workforce has been radically cut, and the RSP township can now accommodate its entire workforce. Fresh Adivasi recruits and RSP Adivasi workers from the resettlement colonies move to the township "for the sake of the children," particularly the better employment prospects they will gain from its higher quality company schools and its more "civilized" atmosphere. One consequence is that Adivasi RSP workers have largely lost interest in their erstwhile neighbors' struggles for jobs in the plant, and often are hostile to them. A second is that these settlements are now almost exclusively inhabited by unorganized labor. The situation is reminiscent of Wilson's (1987) argument that the north American ghetto has become a "sink" for the "truly disadvantaged" as upwardly mobile blacks have moved out of what was once a mixed-class neighborhood, leaving behind a socially isolated underclass without mainstream role models or the capacity to sustain local institutions. Though Strümpell does not put it in these terms, it seems plausible to suppose that the increasingly precarious housing situation he describes is exacerbated by the social isolation of the informal sector workers that remain and the lack of a leadership that is able to effectively articulate their grievances. In any event, the trajectory is one in which a division in the workforce that once was strongly inflected by ethnicity has given way to one that is primarily based on class. It is the opposite of the development that Hoffmann reports from Nepal, where the Maoist agenda has shifted from the politics of class to the politics of ethnicity.

The *naukri/kam* distinction found in Bhilai has strong resonances, and sometimes almost precise analogues, in the local categories documented in several of our case studies. Hoffmann's Nepali informants distinguish between workers with *isthai* and *asthai kam*, fixed employment versus casual work. As mentioned above, Fang's ethnography brings out a sharp distinction between urban and migrant peasant workers. In China, Lee (2007: 130) reports, informal-sector jobs are not regarded as "real work," which is employment in the state sector. That's what they say in Bhilai, where *naukri* is a "proper job" and those without it are often described as *berozgar* (unemployed) even when they toil day and night in terrible conditions.

The way in which these categories may be ideologically freighted is vividly brought out in the vignette that opens Rudnyckyj's chapter. The ethnographer had blundered by referring to his interlocutor, who had a regular post at the Krakatau steel works, as a "worker" (*buruh*), and was indignantly set right: he was an "employee" (*karyawan*), not a worker. There is a world of difference. Employees receive a salary and a variety of benefits, and they have permanent positions from which they are hard to remove. Though the plant is highly overmanned and its workforce is being softened up for neo-liberal restructuring by a management-sponsored Islamic reform program, there have yet to be significant redundancies. Workers get a wage (which in the case of Krakatau contract labor may reach up to half the amount an employee receives) and can easily be "let go." It appears more difficult for a contract worker to become a *karaywan* than for a *karyawan* to become a manager. Contract laborers are assigned the most taxing and danger-ous tasks, often carried out under the supervision of regular workers. The two groups are distinguished by their uniforms and different demeanors; they have different break rooms, sit separately in the canteens, and belong to different unions. Whereas workers are mainly locals, employees are predominantly outsiders, do not understand the local dialect, and regard themselves as superior. They have middle-class lifestyles and consumption patterns, and do not live in the same neighborhoods that workers inhabit.

In Helwan, the steel town south of Cairo where Makram-Ebeid worked, the key distinction in the labor force is between a *muwaẓẓafa* (one who owns a post [*waẓīfa*]) and an *'urzuqīa* (one who does not know what tomorrow's job will be and does only "work" [*shughl*]). A *waẓīfa* is para-digmatically a secure and well-paid government job. Regular EISCO (steel plant) workers "own" it and have been able to pass it on to the next gen-eration by custom and practice. It has now become a "right." Only the children of regular workers are eligible for recruitment. It is now hard to get a temporary contract or even a day labor job in the plant unless one comes from an EISCO family, but is possible to progress up the ladder from day laborer to regular worker (though it is unclear how common that is). That distinguishes this situation from our Indian and Javanese cases, where such mobility is now highly restricted. Given that possibility, and the probability that they are kin, the distinction between EISCO workers who have "posts" and those who do not is less marked than that between plant workers in general and workers in the informal sector outside the plant. The latter are pre-eminently *al-tabābna*, displaced local villagers. The two groups characteristically differ in their lifestyles, household structures, and values and aspirations. EISCO workers consider themselves middle-class and superior to the rough, uncouth *al-tabābna*. Formerly, the two strata were more residentially segregated. That is to some extent breaking down, but closer proximity has not promoted sociability or trust. What has not broken down is the *al-tabābna*'s exclusion from plant jobs. That is largely the product of opportunity hoarding by current workers. Makram-Ebeid describes the relationship as one of exploitation.

While Sanchez wants to stress the growing precarity that affects all segments of labor, and to play down the divisions within it, another reading of his evidence shows a pattern that is very similar to the one just described: a gulf separates Tata workers (regardless of their employment status) from informal-sector workers (like those in the scrapyard he studied). The two kinds of Tata worker are probably kin and members of the same household. It is only to be expected that their ideas and interests should be the same. However, it would seem—at least if we can extrapolate from evidence about the neighboring Tata steel plant—that in the past, large numbers of local Adivasis were employed as contract labor. Permanent workers, predominantly immigrant Biharis, were totally unsupportive of their campaigns for permanent positions (Sanchez 2016: 95). It seems that Tata has since replaced them with Tata "wards" taken on as cut-rate apprentices, and that regular workers now show interest in their plight only because they are their sons.

One obscurity in Sanchez's account is how his stress on the deteriorating conditions of all workers squares with his argument that management has to retain a privileged core workforce if it is to keep its temporary laborers committed to their jobs. It is also unclear what evidence he has for claiming that regular workers are now more precarious. If that is true, how do they get away with the malingering and shirking he describes (ibid.: 138–139)? Admittedly, it might be claimed that the casualization of their sons leaves them exposed in old age, but the fact is that they receive a decent pension and a substantial Provident Fund payout on retirement. What Sanchez does, however, convincingly bring out is the contrast in political attitudes between Tata apprentices and scrapyard workers. While the former have a strong sense of entitlement, of betrayal and outrage at a birthright denied, life teaches the latter that the world owes them nothing and they must submit to their lot with resignation. This is so, he emphasizes, despite there being little to distinguish them in terms of pay (though it must surely make a difference that one's father is a Tata worker and belongs to the same household). These different attitudes point to the essential conclusion that the two kinds of workers regard themselves as existentially different, as belonging to separate worlds. The Tata apprentice's outrage is at his own fate alone. He is indifferent to that of Rakesh and his scrapyard co-workers.; and Sanchez graphically evokes the contempt and derision to which Rakesh is subject on the streets. It seems unlikely that the latter's tormentors would feel licensed to treat a Tata scion so.

In each of these cases, it thus seems plausible to speak of distinct social classes. The cases differ, however, in where the boundaries between the classes are drawn: between workers with urban residence rights and migrant peasant workers, in China; between regular workers and con- tract and informal-sector labor in the Bhilai, Rourkela, and Krakatau steel plants; and between EISCO and Tata workers—regardless of their employ- ment status—and non-company labor in Helwan and Jamshedpur. In other cases, however, class structuration within the manual labor force is fuzzier. Though the picture that emerges from these falls far short of portraying a unitary working class, nor is it possible to identify separate classes of labor.

Keskűla writes of mine workers in Kazakhstan who remain compara- tively well paid (they can afford foreign holidays) and have a strong sense of solidarity, of their distinctive identity, and of being the old Soviet labor elite. Though they predominantly live in their own communities and are all company workers, their separateness is severely compromised because only a minority of their children will get mining jobs. As non-Kazakhs, they stand little chance of obtaining government employment. Even if they speak Kazakh, they have "the wrong eyes." Most are forced into low-paid work or remain unemployed, and must either continue to depend on their parents or emigrate. Their sense of forming a distinct vanguard enclave of labor is being radically undermined.

In nearby Temirtau (Trevisani) and in the Bulgarian case (Kofti), the process of de-structuration has gone further. As we have seen, the pay, working conditions and security of the entire workforce have declined, resulting in a gap between company and contract labor that is narrower than it is in our earlier examples. Even regular employees are now precarious and often work alongside contract labor doing much the same jobs under the same harsh conditions. In the past, Temirtau workers could nominate their own successors, but that privilege has now been rescinded, just as it has been, for all practical purposes, in Pernik, where at the time of Kofti's fieldwork around 80 percent of workers and administrative staff were the children, nephews, or nieces of current or former employees. Today they have little chance of having a regular job, and their parents have little desire for them to follow in their footsteps. In both cases, although managers and workers alike used to live in housing provided by the company (in Temirtau most managers had risen through the ranks), they are now more residentially dispersed, and regular workers are likely to live alongside contract labor. With profound consequences for domestic life, their households are also more likely to contain still dependent adult children, as well as women who have been made redundant. Though Stomana employees are still well-off compared to workers in Pernik's new garment factories, and though in Temirtau the "Mittals" (as regular workers are mockingly known) and contract workers have different political orientations and different attitudes to work, in the broad picture no one is secure, and downward mobility is "a readily possible and typically observable occurrence." The result is low structuration.

As observed earlier, what most obviously sets these two cases apart from our other steel plant examples is that both companies have been privatized and their managements' goals are geared to shareholder returns. (This recalls Lee's argument that management objectives aimed at acquiring "use values" cause workers to be differently placed.) Both cases have to do with a former labor elite whose position of pre-eminence in the hierarchy of labor is now seriously compromised. A priori we might suppose that such workers would be more inclined to identify "downward" with other fractions of labor whose conditions they now share, than "upward" with management and the middle classes. Likely as such a development might seem, however, neither case gives much indication that de-structuration is leading to a wider political mobilization of "the working class."

One reason for that concerns the way class intersects with ethnicity. Although ethnic divisions may inhibit the emergence of more generalized sentiments of "proletarian solidarity" (as the early history of Rourkela suggests), they may help to solidify the sense of common identity shared by workers in a particular niche of the labor market and to set them apart from others. Ethnic identity is often a "market capacity" or its opposite—a market disqualification. Class structuration may be boosted by the overlap between class and ethnicity (Giddens 1975: 111–112). What is certainly striking in our case histories is the way workforce divisions based on differentiation between formal- and informal-sector workers are often congruent with, and reinforced by, divisions based on ethnicity. In Pernik, Roma are over-represented in Stomana's contract labor force, though hardly any have regular positions; and much the same goes for the *Oralman* (people of Kazakh ethnicity who are return migrants from Mongolia and Uzbekistan) in Temirtau. Hoffmann's *paledars* (who have insecure portering jobs) are all ("Tribal") Tharus, whereas those who are sponsored for regular jobs by the Maoist union come mainly from the local Madheshi peasantry. The Tata Motors shop floor is dominated by Biharis, who differ ethnically from both Tata management and the workforce in the Lohar Enterprises scrapyard; while in our Egyptian, Indonesian and Chinese examples there is a high degree of overlap between regular and precarious employment and the distinction between outsiders and locals. At the same time as ethnic identities may subvert "working-class" unity, our case studies suggest that they frequently strengthen *class* structuration *within* it.

Workers as Neoliberal Subjects?

In the ideology of neoliberalism, however, class disappears. Society is supposedly made up of autonomous individuals without collective identities. As Harvey (2005: 2) defines it, neoliberalism is "in the first instance a theory of political economic practices that proposes that human well-being can best be advanced by liberating individual entrepreneurial freedoms and capacities within an institutional framework characterized by strong private property rights, free markets, and free trade." In that framework, individuals are resourceful and creative, take charge of their own fate, give free rein to their entrepreneurial instincts, and adapt to market conditions. If they fail, they have only themselves to blame. It is they who must accept the burden of risk. Welfare is debilitating because it creates a "culture of dependency." Neoliberalism has achieved the status of a "hegemonic" discourse that is disseminated in innumerable ways by innumerable authorities who champion competition, self-reliance, and individual initiative. Its doctrines now pass as "common-sense," its economic "discipline" as "inevitable" (Bourdieu 1998; Harvey 2005; Miller and Rose 2008; Mirowski 2014). Neoliberal subjects fashion themselves (Türken et al. 2016). They are protean beings with chameleon-like qualities. "Flexibility" is a sanctified value, and all commitments are provisional. Harvey (2005: 4) quotes Lyotard's "famous description of the post-modern condition as one where 'the temporary contract' supplants 'the permanent institutions in the professional, emotional, sexual, cultural, family and international domains, as well as in political affairs.'" Even gender identities are now negotiable. Giddens's (1992, 1999) "sociological" analysis of intimacy celebrates this transformation in the personal realm, where couples are now, at any stage, (supposedly) free to terminate their relationship when it is no longer fulfilling. Neoliberalism is a mindset and a way of life.

One striking feature of the literature on neoliberal *subjectivity* is how much of it is really about neoliberal *discourse*. Subjectivity surely conveys the idea of some internal reality, but of the thoughts and feelings of ordinary actors we get little idea. What we learn is what the doctrine requires them to be. Of course, the discourse is much easier to access than the states of mind, but it is not a reliable proxy. The match may be very imperfect. As our ethnography shows, people cannot possibly believe all that neoliberalism tells them, and even if they did, their understandings might prove difficult to predict since the neoliberal agenda is self-contradictory. Although its doctrines and practices might have a significant impact on consciousness, that impact is indeterminate.

Ferguson's (1999) study of Zambian miners at the time of a dramatic downturn in the world market for copper makes it clear that neoliberalism may be chiefly productive of a paralyzing despair—a sense of abjection, of being expelled from the modern world and cast aside by history. These miners were far from being neoliberal subjects in the textbook sense. In a very different context, Gooptu's (2009, 2013) studies of retail workers and security guards in Kolkata shopping malls set out to show how their subjectivities are strongly shaped by the workplace, though the kinds of workers that populate such settings bear little resemblance to the go-getting entrepreneurial neoliberal subjects that figure in the dominant discourse. What the retail staff actually experience is the tyranny of targets, continual scrutiny of their performance, and a gnawing realization that they are in jobs with no future. The security guards continually encounter customers who regard them with contempt. Their training and experience teach them that the quality they most need is "the ability to accept," and that they must fashion themselves for servility. The market, Gooptu concludes, produces the kind of workers it needs; and her picture is of a rather effective ideological project that does indeed succeed in colonizing hearts and minds. Of that, however, it is difficult to be certain. We get little idea of how these workers talk about their jobs outside interview contexts, and no idea of the values they take from the workplace into their lives outside it. To neoliberal ideology in its "pure" form, one might expect some resistance. It is not obvious how its valorization of protean persons is to be reconciled with an ideology that claims that each caste has its own immutable essence.

Neoliberal subjects are the autonomous, self-directed sovereigns of their own persons. They must be flexible, which means disposable. Neoliberalism has shifted the already unequal balance of power between capital and labor, making jobs less secure while work regimes become subject to speed-ups and enhanced surveillance, and demand intensified effort. From Prentice's chapter we learn that although some women in Trinidad's garment industry say factory work is preferable, many others see greater advantage in home-based production, where they can better juggle their income-generating activities with their domestic responsibilities and "cast an eye" on the children—even if it means they are materially worse off.

The kind of person neoliberalism tells workers they should be is in contradiction with the kind of person the neoliberal work regime allows them
to be. This is evident in Trevisani's account of conditions on the Temirtau
shop floor and in Schober's description of the military-style discipline, long
hours, and compulsory overtime that are enforced in the Subic Bay shipyard. It emerges even more strikingly in Morris and Hinz's ethnography of
workers in a multinational car plant in Russia. Their jobs are unskilled and
unfulfilling; they have minimal scope for initiative; and compared to yes-
terday's workers in old-style Soviet factories, they have experienced a loss
of autonomy and must work at higher intensity. Yet at the same time, they
need the higher wages that the car plant offers if they are to be the kind of
get-ahead worker they have always aspired to become. This tension undermines their sense of self-worth. Outside the factory they can hardly bring
themselves to speak of their jobs. In it, they are thoroughly alienated—even
from the union, on which they remain free riders though it has brought
them tangible benefits.

Another disjunction is between the ideology of the entrepreneurial individual and the indubitable fact that nobody can make it alone. Success is
contingent on the ability to mobilize networks of support. Workers in the
Tirupur garment industry take considerable pride in their skills, and gov-
ernment-sponsored training programs foster the idea that their well-being
depends on their individual capabilities. Men in particular are expected
to strive and "get on" by graduating from apprentice to master tailor and
hopefully becoming a contractor or even an owner. But the key to that kind
of success is backing. As Carswell and De Neve observe in their chapter:
"Against the widespread neoliberal rhetoric of individuality, self-reliance
and independent enterprise, our informants reveal themselves as quintessentially non-neoliberal subjects whose lives continue to be shaped by
family relations and domestic responsibilities, and whose entrepreneurial success is as likely to rely on the support of kin, caste and friendship
networks as on individual skill, ability, or drive." Or consider Fang, who
argues that although the young women workers in one of the factories she
studied have insecure jobs, they are not afflicted by their precarity because
they see factory employment as a stepping-stone to becoming independent entrepreneurs. We do not know how often they succeed (rarely, one
suspects), but Fang clearly shows that they imagine they can realize their
aspirations by assiduously cultivating, in the traditional Chinese way, relationships based on *guanxi* with co-workers, bosses, and others—that is,
relationships based on reciprocity, gift giving, mutual obligation and trust,
and often on hierarchical deference. As they plainly see, the only way to
become a successful neoliberal subject is to embrace dependence on old-
style collective support.

Different groups of workers often have quite disparate reactions to the very similar conditions with which neoliberalism confronts them. Though the young female employees in Fang's THS factory (which is located in the Shenzen Special Economic Zone) may not be much concerned by job insecurity, it is a constant source of anxiety for the somewhat older cohort of workers in KSI (which is close to Shanghai). Sanchez's Tata apprentices and scrapyard labor respond to precarity in contrasting ways. Trevisani reports that for company workers in Temirtau the conscientious performance of their duties is almost an act of defiance—an assertion of their determination to keep the plant going despite the machinations of Finance and the London Office. They perform "work as resistance," whereas contract workers "work for subsistence"—to put food on the table. It is the former who work hardest.

Not only are workers' reactions far from uniform, but the lessons they are intended to learn about neoliberal subjectivity may depart radically from the authorized script. In his study of the aftermath of the Gujarat earthquake of 2004, Simpson (2013) shows how the devastation of Kutch allowed powerful political and economic interests from the eastern part of the state to impose their own agenda on it. The earthquake provided both the opportunity and the catalyst for a massive piece of social engineering. It created the space for a radical reorientation of the region's economy along neoliberal lines. By offering tax concessions and cheap land for industry, and giving investors every confidence that it would be extremely unlikely to implement its own environmental and labor laws, the state government turned Kutch into "a large and cut-price industrial estate" (ibid.: 39). But hand in hand with this economic program went a political project that aimed to refashion local society along lines laid down by an assertive ideology of Hindu supremacy. The reconstruction of towns and villages meant that formerly mixed communities could be unscrambled, and new separations between Hindus and Muslims, and between castes and classes, were created. Those who pulled the strings had no interest in nurturing malleable neoliberal individuals with transient commitments. What they wanted were hard-core Hindus.

There are echoes of that in the situation that Rudnyckyj describes. According to the diagnosis of the Emotional and Spiritual Quotient (ESQ) training program that Krakatau steel employees were encouraged to attend, the problems of global competition that the plant has been facing are pre-eminently due to the inadequate Islamic piety of its workforce. For the plant to be restored to health, workers must become better Muslims. This message is conveyed in protracted, carefully orchestrated, intensely emotional mass sessions in which participants are encouraged to weep in atonement, and which combine conventional Islamic teachings with lessons culled from Western self-help manuals and business management-speak.

How far that message is heeded, however, seems variable. While many managers talk of a profound spiritual awakening, workers are generally more skeptical: "Oh no, now we have to cry again!" ESQ training is explicitly intended to inculcate a spirit of individual initiative and self-reliance, and—skepticism notwithstanding—many trainees report that it does. To that extent we can say that it helps to install a neoliberal subjectivity. But at the same time it congeals identities. Elsewhere, Rudnyckyj (2010: 201f.) reports on a remarkable case of spirit possession that occurred during one of the ESQ sessions he attended. The possessed worker was an employee called Arfan, one of whose grandfathers was a Chinese Christian. The spirit that spoke through his mouth did so in "Chinese" (a language of which Arfan was ignorant) and displayed other distinctively Chinese characteristics. Through ESQ, it would seem, he was exorcising the Chinese part of his person to become a more complete Indonesian *Muslim*, a more "properly" anchored person with a more firmly fixed identity. That is not the individual of conventional neoliberal theory.

Neoliberal economies produce precarious workers, and precarity, as previously noted, is inimical to planning for the future and encourages clientelism and dependence on family support. How, under these circumstances, are such workers expected to be autonomous individuals capable of coolly evaluating their (often non-existent) options? Self-fashioning is a project for the relatively privileged, not for those who "do not know what tomorrow's job will be" (as Makram-Ebeid's informants express it). As the contributions by Keskküla, Kofti, and Sanchez poignantly illustrate, the casualization of labor has forced many in the younger generation into prolonged dependence, "infantilizing" them (Keskküla) and strengthening patriarchal authority within the household (Kofti). That might give pause to anybody tempted to suppose that, of Standing's three precariat "factions," it is the educated young robbed of a future who are going to prove the most "dangerous." What it rather suggests is that neoliberal conditions expose the neoliberal subject as a chimera from an imaginary world.

Lee reports that on the Copperbelt it is, tellingly, the older workers with regular jobs who have been best able to set up viable side businesses. The same is true in Bhilai, where BSP wages and credit have capitalized much of the most dynamic entrepreneurial activity in the informal sector. Often it is not, as the theory supposes, those outside the formal economy who start the small businesses that thrive, but those whose moonlighting enterprises are underwritten by it. Whereas regular Stomana workers continue to cultivate land in the nearby villages they come from, and can earn a supplementary income from their membership in collective herding groups (*batchia*), Kofti shows how this is impossible for contract workers due to the unpredictability of their jobs. They are consequently more fully proletarianized and less capable of entrepreneurial initiative. Neoliberal subjects are regularly smothered at birth by neoliberal economics.

The conclusion to be drawn from all this is that in the world created by the neoliberal economy, most people are positively prevented from becoming anything like a "proper" neoliberal subject. It may be true that in certain restricted circles the discourse has achieved a hegemonic status, but any claim that it is now firmly installed as part of the general "common sense" smacks of hyperbole. Such a proposition requires us to suppose that ordinary working people are willing to indefinitely suspend the common sense rooted in their everyday experience, which tells them that such a subject cannot possibly inhabit the same space as they do, and that the ideology and the practices that derive from it do not constitute a seamless and coherent whole. In that realization there is perhaps some glimmer of hope for the future.

Acknowledgments

Thanks are due to an anonymous reviewer, and to Chris Fuller, Chris Hann, Keith Hart, Andrew Sanchez, Alpa Shah, and Tommaso Trevisani for reactions to a draft.

Jonathan Parry is Emeritus Professor of Anthropology at the London School of Economics and Political Science. He has done field research on various topics in different parts of north and central India. His publications include *Caste and Kinship in Kangra* (1979), *Death in Banaras* (1994), and a number of edited volumes. He is currently completing a monograph on industrial labor in a central Indian steel town.

Notes

1. The argument clearly assumes that mobility between the two employment statuses— permanent and temporary—is understood to be possible (and that company policy deliberately fosters belief in that possibility). In Indian public-sector steel plants, the chances of such promotion are now squarely recognized as being extremely remote (see Strümpell in this volume; Parry 2013a); considerations of that kind cannot therefore explain the consent of contract labor.

2. This estimate was reported for 2014/15 by *Business Line* (16 June 2015). It is consistent with comparative data compiled by the Rashtriya Ispat Nigam Ltd for 2015/16, which show that while manpower accounted for 21 percent of total expenditure in Steel Authority of India units, it was a mere 3 percent in two big private companies. Extrapolating from figures provided by D'Mello (1991: 195), labor costs in the Indian

steel industry at the end of the 1980s—that is, before liberalization—had accounted for about 15.7 percent of total production costs.

3. The Marwaris are a well-known mercantile community from Rajasthan who now have huge commercial and industrial interests throughout the subcontinent and in many other parts of the world. Lakshmi Mittal, owner of the Temirtau steel plant, is a Marwari, as is Anil Agarwal, the founder and executive chairman of the Vedanta mining company, which figures in Lee's chapter.

4. Compare Teitelbaum (2011), whose argument on this, and on a number of other points, converges with Agarwala's.

5. See also the current Code of Business Ethics issued by the Magnitogorsk Iron and Steel Works. One of the clauses relating to the "Observance of Employees' Labour Rights" commits the company to fostering "labour traditions and so-called 'labour dynasties'" in the interests of promoting "corporate loyalty, labour discipline and productivity" (http://eng.mmk.ru/upload/iblock/717/Code1.pdf; last accessed 19 October 2017). Publicity material from the United Cement Group's plant at Semei in Kazakhstan proudly includes an account of the Belenko family's association with it over three generations (http://www.unicementgroup.com/news/show/id/27/lang/en.html; last accessed on 19 October 2017).

6. The sources on such practices are legion, but see, e.g., Breman (1996: 66), Sen (2008), Ramaswamy (1988: 29, 39, 181–182, 1994: 116–117), Chandavarkar (1994: 225), Holmström (1984: 214–6), De Haan (1994: 208), Parry (2013a).

7. More precisely, this category includes all who have posts in public-sector concerns but only those private-sector workers with regular employment in the largest, most modern and most bureaucratically organized factories. Only on these do the labor laws have any real purchase, and only such workers are said to have *naukri*.

8. This was the Chhattisgarh Mukti Morcha, mentioned earlier.

References

Agarwala, Rina. 2013. *Informal Labor, Formal Politics, and Dignified Discontent in India*. Cambridge: Cambridge University Press.

Arrighi, Giovanni and John Saul. 1973. *Essays on the Political Economy of Africa*. New York: Monthly Review Press.

Beynon, Huw. 1984. *Working for Ford*. Harmondsworth: Penguin Books.

Bosch, Gerhard. 2006. "Working Time and the Standard Employment Relationship." In *Decent Working Time: New Trends, New Issues*, ed. Jean-Yves Boulin, Michel Lallement, Jon C. Messenger, and Francois Michon, 41–64. Geneva: International Labor Office.

Bourdieu, Pierre. 1998. *Acts of Resistance: Against the New Myths of Our Time*. Cambridge: Polity Press.

Braverman, Harry. 1974. *Labour and Monopoly Capital: The Degradation of Work in the Twentieth Century*. New York: Monthly Review Press.

Breman, Jan. 1996. *Footloose Labour: Working in India's Informal Economy*. Cambridge: Cambridge University Press.

———. 2013. "'A Bogus Concept?' Review of Guy Standing, *The Precariat: The New Dangerous Class.*" *New Left Review* 84: 130–138.

Castells, Manuel. 1996. *The Rise of the Network Society.* Oxford: Blackwell.

Chandavarkar, Raj. 1994. *The Origins of Industrial Capitalism in India: Business Strategies and the Working Class in Bombay, 1900–1940.* Cambridge: Cambridge University Press.

Cooper, Frederick. 1992. "Colonizing Time: Work Rhythms and Labor Conflict in Colonial Mombasa." In *Colonialism and Culture*, ed. N. Dirks, 209–245. Ann Arbor, MI: University of Michigan Press.

———. 1996. *Decolonization and African Society: The Labor Question in French and British Africa.* Cambridge: Cambridge University Press.

Cross, Jamie. 2014. *Dream Zones: Anticipating Capitalism and Development in India.* London: Pluto Press.

De Haan, Arjan. 1994. *Unsettled Settlers: Migrant Workers and Industrial Capitalism in Calcutta.* Hilversum, Netherlands: Verloren.

D'Mello, Bernard. 1991. *Foreign Collaboration in the Public Sector Steel Industry.* Calcutta: Indian Institute of Management.

Dore, Ronald. 1973. *British Factory—Japanese Factory: The Origin of National Diversity in Industrial Relations.* Berkeley, CA: University of California Press.

Dumont, Louis. 1977. *From Mandeville to Marx: The Genesis and Triumph of Economic Ideology.* Chicago, IL: University of Chicago Press.

Ferguson, James. 1999. *Expectations of Modernity: Myths and Meanings of Urban Life on the Zambian Copperbelt.* Berkeley, CA: University of California Press.

Fernandes, Leela. 2000. "Restructuring the New Middle Class in Liberalizing India." *Comparative Studies of South Asia, Africa and the Middle East* 20(1–2): 88–104.

Fortes, Meyer. 1969. *Kinship and the Social Order: The Legacy of Lewis Henry Morgan.* London: Routledge and Kegan Paul.

Giddens, Anthony. 1975. *The Class Structure of the Advanced Societies.* New York: Harper Torchbooks.

———. 1992. *The Transformation of Intimacy: Sexuality, Love and Eroticism in Modern Societies.* Cambridge: Polity Press.

———. 1999. *Runaway World: How Globalisation is Reshaping Our Lives.* London: Profile Books.

Gill, Tom. 1999. "Wage Hunting at the Margins of Urban Japan." In *Lilies of the Field: Marginal People Who Live for the Moment*, ed. S. Day, E. Papataxiarchis, and M. Stewart, 119–136. Boulder, CO: Westview Press.

———. 2001. *Men of Uncertainty: The Social Organization of Day Laborers in Contemporary Japan.* Albany, NY: SUNY.

Gooptu, Nandini. 2009. "Neoliberal Subjectivity, Enterprise Culture and New Workplaces: Organised Retail and Shopping Malls in India." *Economic and Political Weekly* 44(22): 45–54.

———. 2013. "Servile Sentinels of the City: Private Security Guards, Organized Informality, and Labour in Interactive Services in Globalized India." *International Review of Social History* 58: 9–38.

Harriss, John. 1984. "Our Socialism and the Subsistence Engineer: The Role of Small Enterprises in the Engineering Industry of Coimbatore, South India." In *Planning for Small Enterprises in Third World Cities*, ed. R. Bromley, 137–153. Oxford: Pergamon Press.

Harvey, David. 2005. *A Brief History of Neoliberalism*. Oxford: Oxford University Press.

Holmström, Mark. 1984. *Industry and Inequality: The Social Anthropology of Indian Labour*. Cambridge: Cambridge University Press.

Jeffries, Richard 1975. "Populist Tendencies in the Ghanaian Trade Union Movement." In *The Development of an African Working Class: Studies in Class Formation and Action*, ed. Richard Sandbrook and Robin Cohen, 261–280. London: Longman.

Kingston, Paul W. 2000. *The Classless Society*. Stanford, CA: Stanford University Press.

Krishna, A. 2011. *One Illness Away: Why People Become Poor and How They Escape Poverty*. Oxford: Oxford University Press.

Lee, Ching Kwan. 2007. *Against the Law: Labor Protests in China's Rustbelt and Sunbelt*. Berkeley, CA: University of California Press.

Lockwood, David. 1958. *The Blackcoated Worker: A Study in Class Consciousness*. London: Unwin University Books.

Makram-Ebeid, Dina. 2013. *Manufacturing Stability: Everyday Politics of Labour in an Industrial Steel Town in Helwan, Egypt*. Unpublished Ph.D. thesis, London School of Economics and Political Science. Available at: http://etheses.lse.ac.uk/780/.

Miller, Gary. 1992. *Managerial Dilemmas: The Political Economy of Hierarchy*. Cambridge: University Press.

Miller, Peter and Nikolas Rose. 2008. *Governing the Present: Administrative, Social and Personal Life*. Cambridge: Polity Press.

Mirowski, Philip. 2014. *Never Let a Good Crisis Go to Waste: How Neoliberalism Survived the Financial Meltdown*. London: Verso.

Parry, Jonathan 1999. "Lords of Labour: Working and Shirking in Bhilai." *Contributions to Indian Sociology* (n.s.) 33(1–2): 107–140.

———. 2001. "Ankalu's Errant Wife: Sex, Marriage and Industry in Contemporary Chhattisgarh." *Modern Asian Studies* 35(4): 783–820.

———. 2005. "Changing Childhoods in Industrial Chhattisgarh." In *Educational Regimes in Contemporary India*, ed. R. Chopra and P. Jeffery, 276–298. New Delhi and London: Sage Publications.

———. 2007. "The Sacrifices of Modernity in a Soviet-Built Steel Town in Central India." In *On the Margins of Religion*, ed. F. Pine and J. Pina-Cabral, 233–262. New York: Berghahn Books.

———. 2009. "Sociological Marxism in Central India: Polanyi, Gramsci and the Case of the Unions." In *Market and Society: "The Great Transformation" Today*, ed. C. Hann and K. Hart, 175–202. Cambridge: Cambridge University Press.

———. 2012. "Suicide in a Central Indian Steel Town." *Contributions to Indian Sociology* 46(1–2): 145–180.

———. 2013a. "Company and Contract Labour in a Central Indian Steel Town." *Economy and Society* 42(3): 348–374.

———. 2013b. "The Embourgeoisement of a 'Proletarian Vanguard.'" In *Interrogating India's Modernity: Democracy, Identity and Citizenship*, ed. S. Jodhkar, 40–78. Delhi: Oxford University Press.

———. Forthcoming: *Classes of Labour in a Central Indian Steel Town*. New Delhi: Social Science Press.

Parry, Jonathan, and Christian Strümpell. 2008. "On the Desecration of Nehru's 'Temples': Bhilai and Rourkela Compared." *Economic and Political Weekly* 43(19): 47–57.

Peace, Adrian 1975. "The Lagos Proletariat: Labour Aristocrats or Populist Militants?" In *The Development of an African Working Class: Studies in Class Formation and Action*, ed. Richard Sandbrook and Robin Cohen, 281–302. London: Longman.

Polanyi, Karl. 1957 [1944]. *The Great Transformation: The Political and Economic Origins of Our Time*. Boston, MA: Beacon Press.

Pun, Ngai. 2005. *Made in China: Women Factory Workers in a Global Workplace*. Hong Kong: Hong Kong University Press.

Ramaswamy, E.A. 1988. *The Rayon Spinners: The Strategic Management of Industrial Relations*. Delhi: Oxford University Press.

———. 1994. *Worker Consciousness and Trade Union Response*. Delhi: Oxford University Press.

Roberson, James 1998. *Japanese Working Class Lives: An Ethnographic Study of Factory Workers*. London: Routledge.

Rudnyckyj, Daromir. 2010. *Spiritual Economies: Islam, Globalization, and the Afterlife of Development*. Ithaca, NY: Cornell University Press.

Sanchez, Andrew. 2016. *Criminal Capital: Violence, Corruption and Class in Industrial India*. London: Routledge.

Saul, John. 1975. "The 'Labour Aristocracy' Thesis Reconsidered." In *The Development of an African Working Class: Studies in Class Formation and Action*, ed. R. Sandbrook and R. Cohen, 303–310. London: Longman.

Sen, Samita. 2008. "Gender and Class: Women in Indian Industry, 1890–1990." *Modern Asian Studies* 42(1): 75–116.

Sengupta, Arjun, K.P. Kannan, and G. Raveendran. 2008. "India's Common People: Who Are They, How Many Are They and How Do They Live?" *Economic & Political Weekly* 43(11): 49–63.

Simpson. Edward. 2013. *The Political Biography of an Earthquake: Aftermath and Amnesia in Gujarat, India*. London: Hurst.

Standing, Guy. 2011. *The Precariat: The New Dangerous Class*. London: Bloomsbury Academic.

Teitelbaum, Emmanuel. 2011. *Mobilizing Restraint: Democracy and Industrial Conflict in Post-reform South Asia*. Ithaca, NY: Cornell University Press.

Türken, Salman, Hilde Nafstad, Rolv Blakar, and Katrina Roen. 2016. "Making Sense of Neoliberal Subjectivity: A Discourse Analysis of Media Language on Self-Development." *Globalizations* 13(1): 32–46.

Walder, Andrew. 1986. *Communist Neo-traditionalism: Work and Authority in Chinese Industry*. Berkeley, CA: University of California Press.

Waterbury, John. 1993. *Exposed to Innumerable Delusions: Public Enterprise and State Power in Egypt, India, Mexico and Turkey*. Cambridge: Cambridge University Press.

Weber, Max. 1978. *Selections in Translation*, ed. W.G. Runciman. Cambridge: Cambridge University Press.

Wilson, Wilson J. 1987. *The Truly Disadvantaged: The Inner City, the Underclass, and Public Policy*. Chicago, IL: University Press.

Wolcott, Susan. 1994. "The Perils of Lifetime Employment Systems: Productivity Advance in the Indian and Japanese Textile Industries, 1920–1938." *The Journal of Economic History* 54(2): 307–324.

Wolf, Diane. 1992. *Factory Daughters: Gender, Household Dynamics and Rural Industrialization in Java*. Berkeley, CA: University of California Press.

Wood, Geof. 2003. "Staying Secure, Staying Poor: The 'Faustian' Bargain." *World Development* 31(3): 455–471.

1

Varieties of Capital, Fracture of Labor

A Comparative Ethnography of Subcontracting and Labor Precarity on the Zambian Copperbelt

CHING KWAN LEE

Mines a thousand meters deep are unforgiving places. My ethnographic fieldwork in the mines began in October 2012 at the Chambishi mine, now owned by the Chinese state company Nonferrous Metal China, Africa (NFCA). As I shadowed safety officers and maintenance engineers to observe how miners work underground, I found myself utterly unprepared for the oppressive humidity, high temperatures, deafening noise, and pervasive, disorienting darkness. Trekking across uneven, muddy terrains and walking through sometimes knee-deep waters, I struggled to keep my balance and capture my share of the inadequate circulation of oxygen, all the while sweating profusely like everyone else. Sometimes between shifts, right after blasting, dusty, smoky air would move across dark and rugged rocks hanging over a stope ten meters wide that looked like a bottomless dark hole. If Hell existed, this would be it, I said to myself. I had no other vocabulary for this world.

On one of my first few trips down, after more than an hour at a particularly suffocating corner at level 826 meter, I felt as if my lungs had collapsed and stuck together: no air went in, no matter how hard I breathed. I told my colleagues that I would faint if I had to be there another five minutes and implored them to bring me up to the surface immediately, which they graciously did. Even as my lungs recovered, I felt deflated as a fieldworker. Later, when I moved on to the depths of two other mines in this study, Konkola Copper Mines (KCM) and Mopani Copper Mines (MCM)—both owned by London-listed multinationals—I was not only more acclimatized, but also aware that other underground mines were as hot, dark, and dangerous as the Chinese one. The Copperbelt made my old stomping grounds—factories in the sunbelt and the rustbelt of China—look like decent workplaces.

Like the miners, I sometimes forgot which mine I was in, once I went underground. And like me, the miners described their daily work in different mines as harsh, dangerous, and demoralizing. Derek Chanda, a miner at NFCA, joined the industry expecting more money because he knew it involved harder work. He began as a general worker and two years later was trained to drive a locomotive carrying copper ore; then, after another three years, he was promoted to PIC (person-in-charge). Now, after eight years, he is a shift boss at 700 meters:

> The underground is very risky and hostile, full of dangerous elements. At any moment, you face death, like from rock fall. I've seen many accidents. Previously almost every week, someone would be injured in the arm, legs or shoulders. Hard hats have no use when huge rocks fall. They have put in place more safety measures since 2010 ... It's so hot that it is like a grill, an oven. The ventilation is very poor; people feel weak because they cannot breathe well. Like someone has run a long distance. Fainting is common. Air is saturated with gases from the rocks, exhaust air from the trucks, and the dust from the boomer. For facing so many risks every day, we only get peanuts at the end of the month."[1]

MCM's underground is no better than that at NFCA. Victor Chilesite, a contract worker who has worked in different mines, highlighted the pressure to work hard, on top of the physically oppressive environment:

> It's slave-like condition... If you don't drink water, you'd pass out. MCM has safety standards but it gives contractors meters and the contractors only care about meeting the targets. There is a lot of pressure on the workers to meet the target but there are lots of problems everyday: waiting for machines to get repaired, congestion underground, or the machines are too hot and we have to stop for them to cool down. In an hour I can barely make one trip but the target is 10 trips a shift. The supervisors (section boss, shift boss, mine captain) keep shouting at you, 'tomorrow don't go down the mine', threatening to suspend me, when I don't make the target.

Despite doing physically strenuous work for hours on end, most miners did not eat during their shift underground. Following an industry-wide tradition, the mines issued miners two pieces of mine bread, or *kampompo* in Bemba, before they go down. Some companies provided a monthly ration of sugar, cacao, or tea leaves, if the unions managed to include these in their collective agreements. Still, with no official lunch break and only demanding production targets to meet, many would eat at home and save the *kampompo* for their children or spouse. Miners with pocket money to spare would buy soft drinks at the tuck shop near the change house, but many simply put sugar in their own water bottle, shook it, and used this sweet water as their source of energy for the day. With time, as they came to realize, their bodies got used to feeling hungry. An electrician at NFCA explained:

> Many people don't eat underground because the air is too bad. You'll get stomach ache if you eat in all the foul air. I either eat before I go down or after I come up. I feel hungry but I am used to it. A few people eat underground, but you have to find your own time. There is no official lunch break. Hygiene is generally bad underground because people urinate anywhere, and some even defecate at crosscuts [areas that are closed off after production is finished]. They are not supposed to but they do it anyway. You will be fired instantly if you are caught. The cotton masks they give us are not good enough for filtering the soot. It's always black when you take them off at the end of the shift. It's so hot underground that when supervisors are not around miners look for places where there is a bit of cool air or cool water dripping from the rocks.

The same is true of KCM's Nchanga underground, according to a 28-year-old contract scrapper driver:

> We spend 45 minutes walking from the man cage to the work area, and another 45 minutes back at the end of the shift. It's far away. We eat before going underground because there is no break for eating. Some people eat at the gathering area during the five-minute safety talk at the beginning of the shift. Toilets are so far away, near the haulage areas, it takes 30 minutes to get to. So people take a leak where they are when no one is around. If a supervisor caught you, you can be instantly fired. This is serious because airflow is bad enough here as it is.

Political, Legal, Technological, and Racial Disempowerment of Labor

Today, the degradation of work on the Copperbelt, where a multiplicity of foreign investors own and run different major mines, can be traced to four decades of disempowerment by both Zambian state policy and international financial institutions' imposition of structural adjustment. Despite having been a significant force in the struggle for national liberation, organized labor succumbed to the ruling United National Independence Party's corporatist control in the post-independence era. In the name of the national interest, Zambia's first president, Kenneth Kaunda, declared strikes illegal but offered miners paternalism in the form of a "cradle-to-grave" welfare system that subsidized "diapers and burials," food, and housing. When copper prices collapsed after the mid 1970s, the IMF met workers' demands for wage increases and subsidies with staunch resistance. By the late 1980s, the trade union, increasingly alienated from the ruling party, led a society-wide resistance to adjustment and austerity, eventually bringing the union leader Frederick Chiluba to power and ushering in multi-party democracy with the promise of rolling back neoliberalism. President Chiluba then reversed his position and became an ardent supporter of privatization, famously asking workers to "die a little" to revitalize the national economy. It was during Chiluba's reign in the 1990s that labor law reform, part of loan conditionality, laid the framework for today's production regime (Larmer 2007). In one revision after another, the Zambian labor code declared sympathy strikes illegal, splintered the trade union movement, removed the compulsoriness of industry-level collective bargaining, and deregulated the labor market by changing the definition of "casual worker" so that it allowed for a longer duration of casual jobs. Together, these neoliberalization measures accomplished what Marxists would call "primitive accumulation"—subjecting noncapitalist labor and assets to the logic of capitalist profit making—well before Chinese and non-Chinese investors arrived. The past decade has not seen any reversal in the declining power of organized labor, even with the election of the populist president Michael Sata and his pro-poor economic policies.

Along with Zambian laws and politics, global standards for the production technologies and labor processes of mining and construction have also undermined the workplace bargaining power of workers across sectors and investors. With privatization and new investors came mechanization of the mines. Turning away from the extensive use of manual underground labor typical of the late 1960s, the mines in this study have all brought in American and Swedish heavy equipment (brands such as Caterpillar, Sandvik, and Atlas Copco) to achieve higher levels of productivity. Today, the most common underground sight is no longer miners drilling with jackhammers, but operators and drivers mobilizing large boomers, loaders, and dump trucks. Workers have become highly replaceable, though the labor process of mining has not changed: it consists mainly of drilling and blasting for primary and secondary development (i.e., digging new seams to access the ore), stope drilling and blasting for production (extracting the ore), lashing (moving the ore to a tip), and crushing and transporting the ore to the concentrator for processing (extracting copper from the ore). The worldwide trend has been to use subcontractors, who for their part offer only minimal training to short-term contract workers.

Another striking similarity among foreign-owned workplaces is the "colored" glass ceiling. Expatriates dominate senior management in all foreign companies in mining, accounting for 5–10 percent of a company's workforce. Despite widespread rumors, scholarly research has not found any empirical evidence to substantiate the claim that Chinese companies bring their own manual workers rather than hiring local Africans. Strictly speaking, the "color bar" principle (i.e., that no white man should be subordinate to a Zambian) that prevailed in the colonial period is no longer upheld. Still, though, an invisible glass ceiling that is operative to varying degrees ensures that Zambians rarely number among the "chiefs" (chief executive officer, chief production officer, chief operation officer, chief financial officer, etc.). Under Zambian regulations, the human resource manager has to be a Zambian; this is often the highest position held by Zambians at the corporate level. Racial subordination of Zambian managers and professionals is a muted issue today because these employees, who lack collective representation, must resort to individualist strategies for moving ahead on the corporate ladder and therefore are often seen as suspect in the eyes of the Zambian rank-and-file workers in most mines. On the other hand, workers and unions alike agree that companies aggressively discipline expatriates for any racist remarks and demeanors, so interpersonal racism is not a salient problem.

Beneath these similarities in the political, technological, and racial apparatus of production, the three mines differ significantly in the way they do mining. Chinese state capital's interest in long-term, stable production of copper ores, as part of a complex set of imperatives beyond profit maximization, is manifested in the way NFCA invests in exploration, drills for mineable reserves, and makes everyday production decisions. Its peculiarity can only be seen in contrast to the other two mines, driven by what Zambian mining experts call the "trader mentality," in which copper is traded for short-term profit. MCM's parent company Glencore is the world's leading commodity trader, and KCM's parent company Vedanta sees processing (smelting and refining), rather than mining, as its most important profit stream (Lee 2014). Here, I will focus on their adoption of different approaches to subcontracting.

Contract Mining

While all three mines subcontracted mining to cut costs, the much greater financial pressure on KCM and MCM to deliver profit to shareholders drove them to maintain a much larger pool of subcontractors than NFCA's. KCM was particularly notorious for ruthlessly using competition among subcontractors to drive down costs, so much that an internal critical discourse arose among its own managers about the "tyranny of finance." It referred to the Commercial Department's supreme power, overriding that of Operation, to make production decisions (e.g., the purchase of machinery and choice of subcontractors). Though its subcontracting method was based more on performance than cost, MCM resembled KCM in the large extent of its subcontracting. In contrast, NFCA has for the sake of stability used only one mining subcontractor, also from China, since production started in 2003. Some senior managers at MCM attributed this trend to the merger of its parent company, Glencore, a global trader, with Xstrata, a mining major. That is, MCM now stands midway between the producer mentality of NFCA and the trader mentality of KCM. The difference in their practice of subcontracting was literally visible—the presence of large numbers of subcontractors at KCM and MCM made their mines more colorful than NFCA's. The variegated colors of uniforms worn by subcontractors' workers—red, orange, blue, green, and brown, mixed in with the white overalls of KCM and MCM—contrasted sharply with the unvarying army green of NFCA uniforms and the worker's blue of its single subcontractor, JCHX.

The CEO of KCM traced the origin of subcontracting to privatization, but it intensified after 2008:

> From 2000 on, you had the start of a transition to contract mining. Then, with the 2008 meltdown, we began what people call "extensive" outsourcing. It's a matter of survival. We did not have money to buy new machinery for the open pit, for example, so we decided to subcontract to other people who bring in the capital and equipment. It's a matter of capital allocation, to have time and money for core competences. We subcontract primary and secondary development, but production we do it ourselves. We will never outsource processing, the smelter...Subcontracting is here to stay. Mechanization will increase and labor will come down by 20–30% over the next 5 years.

The main attraction of contractors was that they were cheaper than employees—about 20 percent less—because of overheads involved in directly employing people, according to a production manager at Nchanga. But from the perspective of those in production, what made KCM's use of subcontractors problematic was the price competition the company used to select subcontractors. The head of the Commercial Department explained to me that he normally negotiated with two finalists, using each of them as leverage to drive down the other's cost. Trying to contain his frustration and anger, the Nchanga assistant mine manager complained about the "tyranny of Commercial" at KCM: "A lot of times Commercial drives down the price so hard that they actually bring down the contractors. I cannot reject the contractors Commercial picked just based on price. A good portion of them have failed mid-way and they affect me in production. So in the end you are not saving at all."

In 2012/13, for instance, KCM's Nchanga Underground mine used twenty-eight subcontractors to undertake a wide range of tasks in its labor-intensive Lower Ore Body: production scrapping, secondary development, lashing, steel support, tramming, long hole drilling, track and haulage maintenance. Of these subcontractors, 98 percent were local businesses owned by former miners and people unrelated to mining such as teachers, civil servants, and traders. Upper Ore body was highly mechanized and engaged subcontractors who were more capitalized and mechanized. They came from Chile, Peru, and South Africa.

Nobody understood the problems subcontracting inflicted on mining production better than one KCM manager who had been "rehired" after his retirement to solve problems created by subcontractors. Attending one of the production meetings between this KCM manager and its subcontractors was like watching him teach a management course to a group who did not know the basics. Subcontractors were paid at a piece rate per cubic meter; some of them brought their own machines, while others just brought labor. Because their profit margin was low, not more than 5 percent, they could easily go under and could offer only low wages to their staff. The quality of their frontline supervision (site manager, mine captain, section boss) and the morale of labor were therefore always low. At the beginning of the month after employees collected their wages, absenteeism was so intractable that the only solution the KCM manager could find to reduce its impact on KCM was to schedule a mandatory KCM "men to rest" holiday at that time. He and his colleagues were resigned to the fact that low motivation would persist as long as indirect workers were paid some 40 percent less than KCM's direct workers, with whom they worked side by side. Other common problems concerned contractors' delaying of payment to their own workers, which triggered a downing of tools that necessarily disrupted KCM's own production schedule. Contractors offered terms of employment, some providing *kampompo*, PPE (personal protective equipment), and housing allowances, and some not, to workers who practically were doing the same jobs. Turnover was very high, creating gaps in labor supply, especially for jobs that many young Zambians—the "digital kids," as the KCM manager called them—found too tough on arrival at the minesite.

Down the road, MCM also used a large number of subcontractors, despite having moved away from cutthroat competitive subcontracting toward adoption of a performance principle of awarding contracts. As at KCM's Nchanga minesite, at MCM's Nkana minesite each of the three shafts engaged about twenty subcontractors to do charging and blasting, long hole drilling, diamond drilling, grouting, maintenance of rails, de-sludging of water, and so forth. Coordination among contractors was a key problem that arose every day and was brought into bold relief at the daily 6 a.m. production meeting with the underground mine manager's office. Which contractor should be responsible for the prior day's shortfall in production was a question that usually sparked a lot of heated argument.

Like the CEO of KCM, a board director at MCM who had worked from 1975 to 2000 at ZCCM (the Zambian state-owned company before privatization), also recognized that subcontracting, even though it has been an immediate solution to the problem of capital shortage, was still less than ideal.

> The ideal is to do everything ourselves... Under ZCCM there was little subcontracting. By the time of privatization, development was at our nose because there was no working capital to bring in equipment. After privatization, MCM brought in contractors who were capable of bringing capital and equipment. 50% of development was contracted out. But they are under our management. Production and processing is 100% in house. The cost of a direct labor is twice as much as an indirect labor. It's a matter of lesser unit cost of production [the overhead cost—pension, medical, school—is just too much and will eliminate any increase in efficiency in productivity] But contracting is not efficient and a big headache. For instance, when a contractor has the machine to develop an end but needs a loader to lash. He goes to a MCM shift boss and asks for a loader, but the MCM guy also has his own end to lash. He has to decide on the priority, and contractors are usually given second positions... Safety statistics of the contractors count as ours. Their guys are usually only inducted in one week, whereas our people are trained for months and years and know all the safety issues...

The underground mine manager who supervised these contractors complained to me at length about other hidden problems with having subcontractors do all but the actual loading and tramming of ores.

The situation is different at NFCA. Until recently, it engaged only one contractor to undertake underground mining, and it runs the processing (the concentrator), transport, and logistics (haulage, maintenance, and water supply) directly. There are historical, organizational, and market supply reasons for this arrangement, but what is important for my comparative purpose here is that the Chinese model of subcontracting is driven by stable fulfillment of production targets, more than cost reduction. When I described the extent of subcontracting in other mines to the Chinese production head at NFCA, he was shocked and snapped, "I cannot imagine how it is possible. Their managers must become nuts coordinating all these subcontractors. That's not how we do contracting in China. We agree on an output and a price and don't intervene in their production.

> In 1998, when NFCA was set up, its parent company in China had just emerged from a reorganization of China's state-owned mining sector. Historically it specialized in overseas engineering and construction, and it had no experience in underground copper mining. The CEO had brought the project to the company's doorstep thanks to a personal connection he had with the Beijing leadership, but he had to find a partner to undertake mining. NFCA decided the private company JCHX would form the mining department inside NFCA. JCHX, headquartered in Beijing, exists

in Zambia as a department. The NFCA manager explained: "In 2010, they separated from NFCA as an independent company registered in Zambia. I regulate them on two aspects: economic terms which are set by contracts, and then there are technical and safety standards I have to check on a daily basis." Developing together with NFCA, JCHX has now become China's leading international-profile contract miner with an. The Shanghai-listed company recently signed a five-year development and engineering contract with KCM for which NFCA supplied the equipment and JCHX produced the tonnage of ores and maintained equipment.[2] Describing JCHX's relationship with NFCA, its on-site director said it operates as an "appendage" to the client, with very low profit margin but also low risk. Sparing itself the coordination complexities and cutthroat price competition among contractors found in the other two mines, NFCA took on a sole subcontractor on which it placed all production pressure. The result of these differences in subcontracting (as well as in exploration and mine development, as I have explained elsewhere [Lee 2014]) is, according to Zambian experts and officials, that NFCA has been the most stable producer on the Copperbelt. But does that matter for the workers?

Struggles for Permanent Employment

Throughout the mines, the pervasiveness of subcontracting was glaringly illustrated by the composition of their respective workforces. In 2012, the majority of workers in all three mines were indirect employees, or those hired by subcontractors (Table 1.1). The Mine Contractors Allied Workers Union of Zambia, a new union registered in 2010, claimed that 80 percent of mining jobs are now done by contractors' workers. Through different means, mining houses recruit basically three kinds of contractors that bring different productive resources to the mines. At the top of the hierarchy are multinational and regional contract miners, mostly from South Africa or Peru, which bid for contracts that are advertised on the Internet. They are well capitalized to provide full service (machinery and manpower) to the mines to run open pits, tailing leach plants, and underground development. The second tier consists of foreign and local contractors who have

Table 1.1 Basic conditions of three foreign-owned mines on the Zambian copperbelt (2012)

	MCM	KCM	NFCA
Workforce Direct	8,776	8,689	1,209
Workforce Sub-contract	9,800	13,217	1,883
Copper Production (tons)	117,804	200,000	26,178
Ore Grade	2%	3.5%	1.73%

the financial capacity to bring in some equipment, like long haul drills and boomers. At the bottom are the labor hires, that is, contractors who only provide labor. For miners, the terms of service vary widely among these contractors and are invariably inferior to direct employment by the mining houses.

Given the short duration and high mobility of mine employment, many miners have accumulated comparative insights on how the various mines treat workers. While describing working conditions in similarly harsh critical terms, miners noted a major difference between the Chinese and the other two foreign mines: NFCA and its contractor JCHX offer low-paying but stable employment, whereas other mines pay higher salary but are more prone to retrenchment and casualization.

Victor Chilesite had worked for five employers in the past eight years. When I met him, he had just moved from the Peruvian contractor at MCM to JCHX at NFCA and relished the modicum of security this new job brought him. With the Chinese contractor, he has finally landed a permanent job. Victor's career trajectory was typical of many "casuals" (used interchangeably with "contract workers"):

> I started as a track layer with Ramsi [a South African contractor] at Mopani Shaft 1, then with RMS [another South African concern] as loader driver, then as a driller with AAC mining [which is Zambian], operating a jack hammer. From there I became a boomer with Sanvik mining; then as a loader driver and dump truck driver with Reliant [a Peruvian contractor], and am now with the Chinese JCHX. Most were 3 months to one or two year contracts. These companies trained me, but while I was in training I was paid only the basic salary and housing allowance, but not other allowances [food, transport, shift differentials, Sunday overtime, bonus, etc.]. Reliant is worse than JCHX, because there is no rest between 7 days of day shift, then 7 days night shift. They give you targets and you have to stay [underground] until you finish, and then you have to wait a long time for the cage. For Sunday, there is no overtime pay … The Peruvians insult in their language, saying something like "guta mierda" "kalacko". I know it means fuck you … Shift boss always says you have to blast even if you see non-compliance. Every 3 meters there should be support before drilling, but you will find support only every 10 meters, rather than 3. He will make the mine captain sign to shift his responsibility. When MCM people come, they would say don't blast until support is done. But once they leave, Reliant people will ignore MCM people, especially in afternoon or night shifts when they don't walk around that much … The reason I moved from Reliant to JCHX is job security. Reliant only gives one year contracts; at JCHX, you start with a one year contract, then 3 years and then they would offer you permanent … But the air is worse than in Mopani, because they don't wait for dust and fumes to dissipate after blasting. It's a safety issue. There is no ventilation.

Permanent employment for indirect employees in the Chinese mine did not come about because of the employer's largesse. It was the result of worker struggle—two strikes in 2011 that started in JCHX but whose effects inevitably spilled over to NFCA. As mentioned in the last section, JCHX came to Zambia as a contractor for NFCA, but until 2010 it led a shadowy existence as its Mining Department. The Human Resource Department managed one payroll for all NFCA workers, who were represented by the same union branches and included in the same collective agreement. But when JCHX registered as an independent company in 2010, the transition of workers in the Mining Department to JCHX payroll sparked bitter conflicts between workers and the two companies. The contention first focused on severance payment and then turned to issues of equal treatment, permanent contracts for all, and the same pay rate for workers in the same grades across the two companies. Miners went on a week-long strike in February 2011, smashing windows, looting the canteens, damaging security lighting, and even setting fire to the mine police post, paralyzing production. The Zambian minister of mines intervened, demanding that workers resume work and the mine drop charges against the workers who had been arrested for the riot. Management did not honor its promises, and another strike took place in November 2011. It originated in JCHX and then spread to NFCA; production was suspended for about three weeks. At this point, management yielded and agreed to a phased standardization of grades and permanent contracts for all after an initial three years.

Contract workers in other mines also tried to resist casualization, but in contrast to the effort at the Chinese mine, their solidarity was more easily broken due to the large number of subcontractors. In May 2012, some two thousand workers at KCM pulled off a rare strike, putting down tools in protest against the pay discrepancy between KCM's direct and indirect employees. Because they were fearful of losing their jobs and totally unorganized, the incident lasted barely half a shift. Pastor Mwale, who participated that day, explained:

> As a crew boss of Gilgle Mining (a Zambian contractor) I get K1.5 million basic, while KCM pays K6 million. KCM employees receive a production bonus but we don't get anything ... (During the strike) J.J. (the CEO of KCM) came down to the emergency point near the shaft, threatening to dismiss anyone not reporting back to work immediately. He even said the President (Banda) supported this policy against striking workers. He told us to go to your directors to discuss pay and bonuses. You are not KCM employees. Workers shouted that KCM did not care about worker suffering. All you care is to take our money to India. Police were at the gate ready to arrest people and cameras captured the faces of those on strike.

The Chinese NFCA was the only mine where its contractor's workers could get permanent terms of employment, but as in other mines, a big gulf existed in the conditions of service for direct and indirect (subcontractors') employees. Comparing NFCA and its contractor JCHX, Derek Chanda told me that

> NFCA gives higher salaries. At Grade 6, my net income at JCHX is K2.75 million, compared to K2.95 million on the other side. NFCA sticks to its knock off time; at JCHX if I let my people knock off at the official time, I'd be booked (charged) for letting people go on time, and miners will be booked when they come out of the man cage, their cap lamp number will be noted and they will have their salary deducted. They think miners should only resurface at 17hrs ... There is more motivation among workers at NFCA than JCHX. We get loans with Bayport but they do not exceed K2 million, but NFCA has several institutions giving bigger loans, up to K50 millions. My friend is able to do something for the family, like start building a house, but I can't. With K2 million, I can only pay my children's school fees. If I missed my target for my shift, NFCA would ask me to write something to explain. At JCHX, they would just shout at you in front of your juniors.

Also, many workers at the Chinese state mine reminded me that the relative employment "security" at NFCA and JCHX comes at the high price of "low wages." Since its inception, NFCA's salary level for the general workforce has been about 30 percent lower than KCM's, which is the highest on the Copperbelt, and 15 percent lower than MCM's, the second highest. This low-wage regime is the empirical basis for the widespread criticism that the Chinese mine is particularly exploitative; however, some see the relative employment security as compensating for the lower pay. As the mining expert observed, NFCA has never engaged in mass retrenchment, which is global private companies' typical first response to fluctuation in the price of copper as well as to any pressure to cut production costs. During the 2008 financial crisis, NFCA famously announced a "no retrenchment" policy when both KCM and MCM were laying off workers by the thousands. In 2013, KCM twice threatened to retrench a total of 3,500 workers due to low copper prices and a purported "mechanization" plan.

Neither Chinese state capital nor global private capital was particularly benign toward labor, but they did present relatively different bargains: stable exploitation (secure employment at low wages) or flexible exclusion (short-term contracts at higher wages). The roots of this difference are partly historical. The new investors who privatized the mines inherited some distinct labor conditions there, but the differences are also partly due to the respective interests of the two varieties of capital (i.e., Chinese state vs. global private capital).

Take the case of NFCA. Its interest in long-term access and extraction of copper as a physical, not financial, resource puts it in a position to plan for expanded production, necessitating that labor be a stable input.

According to Zambian officials representing the Zambian government as a minority shareholder on the boards of all major mines, NFCA is the only company that has always met its production targets—at other mines, operational and financial problems have prevented achievement of stable production. Paradoxically, NFCA's policy of low wages can also be traced to its logic of encompassing accumulation. The parent company's investment decision to acquire Chambishi had not been totally based on its profitability, and NFCA strained to turn a profit with the inferior ore grade extracted there. It dealt with this situation by adopting a low-wage regime. Also, the mine had been closed for thirteen years, so NFCA had few legacy obligations. NFCA took on only some fifty care and maintenance workers under pre-privatization conditions of service, i.e., permanent status and union membership. The rest of the newly employed workforce was hired on fixed-term contracts at wage rates unencumbered by the standards of the previous employment regime. Lacking any domestic experience with autonomous unions or collective bargaining, the Chinese management tried to stall union recruitment for several years. These practices gave NFCA a notorious reputation as the worst employer on the Copperbelt. Over the years, unions persistently pressured NFCA to match the industry norm in terms of medical coverage for miners' dependents, classification of job grades, and basic salaries, playing a big role in bringing about gradual but consistent improvements. In most years, the rate of salary increment reached through collective bargaining is now on par with other mines. Still, due to the low base level at Chambishi, the Chinese mine remains the lowest paying of the major mines on the Copperbelt.

On the other hand, the global investors that owned KCM and MCM took over large, functioning mines. The comparatively well organized unions and workers at KCM and MCM sent more forceful negotiators to the bargaining table, compelling the investors to offer the existing workforces the same salary levels and conditions of service they had had under state ownership. But while wages are higher in these global private mines, their workers are challenged by these corporations' tendency to downsize and exclude labor altogether. Unlike Chinese state investors, these private corporations were under constant pressure to "show" shareholders that they were responding to copper price fluctuations by cutting costs. Retrenchment and its variant, casualization of labor through subcontracting, is therefore the crucible of labor-management conflicts at KCM and, to a lesser extent, MCM. KCM stopped hiring any direct employees when the financial crisis hit in 2008. Unions and workers found retrenchment a more difficult and elusive battle to fight, as it basically excluded workers from the realm of employment altogether.

Fractured Labor: Alienated Unions and Generational Divide

The Mineworkers Union of Zambia lost its monopoly status on the Copperbelt in 2004, when the National Union for Mine and Allied Workers (NUMAW) was formed. A third union, the United Mineworkers Union of Zambia, came onto the scene in 2010, followed by the Mine Contractors and Allied Workers' Union of Zambia, formed in 2012 in Chingola to represent casual laborers working for contractors. The company versus contract divide is institutionalized by the advent of this newest union for contractors' workers, which operates independently from the other three unions representing permanent workers only. Every year, these unions hold individual or joint collective bargaining sessions with mining companies where they have members. The rising numbers of unions belies their powerlessness vis-à-vis management and their declining status and integrity in the eyes of the rank-and-file members.

Without independent capacity for research or sources of economic data, union leaders found themselves in a defensive, passive position. In the collective bargaining sessions I observed at KCM and NFCA, and according to unionists themselves, the human resource manager typically set the parameters of the salary increment debate by being the sole source of statistics about profit, cost, and production volumes. When companies claimed they were not making money despite rising copper prices, all the unions could say was, "We don't believe you. Our workers know the company makes money on cobalt, not just copper. And the smelter processes ores from other mines, not just our own." Even when management admitted to making profits, they always rejected unions' demand for salary hikes, saying profits were used for reinvestment into expanded production or upgrading of technology.

Powerless to deal with the companies, unionists likewise held little sway with their own members. Many openly expressed distrust of unionists, in numerous ways. One day in Nkana (a MCM minesite) as I was walking with the NUMAW branch chairman and secretary to their office, passing dilapidated buildings that used to be the mine mess, gym, movie theater, and bowling club, some miners shouted at them, teasingly but aggressively, "Chairman, give us our money!" The unionists turned to me and explained that workers all believed union officials got extra pay from the company to compromise during negotiations. When the annual bargaining meetings were stalled for whatever reason, rank-and-file members routinely expressed frustration by throwing stones at them. The popular perceptions of collusion between unions and management stemmed from things like fully paid "overseas study tours" on which unionists visited the headquarters or subsidiary mines of these companies. NFCA offered trips to Beijing and Shanghai to branch and national union officials, KCM took them to New Delhi and mines in India, and MCM showed them some gold mines in South Africa. Managers and unionists from various mines admitted to me that bribery existed, but both sides claimed the money did not change the dynamic of negotiations.

Another important factor in workers' disillusion with the unions was the latter's failure to protect workers dismissed for allegedly instigating strikes or disrupting production. In the name of the national interest, Zambian President Kaunda declared strikes illegal. The 1971 Labor Relations Act made strikes practically illegal, and sympathy strikes were declared explicitly illegal by the Industrial and Labor Relations Act of 1993. Company attorneys and HR managers today are confident that it is lawful to dismiss workers for inciting strikes, and that following the procedures laid down in the company disciplinary code will enable the companies to win any lawsuits brought against them by workers. Unions' hands are tied by these regulations. Workers have occasionally sued union officials too for misinforming them or lying about their participation in work stoppages.

Along with the fault line between workers and unions, generational and status cleavages have fractured miners from within and undermined their collective capacity. This divide is more salient in today's working-class resistance than gender and tribal identities. The industry as a whole is male-dominated, both on the surface and underground. Interviews with miners' wives in Chambishi showed that women, like the rest of the mining community, were usually supportive of higher wages for miners, and some of them admitted to joining in the protests outside the mine gate, just as women did during Copperbelt protests of the 1970s and 1980s (Larmer 2007: 113, 128, 150). I did not have breakdowns of the labor force according to ethnicity or tribal affiliation. Most miners spoke Bemba, the prevailing dialect, and tribal identities were not invoked in any discussion of class conflicts, collective bargaining, or management discourses.

A generational divide in housing was salient in both everyday conversations and the visible spatial order of the mining communities. The housing situations, employment conditions, and life chances of older miners who had joined the mines under state ownership differed meaningfully from those of the younger ones taken on after privatization. In Chambishi, for instance, where many NFCA miners live, the generational divide between miners who benefited from the sales of ZCCM housing stock and their younger counterparts who missed the boat showed up in residential patterns and unequal financial capacity for entrepreneurship. In the Copperbelt today, familial succession to mining jobs appears to be rare; I encountered only one case in which a father and son worked in the same mine. Older and nicer homes built in the ZCCM era, with electricity and plumbing, are found in the township section of Chambishi where veteran miners live. Some of these miners have the financial wherewithal to run small businesses, selling groceries and cell phone recharge cards or supplying parts or services to the mines. They have even formed a small business association based in Chambishi. Adjacent to the township is the Zambia Compound, where younger miners and casual workers live in shoddy mud houses crammed together amidst open sewage. The whole area is strewn thick with white mealie meal bags, which residents piece together as fences to create some privacy. There is no electricity or indoor plumbing. Abject poverty is in plain view—children too poor to go to school play outside their homes during the day, women wait in line to fetch water from a community tap, and young men and women drink their days away in rowdy neighborhood bars serving strong local brews, dirt cheap.

Older miners bought their homes as sitting tenants when ZCCM was privatized. For instance, for a home worth K6 million, a miner was credited 2 percent of the home's price per year of service at the mines, so that a miner with twenty years of tenure would be credited 40 percent of K6 million or K2.4 million, and had to pay the remaining K3.6 million in cash. But since the revised Employment Act of 2000 removed the clause requiring employers to provide housing to employees, young miners who were not given the chance to buy ZCCM housing have had to rent. Still, all mine employees, whether homeowners or renters, receive housing allowances amounting to 35–39 percent of their basic salary. As one veteran miner observed, "Younger miners therefore have been relatively deprived twice."

Pockets of permanent casualization can be found in all mining townships next to the mines: Wusakile near Mopani, Chiwempala and Lulamba near KCM, and Chambishi near NFCA. Informal and unemployed workers have often participated in violent looting when mines went on wildcat strikes. All three mines have experienced strikes that started in the mines and were instantly joined and escalated by laid-off casual workers in the compounds. The latter group wanted to take revenge on the mines, and it had nothing to lose and everything to gain from a strong show of force against the companies. "Even the bartender or the street kids would like to see a bigger pay raise for the miners. When miners have more money, they spend more in the local community," recounted a veteran miner who has witnessed the 2012 strike at KCM. "Some of these are thugs who wanted to steal and vandalize company properties during the riot. They threw stones at workers whom they suspected were going back to work. They terrorized and assaulted union leaders, saying they have accepted bribes from the mines."

Similar dynamics characterized wildcat strikes at NFCA and MCM, where violent and angry casuals and unemployed locals, at the moment of an imminent strike, seized the opportunity to paralyze the mines by attacking miners who tried to return to work. Such grassroots militancy has been a key bargaining chip for the unions, which adopted ambiguous, highly flexible stances towards wildcat strikes. When bargaining sessions reached a stalemate, union representatives threatened management with potential agitations by their members and communities, even as unions were themselves hard pressed to control such non-institutionalized grass-roots disturbances.

A 45-year-old jackhammer operator at KCM who has worked in the mines since 1983 recalled the fear he experienced during a two-day strike in 2006 and a week-long strike in 2007: "Most of the time, during strikes, most miners stayed home. But most agitations are by people related to miners. They would kill me if I went beyond the picket line." In 2009, a three-day strike broke out at KCM. Again, informal and unemployed workers in compounds around KCM were at the forefront of both disturbance outside the mines and, especially, vandalism of Indian expatriates' residences. Township residents and workers were the targets of looting and violence as often as the mining houses were. What transpired during these episodes of strikes and unrest was not cross-class alliance or mobilization among the casuals, unemployed youth, mine workers, and residents of the mining communities. Rather, these incidents resulted from the confluence of uncoordinated interests motivated more by fear and anger than by solidarity, as the most marginalized people in the mining townships inflicted intimidation and looting on miners themselves as much as on the companies.

What is also important is that today, strikes do not spread to the entire Copperbelt as they did before privatization. Human resource managers from the major mines concurred that strikes today were not as powerful as those of yesteryear. A KCM manager observed that:

> Strikes have always been here. Nowadays, they usually happen when negotiations are going on. The miners do that to put pressures on management. Since privatization strikes happen every two years or so. Strikes under ZCCM were more powerful: they paralyzed the Copperbelt and the nation because ZCCM ran so many businesses. Today, one mine strikes the others are not affected. Also, during ZCCM there was only one union, today the unions are split and there is less unity.

Precarious Entrepreneurship and the Culture of Loans

Rather than pinning their hopes on collective struggle, miners have focused their energy on personal strategies of survival. During the nationalization period, sidelines and other entrepreneurial activities among miners and their wives served to supplement miners' income and welfare, or, since the

1980s, as a response to the worsening economic environment. For instance, the women in Patience Mususa's ethnography of the mining town Luanshya reported engaging in peddling agricultural produce, knitting sweaters for sale, and raising poultry in their backyards, before privatization (Mususa 2014: chapter 3).[3] Today's entrepreneurialism is a more central preoccupation among male miners because of the seeming permanence of the precariousness of employment. Hanging onto their current jobs as best they could, many, especially the younger generation, were actively preparing for an eventual exit. Starting around 2007, the most important function of the unions, other than representing their members at the annual collective bargaining table, became arranging micro-loans between their members and banks like Bayport, Barclays, and Finance Bank. The interest rate, around 17–20 percent, was usually a few points lower than the market rate, and the repayment period hovered around one to two years, depending on the length of the employment contract. The mining companies facilitated the loans by setting up an automatic deduction system that allowed the bank to collect its repayment monthly, from workers' paychecks. Permanent workers were able to obtain larger loans than workers on one- to three-year contracts. Casual workers were not eligible for these loans. Human resource managers and the unions reported that more than 90 percent of the work force applied for at least one loan. While yielding to workers' demands, unionists and management alike were concerned that many workers were squandering their money on drinking, womanizing, and secondhand cars, creating problems like marital disputes, absenteeism, and low productivity. When a new HR manager took office at NFCA, she told me her most urgent task was to limit the number of loans workers could obtain through payroll. A considerable number of workers were getting zero take-home salary after all the deductions, leaving them little motivation to even show up for work.

When I visited miners in the compound, I was always greeted by an incongruous sight: private cars parked outside makeshift mud houses whose flimsy roofs were dubiously held down only by rocks or bags of sand. One Saturday afternoon, the whole mining compound population congregated in the stadium adjacent to KCM to watch a local soccer match. The roads outside the stadium resembled an exhibition ground for a jam-packed secondhand car show. I was with a shop steward nicknamed "CNN" who has worked at Nchanga underground for twenty years. He has seen it all, having worked under various corporate regimes, from ZCCM (the Zambian state-owned mining company) to Anglo-American companies and then Vedanta today. But his passion and major source of income was no longer his job at the mine but his television repair shop (hence his nickname). In this small space, which he had rented for the past thirteen years from the privatized racket club, old VHS machines were piled on the shelves and he was completely surrounded by television sets dropped off by his customers. His take-home salary was about 1million kwacha (or 200 dollars), but his repair business brought a monthly 3 million kwacha (or 600 dollars). He deplored that miners these days had no commitment to mining and no hope of reliance on the mines or the government.

When it came to entrepreneurial ventures, older miners who had benefited from the sale of ZCCM housing and become property owners enjoyed a definite edge over younger miners, who suffered from the double jeopardy of being property-less and money-less. In Chambishi township, Victor Mulesu, a 45-year-old mechanic at NFCA, formed and registered a company together with ten business partners in March 2008, taking advantage of the 2006 Citizens Economic Empowerment Program, which offered small and medium-sized businesses a tax holiday, small loans of 200 million kwacha, and consultancy. The company was a member of the Zambian Chamber of Small and Medium Business Association, in which Victor served as chairman. In Chambishi alone, there were nineteen companies owned by miners who ran them part-time. His company was a registered contractor to the mines, providing them with engineering services (building a pipeline, adjusting machinery) and supplying and repairing front loaders, mining materials, and tools. Other commonplace entrepreneurial ventures included restaurants and poultry farms.

Younger and property-less workers also had entrepreneurial dreams but lacked the resources and benefits that their veteran counterparts had been able to accrue during their formal state-sector employment. Chilando, a second-generation miner in his late thirties, eloquently summed up the changing worldview of the Zambian working class among the young: "we are moving from a culture of employment to a culture of entrepreneurship." Chilando's personal experience was emblematic of the radical changes in the conditions and mentality of Zambian labor. His father had worked as an underground miner at Luanshya and returned to his natal village to take up farming after his retirement in 1979, a typical arrangement for the previous generation of miners. Chilando, on the other hand, had no village to retreat to because he was born in the city. He joined ZCCM in 1996 at the age of twenty-four as an underground workman. Articulate and thoughtful, he recalled how

> I was walking through town one day and I stumbled upon Chiluba's visit to Nchanga to announce privatization of the mines and the sale of housing to sitting tenants. He was politicking and people were clapping. People had never expected to own their own homes. Being a Grade 8 (lowest grade) worker and single, I was at the end of the long waiting list. After they sold all the houses, I realized I was left with no house ... Chiluba promised a rosy future which was never realized. But today we do

not see any future … We are on our own. There is no security in jobs. I am using my K800,000 loan to build a house. Once you can settle your family and don't have to pay rent, you can be self-employed. I will venture to set up my business after I build my house. The loans we have now are good for moving forward because they help us build our own homes, buy cars and invest in business opportunities for ourselves or our wives.

This culture of loans is not unique to Zambian miners. In the wake of South Africa's deadly Marikana strike at the Lonmin platinum mine, which claimed forty-four lives in 2012, reports revealed that unsecured and short-term loans had become a thriving industry with an entrenched clientele among low-wage casual workers demanding higher wages (Steyn 2012). It seems that the precarization of livelihoods on the Copperbelt has been aggravated by the advance of financial capital among global mining investors and Zambian laborers, even as the increasing precarity of workers provides banks with a golden opportunity.

Conclusion

A lot has changed since Michael Burawoy's classic study *The Color of Class on the Copper Mines* (1972) in the immediate post-independence years. One salient change has been the configuration of global capital, which has impinged on Zambian economic development in ways irreducible to the classic metropolis-periphery dependence. After independence in 1964, two Western mining companies maintained oligopolistic control over Zambian copper. The Zambian Government nationalized the mines in 1975, and almost instantly a global slump in copper prices plunged the country into heavy debt. Privatization of the copper mines in the 1990s—made possible mostly by coercive structural adjustment programs imposed on Zambia by the World Bank, IMF, and Western donors—internationalized the Copperbelt. By the time I arrived in 2008, many more foreign mining companies were present (ten large-scale copper mines instead of two). They hailed from both the Global South (India, Brazil, South Africa, and China) and the Global North (Canada, Australia, and Switzerland). Of these new investors, the Chinese state-owned company NFCA attracted the most attention, inspiring both hopes and fears among Zambians. Is Chinese capital more beneficial (as the Chinese state has claimed) or more exploitative (as the West claims) than capital from global private capital?[4]

This chapter has addressed this question from the perspective of Zambian miners confronting the global tendency toward informalization.

I have argued that despite having more encompassing goals than does global private capital, Chinese state capital shares with the latter an abiding interest in exploiting and controlling labor. Yet the Chinese state's interest in steady, long-term material production of ores, rather than short-term financial returns from selling copper, leads to a preference for relational subcontracting with a limited number of contractors. The more cohesive contract workforce was able to use strikes to force the Chinese state mine to give them permanent but low-paid employment. Whereas low wages were at the heart of the labor struggles in Chinese state mine, retrenchment of labor underlay most of the labor conflict in mines owned by global private companies.

The multiplicity of foreign investors on the Copperbelt meant that strikes tended to be confined to one firm. The generational divide among miners, buttressed by inequality in homeownership and entrepreneurial resources, further undermined the impact and power of strikes, which, according to participants, were driven more by mob psychology than class solidarity. For the miners, neither Chinese state capital nor global private investors, neither exploitation nor exclusion, offered a real future. Against this background, financial institutions found a ready market for microloans, fueling people's entrepreneurial dreams and fulfilling desires for basic and conspicuous consumption alike.

Ching Kwan Lee is Professor of Sociology at the University of California, Los Angeles. Her research interests include labor, political sociology, development, China, the Global South, and ethnography. She is the author of *Gender and the South China Miracle: Two Worlds of Factory Women* (1998), *Against the Law: Labor Protests in China's Rustbelt and Sunbelt* (2007), and *The Specter of Global China: Politics, Labor and Foreign Investment in Africa* (2017).

Notes

1. All names of interviewees are fictitious. All verbatim quotations are from interviews conducted in Zambia by the author between 2008 and 2014.
2. A company profile can be found in the trade magazine *International Mining*, "JCHX Going International," July 2013, 14–16.
3. I do not have data to shed light on how ethnicity or tribal identity underlines or complicates the company-versus-contract divide among miners. The workforce, both permanent and contract, is overwhelmingly male, and women's earning opportunities, such as petty trade in local markets or vegetable cultivation at home, are confined to the informal economy.

4. I construed these two varieties of capital—instead of "capitalisms"—from the pool of actually existing investors in Zambian copper in the neoliberal era. Deployed as heuristic devices, these ideal types necessarily entail simplifications of the empirical cases, and are by no means exhaustive of all varieties of capital everywhere.

References

Burawoy, Michael. 1972. *The Color of Class on the Copper Mines: From African Advancement to Zambianization.* Manchester: Manchester University Press.

Larmer, Miles. 2007. *Mineworkers in Zambia.* London: Tauris Academic Studies.

Lee, Ching Kwan. 2014. "The Specter of Global China." *New Left Review* 89 (September/October): 29–65.

Mususa, Patience N. 2014. *There Used to be Order: Life on the Copperbelt after the Privatization of the Zambia Consolidated Copper Mines.* Unpublished Ph.D. thesis, University of Cape Town.

Steyn, Lisa. 2012. "Marikana Miners in Debt Sinkhole." *Mail & Guardian,* 7 September 2012, http://mg.co.za/print/2012-09-07-00-marikana-miners-in-debt-sinkhole, accessed 1 May 2014.

2

Miners and Their Children

The Remaking of the Soviet Working Class in Kazakhstan

Eeva Keskküla

Introduction

As Fordist regimes of production have given way globally to flexible accumulation, many full-time permanent employees have been replaced by workers on short-term contracts with reduced benefits and uncertain futures (Harvey 1990). New inequalities have arisen within the industrial working class, and mechanisms of class reproduction have become unsettled. In the Indian context, Holmström (1976) applied the metaphor of the citadel to formal-sector permanent employment, with all those outside it trying to scale the walls. He later complicated his model by replacing the "in/out" binary with the metaphor of a mountain with different levels of security—for each sector of industrial activity, a specific hill on which a core of privileged workers defends its position (Holmström 1984). The small, well-paid, well-educated permanent workforce can be classified as a labor aristocracy or even as a middle class, since contract workers lead a completely different lifestyle (Parry 2013a, 2013b). The two tiers of workers are often differentiated by ethnic background, regional origin, religion, or caste, factors that prevent merit-based entry into the world of secure employment. Yet the children of the old permanent working class are also increasingly to be found as contract workers, sometimes working side by side with their fathers while earning considerably less. In short, the once relatively homogenous aristocracy of labor cannot reproduce itself and has become fragmented, not only on the shop floor but also in the household (Sanchez 2012a, 2012b).

In developed capitalist states, being working-class traditionally meant being at the bottom of a labor hierarchy without realistic prospects of social mobility (Willis 1977). Recently, however, deindustrialization has meant that working-class kids must make do with temporary, poorly paid jobs in the service industry (McDowell 2011; Weis 2013). Heavy industry is becoming a mix of formal large-scale workplaces and informal cottage industry, where workers fight alienation in different ways (Mollona 2009).

Both the Western and the Indian literatures concentrate on the decline of a stable industrial working class and a generational divide where sons can only dream of the security and relative wealth enjoyed by their fathers. Whether they work inside or outside the citadel, their conditions are poorer. The generation of those whose parents held traditional manual jobs but who are now unable to join the old proletarian communities constitutes a significant part of the social formation which Standing (2011; 2014) calls the global precariat. They are often alienated, anomic, anxious, and angry.

This raises the question of how to understand social change where mechanisms of the reproduction of class are no longer at all stable. E. P. Thompson (1980: 9) sees class not as "as a 'structure,' nor even as a 'category,' but as something which in fact happens (and can be shown to have happened) in human relationships." For him, class is a fluid historical relationship that cannot be halted to permit a study of its structure, but must always be embodied in real people and situations. He adds that "class happens when some men, as a result of common experiences (inherited or shared), feel and articulate the identity of their interests as between themselves, and as against other men whose interests are different from (and usually opposed to) theirs. Class-consciousness is the way in which experiences are handled in cultural terms: embodied in traditions, value systems, ideas, and institutional forms" (ibid.).

The Soviet working class has not been regarded as a product of its own making, as Thompson describes the case of England, but rather as a class created from above through particular practices, discourses, or state projects. Scholarly focus has mostly been on the Stalin era, raising questions as to how the revolutionary proletariat was made into Europe's quietest working class (Kotkin 1994: 275)—an atomized mass easy to control (Lewin 1994)—rather than exercising its class consciousness, for example in labor struggles (Filtzer 1986). Fitzpatrick (1993) emphasizes how the Bolsheviks created new categories of class through censuses and identity documents in a state where class structure was weak and subjects lacked a shared identity. Research on the construction of the Turksib railway in Kazakhstan between 1926 and 1931, which embodied the Bolsheviks' commitment to end ethnic inequality and promote cultural revolution, has shown how this project was designed to forge the Kazakh proletariat, bringing not only trains but also the new Soviet man to the steppes (Payne 2001). But even in socialist systems where class has not been an agent of its own making, class consciousness can be created through everyday practices in the workplace (Ngai 2005). When parents have secure employment inside the citadel and their children do not, class experiences differ and the working class is remade. In this chapter I explore how this fact shapes the class consciousness of children who do not share the workplace experiences and rewards their parents have had.

In post-Soviet Kazakhstan, deindustrialization and the outsourcing of labor are consistent with the patterns described above. Coal mining in central Kazakhstan is a partial exception: everyone who gets a job in the mine is a permanent, relatively well-paid employee with social guarantees. In recent years, though, it has become more and more difficult to enter the mining citadel. When the citadel is contracting, who is able to get in, and who is destined for white-collar or precariat existence instead? What are the implications for youth and for working-class consciousness? I explore a situation where precarious sons do not work alongside their securely employed fathers, and where the old working class struggles to reproduce itself and does so in smaller numbers.

Trajectories of Labor

Coal was discovered on the barren, wind-swept steppe of the Karaganda area in the 1920s, and the first mines were opened in the early 1930s with the use of deportees sent to the Karlag labor camp in the 1930s and 1940s for political crimes, *kulak* (rich peasant) status, or belonging to a potentially hostile ethnic group when World War II broke out (Barnes 2011: 34–37; Brown 2001; Pohl 2002). After the camp was abolished, former prisoners and forced settlers who had nowhere to return to built earthen houses in the town of Karaganda and nearby mining villages. They worked in the same workplaces as before (Brown 2001: 47), often living alongside former prison guards. Men worked underground, women on the surface or in light industries established to feed and clothe the miners. For those accused of anti-Soviet behavior, labor in the Gulag was seen as a path to redemption (Barnes 2011). In the post-Stalin years it became a source of glory and abundant income when the former Gulag prisoners were joined by Virgin Lands workers[1] and others seeking a better life in Kazakhstan. The Karaganda coal mines were now of crucial economic significance, producing coal for power generation as well as coking coal for steel production in the largest Central Asian steel plant in nearby Temirtau (see Trevisani, this volume) and for Magnitogorsk.

The mine workers were mostly ethnic Germans, Slavs, and Tatars. Kazakhs mostly worked in agriculture on collective farms, though some were hired by the mines. Well-qualified Russophone Kazakhs who had had formal education and training in mining were respected as "good, civilized Kazakhs." Miners' children went to work in the mines. Some pursued higher education and became mining engineers; others remained simple miners, with less stress and responsibility but often a relatively high salary. New mines were opened throughout the 1960s, 1970s, and 1980s, and wherever a mine was established, settlements mushroomed in the steppe. Housing was scarce in Karaganda itself but could be more easily obtained in one of the satellite towns. The town of Shakhtinsk grew up in the 1960s, sixty kilometers from the city. It was a perfect square, with straight streets running from east to west in the middle of the steppe, dotted by mines all around. The name derives from *shakhta*, the Russian word for mine, and could be translated as "the town of the mines."

In 1997 the mines were sold to a global Indian-owned steel company, Mittal Steel, which later became ArcelorMittal. Due to the restructuring of the economy, demand for coal plummeted and many mines were closed. Only 10.2 million metric tons of coal were mined in the underground mines of Karaganda in 2010, compared to 43.6 metric tons in 1980. In 1990 the coal basin consisted of twenty-six working mines and a workforce of 100,000 people, compared to eight mines (four of them near Shakhtinsk) and 18,000 people in 2010. Many inhabitants had left in the 1990s for their "ethnic homelands" in Germany or Russia. Apartments were abandoned and whole buildings emptied. Those who stayed were able to privatize their apartments. After the mines were privatized, little investment was made in equipment. Miners' salaries, eaten up by inflation, remained low, but benefits such as extended annual leave, compensation for occupational disease and injury, and subsidized vouchers for health resorts were maintained. Miners acknowledge that without privatization, the mines would have closed altogether and they would have had to leave. While Kazakhstan's authoritarian president was focusing on building the new capital Astana, small towns such as Shakhtinsk fell into disrepair, and their infrastructure—roads, street lighting, heating, water, electricity, and public transport—declined dramatically. A large methane gas explosion in a Shakhtinsk mine in 2004 killed twenty-four miners. In 2006, when forty died in another explosion, miners and their families took to the streets to demand better pay, safer working conditions, and investment in both the mine and the infrastructure of the city. Most of their demands were met: miners' wages were doubled, and there was investment in new safety equipment such as gas meters.

In 2013, the company was widely known to be in crisis due to poor sales and the drop in global coal and steel prices after the 2008 global economic crisis. In order to cut costs, recruitment was limited. New workers could be hired to replace those fired due to absenteeism or drunkenness, but not workers who retired or left voluntarily. An acute shortage of labor resulted, and work in the mines was intensified accordingly. The labor force had by now fallen to 14,000, and according to the official discourse, no further layoffs were envisioned. In the Burannaya mine where I did my fieldwork, no one remembered the last significant recruitment. To deter potential applicants, the mine had glued a sign on the door declaring that no hiring was taking place. In the Yulianskaya coal washing plant, cohorts of about thirty people were hired in 2009 and 2010. In a survey covering the careers of thirty-three adult children of miners, I found that only seven (two women and five men) were working in the coal industry. The youngest was twenty-five years old, the others in their late twenties or thirties.

Trevisani's chapter in this volume highlights the increasing disparity between permanent and outsourced labor in ArcelorMittal's steel plant in Temirtau, but no outsourcing has taken place in that company's mining division. Except for canteen and changing room staff, all workers had permanent company contracts. Casualization seems to be common in other mining locations, such as the Chinese-operated copper mines in Zambia (Lee 2009, this volume) and, increasingly, Estonian mines (Kesküla 2012), but this is not the case in Karaganda. ArcelorMittal is primarily a steelmaking company; its acquisition of the coal mines was part of the deal to take over the steel combine in Temirtau. The company lacked the experience to implement cost-cutting operations in the mines. Twenty years after privatization, the Coal Division was still run by locals rather than foreigners. Workers in Temirtau continuously gossiped about "the Indians," but no one in Shakhtinsk had ever seen one. The head of the division was a stern Kazakh with a loud voice who came from a mining village ten kilometers from Shakhtinsk, where many of his deputies lived alongside trade union leaders and miners themselves. Staff of the Coal Division usually argued that mining was a dangerous profession requiring many years of training, with gradual expansion of responsibility as one's knowledge of the mine and expertise increased; thus it was not suitable for low-skilled casual labor. This claim to a local monopoly of expertise made outsourcing unthinkable. It also meant that newcomers without kinship ties, such as Oralmans from the diaspora who had settled in Shakhtisnk with the help of a repatriation program, had very little chance of employment. The few jobs available were allocated to members of local mining families.[2] Most Kazakh newcomers traded at the bazaar or drove old Soviet Ladas that substituted for buses after the municipality's public transport broke down in the 1990s. Small, insulated mining communities offered few opportunities for newcomers, who lacked not only the connections but also the skills for mine work.

Local miners' very strong efforts to maintain closure and keep things way they used to be, as far as possible, might also have been due to the longer history of the mining communities compared to the steel plant. Up to four generations had lived in the area and worked in the mines. Narratives of hardship in the Gulag and deportation were a source of pride and offered as explanations for miners' tendency to be hardworking but also politically passive and apprehensive. Later arrivals from the Virgin Lands campaign in the mid 1950s, who initially were young enthusiasts from elsewhere in the Soviet Union, appropriated and carried on these local narratives. Miners adopted the identity of the vanguard of the Soviet proletariat and were officially depicted as heroes in the Soviet Union (Shlapentokh 1988). Glorifying murals, statues, and newspaper stories constantly reminded them of their special status. Despite extensive outmigration in the 1990s, there was continuity in the community, whose strong, shared identity was based on overcoming hardship but also grounded in the affluence and social respect that accrued in the Soviet period. Despite the chaos of restructuring, the neighborhoods and work collectives of Shakhtinsk had a stronger collective identity and more solidarity than those of Temirtau (Trevisani in this volume).

Outside the Mining Citadel

Given the policies of minimal recruitment but secure employment with reasonably good benefits and salary, employment in the mining sector could be seen as the citadel. Miners desire to continue the reproduction of mining dynasties, both for economic reasons and because of the emotions and histories invested in the mining towns over the years. In the current situation, this can take many years, hefty bribes, and/or special connections. Outside the citadel, miners' children and newcomers tried desperately to enter it. Fields of non-industrial activity, such as the public sector, could be seen as separate citadels with different rules of entry.

Most miners' children who could not enter the citadel stayed in the area, working on the margins of the industrial sector in smaller companies, where wages were uncertain. As noted earlier, I conducted a survey of 50 coal washers and miners, who had 33 children over eighteen that were no longer students (see Table 2.1). Eight of these miners' grown sons were reported to be working as drivers, welders, car service center staff, or sales representatives. Four adult daughters held jobs as shop assistants and hairdressers. Four of the 33 were said to be unemployed, and three daughters were housewives, often an involuntary status for women. Three children had decided to migrate to Russia, in particular to mining areas, where, it was believed, jobs were easier to find, conditions better, and hard-working

Table 2.1 Employment of miners' children

Work sector	Males	Females	Total
Mining	5	2	7
Manual/service professions outside mining	8	4	12
Unemployed	2	2	4
Homemakers	0	3	3
Working in a profession requiring higher education or in the public sector	3	2	5
No data*	0	2	2
Total	**18**	**15**	**33**

*One father had lost contact with his two daughters and was unable to say where they were working.

Kazakhstanis appreciated. Two had higher education and were working in their field of specialization. Sometimes the sons of miners supplemented their earnings in the criminal economy, for example by helping the mine management steal coal with trucks that they worked on during the day. Young women's options were even more limited. Many of them, including graduates, ended up in little shops and bazaars, working for about 100 euros a month and living with their parents.

Those who managed to get jobs in the public sector earned low salaries, around 250 euros monthly, and relied on parents employed in the coal sector to cover major expenses. With qualifications in fields such as nursing, some were able to lead a financially independent, though hardly affluent, life. For a woman, the jackpot was to marry a miner who could sustain the family. Higher education did not guarantee social mobility: of the seven children with higher education, two worked in mining, three had white-collar jobs, one was a sales assistant, and one was unemployed.[3] The survey confirmed the general impression that when only a fifth of miners' children can continue to work in the mining sector (and this share has been still smaller in recent years), then most of the rest either held unstable low-paid jobs outside the citadel or were not employed at all.

Olga, a tall, jovial German woman in her early fifties, had worked in the coal washing plant for nearly thirty years. Her husband, Anatoli, was a miner of Ukrainian origin. Their parents had been deported to the Kazakh steppe, where they experienced hunger and cold. Born in the 1960s, Olga and Anatoli had started their working lives in the 1980s as children of the glorious industrial future. Olga, who had not given much thought to what she wanted to do after school, ended up making the logical choice in a region dependent on coal, the processing of which was considered a woman's job. Anatoli opted for a job in the mine because it was the best paid, most prestigious job in the area (work in construction, transport, and light industry was also available in the 1980s). Having survived the difficult 1990s, when the town was falling apart and salaries were not paid, by 2013 Olga and Anatoli were living fairly comfortably on two incomes and had even enjoyed a holiday in the Emirates (on borrowed money). Nevertheless, Olga worried constantly about the prospects of her two children, both in their early twenties.

As work conditions deteriorated due to reductions in the labor force and aging equipment, many parents no longer wanted their children to become miners. Instead they encouraged them to study at university and specialize in prestigious subjects like law or economics. Olga's son Kolya, who had studied economics, had trouble finding a job after he finished his studies. In 2013 he was commuting for an hour every day to work at a print and copy shop in Karaganda. His income, which depended on the number of orders the company got each month, varied from 200 euros up to 500 euros in a very good month. Olga earned roughly 500 euros as an experienced coal washer, whereas Anatoli's wages were around 900 euros and sometimes higher, depending on the volume of coal produced. Olga and Anatoli paid for Kolya's wedding and took out a loan to help him buy a flat. Real estate prices were calculated in US dollars rather than local currency, so interest payments depended on currency fluctuations. Kolya was thinking about retraining in a more technical field but was not confident that it would help him enter the mining sector. After his son was born, he became his family's sole breadwinner.

Kolya's sister Lena had graduated from a vocational branch of a local secondary school and did not want to study further. A beautiful, slim blonde, she was interested in clothes and enjoyed talking with her friends on the phone, hanging out with them in the city, and going out to the local discotheque. She had worked in a shop for about 120 euros a month until the shopkeeper dismissed her so that a friend of his wife could have her job. Olga admitted that she had not been very serious herself at her daughter's age, but in the Soviet period, not working had not been an option. She recalled that when she first started working in the coal washing plant, she cried herself to sleep every night because the place was so cold, dirty, and noisy. Eventually she got used to it and stayed. She doubted that work in a factory would suit Lena, even if it had been available.

Vova, a miner of Russian origin in his forties who had a twenty-year-old son, said that it would be his dream for his son to work in the mine,

But there is no recruitment. He dropped out of the vocational school. It is his own fault, so let him work in a warehouse for 300 EUR now. We thought he could get a degree from the Karaganda branch of a Moscow University, through distance learning. We went there and got the study materials on a USB stick for 400 dollars. But then we could not open the materials on the USB, although we tried for months. So, no education, just a USB stick for 400 dollars.

Despite their children's aspirations to higher education, miners did not always know what advice to give them. It had been easier in his day, Vova admitted, feeling sorry that his son could not flash rubles to impress girls as he had in his youth. Fathers were perhaps even more worried about their daughters. Vitya, a Russian mine engineer in his late forties, explained: "I live for my daughters. They cannot inherit my job as a mechanic, but I want to leave them something, a café, a shop, at least a stand in the bazaar."

While the majority of miners' children worked at low-paid, precarious industrial and service jobs, a few managed to enter the other citadel on the landscape: the public sector. Gulmira was a Kazakh single mother who had struggled to find jobs for her son and daughter. Her own job at the coal washing plant was physically demanding, but it had allowed her to provide a better future for her children. Her daughter had a public-sector job in Shakhtinsk. The pay was not high, but the position was secure, with opportunities for promotion. It was not quite clear how her daughter had passed the public-sector exams, but it seemed that Gulmira had played a key role in securing this job. With pride, she showed me an expensive fur coat she had bought her daughter: she was a government official after all, and had to look presentable. The last time I visited Gulmira in her humble one-room flat (her investments in her children had left no money for a larger one), she had just come home from the bank: her son had returned from the army and needed a job in the government, so Gulmira had taken out a loan to pay a distant relative to set the son up with a government position.

For miners of Slavic and German origin, the separate citadel of public-sector jobs was even harder to penetrate. Without social networks, children with degrees in law and economics were left with nothing but their parents' debt. Miners' relatives tended to work in mining and could not offer help in other spheres. Some confessed that they lacked the skills to bribe officials, and that public-sector posts were in any case out of their children's reach because "their eyes didn't look right." This refers to the fact that in post-independence Kazakhstan, government posts are mostly occupied by Kazakhs; some knowledge of the Kazakh language and Kazakh connections are preconditions that Russian speakers often lack. Earlier, when language requirements were not as strict, some Russian speakers were able to get jobs in the public sector. Viktoria, whose parents both worked in mining, was a 35-year-old single mother working as an accountant in the local Shakhtinsk administration. She complained that she had to do all the work while her Kazakh bosses, who owed their jobs to their ethnicity, were lazy. Her salary was small, around 250 euros, and she relied on her parents to cover bigger expenses, such as flat renovation. One day, upon returning home to discover that her seven-year-old son had broken the flat-screen TV while playing, she called her mum, very upset. Her mother, who at the moment was ending a twelve-hour shift at the coal washing plant, had to calm her down by promising to buy her a new TV. Viktoria could make ends meet and manage her everyday costs in a relatively secure job in the public sector, but she needed her parents' financial support for any additional expenses.

In the socialist era, most children of workers followed their parents into the mining sector, where jobs were well paid and available. The Russian-speaking population especially considered such jobs historically theirs. As such opportunities for children became increasingly limited, miners worried about their children's economic survival also grew concerned about the continuation of the particular kin-based way of working in the mine and on the factory floor.

Kinship and the Citadel

In times of limited recruitment, even under the company policy of prioritizing family members, entering the citadel depended on fine moral nuances. Partly rooted in the Soviet tradition of honoring labor dynasties, these subtleties also influenced interaction and work organization on the shop floor. In the Soviet Union, labor dynasties were a natural way of life in monoindustrial settings. Tkach (2003, 2008) has argued that the public display of family histories was an ideological tool for implementing a politics of class, family, and labor that presented workers as part of the vanguard of the society, an exemplary model for family and for labor discipline in the post-Stalin era. Such dynasties represented a "labor aristocracy" that was to replace the pre-revolutionary hereditary aristocracy with values of gentility, professionalism, discipline, and local patriotism, the latter being particularly important in mining regions (Kesküla 2014: 63). In monoindustrial settings, family and the workplace were intimately linked (Ashwin 1999: 11). In the case of Estonia, I have argued that the company was seen as consisting of clusters of the miners' own families. Knowing that their grandfathers' and fathers' hard work had helped to build the mines, they claimed a moral ownership of the company (Kesküla 2014). In Estonia, the celebrations of mining dynasties were discontinued after socialism and persisted only informally, but in Kazakhstan the human resources department of every mine could give me a list of dynasties with the names and details of individual family members. Dynasties consisted of generations of both workers and engineers, and were not restricted to one ethnic group. In monoindustrial settings, kinship links were an essential element in creating and reproducing the Soviet working class.

At ArcelorMittal mines, the people on the waiting list for jobs numbered in the hundreds. The list contained details concerning education and work experience, but the most important factor was a "recommendation," which indicated whether or not the candidate had a relative working in the mine. In my survey of 50 individuals, 22—mostly younger workers—said they had obtained their job through their family. Another 21 respondents said they currently had a family member working in the same workplace.

Senior management emphasized the benefits of recruiting family members, and offering secure jobs to local residents who lacked other skills or other ways of imagining life was obviously conducive to political stability. Managers openly admitted to valuing the aspect of social control and reduced costs of formal training: if a parent introduces a child to the workplace, it is the parent's responsibility to train that child. In the coal washing plant, where women made up half of the labor collective, the health and safety official pointed out that mothers, wives, and daughters instruct the men in their families to reduce accidents by complying with health and safety regulations. If a new recruit does not live up to expectations, it is the parents' fault. Furthermore, if someone becomes too active politically—for example, by demanding improvements in employment conditions—it is possible to threaten them with the loss of not only their own job but also those of other family members. Having no alternatives, miners therefore constituted a largely docile workforce.

One day at the coal washing plant, I discussed recruitment with some male workers who sat smoking and bantering in their tool room, as nothing needed urgent repair at the moment. Sanka, a 25-year-old whose mother worked at the plant, was trained as a repair and maintenance person. After signing up for a job in the plant, he spent a year doing his military service, and then another two years working casual, low-paid jobs in Shakhtinsk and other satellite towns until he heard that the plant was recruiting. "I went to the director and he asked me what I liked to do in my free time. I said I liked football and he really liked the answer. I didn't even know back then that the director also liked football."

While Sanka suggested that his leisure interests had some bearing on his recruitment, the director, for his part, preferred to stress the kin link. Another fitter, Aman, reported that "I had some training as an underground locksmith and no job experience, but I was still hired when the director heard that my father was also working there, because he knew that my father could teach me." Things were slightly more complicated when it came to engineers. When Kadyr, a 45-year-old Chechen,[4] graduated from the polytechnic institute, the director immediately offered him an engineer position. His uncle, an engineer himself, forbade the young man from accepting. Kadyr had to start from the bottom. When he began as a simple worker looking after machinery and conveyer belts, his uncle was his direct boss and sent Kadyr to the toughest places to do particularly hard, wet, or nasty jobs. The uncle even had Kadyr do jobs that other workers refused to do because they did not fit their job description. I asked Kadyr why he did not tell his uncle no. "In our culture, you are not allowed to say no to older people, your older relatives. Maybe Russians can tell their uncle to bugger off but we cannot do that."

"And why would your own uncle give you the hardest and nastiest jobs to do?" I asked. "Because I could not say no to him," Kadyr answered. It was acceptable to help children get a job, but beyond this no favors could be expected. "My uncle helped me to find the work but then I had to prove myself," Kadyr explained. Such treatment was also common in Russian and German families. Privileging one's relatives was not immoral, but placing children in responsible positions before they were properly trained for them was.

On the shop floor, kinship constellations took various forms. There were husband-wife engineer couples who had met and fallen in love many years ago and now had their own children working in the plant as well. In the coal washing plant, mothers and daughters, but more often mothers and sons, worked in the same place. In the mine, with its mostly male collective, many combinations of fathers, sons, brothers, cousins, uncles, and nephews worked together. It was common for some family members to be engineers while others remained simple workers. It was also common to have a relative or spouse as one's direct boss. The parent was usually higher up in the mine hierarchy than the child, but I also came across several cases of children who had had the opportunity to obtain higher education and become engineers. Evgeni, an ambitious thirty-year-old of Korean descent, headed a major department in the mine where his father worked as a simple miner. When I asked the father if this caused any problems in a Korean family where one is supposed to listen to one's elders, he just shrugged, smiled, and said it was fair enough that his son was the boss, because the son had the education.

Family members who did the same job were no more likely to help each other than they were to help other members of the team. Zhidkov, who was his wife's boss, could not assign her to jobs that were easier than other women's, as this would have caused an immediate uproar. Children and parents nevertheless looked after each other. A young maintenance man was very happy to work the same shift as his mother, in order to help her lift heavy equipment or coal if necessary. When Oleg and his father, an experienced miner, were on the same work team, the father did not allow Oleg go to the most accident-prone workplaces in the mine but went himself instead. Later, when Oleg had made a career and was relatively high up in the mine management, he had his father "punished" for a minor misdemeanor by transferring him to another brigade where work conditions were safer, without his father's knowledge. Sometimes miners claimed that family members tried not to work the same shifts in case there was an accident, so that at least someone in the family would survive; but this was more myth than actual practice, as working the same shift was more convenient for the household. Whether family members worked in the same or different units depended on the timing of recruitment and the distribution of vacancies. Neither the employees not the company's code of ethics saw working under the direct supervision of a relative as immoral.

In summary, the company continued the Soviet practice of honoring dynasties and recruiting kin, with one major difference: significantly fewer children could get a job in the mine. For most families, this meant the kin-based tradition of working together in the same workplace was no longer possible. The Soviet working class was made by reproducing labor dynasties, but once shifting economic structures kept the children from following a parent's path, class boundaries and identities were altered.

Miners' Models of Class and Class Consciousness

When mine workers talked about class, they often said that they were middle-class, or "middle working class" (*srednii rabochii klass*). I first heard this expression when a woman in a coal washing plant suggested that my book should be called *Middle Working Class in Kazakhstan*. Surprised, I asked her to explain.

> Well, we live well really, compared to other workers. I am not saying that we live as well as the middle class in the government but we have a job, an apartment, those who want one have a car, we can allow ourselves holidays and actually have a proper rest rather than have our health ruined by too much work. It means that we are the middle class among the workers, one that stands strongly on its feet.

This idea was especially common in homes where both spouses worked in the coal industry. Zhenya, a 55-year old miner, explained that the class system had three divisions. At the top were the rich, who did not do anything. Following them were miners and steelworkers, who worked and received wages that were insufficient. He went on to explain that when his wife wanted them to vacation in Turkey, he had taken out a loan that he would have to pay back over the next three years. His friend Anton, a miner in his thirties, continued, "but the lower class is who I see among my neighbors, acquaintances, the ones who live on 60,000 tenge [300 euros] a month." When I asked who was working-class, Anton pointed to himself. "But who else? I go to work, I come from work. That's all I do." Zhenya elaborated that he had worked in the mine for thirty-five years and his shift work made seeing his family very difficult because no one else was home when he was. The miners' model of class society was based on income: they considered themselves middle-class because they earned an average income in Kazakhstani society and could afford more than neighbors who did not work in the coal industry. The adjective "working" (*rabochii*), if it was used, referred to the fact that they actually worked for their income while the rich did not, and the specificity of their work.

"Working," for them, thus had no association with a particular political position. Not even older miners like Zhenya associated it with Soviet political language or new understandings of the political role of the working class. If the miners of Kazakhstan were ever taught to "speak Bolshevik" (Kotkin 1995), they had forgotten how, by the third decade after socialism's collapse. They saw themselves as part of a middle class opposed to a "lower class" composed of people with lower incomes. They were well aware that the particular type of middle class-ness that characterized their existence was defined by reliance on credit. Over half of the workers in my survey were currently paying off loans, which were usually taken for three years and carried high interest rates. They used the money to pay for cars, flats for children, renovations to their own homes, vacations, visits to relatives in Russia or Germany, children's weddings, and parents' funerals. Wages were sufficient to cover everyday needs, but miners emphasized that whereas they could eat everything they desired, anything extra had to be bought on credit. The idea of being middle-class was very strongly related to dual incomes and dependent on the husband's work in the mine, so female coal washers who lost their husbands also lost their middle-class position.

Miners were aware of their lack of a political class consciousness. As they explained, their indebtedness and the dearth of alternative jobs kept them quiet, no matter how bad conditions were at work. Some looked me in the eye and simply asked, "Did you hear about Zhanoozen?" referring to a 2011 incident in which police fired on striking oil workers in Western Kazakhstan, leaving seventeen dead, according to official reports (and many more, according to unofficial ones). Usually miners' protests were confined to a particular brigade or departmental work unit or group, and management and national security institutions swiftly suppressed wildcat strikes by explicitly threatening to fire the militant miners or their kin. Only in extreme situations, like those following the deadly explosions mentioned above, did the power holders tolerate strikes and large demonstrations staged in front of the town hall by miners' families and other inhabitants.

All miners were members of the coal workers' trade union. Every month, 1 percent of their salary was deducted for membership dues. Some acknowledged that the union was standing up for the rights of miners in court cases, but it was more often seen as a provider of welfare benefits like vouchers for health resorts than a political institution dedicated to defending workers' rights. In this respect it resembled the trade unions of the Soviet period. The leader, a former miner of Tatar ethnicity from a mining village nearby, was criticized by some as a corrupt opportunist, while others thought he was doing all he could to stand up to foreign capital in a political climate that did not favor workers' movements. Younger miners took little interest in trade union activities; often they did not know the name of their representative or read the union newspaper. When I suggested to the trade union leader that younger workers seemed barely involved in union activities, he bemoaned their narrow worldview, based on the desire for material goods.

When working with the Russian-speaking working class in Estonia, I identified a model of miners' moral economy, their view of miners' contribution to society and what was expected in return. Miners believe that they are giving their hard labor and health for the benefit of a society that needs coal (or oil shale). In return, they demand respect and a good salary (Keskküla 2012). The basic model also works in the case of Kazakhstani miners. Their mines are dangerous, so they feel the sacrifice even more acutely. Low mechanization means their work is physically harder. Like Russian-speaking miners in Estonia, they feel that their work is not as respected by society as it was in the Soviet period. Miners' wives, whether coal washers or housewives, share the respect for miners' hard work and see their own labor as auxiliary, although it is often just as demanding. Intertwined with this is regret over losing a privileged position as ethnic Russians who believe themselves to be harder workers than the native population. This loss of rewards for their sacrifice brings about a particular genre of constant complaining (Ries 1997). This is a tool for constructing class boundaries and a way to gain dignity and respect (Lamont 2001). They complain about the corrupt elite and politicians, dishonest businessmen who are better off than honest working people, miners' unreasonably high retirement age (63), the poor health care system, and finally Kazakhs' privileged position in the new state. Miners' class consciousness emerges not only from an awareness of the middle-working position that distinguishes them from the elite and those leading less prosperous life styles outside the citadel. It is also created in the work experience that Ngai (2005) emphasizes.

At the mine, each department specializes in a particular task or a particular geographical area. The department (*uchastok*) is divided into brigades (*brigada*) consisting of 20–30 men. Each of the latter is organized by a brigadier, who is not a qualified engineer or manager but an intelligent, experienced, respected worker who receives a salary increment for the additional responsibility. Brigades are named after their leaders, for example Ivanov's brigade or Mukhambetov's brigade. The brigade is typically divided into four shifts that work around the clock (e.g., one repair and maintenance shift and three production shifts) and accomplishment of the objectives brings a bonus for all brigade members. Although socialist competitions between brigades disappeared with privatization, a sense of competition persists.

While the brigade is the core unit that workers identify with, everyday work within a shift is shared in a team (*zveno*) of three to five men to whom workers are particularly close. It is especially important to have skillful and trustworthy men working in this unit, which also has a leader (*zvenivoi*) responsible for work organization and documentation. A team in a tunneling brigade would consist of the combine[5] driver and other miners, ideally four but following layoffs sometimes as few as two. In the basic labor process of a tunneling team, the driver cuts into the wall of coal or rock with the combine. The others make sure that no large pieces of coal or rock find their way onto the conveyor belt, crushing them with a hammer when necessary, and prepare steel arches and other material for securing the mine roof. When the combine has advanced far enough, it stops. The men clear the fallen coal and, balancing on a wooden plank placed on the combine's cutter head, attach the next arches. This dangerous work requires speed, precision, good communication and a lot of trust between workers. Miners' lives are in each other's hands. "Whatever conflicts we might have, at the end of the day, it is your team mate who brings you to the surface if something happens," they say.

Going on holiday, buying a new car, or marking a major life-cycle event are events one should celebrate—if not with the whole brigade, then at least with the *zveno*. Brigade members usually gather after payday at small cafes located in the basements of their five-story residential buildings. Money is collected, and they order *shashlik* (skewers of grilled meat) accompanied by vodka and beer. This is where issues or conflicts that arise at work are clarified and bonds of camaraderie are solidified. The conversation includes personal joking and gossip about the town, but it always returns to the topic of the mine. As miners say, "In the mine we talk about women, and on the surface we talk about the mine." After a few drinks, mates who have died in mining accidents are remembered, and their memory is toasted. Brigade members are often neighbors and relatives. They continue their shoptalk in the brand-new supermarket of Shakhtinsk, where they bump into each other after payday. Informal gatherings of workmates continue in garages where men gather to "repair cars", in saunas, and on outings to the allotments that many miners own.

Women in the coal washing plant are similarly divided into brigades of about 15 people, named after the foreman or forewoman. One brigade works together for a twelve-hour shift from 8 a.m. to 8 p.m., then from 8 p.m. to 8 a.m. the following day, followed by two days off. Each coal washer has his or her own area, equipment, or conveyer belts to service, but they help each other out when particularly demanding tasks arise. During factory downtime, women are sent in large groups to clean or whitewash particular areas of the plant, which gives them time to chat. Breakfast, lunch, and tea are taken together in small, sheltered areas where the coal washers set up tables, benches, kettles, and microwaves. Contributions from home are placed in the middle of the table to be shared by everyone. The breaks allow women to talk about work, to complain about their aging machinery or a rude boss, to gossip about domestic life, and discuss worries about children. Female coal washers also organize café visits on special occasions like International Women's Day or the New Year, when money is gathered from everyone and toasts and eating alternate with dancing to local Russian and Kazakh pop. Thus, miners' class consciousness emerges also from sharing a workplace experience and spending time with colleagues outside the workplace. It is gendered, as men and women often socialize in different labor groups, yet together they are brought to a larger class experience in the home as well as in gatherings with friends and relatives, where male and female mine workers share both the grievances and joys of work in the coal mining sector. Until recently, almost all family members were employed in this sector and Shakhtinsk had a very strong identity as a mining town. Seeing themselves as the middle working class, separate from those below them and above them, and working together was the basis of miners' shared class consciousness. But this is not accessible to most miners' children.

Class Consciousness of Miners' Children?

Miners' children who do not continue working in mines do not constitute a uniform class. They nevertheless share aspects of their parents' understanding of the world, in which a job with a sufficient salary is the basis of a good life. They have the same aspirations to a decent income, to marry young and have children and live in mining towns close to their parents. All generations of ethnic Slavs and Germans share the fear of increased Kazakhization, which they call "nationalism." They feel that they are discriminated against as Russian speakers who might one day have to leave the country because they lack Kazakh language skills. They see themselves as "civilizers" of the Kazakh steppe who built up industry and brought enlightenment to the nomadic locals. They feel superior to Kazakh speakers, even if the tables have been turned and Kazakhs occupy all the positions of power. Miners' children share the three-tiered view of class in Kazakh society. But whereas the parents see themselves as a middle working class that can stand strongly on its own feet, their children in precarious jobs are reluctant to place themselves in any class category. They rather stress that their parents worked in the mine, or that they are on the waiting list for the mine, indicating that their potential future places them in the middle class. This recalls Standing's (2011: 77–78) discussion of the identity confusion of members of the precariat who hold a university degree: they are uncomfortable calling themselves working class and equally uncomfortable adopting their parents' middle-class identity.

Although not working in the sector themselves, the children of miners can still relate to their parents' experience and respect their work. Ierik had studied food technology in one of the vocational schools. He was twenty-three and working in one of the few bars of Karaganda that had put some effort into interior design and served "Western" cocktails to the local elite. He wanted to establish his own business in due course. Ierik was happy not to be working as a miner like his father, because it was such a hard job. The young man described the miners' age of retirement—sixty-three—as an injustice, getting as agitated as if the injustice were being done to himself.

But unlike miners, miners' children lacked a shared class consciousness. Higher education and white-collar aspirations could not be the basis of a positive class identity because education did not guarantee a job. Few wanted to establish their own businesses; to do so was considered foolhardy in uncertain and corrupt conditions. Most preferred to work in a larger company and keep the business as a hobby. They dreamed of a good life with a good salary but had no idea how to achieve these goals. They were uninterested in local and national politics, claiming that it was impossible to change anything in the corrupt system. Some seemed to lack aspirations altogether. Lena was quite happy sharing bottles of beer in the cold hallway with her friends, asking her father for money, and brushing off her mother's suggestions about further study or taking her CV to potential employers. "There are evening courses for nurses offered in town, perhaps you could retrain? Medical staff are always needed," Olga suggested. Lena cringed. "Nurses? To work with sick people? I am not going to do that!" "She could not even marry a miner because she does not know how to cook," Olga sighed while offering samples of her own delicious cooking to Lena and myself. Lena gave her a long, carefree look and continued eating, before announcing that she would carry on living with mum and dad forever. Often, I heard thirty-year-olds talking about twenty-year olds say that the "youth is not the same these days." It seemed that a generation that had had few opportunities to find "normal work" was loath to take on adult responsibility and preferred living as children with their parents. In conditions of precarity, the unemployed children of miners could not hold onto the moral economy of their parents. Their hope was rooted in "household, kin and individual strategies" (Pine 2014) rather than any collective view of a better future. In a situation where their parents' life style was unattainable and sometimes not even desirable, they lacked a sense of direction. But the lack of alternatives left them with little else to do but socialize among themselves, killing time. They were not becoming aware of their class position in the global precariat because they did not think in these terms.

Conclusion

This chapter has shown how, in a contracting industrial sector, miners' ways of living and working together with kin on the shop floor have become more uncertain in the context of deindustrialization and limited recruitment. Work and kinship are tightly interlinked, but nowadays many miners' children are prevented from entering the citadel and sharing the workplace experiences of their parents. Their parents' class consciousness emerged from past experiences of the ideological project of the making of the Soviet working class, in which miners were assigned a special role, as well as from the concrete experiences of working together, shared ideas of kin and company, belonging together, and imagination of being the "middle working class." The children who do not work in the coal industry are excluded from this experience. Besides economic precarity in a mining town and lack of clear vision of the future, they have little in common with each other. In the case of the neighboring steel town Temirtau, Trevisani (this volume) argues that both contract workers and steelworkers' children are outside the citadel, and that contract workers have not developed the language of class and class consciousness. In the case of the mining sector, there are no contract workers, and miners' children take badly paid, precarious jobs outside the mining sector. Others have migrated to Russia, work in the public sector, or are unemployed. As in Temirtau, it can be argued that these people are deprived of both a language of class and class consciousness.

Kasmir and Carbonella (2006) emphasized that scholars in the West have mistaken the decline of the traditional Fordist working class for the end of class per se, because cultural images of what a particular class should look like last longer than actual class formations within capitalism. Yet whereas enduring features of the old stable industrial working class are easily recognized, it is much harder to characterize the diverse population of miners' children outside the coal industry. This generation shares the experience of instability and some aspects of their parents' morality, but it is too diverse to be modeled sociologically. If class is a process rather than a category, then miners' children are part of a process of new classes in the making, and the result is still unclear. Rather than classifying miners' children as part of Standing's precariat, it might be more useful to investigate the *processes of precarization* that affect today's twenty-year-olds much more significantly than they did the parental generation.

The children of the old labor aristocracy in Kazakhstan are experiencing the same trends as those in India and elsewhere. Whether a new global political consciousness emerges out of this remains to be seen. The citadel of Holmström's initial "in-or-out" model still has some measure of validity: the mining sector has not experienced labor outsourcing, and some children are eventually able to join their parents in secure employment. Those who cannot or will not join the citadel may end up either upwardly or downwardly mobile, depending as much on factors like ethnicity and connections as on merit.

The lack of class analysis in postsocialist space in the first two decades since the fall of the Berlin Wall has been noted (Kalb 2015). In Central Asia, scholarly research has mostly focused on ethnicity and clan relationships (Dave 2007; Ismailbekova 2013; Reeves 2014; Schatz 2000) with little attention to labor and class formation. In Kazakhstan, ethnic networks have a big influence over who can enter the public sector, while kinship has comparable influence over who can enter the citadel of secure employment in the mine. Both kinship and ethnicity are crucial to the experience of becoming a miner and thus interlinked with class identity and experience. Local moralities of kin and ethnicity, like global historical processes of the making and remaking of the working class, have important implications for the study of new social processes as postsocialist spaces linked to the global economy.

Acknowledgments

I would like to thank the miners and coal washers of Karaganda area and their children for sharing their work, lives, and cups of tea with me over ten months of research in Northern Kazakhstan (2013/14). Sarah Ashwin and Frances Pine gave helpful feedback on early versions of this chapter. I am grateful to the Industry and Inequality group at the Max Planck Institute for their camaraderie over the years and especially to Tommaso Trevisani for his support in the field and during the writing process.

Eeva Keskküla is Senior Researcher at Tallinn University School of Humanities, where she currently heads a project on health and safety in heavy industry. She completed her Ph.D. at Goldsmiths, University of London and was Research Fellow at the Max Planck Institute for Social Anthropology in Halle from 2012 to 2015. Keskküla has done fieldwork in Estonia and Kazakhstan. Her research interests include anthropology of work, industrial health and safety, gender and gender and work, class, and postsocialism. Her work has appeared in journals such as *Focaal, History and Anthropology*, and *Work, Employment and Society*.

Notes

1. The Virgin Lands Campaign was Khrushchev's plan to increase Soviet agricultural produce by turning the Kazakh steppe into agricultural land. Workers for the project were recruited from all over the Soviet Union (Petrick, Wandel, and Karsten 2013; Pohl 2004).
2. A few outsiders had managed to secure permanent jobs with a bribe. According to rumours, one had to pay 2,000 dollars, or even 5,000 dollars. It was never quite clear whom one had to pay: perhaps the director of the mine, or someone in the management of the company, or even a particular government agency responsible for checking health and safety. Some parents tried to use such opportunities but many lacked the finances or knowledge of who to turn to, or considered this too risky. I am sure that bribery was extensive but it was hard to learn about the details as everyone wished to protect people who had helped them to obtain a job.
3. The seven children (out of 33) who had managed to enter mining comprised four Russians, a Kazakh, a Korean, and a Tatar, indicating that ethnicity did not matter much if one had a parent inside the citadel.
4. According to a long-standing prejudice among Russian speakers, Chechens will not work in industry and prefer trade. Chechens deported to Kazakhstan by Stalin had a reputation for being rebellious and not doing well in hierarchical industry settings (Pohl 2002). Nevertheless, the Kazakhstani coal industry had a few well-known dynasties of Chechens working both underground and on the surface.
5. A tunnelling combine or a roadheader is a machine which is used for boring tunnels. It consists of a cutting head that cuts the coal face and the loading assembly that gathers the cut material and sends it to the conveyor belt. The combine driver sits on a seat on the top of the combine and operates the machine with various knobs and levers.

References

Ashwin, Sarah. 1999. *Russian Workers: The Anatomy of Patience*. Manchester: Manchester University Press.

Barnes, Steven A. 2011. *Death and Redemption: The Gulag and the Shaping of Soviet Society*. Princeton, NJ: Princeton University Press.

Brown, Kate. 2001. "Gridded Lives: Why Kazakhstan and Montana are Nearly the Same Place." *The American Historical Review* 106(1): 17–48.

Dave, Bhavna. 2007. *Kazakhstan-Ethnicity, Language and Power*. Psychology Press.

Filtzer, Donald. 1986. *Soviet Workers and Stalinist Industrialization: The Formation of Modern Soviet Production Relations 1928–1941*. London: Pluto.

Fitzpatrick, Sheila. 1993. "Ascribing Class: The Construction of Social Identity in Soviet Russia." *The Journal of Modern History* 65(4): 745–70.

Harvey, David. 1990. *The Condition of Postmodernity: An Enquiry into the Origins of Cultural Change*. Oxford: Basil Blackwell.

Holmström, Mark. 2007. *South Indian Factory Workers: Their Life and their World*. Vol. 20. Cambridge: Cambridge University Press.

Holmström, Mark., 1984. *Industry and Inequality: The Social Anthropology of Indian Labour*. Cambridge: Cambridge University Press.

Ismailbekova, Aksana. 2013. "Coping Strategies: Public Avoidance, Migration, and Marriage in the Aftermath of the Osh Conflict, Fergana Valley." *Nationalities Papers* 41(1): 109–27.

Kalb, Don. 2015. "Introduction: Class and the New Anthropological Holism." In *Anthropologies of Class*, ed. James G. Carrier and Don Kalb, 5–33. Cambridge: Cambridge University Press.

Kasmir, Sharryn, and August Carbonella. 2006. "Rethinking the Anthropology of Social Class." in *Anthropology News*.

Keskäla, Eeva. 2012. "Mining Postsocialism: Work, Class and Ethnicity in an Estonian Mine." (Dissertation, University of London, London)

———. 2014. "Disembedding the Company from Kinship: Unethical Families and Atomised Labour in an Estonian Mine." *Laboratorium: Russian Review of Social Research* 2. Retrieved 24 October 2017 from http://www.soclabo.org/index.php/laboratorium/article/view/362/1111.

Kotkin, Stephen. 1994. "Coercion and Identity: Workers' Lives in Stalin's Showcase City." In *Making Workers Soviet*, ed. L. Siegelbaum and R. Suny, 274–310. London: Cornell University Press.

Lamont, Michele. 2001. *The Dignity of Working Men: Morality and the Boundaries of Race, Class and Immigration*. London: Harvard University Press/Russell Sage Foundation.

Lee, Ching Kwan. 2009. "Raw encounters: Chinese Managers, African Workers and the Politics of Casualization in Africa's Chinese Enclaves." *The China Quarterly* 199: 647–66.

Lewin, Moshe. 1994. "Concluding Remarks." In *Making Workers Soviet. Power, Class and Identity*, ed. Lewis H. Siegelbaum and Ronald Grigior Suny, 376–390. Ithaca, NY and London: Cornell University Press.

McDowell, Linda. 2011. *Redundant Masculinities: Employment Change and White Working Class Youth*. Chichester: Wiley-Blackwell.

Mollona, Massimiliano. 2009. *Made in Sheffield: An Ethnography of Industrial Work and Politics*. New York: Berghahn Books.

Ngai, Pun. 2005. *Made in China: Women Factory Workers in a Global Workplace*. Durham, NC and London: Duke University Press.

Parry, Jonathan. 2013a. "Company and Contract Labour in a Central Indian Steel Plant." *Economy and Society* 42(3): 348–74.

———. 2013b. "The 'Embourgeoisement' of a 'Proletarian Vanguard'?" In *Interrogating India's Modernity: Democracy, Identity, and Citizenship*, ed. Surinder Jodhka. New Delhi: Oxford University Press.

Payne, Matthew J. 2001. *Stalin's Railroad: Turksib and the Building of Socialism*. Pittsburgh, PA: University of Pittsburgh Press.

Petrick, Martin, Jürgen Wandel, and Katharina Karsten. 2013. "Rediscovering the Virgin Lands: Agricultural Investment and Rural Livelihoods in a Eurasian Frontier Area." *World Development* 43: 164–179.

Pine, Frances. 2014. "Migration as Hope: Space, Time, and Imagining the Future." *Current Anthropology* 55 (S9): 95–104.

Pohl, Michaela. 2002. "'It Cannot be that Our Graves will be Here' : The Survival of Chechen and Ingush Deportees in Kazakhstan, 1944–1957." *Journal of Genocide Research* 4(3): 401–30.

———. 2004. "Women and Girls in the Virgin Lands," in Melanie Ilič, Susan Reid, Lynne Attwood (eds). *Women in the Khrushchev Era*, 52–74. Basingstoke: Palgrave Macmillan, London.

Reeves, Madeleine. 2014. *Border Work: Spatial Lives of the State in Rural Central Asia*. Ithaca, NY: Cornell University Press.

Ries, Nancy. 1997. *Russian Talk: Culture and Conversation During Perestroika*. Ithaca, NY. Cornell University Press.

Sanchez, Andrew. 2012a. "Deadwood and Paternalism: Rationalizing Casual Labour in an Indian Company Town." *Journal of the Royal Anthropological Institute* 18(4): 808–827.

———. 2012b. "Questioning Success: Dispossession and the Criminal Entrepreneur in Urban India." *Critique of Anthropology* 32(4): 435–57.

Schatz, Edward. 2000. "The Politics of Multiple Identities: Lineage and Ethnicity in Kazakhstan." *Europe-Asia Studies* 52(3): 489–506.

Shlapentokh, Vladimir. 1988. "The Stakhanovite Movement: Changing Perceptions over Fifty Years." *Journal of Contemporary History* 23(2): 259–76.

Standing, Guy. 2011. *The Precariat: The New Dangerous Class*. London: Bloomsbury Academic.

———. 2014. "Why the Precariat is not a" Bogus Concept"." *Open Democracy*.

Thompson, E.P. 1980. *The Making of the English Working Class*. London: Gollancz.

Tkach, Olga. 2003. "The Phenomenon of the 'Soviet Hereditary Worker': From Asseveration of Social Class Purity to Workers' Dynasty." In *The Soviet Union — a Popular State? Studies on Popular Opinion in the USSR* ed. Timo Vihavainen, 162–179. St Petersburg: Europeyski Dom.

———. 2008. "Zavodskaia dinastiia kak social'no-kul'turnyi fenomen: sovetskii i post-sovetskii periody. Avtoreferat na soiskanie uchenoi stepeni kandidata socio-logicheskih nauk [Factory Dynasty as a Sociocultural Phenomenon: Soviet and Post-Soviet Periods. Abstract of Ph.D. Dissertation in Sociology]". St.Petersburg: Sociological Institute of Russian Academy of Sciences.

Weis, Lois. 2013. *Working Class Without Work: High School Students in a De-industrializing Economy*. London: Routledge.

Willis, Paul E. 1977. *Learning to Labour: How Working Class Kids get Working Class Jobs*. Farnborough, Hants. Aldershot: Saxon House; Gower/Ashgate.

3

Work, Precarity, and Resistance

Company and Contract Labor in Kazakhstan's Former Soviet Steel Town

TOMMASO TREVISANI

Introduction

On the last day-shift of 2013, the workers of the wagon tippler station at the crushing and sorting factory of the ArcelorMittal steel plant in Temirtau, Kazakhstan, were taking advantage of a mechanical breakdown to have a break in the warmth of their control room. They were awaiting their monthly pay slips more impatiently than usual because of the imminent New Year festivities. One of the aged conveyor belts that carry iron ore from the railway to the factory's stockyards needed repair, so while the senior machine operator alternated phone calls with the console room and consultations with the head of area, the other workers drank tea. Meanwhile the smoking wagons transporting iron ore, freshly thawed in nearby garages and now waiting to be unloaded in the wagon tippling station, were rapidly re-freezing in the icy winter weather. The control room livened up when the shift foreman arrived to hand out pay slips to all present except the two *podriatchiki*, unskilled casual laborers externally contracted to check the doors and brakes of the wagons.

Alexey, the head of area, invited me to join him in anticipation of what he termed the "spectacle": "Just watch how their excitement will turn into disappointment right away," he said, pointing at the operators, loaders, and railcar workers with permanent company jobs as they received their pay slips. Each read his own attentively, many grimacing as they did so. "And now look at the *podriatchiki*," Alexey continued, "how happy they are, although they earn four or five times less. You see, the less you earn, the happier you are." Volodya, a Russian native from Temirtau, and Valikhon, a young Kazakh migrant from Uzbekistan, countered the banter with the deferential smile that subordinates reserve for superiors. They had only recently started working on this shop floor as contract workers and were relieved, after two months, to have received their first payment. Not smiling were Zhenia and Dimitri, two low-rank workers in permanent company jobs. Both had lost bonuses for having been on sick leave. Their salaries, with housing bills, alimony payments, and loan repayments directly subtracted, were uncomfortably close to the contract workers' wages.

In Soviet times pay was handed out over the counter and the figures written in registers open to all. Individual pay slips were an innovation after privatization, but initially workers knew how much others received because the pay slips were given *en bloc* to the work group senior, who passed them around. Later the pay slips were distributed by the shift foreman, who is responsible for checking that individual fines and bonus payments have been accurately implemented. Since recent shop floor restructuring, foremen have more power to decide these matters. Workers no longer show their pay slips to each other, fomenting a culture of secrecy and speculation.

Just as a call from the console room announced that work could be resumed, Alexey summed up by saying, "the Indian wants us all to be happy, therefore he pays all of us pennies," earning the embittered approval of all. Alexey's sarcasm reflected a common attitude among workers: united in their resentment against the foreign owner, but increasingly divided by wages, entitlements, backgrounds, attitudes, and apprehensions. The Indian in question is Lakshmi Mittal, the British-based Indian billionaire, world's largest steel producer, and since 1995 the owner of the steel combine known in Soviet times under the name Karmet—Karagandinskiy Metallurgicheski Kombinat.

Work in this steelworks has always been embedded in a labor hierarchy expressed in manifold and nuanced differences in skill, pay, seniority, gender, and in Soviet times party affiliation. The legacy of the old hierarchy still matters, but in the context of flexibilization (Harvey 1987) it has radically changed in recent years. Compared with the Soviet period, today the plant employs fewer people and produces less, and its industrial infrastructure cries out for investment and better maintenance. This is a typical story of local labor struggling to survive under profit-maximizing global capitalism (cf. Kim 2013; Mollona 2009; Lee 2007; Ngai 2005). In this chapter I focus on how this struggle is affecting workers' social relationships, the content and meaning of their work, and the way it is experienced *morally*.

Echoing a trend discussed by Parry (2013a, 2013b) in the context of India's economic liberalization, the switch from Soviet to capitalist employment regime has opened up a division between securely employed, unionized, more skilled and better paid regular company workers and the poorly paid, less protected, unskilled, and non-organized contract laborers (*podri-atchiki*) who often carry out the most menial tasks in the factory. In Soviet times contract labor existed as a niche phenomenon: a few skilled workers received better pay for carrying out specialized tasks. The situation radically changed under the ownership of Mittal, when low-skilled, poorly paid contract workers appeared in large numbers on the shop floor as substitutes for the work of machines and for workers previously employed under better conditions. In theory, contractors are independent companies that offer their services on the market, but de facto many contractors specializing in low-paid maintenance and repair have been created for and are quasi-internal to the main company, their sole client (cf. Peck and Theodore 2001).

In Bhilai, India, the split between company labor and proletarianized contract labor within a public-sector plant is such that Parry (2013a) identifies different class trajectories. In Temirtau, where the plant is owned by foreign capital, the possibility of capital flight puts labor in a far weaker position, so the two working-class segments tread parallel paths. Contract workers experience exclusion from company workers' rights and privileges and lament employment discrimination. Company workers lament heightened pressure at the workplace and resent the dilapidation of their formerly collectively owned shop floor through what they see as deliberate managerial disregard. However, steel workers' resistance to what they see as "Indian" labor restructuring—that is, the imposition of exploitative and undignified labor relations (associated by workers with Indian capitalism)—is also in part a success story rooted in Soviet labor legacies and in the special interest that the President of Kazakhstan, himself a former blast furnace operator, retains in Temirtau. Over two decades under Mittal, full labor casualization has been averted, contract labor has not been implemented to the extent augured by the company, and job cuts among the regularly employed have proceeded more gradually than in many other postsocialist industrial settings. The division between contract and company workers bears upon broader debates concerning labor casualization and precarity (Allison 2013; Molé 2012; Mollona 2009; Sanchez 2012; Standing 2011). I shall focus on emerging forms of political consciousness, split class subjectivities, and "resistance" patterns within two working-class segments. At the intersection of power, labor, and foreign capital, the circumstances in Temirtau invite comparisons with other styles of capitalist management (see the chapters by Schober and Lee in this volume).

My specific angle of observation is the DSF or *drobilno-sortirovochnaya fabrika* (crushing and sorting factory), the shop floor on which I carried out my fieldwork in 2013/14.[1] The DSF is where the iron ore arrives on wagons or lorries, is unloaded, sorted, crushed, stored and transported to the sintering plant and to the blast furnaces. Preceding the steelmaking departments proper, it has the task of continuously ensuring reception and supply of raw materials. Its task is rendered more difficult by climatic conditions and by technology that is on average fifty or more years old. Due to the pollution and physical demands of labor on this shop floor, company workers earn above the average salary paid to other company workers—reason enough for company management to downsize the regular work-force and replace it with cheap contract labor. I shall show how, against a background of steadily deteriorating shop floor conditions, the relatively better-off company workers come to understand and experience their everyday shift work as a form of self-assertion against the foreign company. I call this *work-as-resistance*: everyday labor execution carries a subtext of values and memories in conflict with those of the higher management. Workers can thereby assert their agency on the shop floor, despite the devaluation of their work. However, their assertion is characterized by a partial, "alienating" autonomy: their ambiguous "resistance" fails to strike the ruling regime and also fails to integrate them and overcome their alien-ation. And because it excludes the contract workers, it ultimately reinforces working-class fragmentation. Due to their different backgrounds and posi-tions at the bottom of the hierarchy of labor, contract workers experience their alienating work in a different way: their labor is *work-for-subsistence* in the crudest sense.

Soviet and Post-Soviet Temirtau

Formerly a Gulag camp within the Karlag (Karaganda Corrective Labor Camp) "archipelago" (Barnes 2011), Temirtau gradually turned into a city during the construction and steady enlargement of its steel works, the largest in Central Asia and one of the largest in the Soviet Union.[2] A first, temporary metallurgical plant was established during World War II with industrial machinery that had been hastily evacuated before the German military advance. Camp detainees and prisoners of war enlarged the settle-ment into a proper city, named Temirtau (i.e., "Iron Mountain" in Kazakh) in 1945. In the postwar period the authorities planned a fully integrated steelworks on the model of earlier plants in the Urals and Siberia (Kotkin 1995; Shaporov and Bondarenko 1983). Temirtau became the object of an all-Union Komsomol (Communist Youth Organization) construction campaign in the late 1950s. Whereas the city's first inhabitants were mainly political exiles, war prisoners, and "punished peoples," the Komsomol-call gave the city a second demographic pillar by attracting enthusiastic young volunteers from all over the Soviet Union. Inaugurated in 1960, the Karaganda Metallurgical Plant was later enlarged into Karmet. At its peak in the 1970s–1980s it was known as "Kazakhstanskaya Magnitka"[3] and celebrated as a symbol of Soviet modernity. The development of this steel industry was motivated by the proximity of large coal and iron deposits in the Karaganda region, but also by the political will to expand the Soviet Union into the "empty" Kazakh steppe. From the very beginning, inequalities in access to privileges and in labor and living conditions caused tensions and protests, "part of a crisis of modernization" (Kozlov 2002: 11) in the post-Stalin years. In the "hot" August of 1959 these conflicts exploded (Bondar 2014). In the postwar Soviet Union, the most serious labor protests to take place until then had been sparked by the privileges granted to Bulgarian workers, which provoked an outraged reaction among other workers housed in large tent camps near the construction site.[4] These early conflicts between established labor and migrants represented a pattern that would repeat itself. After 1959, the harsh working and living conditions characteristic of the early postwar period gave way to socialism's more redistributive and plentiful years. Thanks to the lessons learned in 1959, provisioning, housing conditions, and job opportunities all improved. In the 1960s and 1970s, the city and the combine grew steadily. Attracted by well-paid industrial jobs, a new wave of skilled migrants from all over the Soviet Union added a new layer to the city's demographic fabric. The combine, built adjacent to the city, came to account for a tenth of Kazakhstan's GDP and exported steel to more than twenty different socialist-bloc countries. By the late 1980s, around 47,000 workers were on its payroll, Temirtau at that time counted 245,000 inhabitants. Among the city's proudest boasts was, unique in Kazakhstan, its German drama theater. Housed in the sumptuous Metallurgists' Culture Palace, the theater testified to the presence of a large German community and marked Temirtau as a lively cultural center.

With the collapse (*razval*) of the USSR, Temirtau's ascending curve reversed abruptly. Throughout the 1990s the city was plagued by high criminality levels, rampant alcoholism, and the highest rate of HIV in Kazakhstan. People endured winters with minimal supply of heat, water, and electricity. Empty, decaying houses increasingly spotted the city's landscape. The Germans were among the first to leave *en masse*, attracted to new opportunities opened up by Germany's reunification. Other nationalities also attempted to flee impoverishment by migrating to Western Europe or Russia, but not all were equally successful. Temirtau lost a third of its population after the late 1980s, but it retained its multi-ethnic character: Russians, Ukrainians, Poles, Tatars, Greeks, Chechens, Koreans, and other nationalities shared neighborhoods, kinship, workplaces, and a language. Among those who stayed, the post-Soviet solidarity of needs and mutual help reinforced existing ties. In many respects the situation in Temirtau was better than in other small towns because the combine attenuated *razval* by providing (although intermittently) heat and electricity, jobs, housing, exchangeable goods in lieu of wages, and even a currency (factory coupons were introduced during the early post-Soviet hyperinflation period). "If the combine had stopped working, Temirtau would have died": thus do Temirtauians refer to the period before privatization.

Mittal bought the insolvent steelworks in 1995, when it was on the point of ceasing production in the wake of various local and international businessmen's unsuccessful attempts to privatize the combine (Peck 2004).[5] The takeover deal included repayment of wage arrears to 35,000 workers and international suppliers, and binding plans for the recovery of production capacity (Kavaev and Piyanko 1995). At this time Mittal's group had existed for twenty-five years and was rapidly expanding from family firm into global corporation by acquiring and restructuring publicly owned steel plants worldwide. Temirtau was a decisive step in this process, as it dwarfed all previously acquired plants and almost doubled the company's size overnight.[6] The company's situation improved under the new ownership. By the beginning of the second postsocialist decade, Temirtau had shifted from "economic involution" (Burawoy 2002) to relative capitalist normalcy. From 2003 the city began to grow again, though in 2013 its population was still 65,000 below its late Soviet peak. Its demographic composition was now profoundly altered by regional and international migration.

From the inception of Russian-speaking Temirtau, Kazakhs formed a small minority. This is now changing due to a nationwide trend referred to as "Kazakhization" (Cummings 2005; Dave 2007). Unofficially, this tendency translates into a positive discrimination practice whereby ethnic Kazakhs, reversing Soviet hierarchies, now receive privileged access to power, public-sector jobs, and education. This inequality undermines a constitutionally inscribed and officially celebrated claim to equal and harmonious ethnic relationships. It creates tensions between Kazakh newcomers and the Russian-speaking communities who built and worked in the combine in Soviet years. Until recently, Temirtau has been culturally, demographically, and economically closer to the industrial mono-towns of Central Russia and Siberia than to other urban settlements in Kazakhstan. These are also the native regions of most workers who came to find their luck in Temirtau in Soviet days. But thanks to the arrival of new Kazakh migrants (and their proclivity for larger families), peculiarly "southern" or Central Asian habits and forms of sociality have started to modify the profile of the "Russian" city. In this context, "Russian" and "Kazakh" are often better understood with reference to cultural identities and lifestyles, rather than simply as markers of language or ethnicity.

From a multinational population, the Soviet industrial world forged Russophone working-class communities that shared a strong sociality based on the workplace experience, and on workplace-provided housing, education, and recreation. Kazakhs raised in Soviet Temirtau spoke Russian and "Bolshevik" (Kotkin 1995), as did everyone else. But today's newly arrived Kazakh migrants are seldom proficient in the cultural codes of the Soviet world of heavy industry, and some of them do not know Russian at all. Unlike the wave of involuntary migrants who arrived at the Gulag camps in the Karaganda region in the 1930s, 1940s, and early 1950s, but much like the subsequent waves of migrants who arrived in Temirtau in the post-Stalin decades, this ethnically homogenous post-Independence wave of migrants arrived in Temirtau in search of jobs and a better life. Often from the countryside and from the south of the country or, like the Oralmans,[7] from Mongolia and Uzbekistan, they mostly found work outside of the steel plant's regular company employment.

The older generation of "Russians" perceive uncouth rural Kazakhs as flooding in and feel ousted from "their" city. As Kazakh language, culture, and ethnicity become more important every day, they feel threatened by their lack of prospects and fear for their own and their children's future (cf. Kesküla in this volume). Many, therefore, have activated their networks to find a job, study, or resettle in Russia. Kazakh newcomers, for their part—especially poor Oralmans—feel ousted from "their" country when they realize that despite "Kazakhization," they are comparatively disadvantaged in predominantly "Russian" Temirtau. They especially resent the long established dynasties of steelworkers, who have solid jobs and own apartments whose rent or purchase is no longer affordable for earners of normal wages. As of the early 2000s, Kazakhstan's oil bonanza and a reshaped national economy gradually triggered a real estate bubble (Bissenova 2012). Following a nationwide trend, property in Temirtau that was nearly worthless in 1995 was being traded at exorbitant prices in 2014, creating a divide between (newly arrived) renters and (long established) owners. As in many other parts of Central Asia, though, ordinary homeowners are experiencing the contradiction of apparent wealth in terms of real estate and growing deprivation in terms of what their wages can afford (Trevisani 2014: 251).

During the Soviet period, housing was provided through the workplace, and workers of different rank were likely to share the same neighborhood with their shop floor managers. But once the housing sector was commoditized, residential segregation increased. Migration, urban policies, and the housing market reshaped the cityscape by triggering new socio-spatial differentiations. Some neighborhoods became thoroughly dilapidated; others, visibly disadvantaged. Neighborhoods of expensive villas have appeared in

various parts of the city, including the heavily polluted buffer zone sepa-
rating the combine from the Soviet-era housing estates. Nevertheless, the
division between affluent and disadvantaged neighborhoods is piecemeal
and still embryonic. Interior furnishings are a better indicator of wealth
than location or type of housing. Company and contract workers, whether
tenants or owners, live in more or less crowded apartments in various
conditions of repair in the same high-rise building. Workers and managers
who were neighbors in the Soviet period frequently remain so still, even as
the apartments of former shop floor mates who have left or died are often
occupied by newcomer Kazakh speakers. The presence of these immigrants
brings in new life, but it also creates parallel worlds that intersect only
sporadically in increasingly anonymous housing blocks.

Workers, Company, and State

At first, Temirtau's residents were grateful to Mittal for rescuing their town
and combine at a time of deep crisis. However, one consequence of the
company's restructuring plans was a deterioration of the relations between
the workers and citizens on the one hand, and the foreign managers and
owners on the other. From 1996 to 2013, employment dropped from 30,000
to 15,000. In that same period the number of contract workers grew, oscil-
lating between 2,000 and 3,000 workers. This restructuring process is still
ongoing. The combine—which Mittal once considered "the jewel in my
crown,"—gradually changed its role within the group. After two decades
of mergers and takeovers, ArcelorMittal produced 93.1 million tonnes of
steel in 2014, mostly in Europe and America (ArcelorMittal 2015). Only
about 3 million were produced in Temirtau. During the years of corporate
expansion, the combine had struggled to keep pace with expectations. In
managerial discourse, it turned into a peripheral "troublemaker" whose
key production indicators (which hinge on the ratio between output and
employment) deviated from corporate standards.

Foreign managers and experts[8] justify redundancies by arguing that they
are needed for competitiveness. They condemn the "absolutely communist
mentality of workers and unions." Company workers accuse management
of cutting jobs indiscriminately in a manner detrimental to safety and production, of not adequately investing in maintenance and equipment, and of
deflecting attention from marketing and management failures by putting
the blame on workers. And although the company workers' trade union,
Zhaktau, criticizes company restructuring plans and calls for better conditions in company jobs, contract workers lack an effective voice. Their
"city union," a government-arranged umbrella organization representing

the interests of contract companies' workers *and* owners, is toothless. City-level and regional authorities mediate between company workers and the company by cautioning against overtly anti-social policies, but when workers' claims endanger production, they usually back the company. Stability and tax revenue are the government's priority. Behind closed doors, the President and Mittal regularly discuss the combine's situation.

At the time of my fieldwork, the combine was going through its most difficult period since privatization. The high steel prices of the late 1990s and early 2000s had fallen (in part because of overproduction in China), casting doubt over its future. Contrary to earlier plans to double its output, production was actually declining.[9] The combine was losing market share and faced problems in labor negotiations and in management. Prices were uncompetitive and quality low. Its reputation suffered when a large order of steel rods was found to be defective on delivery. One entrepreneur in Temirtau complained that it was cheaper for him to import steel from Russia than to buy it from the combine next door.

Workers argue that corruption and theft are systemic at all production levels, and that the company purposely avoids financial transparency in order to hide profits from tax officials and trade unions. There is a discrepancy between the company's public outreach campaigns and the very opaque data it publishes about its marketing, finance, and profits. The rumor in the factory is that local management, with the connivance of the higher management, informally channels part of the steel produced for private profit. Such practices were common in the early post-Soviet period, and a former combine director active in the fight against criminality was shot in front of the factory gates in 1992. Local newspapers regularly report on investigations into the theft of steel.

In the rolling mills, where the production cycle ends and coils and rebars are stored, some line managers wear Rolex watches and are said to own several "*kottedzh*" villas (cf. Humphrey 2002: 175ff.) and lead extravagant lifestyles. Corruption affects every shop floor to varying degrees. Theft of scrap metal in the form of old machinery, work tools, or spare parts is the reason behind the security guards that patrol the compound and check people's bags and cars at the factory gates. The scrap metal traders' district begins directly opposite the factory gates of the rolling mills. Value is siphoned away from the factory in myriad ways. At the higher end, this "informal" economy is said to involve offshore accounting, tax evasion, and large-scale theft of finished products with the complicity of certain managers. At the lower end, stereotypical accusations of petty theft of metal are usually directed at contract workers with an Oralman background.

Labor conflict over pay and employment conditions has intensified in step with mounting pressure on jobs and production. In 2012, company workers organized a sit-in in front of the combine headquarters in support of demands for a pay raise, which they obtained. According to the collective labor agreement, company workers are entitled to a bonus in the form of a thirteenth month's salary if they reach their annual production targets on all shop floors. Management, however, also makes the bonus conditional on the results of the sales department. In recent years the bonus was repeatedly not paid out due to economic "crisis," a decision that workers refused to accept.[10] Against this backdrop, heated negotiations took place between the company and the trade union in 2013 and 2014.

In 2014 the company aired plans to fill vacant positions with a number of foreign engineers, and there were rumors about introducing "*autstafing*" (outsourcing)—the practice of hiring non-unionized workers with less protected contracts into regular staff positions through a hiring firm. Some cautious experimenting with *autstafing* in the rolling mills had in practice extended the contract-labor type of precarization to regular staff positions. The company's plans met fierce resistance and eventually moved into the background. But workers fear their future comeback. The trade union, while critical of management, tries to moderate the anger of many workers who feel cheated by the company. It is conciliatory and "understanding" when the company and the government indicate limits. Many workers believe that a real strike could never happen. A total stoppage of production would be illegal, damage the machinery, and provoke a strong governmental reaction.[11] Against the political background of the crisis in Ukraine, the government introduced special laws to prohibit protests or gatherings. In February 2014, the unexpected devaluation of the national currency (tenge) helped the factory (its production costs are in tenge, but it sells in US dollars) and eased the pressure in the negotiations. Suddenly a pay raise of 10 percent became possible for management, though the devaluation of the tenge was twice as much. Prices in the shops rose faster than workers' pay. They felt betrayed again, but their fear of violent repression (comparable to events in the oil industry of Zhanaozen, western Kazakhstan, in 2011)[12] and mistrust of any form of organized protest paralyzed them. Any protests, workers told me, having learned this truth from Russian TV channels, could be manipulated into a "Maidan" and go against their own interests. But workers' passivity must also be seen against the background of their everyday shop floor experiences, to which I now turn.

Shop Floor Restructuring

The DSF is subdivided into two areas: a *verkhny trakt* (upper tract), which ensures reception and storage of iron ores, and a *nizhni trakt* (lower tract), where ores are crushed, sorted, blended, and transported to other departments. Four brigades, subdivided into smaller work groups with specific tasks and competencies, rotate in shifts of twelve hours. At the wagon tippling machines, where the DSF begins, work is in pairs. The junior worker's place is at the rails, where he separates the wagons of the convoys and oversees the tippling, while the senior operates the levers of the console in the adjacent control room. The unblended ore is unloaded into grated, funnel-shaped basins and conveyed from there to a system of overhead transport belts (hence the name *verkhny trakt*), which ends with the ores' discharge onto huge stockpiles. Large-armed excavators mix up the stockpiles while bulldozers push the ores into holes opening onto the conveyor belt system of the *nizhni trakt* below. Here the iron is either directed to the crushing and sorting mills and then stocked, or transported, via chains of conveyor belts extending over several kilometers of underground tunnels, outside the DSF.

DSF operations require many workers with different skills and functions. Conveyor belts, consoles, and cranes are mostly operated by women, while wagon tipplers, drivers of excavators and bulldozers, and electrical and mechanical fitters are male. Company workers' pay is calculated on the basis of a complicated system of pay items and bonuses. Basic pay depends on the type of specialization, seniority, shift, and task. For instance, the pay of conveyor belt operators depends on which conveyor belt they serve. Unequal pay reflects a hierarchy of specialization and seniority. Career patterns are gendered. Typically, male workers enter the factory in low-skilled positions and climb the ladder of rank and specialization over time. Women often start as conveyor belt operators and eventually end up in less wearisome posts (ideally, behind a desk). It takes approximately six months to get to know the territory of the DSF well enough to be able to move around in it autonomously, perhaps three years for a conveyor belt operator to master all the details of her work, and five years for an apprentice electrician to learn the routine work from his master. Formally, skilled jobs require a higher education degree, but in practice education and training take place through apprenticeship to senior workers. For instance, almost all of the shop floor managers started their careers in the DSF as low-skilled workers, climbing the ladder of rank and income over time. At some point they would obtain a higher degree through distance learning, and a position as engineers or shop floor managers. When their bosses retired, quit, or were made redundant in the course of restructuring, these men were promoted to senior positions (see Kesküla in this volume).

Over the restructuring process, the size of brigades was effectively halved. Recruiting stopped, creating a problem of workforce scarcity, aging of the workforce, and interrupted transmission of shop floor jobs across generations. In the first years after privatization, the company had a policy of allowing a worker to indicate a successor upon retirement (de facto formalizing the accepted Soviet-period custom of recommending one's kin for a post on the shop floor). Workers thereby managed to pass their jobs on to family members with the backing of the company, which profited from the intra-generational transmission of skills and values.[13] After restructuring, however, the possibility of "inheriting" a relative's job vanished. In 2010, the DSF workforce consisted of four hundred machine operators, service staff, engineers and shop floor managers. But over the next few years, as voluntary retirement schemes were implemented and vacant positions left unfilled, the workforce was almost halved. The remaining workers had to take over the tasks of those who left and organization charts were flattened by merging units. Workers must now cover more territory and machinery. A conveyor belt operator who was once responsible for one conveyor must today oversee several, which exponentially increases her workload, responsibilities, and risks (cf. Kofti, this volume). At the conveyors, transported ore regularly spills over and can cripple the machines if it is not removed rapidly. Keeping conveyors "clean" today is a labor of Sisyphus. It is done with shovels (and in winter, when the material freezes, with bolts and hammers), whereas in the past, with higher manning levels, regular sweeping was usually sufficient.

After layoffs, the DSF was able to fulfill its tasks only with the help of a fluctuating number of contract workers (59 during my fieldwork) hired temporarily for specific low-skill tasks. Of these contract workers, 56 percent were Kazakhs and 42 percent were women (among company workers a third were women and 16 percent were Kazakhs). The four different subcontracting companies on this shop floor varied according to size, conditions of employment, and the ethnic and gender composition of their workforce. Job cuts have especially affected the DSF's 22-kilometer network of conveyor belts, leading to a significant "masculinization" of the regular workforce, in the past used to be half female, and to a "refeminization" of the shop floor via the deliberate hiring of (lower paid) women in contract jobs, including some who were previously employed as regular workers.

At the DSF, contract workers have replaced broken snowplow locomotives, stone crushing machines, and expensive, newly imported suction excavator trucks that proved unsuited to the Kazakhstani winter. They fill the growing gaps in the ranks of regular workers, who on average are much older and struggle physically to manage their expanding tasks. Contract labor is hired via the higher management, but at the shop floor level the tasks are often redefined. Like a joker in a deck of cards, contract workers are brought into play wherever their labor is most urgently needed. Contract workers do not know the technology and carry out their assignments regardless. Unlike company workers, they regard working a shift as completing a precise assignment received. Because the number of contract laborers is insufficient, menial tasks cannot be entirely delegated to them. Although they occupy different positions in the labor hierarchy, company and contract workers might have to share a jackhammer, work together on a repair, or do the same job with a shovel a few meters away from each other. Although their pay, status, and job security certainly differ, company and contract workers in practice face similar working conditions.

From the control room of the wagon tippler station, Alik, a veteran company worker, points at the stockyards rising behind the rails to recall that "we used to call them the golden mountains." Until a few years ago, upper tract workers were paid per unloaded wagon, shifts met much higher targets than they do today, and pay reflected the piled-up stockyards. But the DSF was delivering more than the blast furnaces could process, creating a costly imbalance for the company. Following the implementation of a time-rate, during its restructuring the DSF became a more polluted, dangerous, and difficult place to work, or in Alik's words: "the dumping ground of the combine." He meant this sentence literally. Unlike in Soviet times, all sorts of industrial waste nowadays ends up reinserted into the production cycle to save money that otherwise would be spent on appropriate waste disposal facilities. For example, *pushonka* is a fine powder produced in the processing of newly introduced low-quality limestone; the pulverized lime is completely useless to the steel production and so light that it cannot be carried on conveyor belts without turning into a cloud of dust suspended in the air. Thus the air in the conveyor belt tunnels becomes saturated with thin particles that quickly cover the machinery. Workers clear their machines by shoveling the *pushonka* back onto the conveyor belts. Knowing it to be useless, workers blame "those higher up" for saddling them with this denigrating work, which they grudgingly carry out, as otherwise the entire DSF would stop. In this and in similar situations workers nod at each other and blame the headquarters for being "irresponsible," "evil," and "harmful" to the shop floor.

Unlike in Bhilai (Parry 2013a), the DSF's staff shortage prevents company workers from retreating into comfortable supervisory tasks. Given the nature of the work in the DSF, "white helmets" (foremen, engineers, and shop floor managers) share dangers and difficult working conditions with workers and must often get their hands dirty. This is exemplified, for instance, by the situation of a shift foreman who, lacking people, cleans off a conveyor by himself. Since workflow disruptions are frequent and accountability grows with seniority, senior positions have also become increasingly demanding, uncomfortable posts. Although many tasks formerly done by regular workers are now done by contractors, company workers ultimately bear responsibility and have to make ends meet with the available means and human resources, bending rules and regulations to achieve the set targets. Restructuring thus materializes as a proliferation of casual, externally contracted jobs with narrowly defined tasks and limited duties that also entails an extension of workload and responsibilities for those who hold the remaining company jobs.

Work Discipline and Resistance

For DSF managers, "making a shift" means ensuring a continuous supply of ferrous materials by allocating and motivating chronically scarce staff in the coordination of intricately interlinked tasks. Company workers (who generally earn a basic 400–500 euros monthly, some as much as 800 euros) are rewarded with a monthly bonus when their work unit fulfills the plan without infringing on health and safety rules. They also receive "*nedoshtat*," a supplementary payment for taking over the tasks of staff positions made redundant.[14] Managers can also augment workers' income by allocating overtime shifts. The upshot is that workers can take home more than their superiors. Bonuses are granted every month, unless the bosses decide otherwise—they can use this instrument to discipline workers.

Contract workers earn a basic 120–160 euros. Most actually do not have a contract, and many work more shifts than company workers, but they never get *nedoshtat* or other bonuses. Rebellious workers are quickly sacked. In theory, contract workers work by volume, meaning that contracting firms should record the cubic meters "cleaned" by their workers. But the accounting is fictitious: pay is based on days worked, irrespective of individual performance. In practice, contract workers are integrated into the command hierarchy at the lowest level and receive assignments from their contract company supervisors, foremen, and regular workers. To motivate contract workers, shop floor managers have introduced a form of piecework called *akkord*, an arrangement that allows them to leave work as soon as they finish the task assigned on that day. This was not part of the original labor agreements, but given their extremely low salaries it has become a diffuse practice aimed at motivating *podriatchiki* and limiting high turnover rates.

Company workers are nostalgic about a past when, in contrast to the current factory regime, "we could just do our work and live in peace." In their perception the labor process has now become one of "suspended punishment" (Ledeneva 1998: 78). The Soviet shop floor was regulated by the model rules of internal labor order, which defined managers' and workers' obligations, creating clear expectations and claimable rights (Conquest

1967: 111ff.). Nowadays workers live in fear of their bosses' moods and are anxious about infringing newly introduced (corporate) health and safety regulations that in practice are impossible to observe while working. For instance, workers' uniforms include protective glass and dust masks, but wearing the latter causes the glass to fog up, effectively leaving a worker in the dark. Dust masks are meant to last for a shift but become a useless burden after just half an hour of work in the dust of a tunnel when conveyor belts are running. Likewise, to keep from slowing down production, workers routinely trespass the protection barriers of running machines to clean up spills, though the rules require the machinery to be switched off.

White helmets and health and safety patrols from headquarters police the shop floor with frequent unannounced visits. Those workers found breaking the rules, or alleviating the boredom of a night shift by playing cards, dominoes, or *nardi* (Kazakh backgammon) are reprimanded and risk losing their jobs. In the past, workers were less oppressed by checks. Given the intermittent work rhythm (long periods of idleness punctuated by intense bursts of activity), a degree of liberty was tolerated, and labor discipline enforcement was principally dealt with within the immediate work group (cf. Ashwin 1999: 146). Restructuring has stepped up the rhythm of work and of control.

The sociality of the work collective (ibid.: 121) has faded, giving way to mistrust, buck passing, accusations of shirking, and permanent quarrels that render working more stressful. At shift briefings foremen read out the complaints of the previous brigade and follow up with discussions about whom to blame. Outside the workplace, workers socialize much less than in the past, generally preferring keeping work relationships and free time separate. Workers have reacted to the new pressures in different ways. Many bow to the new discipline by putting in more effort, acquiescing in new tasks and responsibilities and obeying orders even when they are perceived to be unjust. Others prefer to retreat into a passive routinization of work, insofar as this is possible. Voluntary redundancy schemes have allowed many highly skilled workers to quit. The ensuing manpower shortage is accentuated by departures for Russia (in the past also Germany). Shop floor managers try to stem the hemorrhage of workers. Sonia, for instance, is a conveyor belt operator in her mid fifties who would like to take early retirement, a decision welcomed by the company's personnel department. But her boss, fearing that her post would disappear, refuses to sign the papers on the grounds that she is essential to the functioning of the shop floor. Heads of work units tend to protect workers' jobs and, up to a certain point, will try to cover up bad behavior or shirking in the interest of the immediate work group. Pondering whether or not to file official complaint against one ill disciplined worker, a brigade leader decided not to do so for fear that this would provide headquarters with a welcome pretext for sacking the worker without replacing him. As he put it to me: "any additional worker, no matter whether weak or lazy, is better than none."

The Soviet "pact of plan fulfillment" (Müller 2007) granted a degree of autonomy to workers and shop floor managers in exchange for their support during critical phases of the production process. Restructuring altered this equilibrium and threatened the viability of the workplace. In February 2014, the control room operator Valentina told me that the factory had been suffering from "influenza" for weeks. By this she meant that for the first time, the DSF was having problems keeping up with its basic tasks. New deliveries of ore were being sent directly to other shop floors, preempting the possibility of building up the stockpiles. Never before had the DSF come so close to leaving the blast furnaces short of ore. In the (Soviet and post-Soviet) past, the DSF had secured winter supplies by managing reserves it had built up autonomously. The new managerial optimization logic in the name of efficiency (cf. ibid.: 42) was making this impossible. Although the "fever" eventually passed with the arrival of spring, new just-in-time logistics, penalties for excessive use of leased wagons (a new money-saving measure), and the impossibility of catching up with repairs, given the scarcity of spare parts and personnel, meant that the existential threat to the DSF was real.

Restructuring has also resulted in new shop floor "games" (Burawoy 1979). As I learned at my own cost during my first weeks on the shop floor, workers play "hide-and-seek" with the white helmets, avoiding any person on the shop floor whom they do not know.[15] Experience has taught them that interlopers can only mean trouble (a control, a fine, additional work, undesired questions). For their part, shop floor bosses play "chess" with workers, according to a skilled excavator driver who was replacing a conveyor belt operator on sick leave. Moving workers erratically on an imaginary chessboard meant shifting them from the tasks for which they were qualified to others at managers' discretion. If not compliant, the worker–chess piece can be readily sacrificed in a managerial gambit.

The Soviet shop floor was a crowded place of sociality. Some workers recall going to work as being like "going to a feast." The factory was "a second home" where the home/work separation was attenuated by the quality of relations and the camaraderie between workers, and the work rhythm was intense but also humane (Ashwin 1999). They contrast this to the situation today, in which hard manual work, loneliness, and stressful bursts of activity put enormous pressure on embittered, disillusioned workers. Contradicting the experience and memory of what the shop floor used to be, "solitude, insecurity, familial estrangement, precarious existence" (Allison 2013: 3) have become pervasive on the shop floor. Here, restructuring the post-Soviet factory without altering the factory's materiality has produced advanced capitalist "affects" (cf. Muehlebach 2011; Molé 2010).

Workers' respective types of precarity structure their reactions to the bleak prospects of the industrial working class, though company and contract workers alike fail to transcend their own parochial interests and apprehensions. Contract workers lament their precarious livelihoods and the low-paid, grueling work by which they make a living. Company work, though also alienating, is valorized not only by higher material rewards, but also by a sense of moral (historical) ownership of the means of production. Fear of losing these advantages and "descending" into contract workers' livelihood struggles is part of company workers' experience of precarization, characterized by pressure on their jobs and on their working-class "selves" (Mollona 2009). Against the background of a power constellation unfavorable to workers' demands, contract labor abides in a situation in which the only alternative to "weak" forms of shop floor resistance (Scott 1985) is to quit altogether. DSF company workers' agency consists in "resisting" by enduring in their jobs. Workers' moral experience of work marks another difference from Parry's Bhilai. Under the increasingly challenging conditions that they face on the shop floor, workers experience their ordinary work as a morally "dense" act that carries both an implicit statement of dissociation from the new factory regime of the owner, and a commitment to their workplace and its rich Soviet labor legacies.

What distinguishes company from contract workers, and also from headquarter managers, is that they are repositories of practical knowledge about machinery of a now antiquated Soviet technology (cf. Makram-Ebeid 2012). Since the DSF's founding in the 1960s, a large part of its machinery has been repaired over and over again, without ever being replaced. This machinery still sets the type of labor process and organization. Norms established by Soviet scientific management have not changed fundamentally; they were merely readapted. Company workers know that the company's interest in them is unlikely to outlast the aged machines, doomed to be scrapped sooner rather than later.

In socialist factories, old, complicated machinery strengthened workers' autonomy (Müller 2007: 48). In the DSF, the non-transferable character of workers' skills binds them to their machines: the destiny of the workforce is tied to their capacity to keep their factory alive. As long as the DSF can fulfill its task, knowledge of the obsolete machinery is their best protection against redundancy. Limited attempts to reduce the DSF's task by outsourcing have not been successful so far. However, a precedent has been established in the oxygen shop: its tasks are now outsourced to Linde, a German company that installed a new, fully automatized air separation factory. It now employs 15 highly skilled workers (compared with 227 in the oxygen shop before its closure, and 450 at its peak in 1993) and is managed via Internet from headquarters in the Czech Republic.

In the factory headquarters, managers like to use medical metaphors characterizing the combine as a "patient" that needs to be "treated," and identifying "cancers" that must be "extirpated." Shop floor managers, in their everyday challenge to keep production running, prefer military metaphors from the Soviet era (Gestwa 2010: 325) that equate work with war. Workers are exhorted in briefings to "resist." They are cast as "a demoralized troop," or "wise, old soldiers," or the "last Mohicans." Elsewhere in the post-Soviet world, steel workers who have lost their symbolic and material status have been referred to as "fallen heroes" (Trappmann 2013). But for DSF workers, work started to become truly heroic only after the recent restructuring policy. Here, unlike other postsocialist industrial workers who disengage from shop floor concerns, the experience of working hard to maintain the functionality of the workplace is their "agency of the weak" (Mrozowicki 2011). This form of resistance is not primarily directed *against* a careless management, but *for* the factory's survival and, indirectly, for the protection of better wages, skills, and values.

Old and New Working Class

In Temirtau, recent demographic trends and the new factory regime have fragmented the industrial working class into two segments. One was forged through the making of a Soviet steelworks (Straus 1997). This "old" segment, composed of multinational, skilled company workers, was shaped by the Soviet factory experience and is still earning respectable salaries today. The "new" working class consists of the growing pool of people working as contract workers in unprotected, low-paid, low-skill jobs. These are nowadays almost the only jobs available to people entering the world of industry. Many of these new workers are recent Kazakh migrants with no blue-collar background.

The distinction between the old and the new working class is blurred, if only because most of the old working-class kids end up in new working-class jobs. Old workers can be young, if they have grown up in one of the combine's labor dynasties and inherited their values and their jobs. New workers can be elderly newcomers to the world of industry, forced by necessity into low-paid, unskilled work as *podriatchiki*. The new and old working classes are sociological ideal types, rather than homogenous, clear-cut identities. The new workers seem to share a lack of interest in labor politics, while the old cultivate a collective memory of Soviet work culture.

Company workers bemoan the erosion of their established rights, privileges, and health, which they attribute to the worsening conditions at the workplace and to the fact that nowadays they have to work eight years longer before they can retire; retirement age has risen from 55 to 63 years. Although they earn more than contract workers, comparisons with Soviet times, when education, healthcare, and housing were effectively free, are unfavorable. Old working-class parents have bittersweet feelings about their children's inability to get regular company jobs. Generally, they express hope that they might find jobs elsewhere, deeming their own jobs "thankless." But the lack of opportunities for their children keeps many aging breadwinners at work despite their growing health problems. As the younger generation struggles to find decent jobs, company workers' apartments often house more than two generations. The sense of precarity is intensified by the perceived helplessness of the workers' condition. Neither of their two "masters" (*hozyainy*)—the owner of the combine (Mittal) or the ruler of the country (the President)—can make up, materially or psychologically, for the loss of Soviet forms of security.

In the DSF, old workers voice their dissatisfaction with the management, sense of impotence about the decay of their workplace, and estrangement from the government's way of dealing with the workers' lot (which, however, is more pronounced among the "Russians" than among Kazakhs). Even those old workers who bow to the new pressures feel that their work has become "harder, dirtier and more *ni-blagodarny* [thankless]" than it was in their youth or in the past recalled by their relatives. A veteran worker who spent forty years in the DSF gives voice to widespread opinions and anxieties in the following account:

> A worker should love his job and his factory. No one does here, and how could they? The government sold off the factory. A corrupt, plan-less government. After 20 years of breakdown [of the USSR], what has been built up? We are left without ideals to believe in. The factory is crumbling. Maybe I'm old-fashioned, maybe I'm wrong, but I believe that coal, iron and steel should be state-owned, that the state should care. During the Soviet Union the combine was in good shape. Retirement was at 55 because the machinery did not allow you longer, unless you ruin your health. Thanks to our President we now have 8 years longer to work. I have 20 months left until pension. I can work with my mind, my hands do the work by themselves, but my body cannot keep up anymore. When I started working, there were 55 electricians on our shop floor, always busy with work. Nowadays only three per shift remain. The machines are the same. Educating a skilled worker takes years. This isn't done anymore. How can there be a future?

This account identifies the President of Kazakhstan, frequently referred to as the steelworkers' "patron saint," as the one who "sold off" the factory to foreigners and raised the age of retirement to a level that is unacceptable in view of the physical demands of the work. But the foreign owner attracts more acerbic criticism. In the workers' perception, "the owner does not care about his property as he should"—that is to say, he cares only about the profit that can be squeezed out of his factory: unlike Soviet Magnitka, Mittal is profiting from their work without giving anything back to the workers and their communities.[16]

By contrast, contract workers lament precariousness rather than precariatization. They have never enjoyed the securities now gradually being lost by company labor, and they struggle to survive in the city. There is no scarcity of jobs in Temirtau, but jobs that can sustain what counts as a decent living in the common sense of one's reference group are few and far between (cf. Kim 2013). Employment as a *podriatchik* places one at the bottom of the industrial hierarchy. Unlike company workers, *podriatchiki* are indifferent to the shop floor's decay and quick to change jobs when a better opportunity appears.

As noted above, many contract workers are recent immigrants from nearby villages or the more populated, less industrialized south of the country, or are Oralmans from abroad. They live in rented apartments or commute from villages, so their rent and transport costs come out of their meager wages. The economic divide between old and new workers is also reflected in their different possibilities of accessing and affording debt. Lack of creditworthiness forces many contract workers into risky financial arrangements. At the top end of the hierarchy of debt, shop floor managers take on debt to travel to fancy tourist destinations in Turkey or India. At the bottom end, precarious contract workers borrow money informally to pay for health care and electricity.

Contract workers who do not commute or pay rent in Temirtau had to take jobs as *podriatchiki* because of other pressing economic problems. Some had a troubled past to conceal (prison or alcoholism). Many non-Kazakh women in this segment of the working class were single mothers or divorced. Kazakh women working as *podriatchiki* often complained that they had to work to sustain their families because their husbands were unable to do so. I met several young workers with higher education degrees who could find no better way to supplement the income of their parents' household.

Whereas company workers' complaints revolve around the deterioration of their jobs, contract workers feel stuck in newly created "bad jobs" with no benefits, low pay, and limited duration (cf. Yessenova 2012). The decline of the old working class is not only economic but also cultural. While the new working class may dream of moving to the new capital, Astana, or at least of becoming a company worker by bribing the right person in Temirtau, the Russophone old working class orients itself toward the past or toward foreign countries.

Both immigrants and the children of the regular company workers are outside the "citadel" (Holmström 1984) of secure employment. Contract workers envy the old working class their higher salaries and (relative) job security, and accuse them of egoistically defending their privileges as company workers, perhaps even calling them "the Mittals." But the new-comers have not developed a political language—indeed, many did not even know what a trade union was. Regardless of their ethnicity, today both company and contract, old and new industrial workers live in a situation of uncertainty, fearing downward mobility and wondering whether they will have any place in Kazakhstan's future.

Concluding Remarks

It is difficult to apply Western coordinates of industrial transition in Temirtau because the Soviet model of industrial development was differ-ent, and nowadays also because of the specificity of the encounter between global capitalism and Kazakhstani state and society. The Temirtau combine has survived, thanks to Mittal, but no full restructuring has yet been imple-mented. Mittal's promise to expand production has gone down well with the government, whose main interests are jobs, investments, and revenues, but reality has lagged behind plans. Constrained to maximizing share-holder returns, Mittal has thus far managed to keep both its workforce and the government guessing about its intentions. In this constellation, Temirtau is a case of relatively successful resistance to labor casualiza-tion. Mittal is reluctant to invest; meanwhile, the government maintains an ambivalent stance toward the kind of capital-intensive restructuring that would reduce employment still further. Continuing with the old Soviet machinery and a somewhat reduced workforce is a compromise that suits both sides. Its high price is paid by the remaining workers.

This partial intensification has produced peculiar kinds of laboring persons. It has deepened old inequalities in gender, complicated ethnic hierarchies, and also created new hierarchies within a fragmented, socially declining workforce. Inequalities also exist within the two main segments of the labor force I have identified here, but they do not change the fun-damental pattern: a fragmented working class with divided subjectivi-ties, heading toward uncertain futures. Compared to contract workers, company workers can draw on their history and have a stronger "relational labor consciousness" (Mollona 2009) rooted in the Soviet past and in their better pay, skills, long-term presence, and intense linkages on the shop floor. However, their position too is overshadowed by a growing precarity. Therefore, they work—for wages as the contract workers do, but also to keep the factory from falling apart. Their work has become something altogether different since the shop floor was restructured. Today, carrying out this alienating work despite all difficulties is what confers upon them their identity as workers and structures their working-class selves.

The company workers have developed a specific form of shop floor resistance of the weak, one that is staged as a (pro-workplace) commitment to the cause of preserving a "threatened species"—the Soviet industry worker. Navigating this increasingly difficult environment, workers immerse themselves in "thankless" work, feeling that they have no better choice. If these workers' self-perception could be represented by a single image, it is perhaps that of the orchestra playing on the sinking Titanic. Yet it is easy to see that workers could be quick to give up their self-defeating form of "resistance" if a life jacket were in sight. If, in future, their precarious form of "social contract" with the factory is jeopardized *in toto* (i.e., by shop floor closure or *autstafing*) workers' attitudes might change radically. Until then, for those stuck on the shop floor with their memories (transmitted by kin or from their own experience) of better times, the possibility of asserting oneself, however partially and illusorily, by engaging in "work as resistance" provides an important hold in an increasingly adverse world.

Acknowledgments

I thank Karaganda State University for its support, ArcelorMittal Temirtau for granting access and providing valuable data, the DSF staff for help and hospitality, Massimiliano Mollona for comments on an earlier draft of this chapter, and my colleague Eeva Keskula for feedback and cooperation both in Kazakhstan and in Germany at the Max Planck Institute for Social Anthropology. Fieldwork (September 2013–May 2014; August–September 2014) benefited immensely from the research assistance of Xeniya Prilutskaya.

Tommaso Trevisani is Associate Professor at the Department of African, Asian and Mediterranean Studies, University of Naples L'Orientale, where he teaches Societies and Cultures of Central Asia. He obtained his Ph.D. from the Free University, Berlin, in 2008. In addition to other postdoctoral positions in Germany, between 2012 and 2015 he was a Research Fellow at the Max Planck Institute for Social Anthropology in Halle. Trevisani is the author of *Land and Power in Khorezm: Farmers, Communities, and the State in Uzbekistan's Decollectivisation* (2010). His research interests include agrarian and environmental change; class and industrial work; ritual, marriage and society; and state- and nation-building in socialist and postsocialist Central Asia.

Notes

1. I discuss how I obtained access to the steelworks and the conditions under which fieldwork was conducted in Trevisani (2016).
2. The settlement at Temirtau dates back to the Stolypin reforms. In 1905 a group of German peasants from the Samara region in Russia established a village along the shores of the Nura River. Temirtau, still called Samarkandsky at the time, became a detention camp during the 1930s. A growing flow of deported people, who initially worked on the construction of a hydropower station and a large artificial lake nearby, later erected the city and its industries.
3. Magnitka was the informal name of the Magnitogorsk steel works, the largest of the Soviet Union (Kotkin 1995).
4. The tumult degenerated into riots and looting, and came to an end only after the intervention of the Soviet army. Outcomes included sixteen deaths and 190 arrests on various charges (Kozlov 2002: 39).
5. Details of the deal were not made public, and various versions circulate. It is commonly asserted that Mittal got this huge plant almost for free. According to Frantz (2001), Mittal purchased the plant for 250 million dollars, repaid some debt, and allocated 350 million dollars of his own funds and a 450 million–dollar loan from the European Bank for Reconstruction and Development to the long-term modernization of the plant.
6. Before the purchase of Karmet, the total capacity of Mittal's production sites in Trinidad and Tobago, Indonesia, Mexico, Canada, and Germany amounted to 6.5 million tonnes of steel (Kavaev and Piyanko 1995). Temirtau alone had produced 6 million tonnes of steel in 1989 (Kulikov 1994); but by the time of privatization production had declined to a third of this figure.
7. Oralmans are diasporic Kazakhs who have resettled in Kazakhstan following a government program that supports their "repatriation," especially to areas where Russian speakers are a majority (Diener 2005).
8. People in Temirtau tend to overstate what they see as "foreign infiltration." In 2014 ArcelorMittal Temirtau employed ca. two dozen foreigners (often with a background in other factories of the corporate company), limited to top positions and auditing in the combine's headquarters.
9. Overall production increased between 1996 and 2004 and declined thereafter. Production in 2013 (2.5 million tons) was almost down to the same level it had seen in the first year of Mittal's ownership and well below the level reached in the heyday of Soviet Magnitka.
10. When countering managerial crisis discourse, workers frequently referred to the wedding of Mittal's daughter, celebrated in a castle near Versailles, which cost an

enormous amount of money amounting roughly to the combine's annual salary budget (Roy 2004).

11. Steel plants are particularly vulnerable to unscheduled shutdowns as they put expensive capital equipment, like blast furnaces and coke oven batteries, in immediate danger of serious damage.

12. In 2011 in Zhanaozen, police repression of striking workers ended in a massacre. See Radio Free Europe/Radio Liberty (2011).

13. For this reason, members of "labor dynasties" still receive a (symbolic) bonus payment from the company. A labor dynasty consists of a family with more than one generation of workers (or former workers) employed by the combine.

14. Workers lament that over time, staff positions get canceled without tasks changing. Because tasks are redefined to be feasible with fewer workers, workers, as in the case reported by Haraszti (1977), end up working more for less pay.

15. Over the first weeks of fieldwork workers avoided me on the shop floor (as a guest of the company I was wearing a white helmet). After word spread that I was there on business other than the company's, workers gradually started to accept my presence.

16. The workers' view is very much at odds with the one propagated by the company. Since Mittal came on the scene, it has invested in countless initiatives of public interest (involving, e.g., transport, sport, education, media, festivals, museums, etc.) with the aim of propagating an image of continuity with the socially responsible Soviet enterprise.

References

Allison, Anne. 2013. *Precarious Japan*. Durham, NC, and London: Duke University Press.

ArcelorMittal. 2015. *Annual Report 2014*. www.corporate.arcelormittal.com

Ashwin, Sarah. 1999. *Russian Workers: The Anatomy of Patience*. Manchester: Manchester University Press.

Barnes, Steven. 2011. *Death and Redemption: The Gulag and the Shaping of Soviet Society*. Princeton, NJ: Princeton University Press.

Bissenova, Alima. 2012. "Post-Socialist Dreamworlds: Housing Boom and Urban Development in Kazakhstan." Ph.D. thesis. Ithaca, NY: Cornell University.

Bondar, Anna. 2014. "Temirtauskomu buntu – 55 let." *Vechernaya Gazeta*, 30 June, 2–3.

Burawoy, Michael. 1979. *Manufacturing Consent: Changes in the Labor Process under Monopoly Capitalism*. Chicago, IL: University of Chicago Press.

———. 2002. "Transition without Transformation: Russia's Involutionary Road to Capitalism." In *Locating Capitalism in Time and Space: Global Restructurings, Politics, and Identity*, ed. D. Nugent, 290–310. Stanford, CA: Stanford University Press.

Conquest, Robert. 1967. *Industrial Workers in the USSR*. London: Bodley Head.

Cummings, Sally. 2005. *Kazakhstan: Power and the Elite*. London: Tauris.

Dave, Bhavna. 2007. *Kazakhstan: Ethnicity, Language and Power*. New York: Routledge.

Diener, Alexander. 2005. "Kazakhstan's Kin State Diaspora: Settlement Planning and the Oralman Dilemma." *Europe-Asia Studies* 57: 327–348.

Frantz, Douglas. 2001. "Temirtau Journal; Steel Company Buys a Mill, Gets a Kazakh Town." *New York Times*, 1 August.

Gestwa, Klaus. 2010. *Die Stalinschen Großbauten des Kommunismus: Sowjetische Technik- und Umweltgeschichte 1948–1967*. Munich: R. Oldenbourg Verlag.

Haraszti, Miklós. 1977. *A Worker in a Worker's State*. London: Penguin.

Harvey, David. 1987. "Flexible Accumulation through Urbanization: Reflections on 'Post-Modernism' in the American City." *Antipode* 19: 260–286.

Holmström, Mark. 1984. *Industry and Inequality: The Social Anthropology of Indian Labour*. Cambridge: Cambridge University Press.

Humphrey, Caroline. 2002. *The Unmaking of Soviet Life: Everyday Economies after Socialism*. Ithaca, NY, and London: Cornell University Press.

Kavaev, A., and A. Piyanko. 1995. "Nachalo vselyaet nadezhdy." *Metallurg Temirtau*, 1 December.

Kim, Jaesok. 2013. *Chinese Labor in a Korean Factory: Class, Ethnicity, and Productivity on the Shop Floor in Globalizing China*. Stanford, CA: Stanford University Press.

Kotkin, Stephen. 1995. *Magnetic Mountain: Stalinism as a Civilization*. Berkeley, CA: University of California Press.

Kozlov, Vladimir. 2002. *Mass Uprisings in the USSR: Protest and Rebellion in the Post-Stalin Years*. Armonk, NY, and London: M.E. Sharpe.

Kulikov, Vitaly. 1994. "Fifty Years of Kazakhstan Steel." *Metallurgist* 38 (11–12): 233–235.

Ledeneva, Aleina. 1998. *Russia's Economy of Favours: Blat, Networking, and Informal Exchange*. Cambridge: Cambridge University Press.

Lee, Ching Kwan. 2007. *Against the Law: Labor Protests in China's Rustbelt and Sunbelt*. Berkeley, CA: University of California Press.

Makram-Ebeid, Dina. 2012. "Manufacturing Stability: Everyday Politics of Work in an Industrial Steel Town in Helwan, Egypt." Ph.D. thesis. London: London School of Economics.

Molé, Noelle. 2010. "Precarious Subjects: Anticipating Neoliberalism in Northern Italy's Workplace." *American Anthropologist* 112(1): 38–53.

———. 2012. *Labor Disorders in Neoliberal Italy*. Bloomington, IN: Indiana University Press.

Mollona, Massimiliano. 2009. *Made in Sheffield: An Ethnography of Industrial Work and Politics*. New York: Berghahn Books.

Mrozowicki, Adam. 2011. *Coping with Social Change: Life Strategies of Workers in Poland's New Capitalism*. Leuven: University Press.

Muehlebach, Andrea. 2011. "On Affective Labor in Post-Fordist Italy." *Cultural Anthropology* 26(1): 59–82.

Müller, Birgit. 2007. *Disenchantment with Market Economies: East Germans and Western Capitalism*. New York: Berghahn Books.

Ngai, Pun. 2005. *Made in China: Women Factory Workers in a Global Workplace*. Hong Kong: Hong Kong University Press.

Parry, Jonathan. 2013a. "Company and Contract Labour in a Central Indian Steel Plant." *Economy and Society* 42(3): 348–374.

———. 2013b. "The 'Embourgeoisement' of a 'Proletarian Vanguard?'" In *Interrogating India's Modernity: Democracy, Identity, and Citizenship*, ed. S. Jodhka. 48–78. New Delhi: Oxford University Press.

Peck, Anne E. 2004. *Economic Development in Kazakhstan: The Role of Large Enterprises and Foreign Investment.* London: Routledge/Curzon.

Peck, Jamie, and Nik Theodore. 2001. "Contingent Chicago: Restructuring the Spaces of Temporary Labor." *International Journal of Urban and Regional Research* 25(3): 471–496.

Radio Free Europe/Radio Liberty. 2011. "State of Emergency in Restive Kazakh Town," 17 December 2011, www.rferl.org.

Roy, Amit. 2004. "Welcome to the $78 Million Wedding." *Daily Telegraph*, 3 June.

Sanchez, Andrew. 2012. "Deadwood and Paternalism: Rationalising Casual Labour in an Indian Company Town." *Journal of the Royal Anthropological Institute* 18(4): 808–827.

Scott, James. 1985. *Weapons of the Weak: Everyday Forms of Peasant Resistance.* New Haven, CT: Yale University Press.

Shaporov, A. S., and V. A. Bondarenko. 1983. *Magnitka Kazakhstana.* Alma-Ata: Izdatel'stvo "Kazakhstan".

Standing, Guy. 2011. *The Precariat: The New Dangerous Class.* London: Bloomsbury.

Straus, Kenneth. 1997. *Factory and Community in Stalin's Russia: The Making of an Industrial Working Class.* Pittsburgh, PA: University of Pittsburgh Press.

Trappmann, Vera. 2013. *Fallen Heroes in Global Capitalism: Workers and the Restructuring of the Polish Steel Industry.* London: Palgrave Macmillan.

Trevisani, Tommaso. 2014. "The Reshaping of Cities and Citizens in Uzbekistan: The Case of Namangan's 'New Uzbeks.'" In *Ethnographies of the State in Central Asia: Performing Politics*, ed. Madeleine Reeves, Johan Rasanayagam, and Judith Beyer, 243–260. Bloomington, IN: Indiana University Press.

———. 2016. "Under Suspicious Eyes: Work and Fieldwork in a Steel Plant in Kazakhstan." *Zeitschrift für Ethnologie* 141(2): 281–298.

Yessenova, Saulesh. 2012. "The Tengiz Oil Enclave: Labor, Business, and The State." *PoLAR* 35(1): 94–114.

4

Regular Work in Decline, Precarious Households, and Changing Solidarities in Bulgaria

Dimitra Kofti

Since democracy I do exactly the same job at the same place as before but my salary does not allow me to survive, as it did before. I was sold to various subcontracting companies, as if I was a brick. We, workers, became transferable bricks.

—Kolio, 56-year-old electrician in Stomana[1]

Introduction

Since the early 1990s, most Bulgarian factories have undergone rapid transformation. The most prominent changes in employees' lives include growing insecurity at work, high rates of inflation and unemployment, and the growing divide between regular and casual work. These conditions are familiar throughout the industrialized world (Parry 2013; Mollona 2009), but in the postsocialist world they arrived more abruptly (Dunn 2004; Müller 2007; Kideckel 2008). Many state-owned factories closed down because they lacked funding and lost their clients in the Soviet Union and other Eastern European countries. Others were privatized and went through significant restructuring, which usually meant focusing on core production and subcontracting labor in order to reduce the permanent workforce. Many workers were laid off. Those who remained in factories like Stomana Steel Industry in Pernik experienced new inequalities in the workplace, coupled with gender, ethnic, and age inequalities outside it. In particular, the new division between regular and casual work has significantly transformed household strategies and urban-rural relationships.[2]

Standing (2011) argued that the casually employed "precariat" is distinct from the "salariat," a class that enjoys stable employment in large-scale companies and often aspires to upward mobility. The basic characteristics of Standing's much discussed "precariat" are temporary labor status, lack of unionization, and often a lack of job identity (ibid.: 9). This class division between regular and casual workforce has some resonance with Parry's (2013) ethnography from the public-sector Bhilai steel plant in India. In the past there were opportunities for upward mobility from informal sector "work" *(kam)* to a regular job in the organized sector (*naukri* or "service"), but now the distinction between these two types of workers has hardened into a distinction between different social classes (ibid.). Similarly, in Stomana regular employees enjoy privileges of relative security compared to casual workers, and no upward mobility from casual to regular labor is possible. Yet the distinction is muddied by the overarching fear of capital flight and the possibility of downward mobility for all. Ongoing flexibilization of industrial work in the private sector threatens to bring the regular workers into line with the casual. Moreover, Stomana's regular and casual workers often belong to the very same households, and inequalities between the two employment categories on the shop floor do not translate into sharp divisions outside the workplace.

The fear of capital flight affects all private-sector employees to different degrees. In the case of steel, European production has been hit by increasing imports from Asian markets and by worldwide overproduction (Trappman 2015). In October 2013 the stock market in Athens plunged to levels reminiscent of the worst days of 2008, when the financial crisis first hit the Greek economy. The reason was the transfer of Sidenor, Stomana's mother company and one of the key players in the Greek market, from the Greek stock market to the Belgian in order to avoid the repercussions of the Greek crisis. Workers and managers expressed their worries about the outcome of this move. Greek managers joked bitterly that perhaps they should stop learning Bulgarian and learn French instead. Rumor on the shop floor had it that the Belgians would either come to Pernik to replace the Greeks, or sell the company to a Turkish steel industry that would pay even lower salaries than the "bloody Byzantines," a common term of abuse for Greek managers in Bulgaria (see Angelidou and Kofti 2013). Anything seemed possible, and everyone worried about jobs.[3]

Some of the foreign companies that moved to Bulgaria in the 1990s have already started moving further east in search of even cheaper labor and lower taxation. The company workforce differentiates itself from the casual workforce, but the fear of capital flight generates a common condition of precarity for all employees. By precarity I mean job insecurity and difficulty in planning for the future due to the unpredictability of the market economy in general. In a context of successive crises, many workers pass first from regular to casual employment and then to unemployment. Nonetheless, employment status remains significant.

Following other scholars who have stressed the importance of kinship and household relationships for understanding changing regimes of labor (Mollona 2009; Smart and Smart 2006; De Neve 2008; Narotzky and Smith 2006; Narotzky 2015; Pine 2001), I focus in this chapter on the connections between the workplace and other domains of life. I describe workers' households in Pernik, even those with members who have permanent contracts in the steel industry, as precarious. Tensions of gender and age are intertwined with the regular and casual work cleavage. I show that inequalities at work after privatization deepened intra-family gender inequalities that the socialist state failed to eliminate (Brunnbauer and Taylor 2004).

The Rise and Decline of Industry in Pernik

Pernik, a city 26 kilometers southwest of Sofia, was urbanized in the early 1900s following the establishment of a coal mine in 1892. It became one of Bulgaria's major industrial cities during socialist times. Unlike Soviet steel cities such as Magnitogorsk (Kotkin 1995), but like other Eastern European socialist industrial cities, it developed out of pre-existing conurbations (cf. Alexander and Buchli 2007: 9). During the first half of the twentieth century, young migrants from poor agricultural areas worked in the coal mines seasonally while continuing their agricultural activities. This gradually changed after the construction in 1952 of the Lenin steelworks, now Stomana, a symbol of socialist modernization. The adjoining Lenin district, now known as Iztok (meaning East, because it is located in the Eastern part of the city), provided workers with living quarters within walking distance of the plant.

In the early socialist period the state encouraged workers to abandon their previous agricultural activities (Kalinova and Baeva 2002). Pernik's population growth accelerated (Boneva 2014).[4] Unlike in England, where the shift from agriculture to industry had been abrupt (Thompson 1967), in Bulgaria many workers continued subsistence farming (cf. Hann 1987). Despite the socialist state's attempts to proletarianize the workforce, post-Ottoman linkages between industrial and agricultural activities continued during socialism (Creed 1998; Kaneff 2002; Smollett 1989). Those ties acquired renewed importance in the years after socialism, when domestic food production was a survival strategy for many urban workers. As Tocheva's (2014) recent ethnography suggests, domestic production in rural Bulgaria is imbued with the ideal of self-sufficiency and the value of quality food as opposed to global market products. A common working-class dinner in Pernik includes homemade *rakia* (a 50 percent alcoholic drink), and pickled salad and goat cheese from the village. Most Stomana workers, both casual and regular, had smallholder peasants in their family background.[5] As I shall explain in detail below, the new distinction between regular and casual work has changed this pattern of domestic production, making the casual workers full proletarians for the first time.

With the closure of heavy industrial plants, except Stomana and the power station, small garment factories with owners in Greece, Italy, Germany, and Holland sprang up in their place, often inside modified old factories, operating informally without registering working hours. Fifteen-hour shifts were common in this highly exploitative work environment. I heard stories of doors being locked at the end of the shift when a new "urgent" order had to be met. These companies employed family members of Stomana workers and ex-Stomana workers,[6] who are an ever-present reminder of what lies in store for regular workers if they lose their jobs.

The closure of the mine, which employed approximately 20,000 workers until the early 1990s, was a painful loss for the city. Ex-miners, like the unemployed from other industries, commuted to Sofia to work or migrated abroad.[7] Rural areas in Bulgaria were also depopulated from the early 1990s onwards, as collective farms closed down, but some pensioners returned from cities to their villages of origin. Many industrial and administrative buildings and a smaller share of residential buildings in Pernik were abandoned and became dilapidated as the population fell and unemployment rose in the 1990s.[8] Residential buildings that had housed students of Pernik's technical and metallurgical schools in the socialist era were inhabited by ethnic Roma squatters who came from the countryside and worked mostly as street cleaners or low-paid scrap collectors for contractors who sold to Stomana industry.[9] Roma workers employed in low-skilled jobs during socialism were the first to lose their jobs during postsocialism.

The epochal shift is exemplified in the melting shop of Stomana's core production site, where soon after the fall of socialism a grandiose statue of Lenin at the plant's main entrance was removed and abandoned at the back of the factory yard, and is now rumored to have ended up in the furnace sometime in the late 1990s. As workers often stated: "Lenin was melted in the furnace." They accompanied this remark with both criticism of the previous regime and bitterness about the new working conditions. The raw material in Stomana comes from scrap, which is acquired not only from street collectors but also from the machinery of closed factories. Kremikovtzi, once the largest steel plant in Bulgaria, went bankrupt in the late 2008, three years after it was bought by Pramod Mittal (the brother of Indian steel tycoon Lakshmi Mittal). Stomana managers tell the story of how its machinery was melted in Stomana with pride, but workers were apprehensive that their machines could one day face a similar fate.

Changing Work Conditions at Stomana

Like other industrial workers in socialist Bulgaria, regular workers at the Lenin plant had access to housing, education, child care, health care, and holiday accommodations through their employment. The Lenin Steel Industry was responsible not only for the plant but for the neighboring Lenin district with its blocks of flats and metallurgical schools. Work-related benefits (the so-called social wage; cf. Trevisani and Morris and Hinz, this volume) were gradually cut in the 1990s. In 1992 the plant was renamed Stomana, which means steel. Compared to other factories in Pernik, workers in Stomana were privileged because until its privatization in 1998, the complex also produced bread and other food products that were distributed to the employees. Most of Pernik's workers suffered deprivation during the Bulgarian financial crisis in 1997, but Stomana workers at least managed to avoid hunger.

Until privatization, monetary wages in Stomana, as in other state enterprises, were determined according to skill and seniority. Moreover, networks of non-monetary exchange were important (Kremakova 2011). Inequalities between Party members and those outside the Party reflected their differential access to resources. Those closer to power had more frequent access to vacation resorts and could jump the queue for a company apartment. After socialism, when people in positions of power who came to control state resources privatized them for their own benefit, political inequalities were converted into wealth inequalities (Konstantinov 2000). In a highly obscure deal in 1998, Stomana was bought by a Bulgarian nouveau riche investor rumored to fit this pattern. Privatization was followed by layoffs and shop floor closures. Health risks on the shop floor increased, and union participation diminished. The plant was sold again in 2001 to the Greek steel company Sidenor.[10] The repercussions of the "Greek crisis" put additional pressure on Stomana's shop floor after 2010. Each reduction in wages and wave of layoffs was presented to workers as an unavoidable response to "market pressure" and "crisis." Still, working for Stomana was a source of pride, as it was part of the city's glorious metallurgical history.

After Stomana's privatization, large sectors of production were outsourced to private workshops that arose around and inside the plant. Of approximately 10,000 employees in the early 1990s, approximately 6,000 remained in 2001, and only 960 in 2014. Whereas the first reduction was accomplished through a ban on hiring (in force until 2008), downsizing was later pursued more actively. Many sectors were closed, and new machinery was introduced in place of labor-intensive technologies. Manning levels were reduced even where production did not become more capital intensive. Employees recall that the factory was overstaffed until privatization, whereupon it gradually became understaffed. As of 1998, families were able to choose who would leave his or her job so that at least one regular income was retained per household. The employment of both husband and wife became increasingly rare. Some of the workers initially retained in 1998 were laid off after the factory was sold again in 2001. In both phases, women were more likely to lose their jobs than men, leading to a masculinization of the workforce. By 2014 the gender proportion of the regular workforce was 70 percent male, 30 percent female, whereas in 1992 the approximate figures had been 55 percent and 45 percent respectively.[11]

Many of the workers who kept their jobs were in close relationships (e.g., as godmother, best man, lover, close friend) with people in positions of power. In socialist times, kinship and intimacy had routinely influenced the kind of job one could get. Now these links became important for hanging onto jobs. Under the new regime, you were in a better position if the managers and directors close to you kept their posts. Workers often talked about the importance of connections (*vraski*). Most of the workers' families were ex-villagers from the region, so common village origins played an important role in creating networks of support that continued into the period of my fieldwork. Moreover, the vast majority of workers lived in the Lenin district and developed friendships with neighbors in their apartment blocks. Given this history of residential proximity in the Lenin district, most people had relations with employees at various levels in the hierarchy, including engineers, shop floor managers, and perhaps even the plant's general manager. Mr. Ivanov, a shop floor manager until 2002, was the son of a worker in the melting shop and had grown up in a district block. He had studied engineering and worked in the plant since 1985, climbing the ladder to become a shop floor director. Rumor had it that he was not just a capable engineer but also a beneficiary of the process of privatization, as he was close to the investor who bought the plant in 1998. Workers in his block agreed that they had kept their jobs during the first wave of layoffs in 1998 thanks to Ivanov. When Ivanov left the plant after its sale to Sidenor, several high-echelon white-collar staff in his circle lost their jobs. However, the shop floor workers who owed their jobs to his support after 1998 did not lose them when their patron departed, as they did not hold key positions.

The number of casual workers employed by subcontractors inside the plant had reached 500600 by the time of my fieldwork. Casual workers were invisible in the company's statistics. Their work accidents, although proportionally more numerous, did not count as company accidents. Managers could only guess their numbers, as shop floor managers and engineers were able to make deals with subcontractors without precise documentation. Roma workers were prominent in the new casual labor force, as were young males who worked "temporarily" until they could find a "better job" elsewhere. Pensioners also worked casually, not only to add to their income but also to return to the plant, which felt like "home" to many who had spent their entire working lives there. They were much more respected on the shop floor than their Roma colleagues. Yet, regular workers complained that the company should provide more regular posts for younger workers, instead of re-employing pensioners.

Three main categories of worker could be distinguished in 2014: regular Stomana employees, regular skilled "external" workers, and casual workers.

Regular Stomana employees numbered 960, including managerial staff and skilled workers. Seventy percent were men. Most were ethnic Bulgarians, and a very small minority was Roma (e.g., 1 Roma worker out of 120 in the plate mill). There were two unions, but only 20 percent of workers were members;[12] most had quit after privatization, either because they felt unionism put their jobs at risk or because they generally mistrusted their political representation. Regular workers' wages varied according to position and seniority; average take-home pay in 2014 was around 600 levas (300 euros).

On Stomana's premises, a company called Sigma employed 130 workers and engineers—that is, regular skilled "external" workers—to maintain Stomana's machinery. Although only about 10 percent of its operations were unconnected with Stomana, Sigma was a separate company that in theory competed on the market for Stomana's business. In practice, Stomana worked almost exclusively with Sigma. Most Sigma employees were ex-Stomana workers who had been laid off and moved directly to Sigma, or worked for other subcontracting companies before ending up there. As managers said, "we repositioned the best workers in Sigma." Kolio, the 56-year-old electrician quoted at the beginning of this chapter, was laid off in 1999 and, after working in three other subcontracting companies, ended up with Sigma in 2005. Sigma did not belong to Stomana's owner but to one of his close collaborators. This separation, effected to serve tax purposes and the flexibilization of production, also generated a new hierarchy among the workforce. There were no union members in this company. All Sigma workers were ethnic Bulgarians, including seven women in its administration and one on the shop floor. Salaries were about 15 percent higher than those of the regular Stomana workers, which was a source of irritation and conflict. Initially there was mobility from Stomana to Sigma in the early 2000s, but this soon stopped.

Approximately 600 casual workers were employed in external subcontracting companies. Most were providing Stomana with cleaning services, construction labor, and labor for operations requiring unskilled work. This group consisted mainly of male workers, about 60 percent Bulgarians and 40 percent Roma.[13] Some of these subcontractors employed ethnic Bulgarian workers or ethnic Roma only. The ethnic Bulgarians mainly had been laid off from Stomana, or else were pensioners. The Roma, mostly newcomers to the plant, received lower wages than those paid to former regular ethnic Bulgarian workers. The cleaning contractors hired women, most of whom had previously been skilled or unskilled regular workers. A casual worker (male or female) earned between 150 and 400 levas (75–200 euros) for a month's full-time work, depending on the company and the method of payment. Piece rates (unknown under socialism) were common, shifts irregular, and the exact nature of the work unpredictable, as tasks could change at any time.

Workers were fully cognizant that the changes since 1998 had fragmented the labor force and subverted collective action. Even those in the more privileged and better paid groups would have preferred a more equal structure and larger salaries for all workers. Although Kolio's salary was higher than that of a regular Stomana worker, he was still unable to meet his family's expenses, as one of his sons was unemployed and his wife earned only 240 leva (120 euros) from her work at a garment factory. He also worried that he would not be entitled to receive a pension if he were to be laid off again in the future. Having lost his job in the past, Kolio felt insecure despite having a regular job. He could not take the risk of joining a union or complaining about his working conditions. Some regular Stomana workers active in unions had been fired. The plethora of unemployed skilled steelworkers in Pernik and nearby Kremikovtzi meant that even skilled workers were easily replaceable.

As a regular worker, Kolio had one privilege that casual workers lacked: he had been able to negotiate a bank loan on relatively favorable terms. Indebtedness is an additional reason not to place one's job at risk by unionizing. Around 80 percent of regular Stomana and Sigma workers were in debt to a bank. Most had borrowed to renovate their old apartments, pay for their children's education, or buy a car. Most of the loans were taken out before the 2008 crisis, during which the elimination of bonuses had a dramatic impact on their ability to maintain repayments, diminishing their income by as much as 40 percent. By comparison, casual workers were less creditworthy, less indebted (approximately 40 percent of them), and incurred smaller debts. Sixty percent of the casual workers' loans were taken from money lending companies that offered small sums at high interest rates.[14] Until 2008, regular workers' stable incomes allowed them to maintain a lifestyle distinct from that of casuals, but since the global crisis that distinction has become blurred.

The length of shifts did not change after the layoffs,[15] but the pressure of work on the shop floor intensified. Despite the post-2001 management's strong emphasis on cleaning the plant, painting, and reclaiming the vast spaces where defective products had been dumped, health conditions deteriorated due to undermanning. Substantial changes in machinery began during my fieldwork. New technology had been introduced in the early 2000s, mainly to assist documentation of the steelmaking process and quality control. Production itself still relied on old and still well-functioning equipment, though now with fewer staff. Doctors in Pernik, including those working in the plant, reported a rise in health problems, especially high blood pressure, strokes, and cancer. Though more prominent among casual workers, this rise hit regular employees as well and was attributed to work stress, fear of job loss, and undermanning. Meanwhile the already high pollution levels were exacerbated by the pollution caused by the nearby power plant.[16]

Underlining the changes from a conspicuously overstaffed to an understaffed shop floor, Valio, 47 years old and a plate mill worker since 1988, remembered how workers in his position at the "fridge" would occasionally leave two people on duty and go partying during the night shift. Parties were organized inside the factory to celebrate colleagues' birthdays or name days. In the plate mill, red-hot steel plates arrive at the fridge area to cool. Since the layoffs, a single worker has to walk through the hot plates to document the cooling process with the help of a computer located in a nearby cabinet. The cooling machine regularly turns each plate upside-down, adding high decibel levels to the high temperatures. Given the volume and the rhythm of production, the worker is on move for the whole shift, often with no break. Before the introduction of computers, when three or four people shared this responsibility and documented their work on paper, the mental and physical risks were lower. Like other shop floor positions, fridge workers often said that conditions would be much better if, after the introduction of the computer, the task had been divided between two workers. Regular birthday and some name-day celebrations still took place during my fieldwork. The white-collar staff held them openly during lunch breaks. Surreptitious festivities occurred among engineers and skilled regular workers who could informally take breaks when there was no emergency.

On the shop floor, the new division between casual and regular employment led to conflict about the tempo of work and organization of tasks. For example, in the course of implementing machinery changes, some equipment around the plate mill furnace was replaced, which required a restructuring of the shop floor space. In addition to skilled workers and engineers, subcontractors were needed for cleaning and transportation services. The subcontractor for the cleaning services paid his workers, all of whom were Roma, a low hourly rate of 2 levas (1 euro) while the subcontractor for carrying paid his workers, both Bulgarians and Roma, a piece rate that spurred them to a quicker pace. Coordination was impossible, which led to conflict between casual workers and between an engineer and the subcontractors. In such circumstances, regular workers often described casual workers, especially the Roma, as "devious" or "stupid" and treated them with scorn.

At such times almost all categories of employees had to cooperate, making the tensions manifest. During the transitional period, the company organized several weeklong work trips to bring in engineers and skilled workers from its Thessaloniki factory who, according to management, would ensure that operations were standardized and based on up-to-date expertise. The management further claimed that the Thessaloniki personnel would ensure that there would be no "laziness" or "sabotage" on the part of their Bulgarian employees. Regular workers were annoyed by this Greek presence on "their" shop floor and claimed that Stomana workers were much more knowledgeable. These operations put stress on both the Greek and the Bulgarian workers, but for different reasons. Layoffs were also taking place in the Greek factory, and the Greek workers wanted to prove that their assistance in Stomana was essential. After long days of overtime work, they would go to expensive restaurants in Sofia that Bulgarian workers could never afford. For working abroad, they received several times the pay earned by their Bulgarian colleagues and were lodged in expensive accommodations. This infuriated the Bulgarians, who felt slighted not to be treated as the glorious skilled steel workers of the past. Slogans insulting "Byzantium" and the "Byzantines" were daubed in the plant.[17] However, workers stressed their continuing sense of ownership of the shop floor. A couple of years after privatization, a fire broke out during a night shift at a machine close to the plate mill furnace and could have damaged a large part of the production line. Workers often mentioned the incident, highlighting how they ran to protect the machines rather than fleeing from the fire. They were "still our machines" and "our bread," and not "theirs" (i.e., the Greeks').

One morning during the machinery renovation of 2014, which disrupted regular operations, some regular workers waiting on standby on the shop floor were discussing conditions at work and complaining about Greek managers and "corrupt" Bulgarian managers who were assumed to have benefited from privatization. Sasho, a 38-year-old who had been a regular worker since 1995, started shouting: "They are all thieves, they cut all our salaries and only come here to tell us things we already know." The discussion moved on to workers' low salaries and the related inability to be "proper men" anymore. Sasho, who was single, complained that his salary did not allow him to date a woman and pay the bill, as it had done before privatization. Older men, too, focused on their inability to act "as men" and properly provide for their families. Half of workers' households contained three or four generations. The rest, who lived in nuclear families, maintained relations of mutual support with relatives, providing cash, care, or food. As Valio, the plate mill regular worker, put it: 'I work for the electricity and heating bills, my parents' pension pays the food and my grandfather takes care of the vegetables in the village. I can hardly buy things for my child.' However, regular workers were still the main source of money for their households, which put them in a respectable, powerful position. The discussion then focused on how "they" (the Greeks and the "corrupt" Bulgarian managers) have divided "us," the Bulgarian workforce, into regular and casual workers and created inequalities at work. Both regular and casual workers saw the negative effects of the changes from a state-run to a privately owned factory, and from a socialist to a capitalist regime, in nationalist terms: the foreign managers and employees were viewed with hostility, and Bulgarians in the higher echelons of the administration were described as "traitors" to the national economy. They were often contrasted unfavorably with the managerial staff during the first privatization in 1998–2000, who had resigned rather than implement layoffs.

Though regular workers often treated the casuals as inferiors, there were moments when they included the latter in the wider category of those impoverished by privatization. Sympathy was, however, limited to ethnic Bulgarians. Roma were viewed with hostility as interlopers who were taking Bulgarian jobs. Roma held the lowest of casual posts, and ethnic Bulgarians were not happy to work with "lazy," "devious," "thieving" "Gypsies" (see Creed 2011: 172–179). Along with other changes in the plant's daily life, there was a good deal of theft, for which the Roma were blamed. They were the most isolated group on the shop floor and complained that even though this was how it had always been, now it was worse. Still, Roma casual workers in Stomana were better off than scrap collectors, street cleaners, or the Roma workers at a small private opencast mine in the area, who were paid in coal, or those who were mining informally in the now closed underground mine, where fatal accidents occasionally occurred.

Workers in Stomana, both regular and casual, repeated that in the course of the last two decades they had felt increasingly "lonely" (*samoten*) and that colleagues did not "help each other" (*ne se pomagame*) as they had in the past. This sense of loneliness was intensified by the lack of trust among co-workers. This was not new. In socialist times workers had been afraid of potential informants of the secret police among colleagues; now, mistrust took a new shape in a context of widespread redundancies. They would often also use the negative "*Ne drugaruvame*," meaning "we are not friends, companions and/or comrades." Another common phrase with equally strong political connotations was *"Niamame edinstvo,"* "we do not have unity." Workers recalled the times when co-workers would help a colleague who faced a problem with a machine. They talked about having fun, socializing with colleagues, joking, and flirting. Layoffs had diminished the staff, forcing everyone to concentrate on his or her own job; there were no longer any spare moments. Positions were physically farther from each other on the vast shop floor, so daily communication was limited. This sense of loneliness was intensified by rules against using the Internet or listening to music. Some workers resisted in small ways, facilitated by new technologies like smartphones, but they still complained about the solitude of an eight-hour shift in a noisy environment with minimal human communication. In 1999, a worker's corpse was found in the vast melting shop, three days after his death. The story was repeated to emphasize their isolation. The company declared that the worker had been drunk and fallen from a machine.

In all three of the worker categories I have identified, declining social welfare services have to be compensated by family support (Deneva 2012). Historical traditions of kin solidarity in Bulgaria took new forms as families coped with unemployment and poverty. Even regular workers did not want their children to work in steel, especially after the 2008–2010 crisis. This stance was a response to a situation in which the only mobility was downward. Under socialism, a worker's daughter or son could aspire to become an engineer or to get a managerial position. In Stomana during the period of my fieldwork, 80 percent of regular shop floor and white-collar workers were sons and daughters or nephews and nieces of workers (cf. Keskula, this volume). A large majority of them had obtained technical metallurgical secondary education in Pernik and been employed after graduation, when there was an abundance of jobs.[18] In the post-privatization period, however, their children might find casual employment if they were fortunate, but there was almost no prospect of that employment becoming regular. They viewed such jobs as temporary and hoped for something better in Sofia or abroad. Similarly, engineers did not try to pull strings to secure jobs for their children in Stomana. Like regular workers, the engineers employed in Stomana since the pre-privatization period largely came from steelworkers' or engineers' families. Newly employed young engineers in the post-privatization period were unrelated to Stomana employees and had found their jobs via online announcements. They earned salaries of 800 leva (400 euros), which was below the level of many engineering or administrative jobs in Sofia. They did not view their jobs as the first rung on the Stomana ladder because most key engineering positions were given to Greeks who had previously been employed in the company's factories in Greece. Labor aristocracies elsewhere have attempted to reproduce their status by securing positions for their children (Parry 2013; Makram-Ebeid 2012; Sanchez and Strümpel 2014), but this was not the case at Stomana. Here, parents in all categories of employment wanted their children to study and take up better paid jobs, either abroad or in Sofia, where many foreign companies had moved to benefit from cheap labor and low taxes. A history of reproduction or upward mobility in worker families had ended (cf. Kesküla, this volume).

Outside the Factory

Precarity and new inequalities at work had repercussions outside the factory. Increased casualization of labor resulted in stronger solidarities among household members, along with new hierarchies and enhanced power of regularly employed family members, who were usually male. Moreover, it fractured the solidarity of the neighborhood. Leisure was scarcer, especially for casual workers who needed more than one job to get by. Previous forms of everyday sociality faded. I will discuss these changes by looking at housing and residential patterns, migration, and rural-urban links.

During socialism, steelworkers could rent a flat very cheaply through the plant's 'housing unit' (Zhilishten Fond) in the Lenin district. Since the plant produced building materials, constructing apartment blocks was less expensive than it was for other state companies. Moreover, the municipality of Pernik managed the state-funded House Building Company, which built housing for residents of Pernik.[19] Priority on the waiting list was given to those "more in need," such as those living in multi-generational households. Nuclear families were encouraged. One's position in the list could change, depending on relations of power; the same applied to the size and the position of the flat. Earlier brick socialist blocks closer to the center of the Lenin district, with shops and the factory within walking distance, were preferred to later panel blocks in Teva, a neighborhood up the hill that had to be reached via transportation.

Most nuclear families had moved into a flat by the early 1980s, and when these residential buildings were gradually privatized in the early 1990s, the great majority bought the flats they had rented for years. Priority was given to present occupants, so those who had been allocated the best flats during socialism now became their owners. During those years, Stomana had few orders and it was easy for workers to take unpaid long-term leave. This gave them the opportunity to migrate seasonally to other European countries or to Libya, where skilled Stomana workers could migrate to work for a fixed term. In exceptional cases, this seasonal migration funded the purchase of a second flat.

All the regular and ethnic Bulgarian casual workers' families I met in 2014 owned flats acquired in the 1990s. The only exceptions were Roma, who almost exclusively rented. The great majority of flat owners also owned a small house in their village of origin, or shared its ownership with siblings. Except for the Roma, who were concentrated in particular neighborhoods, and some senior managers and engineers who lived in Sofia, the majority of regular and casual workers were to be found in all areas of Iztok and the nearby neighborhoods, including less privileged ones like Teva, where apartments were allocated to steelworkers. There was no specific concentration of regular workers in more privileged areas and no concentration of casual ones in less privileged areas. After the layoffs of the 1990s, those who did not return to villages or moved abroad continued living in the blocks, each of which housed up to eighty families. The increasing isolation and mistrust on the shop floor were reflected and reshaped here as practices of commensality and mutual aid with non-familial neighbors declined. The sense of unfairness vis-à-vis those who still worked at Stomana changed neighborhood relations.

During socialism, workers in Bulgaria built or reconstructed private houses in their villages with the help of friends and co-workers. Urban families were allowed up to 120 square meters per nuclear family as residential space.[20] As their apartments were below that limit, they used the rest of their allowance to build small houses. If one decided to build a house in the village or on the outskirts of town, colleagues would gather on weekends to provide labor in house-building parties. This practice of mutual aid, which Boneva (2014) describes as an element of continuity with village life, declined during the 1990s. Moreover, during socialism and up until the layoffs, coworkers also worked together on domestic tasks like tiling or painting in the apartment blocks. After the 1998 privatization, this kind of mutual aid ceased in the Iztok district due to new tensions among neighbors. Few could afford to purchase services through the market economy. Rather, maintaining the old house or flat became a central part of the household budget (typically listed as the third priority, after food and bills). Family members carried out urgent tasks during vacations and days off. Casual workers migrated seasonally to Western European countries to pick fruit in order to buy materials for flat renovation; or they worked in construction projects in other Bulgarian cities (i.e., those more dynamic than Pernik). Regular work provided a stable income, but casual work had the advantage of allowing for equally casual migration.

Eventually the housing market became expensive for Pernik workers, especially after the 1997 economic crisis. Younger families started living with their parents in the flats they owned. Sharing space also lowered families' energy costs, a topic of everyday concern that initiated mass protests in Bulgaria in 2013/14. Although there was abundant unused space in Pernik, and although statistics attest to increasing space per person in Bulgaria, especially among ethnic Bulgarians (Ivancheva 2015), this is not reflected in Pernik workers' residential patterns. At least half of both regular and casual workers lived in a household made up of a multigenerational nuclear family who also shared a village house. The usual pattern was for pensioners to live in the village during the warmer months of the year and move into the apartment block with their children and grandchildren in winter. This enabled sharing of bills, especially those for heating. Younger generations lived in the flat for longer periods and visited the village from time to time, mostly in summer. Regular and casual workers were members of the same precarious households. Regular elder workers were property owners and earned more cash than other family members. Casual elder workers were also property owners, and the pensioners among them had additional cash income. Casual young workers without cash or property were obliged to migrate, there being no other way to escape from the lack of job opportunities in the market and from familial generational inequalities.

One in every two workers in Pernik had a close relative working permanently or casually abroad. Two main migration patterns emerged—short-term and long-term—depending on age, employment, and family status. Older regular workers migrated seasonally during the turbulent years of the early 1990s but soon returned and held on to their positions in the plant. Casual workers with children in Pernik also migrated casually to Spain, Italy, France, and Greece, especially after Bulgaria entered the EU in 2007. In addition to such short-term migration, younger, childless casual workers in their twenties worked as unskilled workers abroad, mainly in construction, over longer periods. So too did migrants with university degrees. Especially after wages were slashed in 2008–2010, regular skilled employees who did not yet have family commitments also turned to migration. Krassi, a 36-year-old electro-technician, resigned after twelve years of employment and soon found an equivalent post in a factory in France. He wrote to his colleagues that his salary was smaller than that of a French worker, but still much higher than a Stomana wage. Cases like this, which were much discussed in Stomana, hastened the devaluation of local jobs.

The new division of labor impeded connections with the countryside and agricultural production. Regular workers could maintain ties and even strengthen them due to their greater need for less expensive products. However, few casual workers were able to do so; instead they depended on other family members for access to village produce. Katia, age 48, was a crane driver at Stomana's melting shop, where she had started work after graduating from Pernik's Metallurgical Technical School in 1986. Her parents worked at Stomana until 1993. She met her husband, Ivo, a skilled fitter, soon after she started work. One morning on the Friday shift in the early days of privatization in the late 1990s, her husband, who worked at the plate mill, telephoned to arrange for them to meet between the two shops in order to make an "urgent decision." Friday is the usual day for communicating bad news: Ivo's manager had informed him that one of them would have to leave the factory. It was up to them decide who. Ivo suggested that it should be him because he, "as a man," would find another job easily enough, perhaps at Kremikovtzi, where his expertise from the melting shop was still in demand under its new owner, Mittal. Indeed he was recruited there, but he found himself unemployed three years later. He then became a casual construction worker, and Katia's wages, although by now reduced, became their chief source of household income. Their son Martin, born in 1991, obtained a BA in economics from the University of Sofia while simultaneously working as a private security guard in Stomana. Katia was unhappy with his very low salary and twelve-hour shifts, but this casual employment was better than nothing. They had obtained that position for him through their local network (one of the supervisors for the security contractor was an ex-colleague of Ivo's).

Just as Ivo had been made redundant at Kremikovtzi, Katia too was made redundant, three years after Ivo left Stomana. She cried in her flat for five days after signing the papers in the Human Resources department. Then a friend invited her to attend a party at a local restaurant, hinting that someone she would meet there could be important to her. The unknown man wore a suit and seemed to have good connections in the Stomana hierarchy. Katia assumed he was one of the scrap suppliers. He informed her that her friend, whom he evidently wanted to impress, had told him her story. He told her not to worry and said she should give him a telephone call the next day. When she did so, he told her that "*I was never laid off but had just taken a few days annual leave,*" and that she should turn up to work the next day if she did not want to use up more of it. In the morning, Katia's absence was formally logged and she returned to her job, which, by the time of my fieldwork, she hoped to hang on to for another two years, until the end of 2016. Her classification as a "Class two hazardous worker" would then make her eligible for a pension.

Apart from its wage income, this household was sustained by Ivo's work in his village of origin, 35 km from the city. Katia's sister and brother-in-law, who had managed to hold on to his regular job at Stomana, supplied the extended family with vegetables and *rakia*. As a regular worker, Ivo had continued to participate in a *batchia*, a form of collective for raising goats, sheep, or cows that is common in the Bulgarian countryside (with variants in other post-Ottoman Balkan countries).[21] Each member of the group contributes a number of animals. Ivo's *batchia* consisted of 98 sheep at the time he quit. As the owner of 7 animals, he would have been obliged to contribute some fifteen days of labor during the grazing and milking period from early spring to late autumn. He used his share of the milk for drinking and making cheese that he then distributed to the extended family. Sometimes he sold surplus cheese on the local market. As a regular worker, Ivo was able to plan his schedule so as not to interfere with his *batchia* obligations. However, after becoming a casual construction worker he had to withdraw from the *batchia*. Martin said that he would have liked to replace his father, but he could not do so because he too had no regular job that would have allowed him to calculate holiday time. In the end Ivo had no choice but to sell his animals, a decision with sentimental as well as economic effects, since *batchia* had been a family tradition. Ivo's lack of time and inability to plan ahead even kept him from participating in the daily practices of assistance among neighbors in Pernik. The new division of labor under neoliberal conditions has contributed to the demise of the peasant-workers and cemented their proletarianization. Yet they still depend on familial solidarities and support from those regularly employed to keep going.

Consider the case of Rado, born in 1964, who had been a technician at Stomana's plate mill since he was twenty-three. His wife Mariya, a few years younger, worked as an assistant in a clothing shop in Pernik after being laid off from an industrial machinery plant in 1996. Their son, Giorgi, born in 1988, had studied at Pernik's technical school but was unable to find a job locally and became a construction worker in Sofia. For four years he commuted from Pernik because he could not afford rent in the capital. When the construction sector collapsed after 2010, Giorgi migrated to Belgium, where he found work as an electrician. His income was enough to get by but did not allow him to save money or to send money back to the family as he had initially hoped. Still, this remained his intention. Rado's salary was the most stable income in the household. Mariya's wages were low and paid irregularly. The deregulation of labor encouraged this practice, as shop owners were aware that their employees had no alternatives. Mariya complained that she had become dependent on Rado and often discussed the possibility of leaving Bulgaria for a care job in Spain, where her mother worked.

The family lived in an apartment acquired in 1993 from one of Stomana's housing cooperatives. Rado took out a loan in 2006 to repair the plumbing in the bathroom and kitchen, but repaying this loan was not easy after his salary was cut, and it became even harder when bonus payments ceased in 2008. He visited his native village regularly to take care of his vegetable garden and to contribute to the *batchia*. He also made *rakia* with a village neighbor, another regular steelworker. His continued participation in the *batchia* was facilitated by his 86-year-old father, who still lived in the village, made cheese, and took care of the animals. Theirs was the last mutual aid group left in the village since the disintegration of two others in the mid-1990s. The number of animals had fallen from 120 in late 1998 to only 67 animals in 2014. Owners who could not participate preferred to sell their animals rather than hire a laborer to care for them. They lacked cash to pay for labor, and *batchia* was traditionally based on non-wage labor anyway. Regular Stomana workers were able to supplement their wages by producing vegetables and breeding animals, but it now became impossible for a casual worker to continue animal breeding activities. Some did, however, still make *rakia*, which does not require coordination with a group and takes only a few days.

Household and extended family relations constituted strong unities among Pernik workers. Household practices of solidarity are strategies of survival in conditions of increased economic uncertainty (Pine 2001). But this does not mean that household relationships are necessarily harmonious. The vast majority of the precarious younger generation lives off the few remaining assets and relatively stable income of the older, regularly employed generation and the elders' domestic production.

Conclusion

Many of the tectonic changes of the new casual/regular divide in postsocialist countries have been absorbed by families and by domestic production oriented towards subsistence. Like other ethnographers (Pine 2001; Mollona 2009: 71; Narotzky 2015), I found that strong household solidarities in Pernik are crucial in reproducing the regime of labor flexibility. Fear of capital flight, strong competition from emerging markets, and the possibility of downward mobility for all create uncertain conditions for the workforce. Gender inequalities deepen, as those in a position of power in the family tend to be the regularly employed, who most often are males. Even households with members in regular employment can be precarious when the jobs are patently insecure and no new regular jobs are being created for the next generation. The abundance of skilled workers among the unemployed, the occupation of key positions by foreigners, downsizing, indebtedness, lower wages, and the unpredictability of the financial market put all Pernik steelworkers and their families in a vulnerable position. The most precarious are the poorly paid casual workers, who are forced to take on multiple jobs (sometimes via casual migration), have no time to sustain social relations, and are highly dependent on family members with regular jobs. The outcome for those in this category of employment is a more complete proletarianization than what existed in socialism, one that workers who have held on to their regular jobs still strive to avert by maintaining close ties to the countryside. Despite having so far managed to resist full proletarianization, regular company workers have increasingly come to resemble casual workers in terms of their precarity—especially after the recent economic crisis, which not only reduced their incomes but intensified the fear of capital flight. Although the division between regular and casual workers is rather sharp on the shop floor, they often belong to the same precarious household, blurring the distinction between salariat and precariat (Standing 2011) at home. The clarity of that distinction is modulated by ethnicity: it remains sharp for the Roma, who are excluded from the salariat. Meanwhile, the possibility of downward mobility reduces everyone to aspiring to hold on to what he or she has already.

Acknowledgments

Research for this paper was conducted in Pernik in 2013–2015 at Stomana Steel Industry. In addition to interviews with workers and Pernik residents, a work and household survey was conducted with fifty workers. I am grateful to Stomana workers and their families, to Gavin Smith for his comments on a draft of this chapter, and to Tsvetana Manova for her support and insights during the fieldwork.

Dimitra Kofti is a Research Fellow at the Max Planck Institute for Social Anthropology in Halle. She holds a Ph.D. from University College London and has been awarded fellowships at the Central European University in Budapest and at the University Kliment Ohridski in Sofia. For her doctoral and first postdoctoral project she investigated questions of precarity, flexibility, class, political mobilizations, and changing temporalities in Bulgaria. Her work has been published in journals such as *Focaal* and *Anthropological Theory*. As a member of the Research Group "Financialisation," she is currently investigating questions of value, risk, and indebtedness in Greece.

Notes

1. All research participants' names are pseudonyms.
2. Rural-urban relations in Bulgaria have undergone various types of transformation since the early 1990s, depending on regional economic conditions (Creed 2013) and influenced also by global mobility (Kaneff 2013).

3. Burawoy (1985: 150) described comparable fears among American workers in the 1980s: "The primary point of reference is no longer the firm's success from one year to another; instead it is the rate that might be earned elsewhere ... the fear of being fired is replaced by the fear of capital flight, plant closure, transfer of operations, and plant disinvestment."

4. The population rose from approximately 1,000 residents in 1880 to 12,296 in 1926; 28,545 in 1946; 59,930 in 1956, and 75844 in 1965 (Boneva, 2014: 287–288). The expansion continued until the end of the socialist era. The population fell from 111,244 in 1992 to 85,991 in 2001 (National Statistical Institute of Bulgaria, 2001) and 80,191 in 2011 (National Statistical Institute of Bulgaria 2011).

5. During fieldwork I met only one worker's family that claimed descent from wealthier landowners.

6. In 21 out of 50 workers' households surveyed, at least one member had worked in such a small-scale private company. In 43 out of 50 households, at least one member had worked casually.

7. Estimates of migrants from Bulgaria abroad vary. The Bulgarian National Statistical Institute estimates 600,000, based on the number of de-registered addresses. However, migrants do not always de-register, and given that many migrate inside the EU, accurate figures are difficult to gauge. Half of the households in my survey had one or more members with direct experience of foreign migration.

8. The official unemployment rate in Bulgaria was 1.7 percent in 1990, 12.5 percent in 1991, 18 percent in 2000, and 11.2 percent in 2014. In 2014 the official rate in Pernik was 13 percent, but local social scientists estimated that it was much higher and undocumented, as many underemployed people do not register. Moreover, those who migrate abroad are not classified as unemployed.

9. According to the 2011 census, Pernik's Roma were 2.3 percent of its population. However, the real figure is certainly higher, given that Roma people often conceal their ethnic background to avoid discrimination.

10. According to a report on Foreign Direct Investment published by the Central Bank of Bulgaria in 2009, Greece was the third largest investor in Bulgaria, after Austria and the Netherlands. Investments were made mainly in the banking sector, textiles, financial consultancy, import and export, construction, real estate, and communications. The ongoing Greek crisis has intensified the flight of companies from Greece to Bulgaria.

11. Percentages supplied by the Human Resources manager.

12. According to estimates by the two unions (Podkrepa and KNSB) in January 2014.

13. The actual number of the casual workforce was not documented in 2014; these percentages are my own estimates.

14. These approximations are suggested by my household survey of 50 workers in the plant (35 regular and 15 casual).

15. Most work 8-hour shifts: four days morning (06:00–14:00), four days afternoon (14:00–22:00), and four nights (22:00–06:00), with one or two days off between shifts. Those doing the heaviest jobs in the melting shop receive additional days off.

16. According to the European Environmental Agency report (2013), Bulgaria's air is the most polluted in Europe. Within Bulgaria, Pernik is widely said to be the most polluted city.
17. E.g., "Death to Byzantium."
18. Under socialism, workers' children took up various posts, not necessarily at the same shop as their parents. However, many couples worked at the same shop floor, having first met each other at work.
19. The 'House Building Company' built approximately 1200 flats a year in the 1970s (Manova 2011: 598).
20. In Sofia I have heard of people who fictitiously divorced in order to acquire more space. I have not heard about similar divorces in Pernik, possibly because such ruses were impossible in the smaller city.
21. Older Pernik residents connect the *batchia* to Vlach nomadic traditions (see Campbell 1964). In Bulgaria it is thought to date back to the sixteenth century (Lazarov 2012).

References

Alexander, Catherine, and Buchli, Victor. 2007. "Introduction." In *Urban Life in Post-Soviet Asia*, ed. C. Alexander, V. Buchli, and Caroline Humphrey, 1–39. London: UCL Press.

Angelidou, Aliki, and Kofti, Dimitra. 2013. "Greek (Ad)ventures in Sofia: Economic Elite Mobility and New Cultural Hierarchies at the Margins of Europe." In *Global Villages: Rural and Urban Transformations in Contemporary Bulgaria*, ed. Ger Duijzings, 191–208. London: Anthem.

Boneva, Tania. 2014. "Remembering Communism: Field Studies in Pernik, 1960–1964." In *Remembering Communism: Private and Public Recollection of Lived Experience in Southeast Europe*, ed. M. Todorova, S. Troebst, and A. Dimou, 285–306. Budapest: CEU Press.

Brunnbauer, Ulf, and Taylor, Karin. 2004. "Creating a Family and Reproduction Policies in Bulgaria, 1944–1989." *Continuity and Change* 19(2): 283–312.

Burawoy, Michael. 1985. *The Politics of Production: Factory Regimes Under Capitalism and Socialism*. London: Verso.

Campbell, John K. 1964. *Honour, Family, and Patronage: A Study of Institutions and Moral Values in a Greek Mountain Community*. Oxford: Clarendon Press.

Creed, Gerald. 1998. *Domesticating Revolution: From Socialist Reform to Ambivalent Transition in a Bulgarian Village*. Pennsylvania: Penn State University Press.

———. 2011. *Masquerade and Postsocialism*. Bloomington, IN: Indiana University Press.

———. 2013. "Every Village, a Different Story: Tracking Rural Diversity in Bulgaria." In *Global Villages: Rural and Urban Transformations in Contemporary Bulgaria*, ed. Ger Duijzings, 53–65. London: Anthem Press.

Deneva, Neda. 2012. "Transnational Aging Careers: On Transformation of Kinship and Citizenship in the Context of Migration Among Bulgarian Muslims in Spain." *Social Politics: International Studies in Gender, State, and Society* 19(1): 105–128.

De Neve, Geert. 2008. "'We Are All Sondukarar (Relatives)!': Kinship and Its Morality in an Urban Industry of Tamilnadu, South India." *Modern Asian Studies* 42(1): 211–246.

Dunn, Elizabeth. 2004. *Privatizing Poland: Baby Food, Big Business, and the Remaking of Labor*. Ithaca, NY, and London: Cornell University Press.

European Environmental Agency. 2013. Air Quality in Europe-2013 Report. EEA Report, 9/2013. Retrieved from https://www.eea.europa.eu/publications/air-quality-in-europe-2013.

Hann, Chris. 1987. "Worker-Peasants in the Three Worlds." In *Peasants and Peasant Societies*, ed. T. Shanin, 115–120. New York and Oxford: Blackwell.

Ivancheva, Mariya. 2015. "From Informal to Illegal: Roma Housing in (Post-)Socialist Sofia." *Intersections: East European Journal of Society and Politics* 1(4): 38–54.

Kalinova, Evgenia, and Baeva, Iskra. 2002. *Bulgarskite prekhodi, 1939–2002* [Bulgarian transitions, 1939–2002]. Sofia: Paradigma.

Kaneff, Deema. 2002. "Work, Identity and Rural-Urban Relations." In *Post-Socialist Peasant? Rural and Urban Constructions of Identity in Eastern Europe, East Asia and the Former Soviet Union*, ed. P. Leonard and Deema Kaneff, 180–199. New York: Palgrave.

———. 2013. "Rural-Urban Relations in a Global Age." In *Global Villages: Rural and Urban Transformations in Contemporary Bulgaria*, ed. Ger Duijzings, 33–51. London: Anthem.

Kideckel, David A. 2008. *Getting by in Postsocialist Romania: Labor, the Body, and Working-Class Culture*. Bloomington, IN: Indiana University Press.

Konstantinov, Yulian. 2000. "Survival Strategies in Post-1989 Bulgaria." In *Karl Polanyi in Vienna: The Contemporary Significance of the Great Transformation*, ed. K. McRobbie and K. Polanyi-Levitt, 132–146. Montreal: Black Rose Books.

Kotkin, Stephen. 1995. *Magnetic Mountain: Stalinism as a Civilization*. Los Angeles, CA: University of California Press.

Kremakova, Milena. 2011. "What Do Market Mechanisms (Really) Mean? A Study of Bulgarian Maritime Livelihoods after 1989." In *Rethinking Work: Global Historical and Sociological Perspectives*, ed. R. Behal, A. Mah, and F. Babacar. New Delhi: Tulika.

Lazarov, Valentin. 2012. "Letni Sdruzhenia za Obshto Otgledane i Doene na Ovtse u Bulgarite I Ozven Dneshnite Granitsi na Bulgaria." [Summer associations for collective sheep breeding among Bulgarians, within and beyond the current boundaries of Bulgaria]. In *Kulturno-Istoritshesko I Ezikovo Nasledstvo na "Sasedna" Bulgaria* [Cultural, historical and linguistic heritage in the neighborhood of Bulgaria], ed. Margarita Mladenova, Valentin Geshev, 294–321. Sofia: St. Kliment Ohridski University Press.

Makram-Ebeid, Dina. 2012. *Manufacturing Stability: Everyday Politics of Work in an Industrial Steel Town in Helwan, Egypt*. Ph.D. thesis. London, GB: London School of Economics and Political Science.

Manova, Tsvetana. 2011. *Sokove ot Korena: Etnolozki Interviuta* [Stories from the roots: Ethnologic interviews]. Pernik: Dvoretch na Kulturata.

Mollona, Massimiliano. 2009. *Made in Sheffield: An Ethnography of Industrial Work and Politics.* New York: Berghahn Books.

Müller, Birgit. 2007. *Disenchantment with Market Economics: East Germans and Western Capitalism.* New York: Berghahn Books.

National Statistical Institute of Bulgaria. 2011. Population and Housing Census in the Republic of Bulgaria 2011. http://www.nsi.bg/census2011/PDOCS2/Census2011final_en.pdf.

National Statistical Institute of Bulgaria. 2001. Population and Housing Census in the Republic of Bulgaria 2001.Retrieved from http://www.nsi.bg/Census_e/Census_e.htm.

Narotzky, Susana. 2015. "The Payoff of Love and the Traffic of Favours: Reciprocity, Social Capital, and the Blurring of Value Realms in Flexible Capitalism." In *Flexible Capitalism: Exchange and Ambiguity at Work*, ed. J. Kjaerulff, 268–310. New York: Berghahn Books.

Narotzky, Susana, and Smith, Gavin. 2006. *Immediate Struggles: People, Power, and Place in Rural Spain.* Los Angeles, CA: University of California Press.

Parry, Jonathan. 2013. "Company and Contract Labour in a Central Indian Steel Plant." *Economy and Society* 42(3): 348–374.

Pine, Frances. 2001. "Retreat to Household? Gendered Domains in Postscialist Poland." In *Postsocialism: Ideals, Ideologies and Local Practices*, ed. C. Hann, 94–113. London: Routledge.

Sanchez, Andrew, and Strümpell, Christian. 2014. "Sons of Soil, Sons of Steel: Autochthony, Descent and the Class Concept in Industrial India." *Modern Asian Studies* 48(5): 1276–1301.

Smart, Alan, and Smart, Josephine. 2005. "Introduction." In *Petty Capitalists and Globalization, Flexibility, Entrepreneurship, and Economic Development*, ed. Alan Smart and Josephine Smart, 1–22. New York: State University of New York Press.

Smollett, Eleanor. 1989. "The Economy of Jars: Kindred Relationships in Bulgaria; An Exploration." *Ethnologia Europaea* 18: 125–140.

Standing, Guy. 2011. *The Precariat: The New Dangerous Class.* London: Bloomsbury

Thompson, E.P. 1967. "Time, Work-Discipline and Industrial Capitalism." *Past & Present* 38(December 1): 56–97.

Tocheva, Detelina. 2014. "'They work in a Closed Circle': Self-Sufficiency in House-Based Rural Tourism in the Rhodope Mountains, Bulgaria." In *Oikos and Market: Explorations in Self-Sufficiency after Socialism*, ed. S. Gudeman and C. Hann, 137–161. New York: Berghahn Books.

Trappman, Vera. 2015. "Steel in the European Union in the Wake of the Global Economic Crisis." In *Foreign Investment in Eastern and Southern Europe After 2008: Still a Lever of Growth?* ed. B. Galgoczi, J. Drahokoupil, and M. Bernaciak, 355–375. Brussels: European Trade Union Institute (ETUI).

5

Precarious Labor and Precarious Livelihoods in an Indian Company Town

CHRISTIAN STRÜMPELL

Introduction

One evening in February 2006 I sat with Bhola, a 35-year-old steel worker, in his quarters in the spacious, green, clean company township his employer maintains for its regular workforce at Rourkela in the eastern Indian state Odisha. Bhola had grown up just a stone's throw away, in a village on the edge of the township. On that evening he lamented that his father, who had also been employed by the company, had not left the *basti*, as such settlements are called, in order to raise his children in the township. "Here," Bhola explained, "we would have attended proper schools, would have learned proper speech and manners, and I often think how much better my life would have been!" Bhola's complaints referred to the difficulties he had experienced in obtaining a regular job with the company that had already employed his father. For manual workers, this company offered by far the best employment conditions available.

Bhola's employer, the Rourkela Steel Plant (RSP) is a public-sector undertaking established in the 1950s by the Government of India under Prime Minister Nehru. Domestic steel production was considered essential to making India economically autonomous and buttressing the country's newly gained political independence (Khilnani 2003 [1997]: 61–106; Nayar 2004 [2001]: 50–85). RSP, like all public-sector industries, was to be a cornerstone of Nehru's sociopolitical agenda of balancing regional inequalities. The plant was intentionally located in a rural backwater, an "elsewhere" between the metropoles (cf. Roy 2007). It would help to relieve pressure on the countryside by providing large-scale employment, and its workforce would become a "model" citizenry. The area was still sparsely populated, and the plant's workforce would include significant numbers of immigrants and unite people of different regions, castes, and religions. As a public-sector undertaking, RSP would provide relatively well-paid and secure employment, including accommodation in the well-equipped township adjacent to the plant. This, it was expected, would inevitably transcend workers' loyalties to caste, region, and religion, and transform them into modern, secular, socialist citizens (cf. Parry 1999, 2009).

Over the decades, the employment conditions RSP offered were indeed munificent compared to those at other public-sector companies, as well as at the large number of private-sector factories that were soon attracted to Rourkela. Furthermore, RSP offered such employment to a relatively large number of people. In 1981, it had 38,701 employees on its direct payroll while the population of the larger town, including the company township and other "planned" or "unplanned" colonies, stood at 322,610.[1] Ten years later there were 36,049 RSP jobs for an urban population of 398,692. By 1986, other central or state government public-sector enterprises in the town were employing around the same number of people, while private industry had a regular workforce of around 25,000 (Barick 1989: 65). Clearly, it was a common experience in Rourkela to have regular employment in the "organized" formal sector, which comprises relatively large-scale, capital-intensive industries that are registered, pay sales and income taxes, employ 100 or more regular workers entitled to union representation and enforceable standards of working conditions, and are predominantly run by the state (cf. Parry 2009: 180). Accordingly, many young people could aspire to such employment conditions. However, the situation in Rourkela changed dramatically in the 1990s, when the Government of India—under pressure from global financial institutions as well as domestic forces (Nayar 2004: 129–155)—officially turned away from Nehruvian "socialism" toward "economic liberalization." RSP still offered secure, remunerative employment, but—like other public-sector undertakings—it drastically reduced its regular workforce. By 2009, its manpower was reduced to 19,500, a number that was set to decrease even further. Many young people were forced to abandon their expectations of regular employment in Rourkela and leave the place, or else accept jobs in the informal sector. By contrast with the situation in India at large, where 90 percent of the total labor force had always had to rely on the "unorganized" informal sector (Breman 1994; Parry 2009: 180), and where precarious labor has always been unexceptional (Cross 2010), the increasing precarity in Rourkela represents a reversal of expectations. In this respect, the process unfolding at Rourkela resembles the experience of the organized working classes in the "West" (Standing 2014 [2011]).

However, increasing precarity has not affected the whole of Rourkela's working classes in the same way. After liberalization, RSP also enhanced the educational credentials demanded from applicants. Since then, as Bhola's statement makes clear, company accommodation in the township is considered crucial to getting the education required for regular employment. Indeed, it is a major perk of the job, not only because the housing is of good quality and the rents and services (like water and electricity) are heavily subsidized, but also because the township is where the company's well-equipped hospital, health centers, and schools are located. In 1982, the Steel Authority of India Ltd (SAIL)—the holding company responsible for several public-sector steel plants—was spending more than 50 percent of its budget for welfare and social amenities on townships and schools (Mohanty 1988: 122f.). Until a decade ago, however, the RSP township had far too little accommodation for all of its regular employees. Roughly half lived in villages, slums, and other settlements on its periphery.

As I shall show, this divide between township and surrounding settlements was congruent from the start with an ethnic divide between migrant workers of various castes from Odisha's coastal lowlands and other Indian states, and the local population, who were predominantly Adivasis (i.e., "tribals" of supposedly autochthonous origin). Initially, however, this residential segregation of ethnic groups did not divide the regularly employed public-sector RSP workforce from the other, less privileged informal sector labor. In the township, regular RSP workers were among themselves. But outside it they lived cheek by jowl and shared in a common neighborhood life. Only upon economic liberalization and the ensuing changes to the Indian public sector did the spatial segregation begin to reflect the divide between the two types of worker. When RSP radically reduced its regular workforce, the educational credentials required to join it were made more rigorous. With the reduction in manning, the township was now large enough to accommodate all regular company workers, and the Adivasis amongst them now rushed to move in for the sake of their children's educational prospects. The spatial distance established between regular RSP workers and precarious informal-sector workers of Adivasi ethnicity distanced the former from the demands for regular employment made by those they had left behind. Furthermore, while Rourkela's still largely Adivasi *basti*s were being turned into "sinks" of informal-sector labor (cf. Parry 2013b: 71), the town witnessed an intensifying spate of urban development projects that threatened the inhabitants of the *basti*s with eviction. Not only do they now have very little chance of landing a regular RSP job, but their very existence in their natal settlements is in jeopardy.

This chapter shows that precarity is not exclusively rooted in the realm of work and employment, as Standing's (2014) account suggests, and that the postcolonial Indian state and contemporary urban development processes exacerbate precarity.

Local and Foreign Workers

From its outset in 1955, the construction of the steel plant and township was marred by technical problems. To realize the project, the Government of India required expertise, equipment, and capital from its foreign partners. After prolonged negotiations with several prospective partners it contracted with a consortium formed around the West German steel corporations Krupp and DEMAG. These companies lacked prior experience assembling a steel plant–cum-township on a "green field" site in a cultural environment very different from their own. The Indian authorities and civil construction companies were in no position to help. The ensuing misunderstandings and overambitious technical aspirations resulted in major delays in preparing the ground for construction, delivering the necessary equipment, and commissioning individual units.[2]

These organizational difficulties were aggravated by serious social problems. Construction work was interrupted by violent attacks on immigrants from Bengal, Punjab, and Tamil Nadu, perpetrated by *goondas* (hooligans) of the Odia ethnic group. They had been shipped in by Odia petty capitalists and steel plant officers to intimidate competitors from outside Odisha who dominated the local construction industry as well as the RSP executive cadres. Odia construction workers were easily mobilized to join these attacks. Elderly Odia workers remember the *goondas* as "heroes" who protected their compatriots, who were working for derisory wages as unskilled laborers under "foreign" contractors and supervisors from Bengal, Punjab, and other Indian states. Skilled workers, almost all of whom were from outside Odisha, earned up to ten times more than others as the West German companies competed with each other to recruit those with industrial work experience. Despite the Nehruvian objective of an economically secure public-sector industrial workforce (cf. Parry 2009), RSP was built in collaboration with foreign capitalist companies that employed workers according to market principles.

The conflicts between Odia RSP officers, contractors, and workers on the one hand and the "foreigners" on the other were exacerbated by the political situation in Rourkela and in Odisha more widely. In 1958, an enquiry committee of the Odisha State Assembly accused RSP management of discrimination against the people of Odisha and demanded that it keep its promise of regional development and give Odias priority in employment.[3] The incursion of non-Odias was bitterly resented. Protection of the "Odia nation"—especially from the Bengalis, who had administered large tracts of Odisha during colonial times, allegedly much to the Odias' disadvantage— was a deep concern for many educated Odia (Bailey 1998: 31) and became a unifying agenda for major political parties in the state that otherwise catered to very different constituencies. The Congress party could count on support only in the coastal lowlands of eastern Odisha, whereas the western uplands where Rourkela is located were the stronghold of the Ganatantra Parishad, a party dedicated to protecting the region from the lowland immigrants who had flocked there after its incorporation into Odisha in 1948 (Bailey 1963: 161–218). Several royal houses had ruled the hill region under the "indirect" control of the British. After Independence, they initially resisted integration into the Republic of India but ultimately buckled under pressure from local popular movements and from the Indian state, which offered financial incentives for a "merger." Meanwhile, the kings and their entourages of Odia landlords, administrators, and lawyers resented both the coastal Odias, who allegedly displayed the "mentality of conquerors" (Bailey 1959: 1471), and the Bengalis and other outsiders brought in by the RSP. The Ganatantra Parishad party, a product of these resentments, successfully challenged the supremacy of the Congress Party in the state for several decades, and in Rourkela it supported local villagers' protests against their displacement.

The Ganatantra Parishad was soon joined by rival parties, including socialists and a "tribal" party that aspired to set up a new tribal state of Jharkhand in the region.[4] The majority of Rourkela inhabitants belonged to several different indigenous tribes that all considered themselves distinct from Odias. Most mistrusted the self-proclaimed guardians of western Odisha as much as they did those of "the Odia nation." After protracted negotiations and violent confrontations, an agreement was reached. It promised each displaced household not only monetary compensation but also regular employment in RSP for one of its able-bodied male members; a housing plot in one of three "resettlement colonies" to be established close to, but separate from, the company township for those wishing to take up such jobs; and land in "reclamation camps" further away for those preferring to remain in agriculture. In this way the construction of the steel plant and township, with their unprecedented employment and business opportunities, fueled pre-existing ethnic and intra-regional tensions that were heightened by the arrival of thousands of migrants from other parts of India. One important effect of this was the segregation of the local, largely tribal population in separate residential areas outside the RSP township.

From 1959 onward, as RSP started its operations and recruited its regular workforce, relations between "locals" and "outsiders" remained volatile. Though the plant had taken on 23,000 workers by 1965, competition for jobs was strong and usually framed in ethnic terms. Outbreaks of violence were frequent and reached a sad climax in 1964 in a communal riot in which around two thousand Muslims were murdered by mobs that included Punjabis, Bengalis, Odias, and Adivasis, all of whom considered the Muslims outsiders.[5]

Strained ethnic relationships also reverberated in RSP labor politics. The two major rival trade unions were associated with Odia and non-Odia workers respectively. Indian labor laws "recognize" only the union with the largest membership in an enterprise as the sole representative of its workforce in collective negotiations. With the support of the state government, whose labor department verifies the union membership lists, the "Odia union" was formally recognized as the representative union in 1967. Around the same time, it became mandatory for public-sector undertakings to recruit manual workers exclusively through local employment exchanges under the state's labor department. In this way the Government of Odisha finally gained control over access to RSP employment, and Odia applicants were privileged. In the late 1960s and early 1970s, the plant commissioned some new units and again recruited regular workers in large numbers. Between 1966 and 1974, the regular RSP workforce grew from 23,000 to 35,000 workers, and most of the new recruits were Odias. Furthermore, the recognized union was able to help Odia workers receive more favorable treatment. From the shop floor to the plant level, and with few exceptions, union office holders were Odias. When it came to promotions, holidays, or the allotment of quarters, hospital beds, or any other benefits in which the recognized union had a say, it would first support its "own people." Not all Odia workers supported or received favors from the union. However, many now retired Bengali and South Indian workers I talked to were convinced that they had experienced ethnic discrimination in which the union had been at least complicit.

I never heard anybody in Rourkela claim that the earlier animosities between hill-dwelling and coastal Odias were ever significant in union politics or in the competition for RSP jobs. Many people viewed Rourkela as a place where Odias as a whole had reinvigorated their identity by successfully asserting themselves against "foreign" (especially Bengali) domination. For Odia nationalists, Rourkela became an icon of modern Odisha, as well as of modern India in general.

By contrast, Adivasi suspicions of Odias from east and west alike gained new vigor in and around the RSP as early as the early 1960s. Odia regard the Adivasi as part of Odisha (Sengupta 2007). However, relatively few were taken on when the employment exchanges controlled the pool of candidates for the expansion of the RSP workforce between 1966 and 1974. As was standard practice already, those Adivasi who were recruited to regular jobs, or given jobs in compensation for their displacement, were posted in mechanical maintenance departments or, more often, in "hot shops" like the coke ovens, blast furnaces, and steel melting shop, where working conditions are particularly tough (cf. Behera 1996). Officers in the RSP personnel department considered Adivasis especially (and perhaps exclusively) suited for hard physical labor, an understanding shared by non-Adivasi workers on the same shop floors who, with the consent of their superiors and the union, routinely ordered their helpless Adivasi workmates about.

RSP employed only a small number of Adivasi in white-collar jobs, and they too felt unfairly treated at work. In the late 1960s they founded a union of their own that challenged the recognized Odia union and quickly received support from the large number of Adivasis working in the hot shops. That union came to be called the "Jharkhand union"—a reference to the tribal state to which many Adivasi aspired. This union received strong support from many Bengali, Punjabi, and other non-Odia RSP workers who felt alienated from the recognized union. Unlike the Adivasis, however, these workers were not concentrated in specific units or positions. The Jharkhand union failed to establish a majority among RSP workers because—according to many of its erstwhile supporters—the state government's labor department, which verifies membership figures, again backed the Odia union.

Most Adivasi RSP workers not only worked in tribal jobs but also lived in places considered tribal. Two-thirds of those who lost land to RSP belonged to one of the tribal groups in the area. Consequently, most inhabitants of the resettlement colonies were Adivasis, and their predominance in these settlements increased when other Adivasis from the surrounding villages who had come to find work in Rourkela moved into the colonies, where most of them had relatives. They came to be regarded as tribal places conspicuously different from the RSP "garden city" with its schools, parks, clubs, and health centers. Indeed, whereas the company funded the township with relatively great generosity, the resettlement colonies fell under the jurisdiction of the notoriously underfunded Odisha state government. It cleared and leveled the ground, marked out streets, and built a few school buildings and sank wells. Houses, however, had to be built by the displaced people themselves with money provided in the compensation package.[6]

Some local villagers, mostly Adivasis, did not have to leave their houses because RSP had acquired only their fields. Some lost all their land and moved away, only to return to their old village site when they realized after a couple of years that it was still vacant.[7] When it turned out that not all of the appropriated land was required for the development, around 4,000 acres were returned to the state government as unutilized "surplus land." Some of the land it retained remained vacant, and the displaced unofficially reclaimed parts of the latter to establish houses, cultivate rice, keep animals, and make kitchen gardens. Many Adivasis earned additional income from informal activities like liquor distillation or construction work, and quite a few also had regular RSP jobs. Much of my fieldwork focused on one such re-established village, the *basti* of Nag Nadi, where to his regret Bhola had grown up. In the mid 1980s, according to the census I carried out in 2005, 43 of 68 households contained at least one regular RSP worker. In all these *basti*s, as in the resettlement colonies, Adivasi permanent workers lived alongside casual workers. By contrast, Odia RSP workers, most of them from the coastal lowlands, lived in the township, as did immigrants from other states. Both the work situation at the RSP and the living situation in the town had important political ramifications. Adivasis had claimed a preferential right to the many jobs RSP offered in the late 1960s because the industry was built on their forefathers' land, and because promises of regular RSP employment as compensation for their displacement had not been kept. They received support from the above-mentioned Jharkhand union and achieved their most significant success in 1971, when around 300 locals were recruited after the steel minister in Delhi directed RSP to employ at least one person from each displaced household.

Some years later, several thousand contract workers employed in the plant through a chain of contractors and subcontractors laid claim to regular RSP jobs. Though there is also Odia, Bihari, and Telugu contract labor, most of it is Adivasi and local (cf. Omvedt 1981). In the 1970s regular steelworkers' wages began to rise substantially (Mohanty 1988: 185–199). Like many other public-sector companies, RSP increasingly resorted to much cheaper contract labor for repair and maintenance jobs.[8] Few such workers have union protection from arbitrary dismissal, receive sick pay, or enjoy any of the other benefits and perks to which regular workers are entitled (cf. Parry 2009, 2013a). Though the law obliges a company to employ regular workers for all jobs that are "permanent and perennial" to its production process, RSP—like many other companies in both the private and the public sector—regularly deploys contract labor alongside regular RSP workers on the very same tasks. In 1986 some contract workers approached Panicker, an RSP clerk from South India who had gained a reputation for his courage and legal acumen, to file a suit for the regularization of the RSP contract labor force, which comprised around 10,000 workers at the time. In 1995, after interminable legal proceedings and much intimidation by the RSP management, the Supreme Court ordered RSP to take 4,500 of them on as regular workers.

Even before this triumph, Panicker had gained enough popularity among RSP workers to found a new union with the aim of overthrowing the recognized union. Many office holders of the Odia union, Panicker and many others claimed, had been bribed into acquiescence to the contract labor system and involved in attempts to intimidate him and his associates. By the late 1980s the Odia union had lost credibility even among many Odia RSP workers, and an election to decide which union had majority support was won by Panicker's union.

In the early 1990s, some residents of the *basti*s and resettlement colonies revived claims to regular RSP employment as compensation for their earlier displacement. Because of his previous successes, especially on behalf of largely Adivasi contract labor, Panicker's aid was solicited. On his advice they filed a case for preferential employment for all those displaced by RSP and pressed those claims with large demonstrations and sit-ins. Though their demands were not completely fulfilled, they achieved further concessions from the RSP and the state government. One RSP job was allocated to each of around 1,000 households whose land had been acquired in the 1950s, but who had not yet been provided with compensatory employment. Bhola was among them.[9] The action of the early 1990s replicated that of the 1970s, and success in each case probably owed a lot to the support extended by a new union.

Economic Liberalization and the Second Generation of RSP Workers

In the same era when several thousand contract workers and displaced people were struggling for regular RSP employment, public-sector industries were going through a major transformation. In 1991 the Government of India embarked on a policy of "economic liberalization" that broke with several tenets of Nehruvian socialism (Nayar 2004: 129–155).[10] A crucial part of this process was the restructuring of SAIL, the central government holding company, as a competitive player on the global steel market. This entailed the reduction of the regular workforce in SAIL units like RSP but did not diminish the munificent—by Indian standards—wages and fringe benefits the workforce enjoyed, or its high degree of job security. Since the first generation of RSP workers was about to turn sixty, the age of retirement, manpower reduction was achieved by natural attrition supplemented by a "voluntary retirement" scheme (Strümpell 2014). RSP did recruit new workers during this period, but they were far fewer than the retiring workers. By 2014 there were only 15,000 permanent employees. Furthermore, although a significant share of first-generation retirees were illiterate, starting in the 1990s RSP demanded matriculation (i.e., successful completion of the tenth grade) as a minimum qualification. De facto it only recruited people with much higher educational credentials—commonly those with a certificate from an industrial training institute, a diploma from an engineering college, or a degree. Thus, the prospects of regular employment with RSP shrank dramatically in the 1990s, and recruitment became the privilege of the formally educated.

These changes had very uneven social effects. Differences in educational qualifications mapped quite neatly onto Rourkela's ethnically segregated townscape, since it is taken for granted that the *bastis* and resettlement colonies are largely populated by the "uneducated," the "matric fail." The largely Odia residents of the RSP township are much better schooled. They were optimistic that their grown-up children would make it into regular employment elsewhere, and some indeed had already found jobs in the South Indian IT industries. By contrast, in Nag Nadi, the *basti* Bhola grew up in and the one I know best, no one passed the tenth class until 1992, by which time matriculation was insufficient in practice to obtain an RSP job. Jobs were obtained only through the political action described in the preceding section.

During my research in Rourkela between 2004 and 2008, displaced people again held large rallies and filed court cases. Only half of the 1,000 households promised a job in 1995 had actually been given one, and the displaced people's associations demanded faster implementation. They also claimed that the list of households from whom the Odisha state government had acquired land in 1954 was faulty: it was based on the census of 1951, but several of the listed households had fissioned by the time of land acquisition. This time around, however, few regular RSP workers, whether Odia or Adivasi, had any sympathy for these claims. Many said it made no sense to employ such people, because it was a burden to work with them and they were all "uneducated." With an RSP pay packet they would only get drunk more often, it was alleged, and then their tasks would have to be carried out by somebody else and collective production bonuses would fall. Those who voiced such sentiments were all educated. To be sure, even during the earlier agitation at the beginning of the 1990s, not a few RSP workers had been unsympathetic or even hostile. It was those who lived in the same neighborhoods, and those who felt marginalized by the recognized union, who had supported the claimants to regular jobs at RSP. By the mid 2000s, things had changed.

Odia nationalism, which had once antagonized non-Odia RSP workers, had waned, and its impact on RSP's recruitment policy and on shop floor relations was more muted. Once economic liberalization was under way, attracting international corporate capital to Odisha became the chief concern of state government and the elite (Sengupta 2007). As of 1989 the local employment exchange considered applications only from persons holding a residential certificate, which was predicated on twelve years of uninterrupted residence in the state. Young migrants from other states were often disqualified because they had spent part of their childhood or adolescence in their home states. At this point, then, almost all RSP workers were either Odias or Adivasis from Odisha. By the mid 2000s the generational change of the RSP workforce was almost complete. Only a few RSP workers still lived in *basti*s and resettlement colonies, and they were about to retire. Many had retired already, and the few sons who had followed in their fathers' footsteps as regular RSP workers had all moved into the township. Adivasis from other parts of northern Odisha who had joined RSP in large numbers during the 1990s had settled in the township and not, as in previous generations, joined relatives outside it. Though the *basti*s and resettlement colonies remained largely Adivasi areas, they were now ever more exclusively inhabited by informal-sector workers making a living from precarious (self-)employment as construction workers, drivers, tailors, distillers and sellers of illicit liquor, contract workers in the RSP or in private-sector factories, or petty contractors or *goonda*s—jobs that are often supplemented by some kitchen gardening and rice farming. So whereas many Adivasis now lived in the township, hardly any RSP workers were left in the *basti*s or resettlement colonies. So even though the distinction between the *basti*s and resettlement colonies on the one hand, and the township on the other, became more muted in terms of the ethnic segregation between Adivasis and the rest, in class terms the residential segregation had sharpened significantly.

"Educated" and "Uneducated" Workers

Like Bhola, all new township settlers I talked to mentioned their children's educational prospects as the reason for their residential choice. *Basti*s like Nag Nadi are officially considered illegal encroachments, so they have no schools at all. In the 1980s a housing colony was established adjacent to Nag Nadi (see next section below), and the children of the *basti* started attending schools there. Even in the resettlement colonies schools were not opened until the 1970s. The township, however, had them from its start. Moreover, the resettlement colony schools are run by the state government, which means they are poorly funded and staffed and have lower standards, compared with company schools in the township. Quite apart from its schools, life in the township is itself considered an education. Residents live surrounded by "educated" neighbors who see to it that their children study and learn proper speech and manners. Conversely, proper education of children is held to be almost impossible for someone living in Rourkela's slums or resettlement colonies, where money is drunk, not saved, and parents give no thought to the future. Many Odias regard the Adivasis' lack of interest in education as part of the natural order of things and find it unremarkable that *basti* people should be poorly educated. It is indeed the case that some of the latter spend a significant proportion of their meager earnings on drink and pay little heed to school attendance. It is difficult to map out a future when life is so insecure (cf. Parry 2013b: 68f.). My general impression, however, is that education is a major concern, not only for regular RSP workers but also for many in the informal sector who live in *basti*s and resettlement colonies, and regardless of whether or not they are Adivasis—an impression supported by evidence from all over India (cf. Jeffrey, Jeffery, and Jeffery 2005). Of course, the kind of education parents are able to offer their children depends on the kinds of schools and tuition classes they have access to. The pay and perks of a regular RSP worker provide an obvious advantage in that regard, as does an "educated" environment of the kind that the township provides. It is hardly surprising that the "Panicker people," like the displaced people who finally got RSP jobs, deserted their *basti*s for the township as soon as space became available there.

Only in the early 2000s did RSP become able to accommodate its entire workforce, which by then had shrunk to less than 24,000. Its residential quarters are spread over nineteen sectors, each divided into an unequal number of blocks. One such block was built in the early 1990s for the international personnel expected to play a key role in modernizing RSP in those years. One sector, which initially housed the workforce of the Rourkela Fertilizer Plant, metamorphosed into an additional RSP township sector, but only after the plant was closed in 2003. The township has always accommodated some non-employees, and quite a few employees illicitly sublet their company quarters. From the early 1970s to the early 1990s, the township accommodated little more than half of the company's regular workforce.

But the size of the township does not in itself explain why, in earlier days, some RSP workers moved into the township while others did not. Bhola's father became a regular RSP worker in 1962 and was entitled to a township quarter, but did not consider moving. Many older workers allotted township quarters in the 1970s or 1980s preferred to rent them out unofficially because they preferred living in the *basti* or the resettlement colony. People from the better parts of Rourkela took this as a clear sign that "these people" have no interest in education. Managers regularly alleged that "such people" sublet their quarters with the sole aim of obtaining extra money for liquor. Indeed, the handful of RSP workers who now remain in Nag Nadi have all been allotted RSP housing, and they all sublet for a monthly rent of around 700 rupees. But unlike comparative youngsters like Bhola, those who stayed on in the *basti* were coming up for retirement. Their children were beyond school age, so they did not have the same incentive to move.

Retired Adivasi RSP workers, like Bhola's father, explain their reluctance to move by pointing out that their houses in the *basti* are larger and more comfortable than the township quarters to which RSP workers of their grade would have been entitled, and their garden plots and fields are nearby. Women especially tend to prefer to stay where they are. In the township, many elderly women in particular felt confined and condemned to enforced idleness. Even nowadays, Adivasi and Odia neighbors in the township seldom maintain close links. In the past Odias, as well as other non-Adivasis, were often outspokenly disdainful of Adivasi culture and customs. Though I was never told so explicitly, it seems likely that Adivasis saw this as a further disincentive to living in the township.[11] Before the 1990s, there was of course no sign that India would liberalize its economy, that SAIL would reduce manpower so drastically, or that regular permanent employment would be restricted to those with far better educational qualifications. The many Adivasi RSP workers living in *basti*s and resettlement colonies had little reason to worry much about school standards or put up with snooty neighbors.

Nowadays, Adivasis living in *basti*s and resettlement colonies also complain about the snootiness of their erstwhile neighbors who have moved into the township. Adivasis living in the township remain tied to them by kinship and the ritual and social obligations that come along with it. But the education they seek for their children entails maintaining a distance from the "uneducated." If they socialize, the Adivasi regular RSP worker or his wife makes sure that they do so in *basti*s or resettlement colonies. Such people won't feel comfortable in the township quarters, town residents say: they are not used to sitting at a table, so they will not like eating there. The construction or contract workers from the *basti* suspect that their posh relatives' reluctance to entertain them in their company quarters is not due to worries about their guests' comfort, but to anxiety about their reputation among their township neighbors. It remains to be seen whether and how this growing distance will affect marital choices in the future. It very likely will, but at the time of my research their children had not reached the age of marriage. The divide is already reflected in their political relationship, however. Unlike before, Adivasi RSP workers no longer come out in support of displaced people's claims for regular employment. In fact, Adivasi RSP workers living in the township and their Odia colleagues are equally likely to consider it a burden to work with people who live in *basti*s and resettlement colonies and allegedly are regularly drunk and absent.

From the start, the Adivasis were marginalized by Nehruvian industrial modernity. Considered a class of uneducated laborers, those who were provided with regular RSP employment found themselves at the bottom of the shop floor hierarchy despite their legal status as permanent public-sector steelworkers. They were also pushed into the *basti*s and resettlement colonies at the fringes of the township, where the next generation was reproduced as a class of uneducated laborers. In the wake of economic liberalization in the 1990s and the subsequent restructuring of India's public sector, this class was excluded from regular employment and left with no alternative to precarious (self-)employment in the informal sector. The few people from the *basti*s and resettlement colonies who still had RSP jobs left these places for the sake of their children's future. The RSP workforce as a whole now lived segregated from precarious informal-sector workers, even as it distanced itself politically from the latter's claims for RSP employment.

Urban Development, Informal Livelihoods, and Precariousness

The largely Adivasi inhabitants of Rourkela's *basti*s were rendered even more precarious by urban development projects pursued over the last forty years. A few years before the first generation of RSP workers started retiring in large numbers in the late 1980s, three housing colonies were established by the Odisha State Housing Board, the Rourkela Development Authority, and the Housing and Urban Development Corporation (all statutory government bodies). Their purpose was to relieve pressure on Rourkela's overall housing stock, and specifically for retiring RSP employees who wanted to remain in Rourkela but had to vacate their township quarters. The three colonies differ in size. Chhend is the largest, with a current population of about 45,000. Basanti has about 35,000 and Koelnagar, 20,000.[12] They also differ in social composition. Koelnagar has a large number of retired RSP executives and a higher proportion of migrants from outside Odisha. In the other two colonies, retired lower-level executives and manual workers from Odisha predominate. All three are planned urban development projects that provide the same public amenities as the RSP township, though less well-funded and of lower quality.

Chhend, built in 1984, was contiguous with Nag Nadi, my base in Rourkela between 2004 and 2009. On my return in 2011, shortly after India's decennial census, Nag Nadi had around 250 households, almost all of which were Scheduled Tribe Mundaris. The settlement had existed before the RSP was planned, and in 2004 its elderly inhabitants still remembered their eviction in the 1950s. They had moved to a resettlement colony two kilometers away from the steel plant, but some had returned to their old village site in the mid 1960s to avoid the ethnic violence that swept the colony in the wake of the Rourkela communal riots in 1964, and because they wanted to reclaim their fields and work them, besides working the regular RSP job that most of them had. Some of their fields were lost when Chhend was constructed in the early 1980s. They had tried to obstruct the building site, but the police broke up their protest and detained the demonstrators. In 2005, when some of them lost land again—this time due to a housing development that the State Bank of India was building for forty senior officers—their resistance was again quickly broken with the help of a powerful *goonda* who appeared at the site and recruited a few young aspiring *goonda*s from Nag Nadi itself. The expansion of the town affects other *basti*s similarly. Yet the new urban housing colonies also provided *basti* dwellers with opportunities to earn informal income in various ways. Masons, carpenters, and painters from Nag Nadi helped to build Chhend colony. Their reliance on such informal wage labor or self-employment is, of course, a consequence of their shrinking access to land and their lack of access to regular RSP employment.

Urban development and the ensuing conflicts over land gained new momentum in 2013. Rourkela was considered for an administrative reclassification from municipality to municipal corporation. The issue was highly controversial, though everybody agreed that "if Rourkela turns into a municipal corporation, you won't be able to recognize it in five years' time." But while many were enthusiastic about the town's prospects if the change went ahead, others were extremely apprehensive. Enthusiasts were typically residents of the housing colonies, whereas denizens of the *basti*s and resettlement colonies were anxious. Municipal corporations enjoy higher status than municipalities and receive much larger grants from the state government. However, a municipal corporation must have a minimum population of 300,000, and the Rourkela municipality had only 270,000 inhabitants. The whole Rourkela urban agglomeration is of course much larger, but of its 550,000 inhabitants, 210,000 live in the RSP township and a further 70,000 in several adjacent villages with *gram panchayat*s (village councils) of their own. The RSP township was to remain under the jurisdiction of SAIL, so the only way to make up for the deficit of 30,000 inhabitants and to become eligible for the status of a municipal corporation was to absorb some of the surrounding village (*panchayat*) areas.

Many *panchayat*s rejected that option because corporation status was thought to entail substantially higher taxes on land as well as higher charges for electricity and water. In the resettlement colonies, people also worried that they would lose their homes because they still did not have title deeds for the house plots they had received as compensation for their displacement in the 1950s. This fear was particularly acute in *basti*s like Nag Nadi, where inhabitants had already learned that they would be considered encroachers without any rights to compensation, should the municipality decide to "develop" their area. Under a municipal corporation, they reckoned, development would inevitably accelerate. As encroachments, moreover, such *basti*s did not have constituted *panchayat*s that were entitled to reject their integration into the new corporation.

Resistance to the proposal took the form of demonstrations, sit-ins, and blockades of local market centers and rail connections. These provoked the usual police violence. On one occasion a violent clash with armed police in the vicinity of Nag Nadi was followed by the arbitrary arrest of dozens of *basti* residents. Middle-class housing colony residents generally denounced this opposition and put it down to the irrationality of the "uneducated," "wild" Adivasi who live in such places, or alternatively to their innocent gullibility, which allowed them to be easily manipulated by cynical politicians. For their part, most *basti* dwellers were pessimistic about their chances of success. They now questioned not only their chances of remaining part of the public-sector steel workforce, but also their very existence in the town. Their sense of precarity derived not only from the precarious (self-)employment on which they are forced to rely, but also increasingly from the precarity of their homes and of their other sources of livelihood.

Conclusion

Ever since the 1950s, "autochthony" has figured prominently in people's claims to the relatively privileged regular employment that RSP provides. Claims were raised by people identifying as Odia or as Adivasi, but with varying levels of success. Early on, the Odisha state government had strongly supported "local" people's claims to RSP jobs. It argued that RSP was supposed to foster regional development and bring regular, remunerative employment to the people of one of India's most backward regions. This assertiveness had to do with the political situation prevailing in the state at the time: in 1948, less than a decade before the advent of RSP, Odisha's western uplands (where Rourkela is located) merged, not quite voluntarily, into a single political entity with the coastal lowlands, which itself had just received autonomous political status within India after a long struggle for independence from colonial Bengal. In this climate, every political party had a strong interest in presenting itself as a guardian of local interests vis-à-vis outsiders. Meanwhile, different groups drew boundaries in different ways. Some aimed to safeguard Odia interests against those of other states or the central government, some to protect Odisha's western hills against colonizers from the state's coast, and some to shield the Adivasi people of the uplands against all non-Adivasi, but primarily Odia.

When the RSP arrived in the contested border region of northwestern Odisha, together with thousands of migrants from other parts of Odisha and elsewhere, it became vital for the government of Odisha to advocate RSP employment as serving the interests of local people. The result was that the Odia who staffed government departments allocated jobs only to Odia and disregarded local Adivasi interests. Later on, though, autochthonous Adivasis had some success in securing regular RSP jobs when large numbers of non-Odia RSP workers were antagonized by Odia nationalism. In the wake of India's economic liberalization in the 1990s and the subsequent restructuring of its public-sector industries, the RSP workforce took on a different shape. The first generation of RSP workers retired, and the new one recruited in its place was less numerous and expected to have higher educational credentials. Since the largely Adivasi people in Rourkela's *bastis* and resettlement colonies have been disadvantaged in schooling, they have again lost out. From the start their residential areas were segregated from the RSP township, which provided its largely Odia inhabitants with high-standard educational institutions, in addition to hospitals, recreational facilities, and civic amenities.

Nowadays the RSP workforce and its unions are no longer willing to support the claims of the people from *basti*s and resettlement colonies, as at least some of them did in the last century. Economic liberalization has somewhat muted the Odia nationalism around the public-sector undertaking, and the RSP workers from other states who were antagonized by it have retired and moved away. Furthermore, Adivasis who work for RSP have withdrawn into the township for the sake of their children's education and future employment prospects. They now distance themselves socially from their uneducated erstwhile neighbors in *basti*s and resettlement colonies, and politically from their claims for compensatory RSP employment. In this relationship, class has taken precedence over ethnicity, depriving the precarious laborers in Rourkela's precarious boroughs of a once-close ally.

Acknowledgments

My field research in Rourkela extended over roughly thirty-two months and was conducted at intervals between 2004 and 2014. I gratefully acknowledge the support of the German Research Council

(Deutsche Forschungsgemeinschaft), the Max Planck Institute for Social Anthropology, Heidelberg University, and the Work and Human Lifecycle in Global History research center at Humboldt University, Berlin. I am also indebted to Rajat Singh and Ganesh Hembram for their invaluable research assistance.

Christian Strümpell holds a replacement professorship at the Institute of Social and Cultural Anthropology at Hamburg University. He earned his Ph.D. in Social Anthropology at the Free University of Berlin in 2004 and has held research positions at the Max Planck Institute for Social Anthropology, Halle, at the South Asia Institute at Heidelberg University, and at the research center *Work and the Human Lifecycle in Global History* at Humboldt University, Berlin. He has conducted ethnographic research on industrial workers in India and Bangladesh, and published in journals such as *Contributions to Indian Sociology*, *Economic and Political Weekly*, *Citizenship Studies*, and *Modern Asian Studies*.

Notes

1. Some RSP workers and regular workers in other enterprises lived in the surrounding countryside, but these were a minority.
2. For a detailed West German account of the construction of the Rourkela Steel Plant, including the misbehavior of West German personnel on and off the construction sites, see Sperling (1969).
3. The Odisha state government committee enquiring into grievances at Rourkela in 1959 demanded regular RSP employment for "Odishans" (then Orissans), i.e., people from Odisha defined on a territorial basis to include Odias as well as Odisha's Adivasis (Mardaraj Deo 1959: 9). However, in the very same report the committee often used only the ethnic term "Odia" (ibid.: 10), which in common parlance excluded Adivasis (cf. Strümpell 2011; Weiner 1978: 299–324).
4. For a detailed discussion of the history of the Jharkhand Movement and varying perceptions of the Jharkhand state, see Corbridge, Jewitt, and Kumar (2005 [2004]); Shah (2010).
5. For a detailed account of ethnic violence in Rourkela and a comparison with the very different scenario around the RSP's sister undertaking in Bhilai, Chhattisgarh, see Parry and Strümpell 2008.
6. The authorities erected a few showcase dwellings, some in the "traditional," "tribal" style of their abandoned houses; see Sperling (1963: 20).
7. In 1955 the state government had acquired around 20,000 acres from thirty-two revenue villages for the steel plant and township. In 1959 another 11,000 acres were acquired from a further thirty-one revenue villages for the Mandira Dam and Reservoir that supply Rourkela with water (Xaxa 2006: 121). The number of

households displaced by RSP is more difficult to assess. Ratha and Behera (1990) give a figure of 2,465 displaced households. An official letter from a high-ranking Rourkela administrator says 2,976. The Mandira Dam displaced another 8,785 people from 941 households (Xaxa 2006: 101). The land was handed over to Hindustan Steel Ltd., the central government holding company (the predecessor of SAIL). Some land was also handed over to the Indian Railways for the construction of a railway marshaling yard and its associated township. The yard was required for handling the transport of raw materials for the plant and its finished products.

8. In 2008 a regular RSP worker in grade 8 (out of 11), after roughly twenty years of service, was earning a gross monthly wage of around 20,000 rupees. A contract worker earned slightly more than 3,000 rupees if he was employed throughout the month, which was by no means certain.

9. The agreement revealed that until then almost one-quarter of the households displaced in the 1950s had remained uncompensated by RSP employment.

10. Several sectors of the economy had been "liberalized" by stealth much earlier (Nayar 2004: 86–128; see also Münster and Strümpell 2014; Neveling 2014).

11. Many Mundas, Oraons, and other Adivasis often expressed their admiration for Santals on account of their "boldness" in speaking their tribal language in front of others. It is probably not by chance that quite a few Santal RSP workers moved into the RSP township as early as the 1960s.

12. These figures are only approximations and include people from *bastis* in or on the fringes of the colonies that come under the same wards. None of these settlements was built on completely vacant land that was strictly "unutilized surplus." Their construction entailed evictions from *basti* hutments, gardens, and fields. Unlike in the 1950s, however, this time people faced eviction without any entitlement to compensation. Officially, they were encroachers on government land.

References

Bailey, Frederick G. 1959. "The Ganatantra Parishad." *Economic Weekly* 11(43–44): 1469–1476.

———. 1963. *Politics and Social Change: Orissa in 1959*. Berkeley, CA: University of California Press.

———. 1998. *The Need for Enemies: A Bestiary of Political Forms*. Ithaca, NY: Cornell University Press.

Barick, Bidyadhar. 1989. "Labour Market Study in Rourkela." In *ILO-ARTEP, Employment and Structural Change in Indian Industries: A Trade Union Viewpoint*, 65–70. New Delhi: ARTEP.

Behera, Deepak K. 1996. "Plight of the Tribal Workers of Rourkela Steel Plant of Orissa." *Man in India* 76(3): 239–251.

Breman, Jan. 1994. *Wage Hunters and Gatherers: Search for Work in the Urban and Rural Economy of South Gujarat*. Delhi: Oxford University Press.

Corbridge, Stuart., Sarah Jewitt, and Sanjay Kumar. 2005 [2004]. *Jharkhand: Environment, Development, Ethnicity*. New Delhi: Oxford University Press.

Cross, Jamie. 2010. "Neoliberalism as Unexceptional: Economic Zones and the Everyday Precariousness of Working Life in South India." *Critique of Anthropology* 30(4): 355–373.

Jeffrey, Craig, Roger Jeffery, and Patricia Jeffery. 2005. "Broken Trajectories: Dalit Young Men and Formal Education." In *Educational Regimes in Contemporary India*, ed. R. Chopra and P. Jeffrey, 256–275. New Delhi: Sage.

Khilnani, Sunil. 2003 [1997]. *The Idea of India*. London: Penguin Books.

Mardaraj Deo, Ramachandra, et al. 1959. *Report on Rourkela*. Cuttack: Orissa Government Press.

Mohanty, Pravat K. 1988. *Collective Bargaining in the Steel Industry*. Delhi: Discovery.

Münster, Daniel, and Christian Strümpell. 2014. "The Anthropology of Neoliberal India: An Introduction." *Contributions to Indian Sociology* (n.s.) 48(1): 1–16.

Nayar, Baldev R. 2004 [2001]. *Globalization and Nationalism: The Changing Balance in India's Economic Policy, 1950–2000*. New Delhi: Sage.

Neveling, Patrick. 2014. "Structural Contingencies and Untimely Coincidences in the Making of Neoliberal India: The Kandla Free Trade Zone, 1965–1991." *Contributions to Indian Sociology* (n.s.) 48(1): 17–43.

Omvedt, Gail. 1981. "Steel Workers, Contract Labourers and Adivasis." *Economic and Political Weekly* 16(30): 1227–1229.

Parry, Jonathan P. 1999. "Lords of Labour: Working and Shirking in Bhilai." In *The Worlds of Indian Industrial Labour*, ed. J.P. Parry, J. Breman, and K. Kapadia, 107–140. New Delhi: Sage.

———. 2009. "'Sociological Marxism' in Central India: Polanyi, Gramsci, and the Case of the Unions." In *Market and Society: The Great Transformation Today*, ed. C. Hann and K. Hart, 175–202. Cambridge: Cambridge University Press.

———. 2013a. "Company and Contract Labour in a Central Indian Steel Plant." *Economy and Society* 42(3): 348–374.

———. 2013b. "The 'Embourgeoisement' of a 'Proletarian Vanguard'?" In *Interrogating India's Modernity: Democracy, Identity, and Citizenship. Essays in Honour of Dipankar Gupta*, ed. S.S. Jodhka, 40–78. New Delhi: Oxford University Press.

Parry, Jonathan P., and Christian Strümpell. 2008. "On the Desecration of Nehru's 'Temples': Bhilai and Rourkela Compared." *Economic and Political Weekly* 43(19): 47–57.

Ratha, S.N., and Deepak K. Behera. 1990. "Displacement and Rehabilitation: Data from the Resettled Colonies around the Steel Plant at Rourkela, Orissa." *Man in Asia* 3(1): 10–23.

Roy, Srirupa. 2007. *Beyond Belief: India and the Politics of Postcolonial Nationalism*. Durham, NC: Duke University Press.

Sengupta, Jayanta. 2007. "Imagined Chronologies: Perceptions of 'Development' as a Tool in Mapping Oriya Identity." In *Time in India: Concepts and Practices*, ed. A. Malinar, 287–313. New Delhi: Manohar.

Shah, Alpa. 2010. *In the Shadows of the State: Indigenous Politics, Environmentalism, and Insurgency in Jharkhand, India*. Durham, NC: Duke University Press.

Sperling, Jan Bodo. 1963. *Rourkela: Sozio-ökonomische Probleme eines Entwicklungsprojekts* [Rourkela: Socioeconomic problems of a development project]. Bonn: Eichholz Verlag.

———. 1969. *The Human Dimension of Technical Assistance: The German Experience of Rourkela, India*. Ithaca, NY: Cornell University Press.

Standing, Guy. 2014 [2011]. *The Precariat: The New Dangerous Class*. London: Bloomsbury.

Strümpell, Christian. 2011. "Social Citizenship and Ethnicity around a Public Sector Steel Plant in Orissa, India." *Citizenship Studies* 15(3–4): 485–498.

———. 2014. "The Politics of Dispossession in an Odishan Steel Town." *Contributions to Indian Sociology* (n.s.), 48(1): 45–72.

Weiner, Myron. 1978. *Sons of the Soil: Migration and Ethnic Conflict in India*. Princeton, NJ: University Press.

Xaxa, Celestine. 2006. "The Life and Struggles of the Displaced Adivasis of Sundargarh District in Orissa." *Sarini Occasional Papers: Adivasis of Rourkela. Looking Back on 50 Years of Indo-German Economic Cooperation; Documents – Interpretations – International Law, no. 4*, 97–119. Retrieved 31 March 2015 from www.adivasi-koordination.de/dokumente/RKLReader.pdf.

6

Regimes of Precarity

Buruh, Karyawan, *and the Politics of Labor Identity in Indonesia*

Daromir Rudnyckyj

"We're not workers, we're employees!" Umar defiantly told me as we discussed events at Krakatau Steel's hot strip mill. We were sitting in his compact house on the outskirts of Serang, Banten's new provincial capital, discussing a political movement that he had been pivotal in founding at Krakatau Steel, a major state-owned enterprise in Indonesia and one of the largest steel companies in Southeast Asia. I had met Umar, a large man with a voice and demeanor that matched his imposing presence, midway through my fieldwork in Banten. Originally from Palembang on the island of Sumatra, he had followed his brother to the province, ultimately gaining employment at Krakatau Steel in 1985. After several months of pestering, he had finally consented to tell me the story of how he and several others at the hot strip mill had tried to improve labor conditions and remuneration by starting an employee activist group outside the formal union structure.

We had just begun our conversation when I irritated Umar by referring to him and his colleagues as "workers" (*buruh*). He responded gruffly that "we're not workers, we're from a state-owned company! Employees (*karyawan*) are different from workers!" The distinction between workers and employees that Umar took as self-evident had not been explicitly expressed to me until this moment in my fieldwork, and his indignation resulted in the following exchange:

DR: I see. So you are employees. What's the difference?
Umar: Employees have permanent positions (*berkeja tetap*) ... they
        usually have a salary, maybe benefits (*kesejahteraan*).
DR: Oh, I see. So they are better off compared to normal workers?

Umar: The connotation of workers is … employees who can be let go (*karywan yang kerja lepas*).

DR: What do you mean, "let go" (*lepas*)?

Umar: Not stable, they can be laid off whenever (*di-PHK[1] kapanpun*), their wages are small, their benefits are not so good. They always make demands and demonstrate in front of the parliament when they are laid off. That's the difference.

DR: OK, so "employee" means that you can't be laid off at any time. That's the definition of a state-owned employee?

Umar: Well, we can be laid off, but there is a long process … It takes a long time to lay us off … it is not as easy as with workers. That's a worker. If you say, "you're a worker, you're an employee" there has to be a distinction.

This chapter contextualizes the distinction that Umar was making. I show how it was grounded in the labor politics characteristic of Indonesia's authoritarian regime and its rabid anti-communism. I briefly describe the historical context of this distinction and the significance of Krakatau Steel, the specific geographical context in which I encountered it. I then describe the labor hierarchy at Krakatau Steel and the division of workers into two distinct categories. Most visible were the "permanent" (*tetap*), salaried employees with benefits, but the company also relied on the labor of "contract workers" (*pekerja kontrak*), who were hired and paid by third-party "suppliers" and occupied a far more precarious position in terms of both the conditions of their work and the labor they performed. I argue that this distinctive labor strategy was a key political strategy of the authoritarian regime, which sought to foreclose workers' political activism—initially to suppress communism and later to make the country an attractive destination for foreign direct investment concordant with an export-led growth development strategy. The chapter concludes with a description of how even "permanent" workers were being subjected to a new regime of precarity through a program of institutionalized, factory-sponsored Islamization.

I argue that laborers at Krakatau Steel were faced with two distinct regimes of precarity. The initial regime segmented company employees into a group of permanent, salaried employees and another group of contract laborers, who had less training and no company guarantees. It was this latter group that was subjected to labor discipline through precarity, insofar as the steel company made little investment in their skills and their positions were tenuous and impermanent. Quite simply, they could be let go at any time. However, following the collapse of the Suharto regime and growing pressure on Krakatau Steel to become self-sufficient, permanent employees too were exposed to a regime of precarity. Unlike that of the contract laborers, their regime entailed subjection to the specter of the free market and threats that the company would not survive increasing competition (Rudnyckyj 2009a). Thus, company managers repeatedly mentioned that the number of jobs at the factory far exceeded the volume of labor actually required and threatened workers with the probability of widespread layoffs. Here my emphasis is on the techniques that managers deploy to create what I refer to as regimes of precarity at Krakatau Steel.

Labor Politics and Indonesian Anti-Communism

Umar's indignation at being called a worker highlighted the politics and representation of labor in Indonesia following the end of the Suharto regime. For the most part, scholars of Indonesia have been puzzled as to why organized labor did not play a larger role in the political transformations associated with *reformasi* (reform) and their aftermath, even though between two and six million Indonesian wage laborers lost their jobs in wake of the economic crisis (van Dijk 2001: 94). In the years leading up to Suharto's downfall, some had predicted that workers would play a leading role in the nascent pro-democracy movement (Hadiz 1997). However, as Jeffrey Winters (2000: 148–149) has noted, "labour had failed to step into the new political space ... not only did no major parties try to mobilize workers qua workers, the word '*buruh*' (worker) was scarcely ever mentioned by any political elites during the election campaigns." Many regard the absence of an active working-class political movement after the authoritarian state's demise as a conundrum.

Umar's response also underscored the success of the Suharto regime's efforts to discourage left-wing political activism based on labor solidarity and class consciousness. His insistence on the contingency of work compared to the stability of employment reveals that precarity was central to how worker identity was defined. This distinction was a key technology used by the Suharto regime to divide workers and preclude political alliances grounded in labor. Indeed, the regime had come to power in the aftermath of an alleged attempt by Indonesian communists to seize power in the 1960s. At Krakatau Steel and across the country, workers with any connection to communism had been blacklisted and in many cases imprisoned. At Krakatau Steel I interviewed one former employee of the company who, prior to the 1965 coup, had served as a screener to weed out prospective company employees who were "of the extreme left" and "extreme right." By the former he meant anyone who had been affiliated with the Indonesian Communist Party. In fact, he explained, a prospective employee whose parents or even extended family members had been in a labor union sympathetic to the Communist Party prior to 1965 would likewise be denied employment at Krakatau Steel, even if the given applicant had personally never claimed membership in such an organization. The "extreme right" referred to Muslim militant groups that had fought to establish an Islamic state in Indonesia in the 1950s and 1960s. Ever fearful of the threat of communism, the Suharto regime carefully created divisions among the Krakatau Steel workforce to foreclose any potential activism. Furthermore, following other Asian Tigers and the export-led growth models of development that had been so successful in neighboring parts of East and Southeast Asia, the state sought to create a working population that was docile, politically impotent, and hence attractive to foreign capital.

Krakatau Steel and Indonesian Modernization

Krakatau Steel is located in Banten, at the western edge of the island of Java. As a province Banten is new, founded in 2000, but it is based on the boundaries of an early modern Islamic sultanate. In the sixteenth and seventeenth centuries, Banten was a cosmopolitan node in the trade networks that connected the Java Sea with the Indian and Pacific Oceans (Guillot 1992). After the Indonesian revolution of 1945–1949, the region was the site of several development initiatives. Having decided to build, with Soviet support, Indonesia's first steelworks, the nationalist Sukarno government chose to locate it in Banten, mainly because of the province's accessibility to sea-based trade networks (Purwadi et al. 2003). Thus, when construction of the first steelworks on the site, known as PT Trikora, started in the early 1960s, it was Soviet engineers who offered the primary outside expertise. Although construction ceased following the 1965 military coup that brought Suharto to power, it was resuscitated in the early 1970s—this time without Soviet aid—as a centerpiece of national development under the import substitution industrialization prong of Indonesia's New Order development strategy (Hill 2000; Rock 2003).[2]

The planners now sought to expand the factory, renamed Krakatau Steel, onto land that was the site of several coconut groves farmed by smallholding agriculturalists, who received cash payments to relocate beyond the periphery of the vast new industrial zone. The site was also home to the Al-Khairiyah madrassa, the most important religious school in the region. The head of the school, Kiyai Rachmatullah, consented to move it to the adjacent village of Citangkil. In return, the company agreed to construct new buildings. Though they likely looked impressive in the 1970s, by the mid 2000s they had fallen into obvious disrepair and looked forlorn and neglected. Nonetheless, Krakatau Steel was central to the project of modernization that preoccupied Indonesia's longtime strongman president, Suharto, and the company thus became the backbone of a sprawling industrial region adjacent to the town of Cilegon.[3]

Krakatau Steel played an important role in the Indonesian national imaginary because it produced a material that was viewed as absolutely critical to the state's nationalist project of modernization. It occupied an iconic position in the nation and was frequently visited by the Indonesian President and other official dignitaries.[4] Indeed, Krakatau Steel was a paradigmatic site for the emergence of what Ferguson (1999) has referred to as "faith in development": the optimistic modernist conviction that importing technology to facilitate industrialization will bring economic growth and enhanced living standards. The 1998 Asian financial crisis, the end of the Suharto regime, and the increasing integration of Indonesia into a wider global economy have called that faith into question.

From the 1970s until the mid-1990s, Krakatau Steel had been the recipient of billions of dollars in state development funds. In those years state investment guaranteed the company's viability by enabling it to keep up with advances in steel production technology. However, such investment came to an end in 1998 after the near bankruptcy of the Indonesian government. Tariffs on imported steel that had long protected the company from international competition were fully eliminated in April 2004, and China emerged as a threat to the Indonesian steel industry. Employees feared that once the Chinese economy began to slow down, China would flood the Indonesian market with cheap, imported steel. At the same time, new legal protections for workers offered unprecedented possibilities for factory employees' political mobilization, including the formation of a new labor union. Finally, and perhaps most ominously for some employees, the Indonesian government explored the possibility of privatizing Krakatau Steel, which, if pursued, could trigger sweeping job losses for members of a workforce who had previously been able to count on lifetime employment.

These changes represented a re-evaluation of Krakatau Steel's symbolic and material relationship to the nation and its project of developmental modernization. Given the structural changes taking place, the company's existence could no longer be justified with reference to its status as an icon of modernization and industrialization. The re-evaluation of the company's position in the nation was often evident during the period of my research for this project (2003–2005, with a shorter return visit in 2008). A foreman in the slab steel plant at Krakatau Steel explained to me that prior to the late 1990s, "the social was the most important and profit was secondary," but "now profit is number one and the social mission [*misi sosial*] is number two." He said that this "social mission" was premised upon *padat karya*, literally "dense work," which refers to the past practice of hiring more workers than necessary to operate a business. This practice was common at many Indonesian businesses, including both state-owned enterprises and private corporations. At Krakatau Steel, a thinly veiled debate pitted those who sought to preserve the company's earlier mission to "support the livelihoods of the masses" (*hajat hidup orang banyak*) against those who wanted to make the company competitive in an increasingly global steel market by subjecting its operations and workforce to stricter cost-benefit calculations.

As noted already, construction had lapsed after the military coup of 1965 and Indonesia's turn away from the Soviet bloc and toward the West. The period between 1972 and 1995 marked the heyday of Krakatau Steel, when the company and its workers were flush with cash and halcyon fantasies of industrial utopianism. Under the patronage of B.J. Habibie, the longtime minister of research and technology and later vice-president, the Suharto government had spared little expense to bring the most up-to-date, high-technology steelmaking equipment to Krakatau Steel. After construction of the first direct reduction plant in 1972, a series of new plants were brought on line. By 1979 the billet plant and wire rod mill were completed. In 1983 President Suharto officially opened plants constructed under the company's "second-stage development" plan, including the steel slab plant and the hot strip mill. In 1993, the expansion and modernization of the hot strip mill led to a corresponding expansion in both the organization of the company and the number of managerial jobs. Suharto again visited the company after a major expansion of the facilities in 1995, when the third direct reduction facility (Hyl 3) and another slab steel plant were completed ("Krakatau Steel Expands" 1996). Whenever the company built new plants, there was a corresponding expansion of managerial positions for employees who had worked at the factory and felt entitled to promotions.

Karyawan and *Buruh* at Krakatau Steel

Precarity did not just differentiate laborers at Krakatau Steel from the low-skilled workers at factories dedicated toward export production. It was also evident in different categorizations of workers within the steel company itself. The factory hired two distinct classes of workers. On the one hand, "permanent" (*tetap*) or "organic" (*organik*) workers who called themselves *karyawan* (employees) had guaranteed employment, earned salaries, and drew a full range of benefits. On the other hand, a less visible category of worker at Krakatau Steel included the permanent employees referred to as "contract workers" (*pekerja kontrak*) or *buruh*, which translated literally can mean "labor "or "laborer," connoting the physical work that these employees often performed. Although they took their orders from organic Krakatau Steel employees, these workers were actually hired and paid by third-party subcontractors. Thus, they were employed only on a fixed-term basis and did not receive any supplementary benefits as part of their compensation.

Krakatau Steel employed about ten thousand people during the period of my research in the mid 2000s, but only about six thousand of these were full-time, organic employees. The remaining four thousand fell under the category of contract employees. These workers often performed the most laborious and hazardous tasks at the factory. I routinely saw contract employees arc welding and doing other dangerous jobs without proper safety gear. The organic employees, in contrast, were less frequently involved in physically demanding tasks and generally staffed the control rooms of the various plants. They often attributed the difference in their respective labor conditions and pay to their superior education and training. However, ethnicity was another axis of difference. For the most part, organic Krakatau Steel employees were not from Banten, but were born in other parts of Indonesia. Most identified as either Sundanese or Javanese and did not speak the local Bantenese language. They called themselves "newcomers" (*pendatang*) to Banten and saw themselves as superior to the Bantenese, who were viewed as uncouth, rough (*kasar*), and uneducated. Although Krakatau Steel had been established in the 1970s, local Bantenese were not hired as organic workers at Krakatau Steel until the mid 1990s. The contract employees were overwhelmingly local Bantenese from the region surrounding Cilegon. Many hoped that their experience working as contractor laborers would eventually lead to a permanent position at Krakatau Steel, but by the 2000s, with state largesse on the wane, this was becoming an increasingly dim prospect.

Within the plant itself, the two categories of workers were easily identifiable. The permanent workers strutted around the various mills of the factory in smart-looking blue-collar uniforms consisting of a dark blue denim work shirt and matching pants. Employees referred to this uniform as "Levi's," as they resembled the popular American brand of blue jeans. Indeed, on occasion I saw some employees match their denim tops with commercially available blue jeans. The shirt featured the employee's name embroidered in dark blue on a white patch sewn over the right breast pocket. A matching patch noting the specific mill where the employee worked was sewn on the upper portion of the right-hand sleeve. The company name—PT Krakatau Steel—was embroidered in red above the left breast pocket. The smartly dressed look of the staff lent an air of professionalism to the factory operations, especially at some of the newer mills, such as the slab steel plant, hot strip mill, and cold rolling mill. The operations uniform was capped by

Figure 6.1. A group of "organic employees" after *asar* (afternoon) prayers at the mosque outside Krakatau Steel's hot strip mill. Note the formal "Levi's" uniform, official workplace badges, and patches.

a smart-looking white work helmet with the Krakatau Steel logo featured prominently above the visor.

In contrast, contract workers could be discerned by the absence of any standardized uniform. In most cases they did not wear uniforms at all and worked in worn t-shirts or soiled work shirts. Their helmets were obviously of low quality and seemed unlikely to offer any protection in the event of an accident. In an interview, an activist in the labor union representing these workers complained that they were not entitled to the same safety provisions as organic employees. He showed me the boots that were provided by the subcontractor that had hired him. Although the workers received them free of charge, he noted that they did not meet the same safety standards as the boots given to organic employees. Contract workers mostly avoided eye contact with me and avoided interaction as I conducted my fieldwork. They showed deference to organic employees who gave them orders.

The differences between the two categories of workers were also evident in the way they were represented. The very possibility of labor organization had been ruled out under the Suharto regime, but after the political transformation of 1998, both organic employees and contract workers moved

Figure 6.2. A group of contract workers at Krakatau Steel's direct reduction plant. The absence of uniforms, badges, or logos on their helmets makes these workers easily identifiable in contrast to formalized, "organic" employees.

quickly to establish representative bodies. Organic employees at Krakatau Steel were already members of Korpri (Korps Pegawai Republik Indonesia, the Republic of Indonesia Civil Service Corps), the civil servants' "representative" organization. Korpri was established in 1971 as the representative organization for all Indonesian civil servants. Employees of state-owned enterprises were required to join this organization and could not establish independent unions. Korpri was designed to support the political goals of the authoritarian state. At Krakatau Steel, the structure of Korpri mirrored that of the corporate hierarchy: the chairman was a director, the second in command was a general manager, the third in command was a manager, and so forth.

Following Suharto's resignation and the events collectively referred to as *reformasi*, Krakatau Steel employees dismantled Korpri and formed a new representative organization. A claim to the designation "employee" was evident in the formation of the new union, which was called the Serikat Karyawan Krakatau Steel or the Union of Krakatau Steel Employees. Thus, even with the freedom of association that came in the post-Suharto period, the language that the regime had chosen to divide workers at the company persisted, as organic laborers adopted the identity conferred on them by the previous authoritarian state. Not all workers were content with this new arrangement. In previous work I have described an employee activist group that acted independently of the union in seeking to improve labor conditions inside the hot strip mill at Krakatau Steel (Rudnyckyj 2010: 221–252). These activists objected to the fact that, as in the Korpri hierarchy, the union organization did not distinguish between labor and management. From the level of operator to general manager, all employees of Krakatau Steel were members of the union. This included everyone who was formally employed at the company, excluding only the five directors and the CEO. Furthermore, as in Korpri, the new union's powerful executive committee was made up of employees who held managerial positions, rather than lower-level operators. The latter thus felt that the union was unable to represent their interests.

Whereas organic workers were represented by a "Union of Employees," contract workers formed an organization of their own once the Suharto regime had ended. Explicitly proclaiming the identity of workers, this new body called itself the Serikat Buruh Krakatau Steel (SBKS) or the Union of Krakatau Steel Workers. Thus, the distinction that Umar insisted upon in this chapter's opening vignette was formalized in the actual institutional identities of the respective representative organizations of each category of company laborer.

Precarious Work

Being a worker at Krakatau Steel was far less prestigious and less stable than being an employee. Although both groups performed labor within the various mills of the factory compound, often alongside one another, workers' compensation was inferior to that of employees. Workers, who were not directly employed by Krakatau Steel but by the company's subcontractors, received salaries and benefits equivalent to half or less of what organic employees received. In essence, these workers were equivalent to the temp workers who became a staple of western economies in the 1980s and 1990s.

I met one contract worker, Dadang, in the decrepit headquarters of the SBKS. He had been active in the formation of the union for contract workers and spoke bitterly about their conditions. Having begun working at Krakatau Steel nearly twenty years before our conversation, he had expected to be "made organic" at some point, but those hopes had never been realized. He claimed that "we do the same work [but] don't have the same privileges as organic workers," who regarded them as *pembantu* (servants) and *sapi* (cattle). He and his colleagues were officially classified as *tenaga kerja borongan* (contract manpower), but this, he complained, was "not logical": if they were merely contract manpower, then "we should receive our orders from a second party, not directly from Krakatau Steel employees."

Dadang said that conditions for contract workers had improved somewhat following the fall of the Suharto regime. Prior to 1999 there had been no union representation whatsoever for contract workers at Krakatau Steel and no benefits beyond their wages, but after the union was established they received health, accident, and life insurance and became eligible for a pension plan through Jamsostek, a national state-owned company responsible for managing private-sector social insurance. In addition, in 2001 SBKS organized two strikes, and after the second strike, the workers won a yearly bonus of half a month's pay. Furthermore, Dadang told me, prior to 2001 more than a hundred "labor supply" companies had provided temporary workers to Krakatau Steel. Upper-level and mid-level managers at the company were authorized to sign off on purchase orders establishing shell companies that served as suppliers for everything from spare parts to office computers and manpower. Typically they would charge a substantial premium over the actual price of the goods and services and treat the surplus as profit. One manager told me that several of the labor supply companies were in fact owned by managers at Krakatau Steel, but that in 2001, in an effort to cut costs and introduce efficiency, the company required that these firms be consolidated. Consequently, they were merged into four companies.

Dadang said that although it was not uncommon for contract workers to work for many years at the factory, as he had, they had no job security and could be "let go at any time" (*di-PHK kapan saja*). He estimated that approximately 70 percent of the contract workers were indigenous Bantenese (*pribumi*). Company managers claimed that Bantenese "lacked the education" needed to work at a modern factory, which was why the company had hired better educated applicants, mainly from the Javanese and Sundanese ethnic groups. However, as Dadang attested, Bantenese were regularly hired to perform physical tasks as temporary contract workers.

The process of becoming an organic employee at Krakatau Steel begins with an entrance exam and continues with an apprenticeship in which an employee receives extensive training in company operations. Dadang said that although he had wanted to take the test required of potential new organic employees, he had never been granted the opportunity to take it. Foremen and supervisors often discriminated against contract workers. Considered unskilled, they "never were given the opportunity." Those who did get the chance usually did so through personal connections. "They have a relation who works for the company and they bring them there." Dadang did not have connections.

Local and national politics also contributed to the precarious position of contract workers. The ongoing process of political decentralization in Indonesia made it more difficult for contract workers to have their voices heard because the Krakatau Steel management had cultivated relationships with local political elites to ensure that they would support the will of management.

> Now, power is with the mayor ... Krakatau Steel is more inclined toward the local government compared to the central government, because if there is a problem the company will directly ask for the assistance of the local government to resolve the problem ... We are under the pressure of the local government. For example, if we want to make an action [strike], we have been prevented by the local government.

Perhaps the increased clout of local leaders had been expected to benefit contract workers, but Dadang suggested that most of these functionaries used their increasing influence to benefit themselves and their allies instead of the local population. Many Indonesians alleged that the decentralization did nothing more than to enhance the power of "little kings" (*raja kecil*) who mimicked the "corruption, collusion, and nepotism" (*korupsi, kolusi, dan nepotisme*) of the deposed "big king" (*raja besar*) Suharto, who had used his political position to secure economic advantages for his family and cronies. The "little kings" who rose to prominence as a result of decentralization used their power to benefit themselves, often to the detriment of contract workers at Krakatau Steel. For example, Dadang said that during the SBKS strikes, the mayor of Cilegon had direct control of a semi-formalized security force composed of *jawara*, locally venerated strongmen skilled in local martial arts who are reputed to have supernatural abilities. Popular representations depict these imposing figures as physically powerful men with thick, drooping moustaches who dress entirely in black. After the end of the Suharto regime, *jawara* took over many of the security functions formerly handled by the army. Krakatau Steel managers and their allies in local government deployed *jawara* to intimidate SBKS members who had gone on strike.

Clearly, contract workers occupied a second-class status. Organic employees operated all the factory's sophisticated machinery and uniformly worked from control rooms that often were air-conditioned and in any case were far more comfortable than the noisy, dirty nether reaches of the plant. Whereas organic employees performed some tasks requiring physical effort and exposure to the discomfort of a massive industrial pro-

Figure 6.3. A contract worker operating the furnace door of an electric arc furnace at Krakatau Steel.

cesses, none of the contract workers occupied any of the plum jobs that involved monitoring the production process from the relatively more comfortable control rooms. There were even separate break rooms for the different categories of labor. Those reserved for organic employees were not especially well appointed by Western standards, yet they were much more comfortable than those designated for contract workers. The tile floors and finished walls of the former contrasted markedly with the plywood walls and general decay of the spaces where contract workers sought refuge from the sweltering, dusty conditions of the factory.

Although contract workers and organic employees were separated and hierarchized, from time to time they were called on to work together. For example, on one occasion I was interviewing Hidayat adjacent to the electric arc furnace in the slab steel plant, where iron pellets were melted down to create the fluid steel that was subsequently cast into massive slabs. Our conversation had taken place entirely in Indonesian, but suddenly he leapt to his feet and exclaimed, "Uh-oh, problem!" in heavily accented English. Grabbing his white, factory-issued helmet, he ran over to furnace 2, the more recent of two electric arc furnaces that, according to Hidayat, had "better technology" but "worse performance."

It turned out that the door of furnace 2 was stuck because the lower wall had fallen forward. I then watched the heart-stopping spectacle of Hidayat, along with two organic colleagues and two contract workers, attempting to wedge a plate between the precariously leaning furnace wall and the pusher. Although the group was clearly working together to fix the problem, from my vantage point in the control room it appeared that the contract workers did the bulk of the manual labor, hoisting heavy bars and trying to force the plate into place while unsteadily balanced on the roll table. All the while the furnace was stuck partially open with its ferocious fire glowing furiously inside, looking extremely perilous. It took the five workers, pushing and grunting in the heat, over 45 minutes to resolve the problem and reseal the furnace. When Hidayat returned to the control room, he was sweating profusely and looked completely exhausted.

While the distinction described here between Krakatau Steel workforce members identified as employees and those identified as workers must be contextualized within the specific history of Indonesia, it echoes distinctions in industrial labor elsewhere. For example, Parry has shown how workers at the Bhilai Steel Plant in the Indian state of Chhattisgarh differentiate themselves according to those who possess "secure employment" (*naukri*) and those who subsist on "insecure wage labor" (*kam*), the former constituting what he evocatively refers to as a "labor aristocracy" (Parry 2013: 363). At the Egyptian Iron and Steel Company, Egypt's largest state-owned enterprise, Makram-Ebeid found a similar distinction (see Chapter 7). Parry argues that the Indian distinction "cuts across the manual/non-manual divide" (Parry 2013: 349) and that the two categories of employees should be viewed as members of distinct social classes. The distinction between worker and employee at Krakatau Steel likewise could be understood in class terms. Organic workers sometimes performed manual labor but enjoyed many of the benefits of a middle-class livelihood, including homeownership, private automobiles, pensions, and the ability to participate enthusiastically in Indonesia's burgeoning consumerism. The material livelihoods for contract workers were nowhere near as comfortable. Furthermore, at Krakatau Steel the distinction between two categories of labor was largely taken for granted. Although no managers ever indicated to me that it was a deliberate technique to divide employees, the segmentation has obvious benefits for management in that it splits workers into different groups, thereby inhibiting their ability to realize common interests. The separation between the two groups was readily apparent in interactions during the workday. Organic employees generally gave orders, while the contract workers followed them. At company canteens, each group generally sat and ate separately from the other. Since organic employees were typically from outside Banten, they did not speak the local Bantenese dialect used by most of the contract workers. Outside the factory, the two groups lived in separate neighborhoods. Organic workers at the operator or foreman level typically lived in newer housing developments that had been privately constructed in the Cilegon region, whereas contract workers lived in already established neighborhoods and villages with older housing stock of inferior quality. Organic workers with a higher level of supervisory capacity were provided with housing that had been constructed by Krakatau Steel.

New Regime of Precarity

Krakatau Steel had long been able to count on reliable infusions of state investment, generously forwarded to the company under the presumption that domestic steel production was indispensible to Indonesian development and modernization. Organic employees benefited from this state largesse. They had the best jobs and working conditions, the highest salaries and the most generous benefits. However, after the end of the Suharto regime and the new economic climate brought about by the economic crisis that swept across Asia in 1997/98, it was unclear how much longer they could count on enjoying the relatively generous labor conditions and remuneration packages to which they had become accustomed. During my fieldwork, messages promoting austerity were pervasive. Signals of the need for belt-tightening often invoked the specter of future job cuts. Despite a history of workforce reductions implemented through phased retirements in the 1990s, there were no widespread layoffs of organic employees. However, company employees were routinely reminded that such layoffs were always possible. For example, several employees mentioned to me a 1995 study of the company by the global management consulting firm Booz, Allen, and Hamilton. Its report asserted that of the 6,000 permanent employees, fully 1,500 were superfluous—in other words, one-quarter of the company's organic employees could be replaced with little effect on output. These conclusions were well known, even if they were yet to be acted upon.

By the mid 2000s, there were clear signs that the company was preparing its workforce for layoffs. This was most evident in a new employee-training program that sought to cultivate the Islamic piety of employees. This program, called Emotional and Spiritual Quotient (ESQ) training, was the brainchild of Ary Ginanjar, a charismatic businessman who developed a "spiritual reform" empire in Indonesia based on his conviction that Islamic piety was the key to individual and national success in an increasingly global economy. Through human resources management training sessions, a series of books and videos, media appearances, a vast network of inter-linked businesses, and most recently the ESQ business school, Ginanjar contends that a business and work ethic conducive to commercial success is latent in the five pillars of Islam and the six pillars of Muslim faith (*iman*). He has drawn other ideas for the program from business management, self-help, and personal growth discourses, such as *The Seven Habits of Highly Effective People*, which has greatly expanded in North America, Europe, and Asia in recent decades (Matza 2009; McGee 2005; Thrift 1998). Throughout the multi-day training sessions that his company offers, Ginanjar stresses that Islamic piety should not be restricted to religious worship, such as daily prayers. Rather, Islam should animate all of one's worldly activity, from interactions with one's family to everyday work. Ginanjar told me that "at the root of Indonesia's political and economic crisis is a moral crisis," saying that "although most Indonesians are Muslims," they do not adhere to the tenets of Islam, "so at the moment here religion is only like a ritual ... just a ritual without spirituality." He conceives of his spiritual reform initiative as a way to redress the moral crisis at the root of Indonesia's developmental crisis.

ESQ training sessions were held once or twice per month at Krakatau Steel, most often in the large, multipurpose room of the factory's edu-cation and training center. The sessions usually ran from Friday through Sunday. The first two days started at 7:00 a.m. and lasted until just before the Maghrib prayers, which usually begin around 6:00 p.m. The final day included the gripping climax of Ginanjar's program: a simulation of three of the main rituals that take place during the annual hajj pilgrimage to Mecca. Most compelling for participants was a recreation of the circula-tion around the Kaaba, the central shrine in the main mosque in Mecca. An SUV-sized replica of the kaaba was placed in the center of the room, and participants rotated around it, chanting, "there is no God but Allah" in Arabic. Participants re-enacted the stoning of jamrat al-aqabah, in which pilgrims hurl rocks at three representations of the devil, by hurling small wads of paper at three demonic images elaborately drawn and posted on flip charts. They also simulated the *sa'i*, a ritual that consists of running seven times back and forth between the hills of Safa and Marwah in Mecca, by running back and forth across the room seven times. These re-enactments were designed to intensify the Islamic piety of corporate employees and, in so doing, to increase their corporate productivity. This final day ran until almost midnight.

A sophisticated Microsoft PowerPoint presentation provided the struc-ture for the training and consisted not only of graphs, charts, tables, and a litany of bullet points, but also spliced film clips, colorful photographs, and popular music. The information conveyed was culled from a variety

Figure 6.4. A sign prominently displayed above a glowing strip of steel in Krakatau Steel's hot strip mill reads "hard work is a component of our religious worship."

of websites, including those of the Harvard Business School. The training was delivered primarily as an interactive lecture in which the main trainer alternated between engaging with the audience in the familiar style of a television talk show host and then proceeding to deliver fiery, profoundly emotive lectures asking for collective forgiveness from Allah.

These elaborate spiritual training programs mix the latest human resources management theory with collective prayers and lessons in Islamic history. Ginanjar asserts that a work ethic conducive to business success is present in the five pillars of Islam. For example, the fourth pillar, the duty to fast during Ramadan, is recast as a directive for self-control and individual accountability. The third pillar, the duty to give charity, is taken as a divine endorsement of "synergy" and exercising "win-win" approaches in both business transactions and relations with co-workers. Ginanjar describes the prophet Muhammad as the model for a successful corporate executive, and participants are encouraged to emulate his example in business and trade.

ESQ has grown spectacularly in the past fifteen years; by 2017 well over 1.5 million people had completed the training program. Krakatau Steel was one of the first companies to embrace it as the program spread across Indonesia to some of the country's most prominent governmental institutions and state-owned firms, including Pertamina (the national oil company), Telkom (the country's largest telephone company), and Garuda (the nation's flag air carrier). Current and former military generals are avid participants in ESQ, and several sessions have been conducted at the army's officer candidate training school in Bandung. ESQ recently met its goal of becoming a national movement, establishing branch offices in 30 out of 33 Indonesian provinces. In 2011 the ESQ Leadership Center completed a 25-story office tower and convention center in South Jakarta funded in part through investment shares sold to past participants. The convention center portion of the building housed a purpose-built room to accommodate large-scale spiritual training programs. In 2013 Ginanjar opened the ESQ Business School to train young Indonesians in his secrets of business success. Capping this list of achievements, ESQ has "gone global." The first overseas ESQ training was held in April 2006 in Kuala Lumpur, and by 2007, regularly scheduled ESQ trainings were being delivered bimonthly in Malaysia. Former Malaysian Prime Minister Mahatir Mohamed endorsed the program. ESQ training has also been conducted in Singapore, the Netherlands, Australia, Brunei, Saudi Arabia, and the United States.

Islam, Neoliberalism, and Theories of Precarity

A major theme of the training was that employees should be ready to face uncertainty and change by being proactive and entrepreneurial. Rather than fearing the prospect of the company's declining fortunes and future job losses, employees were enjoined to see these as challenges to their religious piety. In making this connection the program liberally combined management science with Islamic piety to represent changing economic conditions as a challenge posed by Allah. For example, a key point in the training occurred toward the end of my fieldwork, on the third day of a training session in which I participated at Krakatau Steel. Ary Ginanjar had made his brother, Rinaldi, responsible for providing the training at the company.

The precarious condition of the factory was illustrated in film clips from *The Message*, a 1976 film about the life of Mohammed that stars Anthony Quinn as Hamza, the prophet's uncle, and Irene Papas as Hind, Mohammed's leading antagonist in Mecca. Mohammed is invoked as a model for a modern CEO: a visionary leader who inspires his followers despite tremendous adversity and persecution like that endured by the first Muslims. Several times Rinaldi brought up the fact that the first Muslims faced the possibility of destruction of the faith as a whole. Then, drawing on the theory of precarity described in a *Harvard Business Review* article, Rinaldi asserted that the rapid expansion of Islam during the religion's early years was attributable to uncertainty. Early Muslims did not know whether or not their efforts to spread the religion would succeed, yet their leaders were able to convince them that their struggles were not in vain. Rinaldi translated this message of striving in the face of adversity into everyday practice by comparing work to a religious endeavor. "Never forget, we all work for Allah," Rinaldi shouted while a series of quotes from the Quran flashed on the screen. He exhorted company employees to "become representatives of Allah at Krakatau Steel" and consider their labor "a vehicle to meet Allah."

During the ESQ training, employees were exhorted to see their new precarity not as a threat but as a challenge presented by Allah. One of the pressing issues facing the company during my fieldwork was an Indonesian government plan to eliminate tariffs on imported steel, forcing Krakatau Steel (the largest domestic producer), to compete internationally with producers in China, Korea, and Japan. During one training session, Ary Ginanjar asked in his booming voice, "What should our attitude toward this change be?" Then, immediately answering his own question with equal resolve, he told the employees that "we should view it as a challenge not as an obstacle [*hambatan*]! ... This is a challenge presented by God to test Krakatau Steel employees ... These are ways that Allah reminds us [*Allah meningkatkan kita*] that ... It is the era of globalization and competition ... it is not the government but Allah [that is testing us]." Later, during another training session, Rinaldi took up this same theme, saying that by bravely facing the uncertainty of a new tariff regime, Krakatau Steel employees could demonstrate that the "servants of Allah are ready for the free market [*hamba Allah sudah menunggu pasar bebas*]." Thus, the end of state support and the newly competitive global market characteristic of the new regime of precarity were likened to a spiritual challenge.

Krakatau Steel managers also conveyed the notion of embracing precarity. One manager, Fajri, told me that between 1975 and 1985, as a way of incubating the growth of Krakatau Steel, every steel company in Indonesia had to market its steel through Krakatau Steel. Thus, although Krakatau Steel did not hold a monopoly on steel production, it did hold a monopoly on its marketing. In Fajri's words, Krakatau Steel was "the king of steel [*raja baja*]!" However, he noted, their monopoly had led to very poor customer service. There was no competition, so there was no pressure to provide good service. In language that directly echoed what was said in ESQ training, Fajri described the "culture" of the company as one of "being served, not serving [*dilayani, bukan melayani*]." Customers who wanted their steel delivered quickly often had to pay a bribe to the marketing department to receive such expedited service. Fajri said that "now with globalization, with the free market, we must be competitive, the steel business must be competitive. We must serve the customer, if not we will be destroyed, there won't be anyone to buy." In this way he highlighted the precarious situation of the factory, now that it was increasingly forced to compete in a global economy. Similarly, all the employees were to internalize this threat and use it to motivate themselves to face the future. He conveyed precarity by repeatedly invoking a language of "risk [*risiko*]" in our conversation. Fajri said that ESQ prepared employees to take risks, even to the point where they might "disagree with their superiors" and not just follow them "like sheep."

The theme of embracing uncertainty and the unknown in the face of adversity and increasing precarity was emphasized by another human resources manager, Eliani. As we discussed the new economic climate that Krakatau Steel was operating in, she told me that the biggest challenge was preparing employees to accept their precarious positions. She stressed that employees had to prepare themselves for the possibility of being laid off, stating:

> the mentality must be different. People must be more ready to be fired [*lebih siap di-PHK*]! This means changing the mind-set … In state-owned enterprises, employees think that they can depend on the company for a long time. It is safe [*aman*], people can wait around for their pension … ESQ prepares people to face changes, in a way in which they are not afraid [*tidak takut*]. They will be certain that Allah is the most generous [*pemurah*]. Their faith will be bigger.

Spiritual reform was envisioned as a means of incorporating Krakatau Steel employees, long used to generous salaries, stable working conditions, and job security, into a regime of precarity characteristic of the liberalizing economy, even though disruptions in the material conditions of organic employees were still only dimly on the horizon. In this sense, the spiritual training program was actually a mechanism to prepare employees for the possibility of future layoffs and other structural transformations in the composition of the company's workforce.

The effectiveness of spiritual reform varied according to who participated in it. For the most part, it appeared to have a stronger effect on managerial workers than on workers at the foreman and operator level. Many upper-level workers spoke of profound personal transformations that they had felt following their exposure to ESQ. For example, a senior Krakatau Steel manager, Djohan, likened his experience during ESQ to a pilgrimage he had previously made to Mecca. He told me "after I did the *hajj*, I started to do *tahajud*[5] prayers … This was the first time I cried during prayer. I had no idea why I cried. This happened again after ESQ … My heart saw that God sees us." He then explained that after the training he began to regard his economic practices as connected to religious obligations. Prior to his participation in ESQ, he explained, on business trips he had pocketed any outstanding per diem allowance. However, after undergoing the training he realized that this was contrary to the central Islamic value of honesty. "It is not my money, but the company's money," he declared, adding: "If everyone did it the company would not exist anymore." Stories of such transformations were common among members of the upper ranks of the company hierarchy.

However, lower-status employees were not so receptive to the training. When I began fieldwork in 2003, the company's initial plan was to enlist every member of Krakatau Steel's workforce in the training in groups of 250–300 employees. The first to begin the training were at the top of the company's managerial hierarchy, not at the bottom like the operators and foremen. I asked Nuranto, one participant, why this was. At first he tried to avoid the question, but when I pressed him, he told me at first that it was because the program used lots of technical concepts and foreign words, and less educated employees might not understand all the content. Later, though, he leaned over and murmured, "You know, some of the problems—the corruption, the collusion, nepotism—these things are worse at the top than they are at the bottom."

In fact, lower-level employees appeared much less receptive to the training than managerial employees. The later sessions I attended, which took place after most of the managerial-level employees had been exposed to the training, took on elements of the casual informality that is characteristic of other theatrical events in Indonesia. Indonesian *wayang* (shadow puppet) theater, for example, is often marked by the casual way in which audience engages with the performance. During these shows, which often last all night long, attendees wander in and out, carry on conversations, eat and drink, smoke, sell things to each other, and tend to their children. One ESQ training session I attended toward the end of my fieldwork had the nonchalant air of a *wayang* performance. The audience was primarily composed of operators, and by the afternoon of the second day there was almost continuous conversation going on in the back of the room near where I sat. Minders repeatedly circulated around the back, imploring participants to be silent. When the lights were turned off to create a mood conducive to a particularly spiritual portion of the training, someone called out, "Oh no, now we have to cry *again*!" By contrast, the audiences in the earlier sessions I had attended, primarily attended by management-level employees, were considerably more docile. They responded readily to visual cues and oral exhortations, alternately cheering, crying, or listening attentively at the right times. Conversation and back talk were rare, and participants seemed more effectively moved during the emotionally intense portions of the training.

The common explanation for this was that less educated employees could not understand all the arguments that were presented. However, another reason for ESQ's failure to powerfully affect those at lower levels of the company hierarchy may have been that they had less for which to atone. They had not benefited from the largesse of the New Order state to the same degree. Though they had been given decent jobs, they had never had the opportunity to obtain education or training overseas under company sponsorship. Lower-level employees were eligible for fewer company benefits and had fewer opportunities for promotion. They had never been in a position to personally profit from company activities by setting up shell companies with advantageous trading arrangements. Appeals to plead for collective forgiveness rang hollow, for this group.

Conclusion

Umar's defiant refusal to be labeled a "worker" represented a type of subjectification characteristic of Indonesia's authoritarian government during the Suharto period, when the state sought to manage the political potential of industrial workers at state-owned firms by dividing them into hierarchically differentiated categories. At Krakatau Steel, organic employees were beneficiaries of the developmentalist state in that they were granted better jobs, higher compensation, stability of employment, and higher status compared to the contract workers who worked alongside them. Organic employees were also absorbed by the political will of the state insofar as they were incorporated into Korpri, the representative organization for civil servants, and the broader political machinery of the ruling party. Contract workers, however, had no job security, inferior wages and working conditions, and only a dim glimmer of possibly obtaining permanent employment as organic employees at Krakatau Steel. Part of Umar's conviction in his own self-worth as an "employee" was that he performed a type of labor that was indispensible, in comparison to "workers" whose precarity was marked, according to Umar, by the prospect that they could be "laid off whenever."

Nonetheless, Umar's attachment to identifying as an "employee" rather than a "worker" was a vestige of a political economic configuration that was clearly on the wane, where it had not already disappeared. The end of the Suharto regime (and earlier the Cold War) meant that the state no longer took an active role in manipulating industrial workers to ensure their support and complicity with the will of the state. Indeed, Suharto's downfall ushered in a period of unprecedented democratic freedoms, including rights to free association and free speech. The Asian financial crisis and increasing global economic integration increasingly called into question the presumptions of state-led modernization. In this new configuration, creating a regime of precarity was no longer part of a strategy to manage the political agency of industrial workers. Instead, management sought to subject all company workers to the logic of precarity, and in so doing discipline them to conform to the will of the company. This was accomplished by what I have referred to elsewhere as a "spiritual economy" (Rudnyckyj 2009b). In creating this spiritual economy, new management trainers-cum–religious proselytizers like Ary Ginanjar emphasized ethics in Islam that were conducive to a regime of precarity. This meant representing the economic changes confronting workers as "a challenge presented by God to test Krakatau Steel employees." Workers were reminded of the precarious situation faced by early Muslims, who followed the expansionist aims of the prophet Muhammad without any guarantee that their efforts would be successful. These lessons were reinforced by invoking the science of motivation as discussed in business management texts like the *Harvard Business Review*. Thus, the stability and guarantees of the Suharto period were replaced by a regime of precarity in which, in Eliani's words, "employees must accept they could be laid off whenever."

Acknowledgments

This research was conducted over a period of twenty-four months between 2002 and 2008, with the majority of the fieldwork conducted between 2003 and 2005. I extend my sincerest gratitude the employees and workers at Krakatau Steel who facilitated my fieldwork and regret that, in order to ensure their confidentiality, I am not able to thank them individually. I also extend my deepest thanks to Ary Ginanjar, Rinaldi Agusyana, and the rest of their staff from the ESQ Leadership Center for kindly and patiently addressing my entreaties. I am grateful for constructive criticism and insightful comments on this chapter from Chris Hann, Jonathan Parry, and the other contributors to this volume. This research was made possible with material support from the Wenner-Gren Foundation for Anthropological Research, the Social Science Research Council, the University of California's Pacific Rim Research Program, Fulbright-Hays, and the University of Victoria. I am grateful to all of these institutions for their support.

Daromir Rudnyckyj is Associate Professor in the Department of Anthropology at the University of Victoria. His research addresses globalization, religion, finance, development, Islam, and the state in Southeast

Asia, focusing on Indonesia and Malaysia. His forthcoming book, *Beyond Debt: Islamic Experiments in Global Finance*, analyzes Malaysian efforts to create a global alternative to the conventional financial system and make Kuala Lumpur a central node in this emergent network. His previous books include *Spiritual Economies: Islam, Globalization, and the Afterlife of Development* (2010) and the volume *Religion and the Morality of the Market* (co-edited with Filippo Osella, 2017). He was awarded a Sharon Stephens Prize by the American Ethnological Society in 2011.

Notes

1. PHK is an abbreviation for *putus hubungan kerja*, which literally translates as "to sever the work connection."
2. The New Order lasted from 1965 to 1998. Suharto coined the term to contrast his rule with the "Old Order" under Sukarno.
3. Suzanne Naafs (2012) provides a useful illustration of the social dynamics of this region of Java following the end of the Suharto regime.
4. Krakatau Steel's historical significance for Indonesian nationalism is well illustrated by Suzanne Moon (2009).
5. These are special prayers that are executed in the middle of the night. In the five-fold Islamic classification of human action, *tahajud* prayers are not mandatory (*wajib*), but are encouraged (*sunnah*).

References

Ferguson, James. 1999. *Expectations of Modernity: Myths and Meanings of Urban Life on the Zambian Copperbelt*, Perspectives on Southern Africa 57. Berkeley, CA: University of California Press.

Guillot, Claude. 1992. "Libre Entreprise Contre Économie Dirigée: Guerres Civiles À Banten, 1580–1609." *Archipel* 43: 57–72.

Hadiz, Vedi R. 1997. *Workers and the State in New Order Indonesia*, Routledge Studies in the Growth Economies of Asia 11. London: Routledge.

Hill, Hal. 2000. *The Indonesian Economy*. Cambridge: Cambridge University Press.

Matza, Tomas. 2009. "Moscow's Echo: Technologies of the Self, Publics, and Politics on the Russian Talk Show." *Cultural Anthropology* 24(3): 489–522.

McGee, Micki. 2005. *Self-Help, Inc.: Makeover Culture in American Life*. New York: Oxford University Press.

"Krakatau Steel Expands in a Big Way." 1996. *Metal Bulletin Monthly* 5: 77.

Moon, Suzanne. 2009. "Justice, Geography, and Steel: Technology and National Identity in Indonesian Industrialization." *Osiris* 24(1): 253–277.

Naafs, Suzanne. 2012. "Navigating School to Work Transitions in an Indonesian Industrial Town: Young Women in Cilegon." *Asia Pacific Journal of Anthropology* 13(1): 49–63.

Parry, Jonathan. 2013. "Company and Contract Labour in a Central Indian Steel Plant." *Economy and Society* 42(3): 348–374.

Purwadi, Dibyo Soemantri, Alfuzi Salam, Purwo Djatmiko, Sulaeman Ma'ruf, and Zainal Muttaqien. 2003. *Sejarah P.T. Krakatau Steel: Memelihara Momentum Pertumbuhan* [The history of P.T. Krakatau Steel: Maintaining momentum for growth]. Yogyakarta: Pustaka Raja.

Rock, Michael. 2003. "The Politics of Development Policy and Development Policy Reform in New Order Indonesia." *William Davidson Institute Working Papers* 632. Ann Arbor, MI: University of Michigan Business School.

Rudnyckyj, Daromir. 2010. *Spiritual Economies: Islam, Globalization, and the Afterlife of Development*. Ithaca, NY: Cornell University Press.

———. 2009a. "Market Islam in Indonesia." *Journal of the Royal Anthropological Institute* (n.s.) 15(s1): 183–201.

———. 2009b. "Spiritual Economies: Islam and Neoliberalism in Contemporary Indonesia." *Cultural Anthropology* 24(1): 104–141.

Thrift, Nigel. 1998. "The Rise of Soft Capitalism." In *An Unruly World?: Globalisation, Goverance and Geography*, ed. A. Herod, G. O'Tuathail, and S. Roberts. London: Routledge.

van Dijk, Kees. 2001. *A Country in Despair: Indonesia between 1997 and 2000*. Leiden: KITLV Press.

Winters, Jeffrey. 2000. "A Review Essay: The Political Economy of Labour in Indonesia." *Indonesia* 70: 139–150.

7

Between God and the State

Class, Precarity, and Cosmology on the
Margins of an Egyptian Steel Town

Dina Makram-Ebeid

In Autumn 2013, after management had deferred annual bonus pay and proposed paying it in installments, workers at Egypt's oldest and largest state-owned enterprise, the Egyptian Iron and Steel Company (EISCO), stormed the industrial relations department and began a factory occupation. A few days later, I interrupted my visit to the protesting workers and headed towards the fruit sellers outside the gate. While I was buying oranges for the protesting workers, the vendors told me alternative stories about the occupation. For example, a middle-aged vendor said something along the lines of, "What are these twats complaining about? I would do anything to work in their place, or to get my son in." Raising his voice, he continued: "They are *muwazzafīn* [blue-collar employees in the governmental or public sector, or white-collar employees] and they are complaining! Well, give me their job and I'll work solidly without grievances!"

In this chapter I examine various experiences of cumulative precarity in Helwan. If precarity, as Butler (2009: 14–15) puts it, means "that one's life is always in some sense in the hands of the other," I ask how people who spend their lives in and around this steel plant articulate this lack of control. This leads me to focus on popular cosmological beliefs. Workers' discursive traditions and everyday religious practices place notions of work within wider understandings of the universe. Their reflections reveal that precarity is relative to the side of the factory wall they inhabit. I distinguish two different experiences of precarity in the steel town. The first articulations came from steelworkers whose permanent jobs in the plant are slowly losing economic value. The second were produced by daily-wage workers who live on the fringes of the plant. Experiences of precarity share a lot of similarities, yet still they differ, not least because steel jobs shield workers from police brutality and offer them more leverage over their life outside the plant. The divergence is expressed in workers' language of class, which emerges from their religious meditation on the nature of uncertainty in the world.

In Egypt, as in many countries where Islam is the dominant religion, *rizq* (God-given means of subsistence or livelihood) is often considered to be as important as one's actual labor. *Rizq*, as the Quran teaches, is unpredictable and irregular, ordered and distributed by God alone. I look at ideas of *rizq* as a prism for people's reflection on their vulnerabilities in life. Their enunciations of *rizq* render the uncertainties of work tangible.

Rizq is arbitrary, in the sense that it bears no relation to deservedness and is entirely the product of God's mysterious will. Everybody is subject to it, and indeed everybody invokes it on occasion. However, when I started my research in the steel plant in 2009, permanent workers seldom invoked notions of *rizq*. Instead they stressed that the state provided their subsistence. When they did invoke the notion of *rizq*, they did so strategically to shame managers into not cutting their pay, as to do so would be to interfere with something ordained by God. Managers, for their part, would strategically invoke *rizq* to justify shop floor inequalities, which must also be a matter of God's will. In recent years, however, as steelworkers' livelihoods have become more precarious, they cite the notion of *rizq* more frequently. Their discourse about what ultimately determines their living standards and their life chances now sounds more like that of *al-tabābna*—the natives of al-Tibbin, the original land on which the steel plant was built, who now live on the margins of the steel plant and have highly precarious jobs. Despite this similarity, crucial differences persist in the way each group references *rizq*. Most importantly, steelworkers rarely imply that *rizq* is the most decisive aspect of their livelihoods.

al-Tabābna', the autochthons, stress their total dependence on *rizq*. Indeed, they take the concept of *rizq* to another level by labeling themselves *'urzuqīa* (those who do not know what next day's job will be, who live from hand to mouth and rely entirely on *rizq* as sustenance from God). Etymologically, *'urzuqī* (the singular of *'urzuqīa*) derives from the root verb *razaq* (to provide sustenance) and the noun *rizq*. In colloquial Egyptian Arabic, *'urzuqī* is an adjective that makes dependence on *rizq* into an identity by suggesting an embodiment of the concept through which one's main persona becomes the receiver of *rizq*. By referring to themselves as *'urzuqīa*, precarious workers from *al-tabābna* suggest that, unlike steelworkers who consider *rizq* an important factor in their lives, most dispossessed members of *al-tabābna* see *rizq* as by far the most crucial aspect of their lives. Appropriations of "*rizq*," I shall argue, constitute a local language of class that distinguishes between steelworkers and the precarious autochthons outside the plant. At the core of this distinction is an understanding of property relations that goes beyond the

Western/Eurocentric focus on objects/things. Further, although these appropriations highlight class dynamics, they downplay the state's role as a facilitator of capital accumulation by a few, and thus as the cause of enduring inequalities in the community of *al-tabābna*.

My enquiry into the relations between work and cosmology for these different categories of Muslims is inspired by da Col's (2012) proposition that anthropologists have not sufficiently explored the cosmological imagining of luck, fortune, and fate that underpins alternative economies. My task is also shaped by Mollona's proposal that anthropologists of the global factory "must look at the spatial and temporal interconnectons between the visible, stable, respectable labor at its core and the precarious, invisible and degrading labor at the margins" (Mollona 2009: xxi). Social history narrated from the fringes—here understood as the economies that thrive around major industries—thus reveals a breadth of precarious encounters and complex relations between them.

The difference between steelworkers and those toiling around the plant is obvious in everyday language. Egyptians often contrast the *muwazzaf* with the *'urzuqī*. The former owns a *wazīfa*, that is, a white-collar or blue-collar job in the public and governmental sector; whereas the latter relies entirely on *rizq* as sustenance from God. They are at opposite ends of the hierarchy of labor. The starkly visible workers at the Helwan plant are *muwazzafīn* (plural for the masculine *muwazzaf* and feminine *muwazzafa*), while the workers in the informal economy on the fringes of the company town are *'urzuqīa* (plural for the masculine *'urzuqī* and feminine *'urzuqīa'*). The two groups diverge in their life cycles, household structures, and aspirations, and as I have argued elsewhere, they have the potential to be different classes (Makram-Ebeid 2015a). The *muwazzafīn* tend to work later in life and marry at a later age than the *'urzuqīa*. Their households are on average smaller in size, and their adult offspring are less likely to reside in the same house. The *muwazzafīn* tend to have higher expectations about the marital and familial lives they ought to lead, which extend to the educational qualifications their household members acquire, the consumer goods they own, and the spouses they choose. They also have different concepts of work: *wazīfa* (office or job) in the case of both white-collar and blue-collar steelworkers, and *shughl* (work) for everyone else. At EISCO, permanently employed workers and their sons, relatives and *baladiyyāt* (those who originate in the same village, town, or district) tend to think of their jobs as property and themselves as members of the middle class. This is crucial to the distinction between the two kinds of workers. Daily-wage workers' experience of precarity is partly a result of their indirect exploitation by steelworkers who prevent others from accessing jobs in the plant. By supporting the position that workers' children should be given priority in hiring at the plant when job openings are already very rare, steelworkers restrict the daily-wage workers' access to the steel jobs that provide security and stability. I shall show how, despite increasing references to divine agency, regular workers remain largely shielded from the vulnerabilities of the *'urzuqīa* among *al-tabābna*. The precarity of the latter must be seen in the light of the wider class struggle in the community. *al-Tabābna* experience double exclusion: they are kept out of the Helwan plant jobs and also off their land—for as they see it, they are landowners who were illegitimately pushed to the margins of the town. This perspective explains their expression of their claims on the plant, which vary from regular and organized robberies to attempts to recapture their land.

Guy Standing (2011) presents the precariat as part-time workers and those who depend on daily wages earned through insecure contracts or internships. Precarious workers are said to be increasingly substituting the more stable workers who have contractual rights, access to health care, and stable pay. But as Jan Breman (2013) has pointed out, Standing's writing on precarity is focused mainly on Western/OECD countries and uses a definition of work that privileges post-1945 developments while neglecting labor relations in the Global South. Breman argues that precarity has always been the norm; hence, the analytical challenge is to understand how the lives of those who work in the "new" organized sectors relate to lives lived in the "old" informal economies. For the case of India, Holmström (1976, 1984) depicted how kinship relations mitigate the separation between these two kinds of workforce, Parry (2013) argued that class distinctions at Bhilai rely on the fact that steel jobs have become a quasi–property right, and Strümpell (2014; this volume) analyzed the process of accumulation by dispossession rooted in divisions triggered by the regional postcolonial state of Odisha. Inspired by this body of work, I show that the lives of those who have been excluded by the plant, which appear marginal to the official history of Helwan, are integral to the class politics of the town.

Seven Decades of EISCO

Helwan emerged as an industrial hub under President Nasser in the 1950s, and EISCO was its main landmark. From a peak of about 25,500 workers in 1982, EISCO's labor force was gradually slimmed down to 13,200 by the end of 2009.[1] It nevertheless remains one of the largest factories in Egypt. By the end of my research in 2010, only 102 women worked in the plant. Part-timers, three of whom were female, made up just 17 percent (2,300 workers) of the total labor force. About 800 men who worked as daily laborers in the plant were undocumented in the plant's records. They were mostly relatives of EISCO workers who had been unable to secure either a permanent job or a part-time one.[2]

EISCO resembles renowned steel plants like Stalin's Magnitogorsk, Nehru's Bhilai, and Suharto's Krakatau in that it embodies ideals of modernization and nationalist self-determination (Kotkin 1997; Parry 2003; Rudnyckyj 2010). The plant extends over 4,000 acres, not including the company town that accommodates roughly three thousand EISCO households. Three generations of EISCO employees turned al-Tibbin into their new home. While most employees came from governorates all over Egypt, some who hailed from villages to the west and south of the plant continued to be peasants as well as workers. A small minority of workers live in distant parts of Cairo. Very few live in the vicinity of the plant historically occupied by *al-tabābna* because of the area's reputation as a problematic, impoverished part of town.

In the initial land grab, *al-tabābna* were driven off their land to the margins of the company town of al-Tebbin, where they occupied informal housing generically referred to as *bīyūt ʾahālīa* (family-built houses). Hence, they continue to refer to themselves as *ʾaṣḥāb al-ʾarḍ* (the owners of the land). Some large families of *al-tabābna* received compensation for seized land, often below market rates. Many who were entitled to compensation found it too little to bother to claim. Other, smaller families were resettled in state-provided housing in a new quarter close to the plant. Some of the latter held titles to land, but many who did not could still prove they had lived on the land for a significant period of time. Most, left dispossessed, occupied the fringes of the town and turned to illegal trades to make ends meet. *al-Tabābna* are thus divided into two groups. The first is made up of members of powerful large families who kept small pockets of land around the plant—not seized by the state—who are involved in large organized crime networks and have strong connections with the police and the local municipality. The second group encompasses the rest of the community, who struggle to put food on the table and depend on the powerful men of big families. Both groups of *al-tabābna* are considered disreputable by the EISCO residents of the company town. Steel households distinguish themselves from *al-tabābna*—especially when economic downturns jeopardize their relatively high social status— by treating *al-tabābna* with condescension, referring to them as "rubbish," "*sūqiyīn*" (people of the market), or "thieves."

al-Tabābna give various reasons for not taking up jobs at the plant. Some claim they are discriminated against because of their associations with powerful local families, their involvement in crime and access to arms, and their general reputation as troublemakers. Others did not want to work for the plant that robbed them of their land. Many earnestly said that *al-tabābna* do not like working for any boss and prefer working with their kin. The majority suggested that EISCO salaries in the early days had not been tempting enough. Reasons vary, but few *tabābna* toiled in the plant.

In 2009, there were thus four main types of workers in Helwan. Most workers on the shop floor had permanent contracts. Some had the temporary contracts introduced by the labor law of 2003. Some were hired on a daily basis. And outside the plant, most workers in the informal economy were also paid by the day. As my research progressed I realized that labor politics inside the plant were closely tied to the labor histories of those living around the plant and exploited by it. Precarity becomes clearly hierarchical when the vulnerability of some depends on the security of others. The original sin behind the inception of EISCO, which robbed autochthons of their land and livelihood before a single proletarian had set foot in the plant, was muzzled by a collaboration of silence about this theft.

Labor Histories in Helwan

The architectural character of the company town changed in 2011, when the collapse of the police at the start of the revolution allowed residents to enlarge the previously identical grey buildings originally built by the plant.[3] Some steelworkers bought land from *al-tabābna* and constructed multistory family houses outside the company settlement. Empty and contested spaces in the company town were taken over by *al-tabābna*, who built similar houses. Agricultural land in the vicinity of the plant almost vanished. Even more members of *al-tabābna* moved into EISCO buildings, a trend that had started in 2006 following the privatization of the company town. But although the mutual dependence between steelworkers and *al-tabābna* increased, it did not generate greater trust. Negative stereotypes persisted in everyday language and became sharper with the increasing instability after 2011, while the new proximity of "untrusted" *tabābna* in some buildings threatened the viability of the residential saving groups that financed the major life-cycle expenditure of workers' households.[4]

To understand the tense relations between steelworkers and *al-tabābna*, it is necessary to recall the history of structural adjustments since 1991, which slashed subsidies at EISCO and prompted the decentralization of the plant's management. Machinery was not updated in most mills, the shop floor became dependent on low-quality spare parts, and blue-collar workers and engineers were pitted against each other. Flexibilization further intensified as of 2003. To ensure workers' acquiescence to these reforms, priority in employment was even more rigidly restricted to workers' children. In previous generations, entire families had been employed at EISCO. As unemployment soared and jobs became scarce, this custom was turned into a right. "Workers waste their health and life in the plant," most workers said, "and the plant should thus reciprocate by at least employing their children in return."

A ministerial decree annexed to the labor law of 2003 proposed that new temporary contracts should be made permanent within three years. This held out the prospect of overcoming the consequences of a sixteen-year moratorium on hiring that had turned contractual differences into generational ones. In addition to the distinction between the "fathers," who were the permanent workers, and the "sons," who were the temporary and daily workers, a new hierarchy was created between "fathers with value and fathers with none." The fathers "with value" were reputedly the astute ones who had managed to have their children taken on as temporary workers, while those "without value" were only able to put their sons' names on the list of daily laborers, from which they might one day rise to obtain temporary contract and then eventually a permanent job. Thus, to even secure a daily laborer position, one had to have a father, relative, or *baladiyyāt* (fellow villager or townsman) employed in the plant. Very few daily laborers and fixed-term temporary works lacked any relation to permanent steelworkers, and when such outsiders did join as daily workers, they did not last long—especially once they understood the slimness of their prospects of upward mobility in the labor hierarchy. The pay of a daily worker in the steel plant was lower than the average daily pay in industrial and construction work, so becoming a daily worker in the steel plant only made sense if it was to yield future rewards of temporary, and then permanent, jobs. It is difficult to be certain about the daily laborers because of their absence from plant records, but most of the workers in the steel-and-sheet-rolling mill on which my ethnography focused did eventually secure temporary and permanent contracts. Some waited for months, others for years, before getting a temporary job in the plant. Eventually, the politics of parliamentary elections before Mubarak's ousting was the political nudge that rendered most daily and temporary workers permanent at EISCO.

In 2010, a few months before the last parliamentary elections under President Mubarak, young workers who had joined the steel plant since 2007 as either temporary or daily workers were given tenured contracts. Managers explained this move, which contradicted the general trend of flexibilization, as Mubarak's last gasp—a stratagem to buy support for his ruling National Democratic Party. While contractual labor rights were radically undermined in other sectors of the Egyptian economy (such as textiles), sites like EISCO that were loaded with nationalist symbolism were key factors in electoral calculations. The militant history of EISCO—which in 1989 was the site of the largest strike in Egypt's postcolonial history—contributed to these calculations. A top manager said the regime feared that "if EISCO rises, Helwan rises and if Helwan rises, the whole of Egypt rises."

Yet the workers awarded permanent contracts in 2010 were the ones who had led the industrial actions of 2013 and 2014. "This plant is our future. It is ours. Not that of older workers. Their future is behind them," young workers repeatedly told me during the occupation I mentioned at the beginning of this chapter. Their fears, I have suggested elsewhere (Makram-Ebeid 2015b), are engendered by their long-term history of job insecurity. Having worked in insecure conditions for years before joining EISCO, young men are all too aware that their future might resemble their past. Worried that cutbacks in the annual bonus pay and perpetual coal shortages were signs of plant liquidation, they occupied the factory in 2013 and went on a full strike in the following year.[5] Most workers, especially young ones, were heavily indebted due to a complex system that enabled them to feign the purchase of goods in installments from the plant cooperative while in reality receiving instant cash from a loan shark who in turn resold these goods on the market.

No matter how fragile the position of the factory workers, however, they were less vulnerable to continuous police brutality than were *al-tabābna*. The newly tenured workers at EISCO were in the age range pestered by police security, but their jobs afforded them protection from the daily violence and humiliation central to the experience of other young males in Egypt. Steelworkers' jobs were registered on their national identity cards, which they carried with them along with their company cards. These cards spared them from harassment during random police checks while using public transportation or being in the vicinity of spontaneous police patrols, which often resulted in arbitrary arrests. A permanent EISCO job meant that the person was well-off and probably backed by union membership or managers who would pursue the matter.

Ahmed, who had initially joined EISCO as a daily worker, reminded me early on, before becoming a permanent worker, that "for a young man like us, life is a second." By "life is a second" he meant that if one fell into the hands of police officers for any reason, one's life was wasted in a second through trumped-up charges and a sentence ranging from a few months to years in prison. Prior to joining the plant, police officers had ordered Ahmed to strip down in the midst of his community following a quarrel with a relative of a policeman. Humiliated and imprisoned for a few months under false allegations of drug possession, he later formulated his grievances in wider terms by reminding me that: "before it was a revolution, the uprising, on January 25th [previously Police Day] was against police violence." A few days into the revolution, young people freed prisoners and attacked and set fire to police stations across Egypt. Many of these rioters had been victims of police violence. EISCO jobs gave steelworkers financial security and a status that kept the security state at bay. Considerations of precarity in Egypt must thus include exposure to police violence. Throughout the Arab world, the role of the police is an overlooked aspect of precarity that correlates strongly with position in the labor hierarchy.

Histories on the Margins

Ramy Ragab is a household name in al-Tibbin. Its mention creates rifts right away, as he is either idolized or loathed. A relative with large landholdings from *al-tabābna* considers him a pious man, *hajj* Ramy. Other locals too respect him for making regular sacrifices and distributing the meat to the poor. Ismail Matar, a poor man belonging to a large local family distantly related to that of Ramy, has another story to tell. Ismail works as *'urzuqī*, mainly for Ramy, whose fortune derives from trading in scrap and other dubious links to EISCO. Ramy inherited land, and a brother-in-law who works in a bank helped him take out large capital loans and secure a commercial license, which allows Ramy to tender when EISCO disposes slag by the ton. His power also derives from diversifying his capital and his monopoly over the sale of certain steel products, in which he colludes with staff in the sales department, which has a notorious reputation for corruption.

Ramy collects slag and scrap with a tractor, and many collaborators share in his profits, from management and security personnel to the truck drivers and workers who hide valuable materials for him. The tractor is unloaded in the nearby hills to allow people like Ismail to extract valuable items and deliver them to Ramy. The work is highly competitive and the outcome unpredictable: sometimes one can secure a whole month's salary of around a thousand Egyptian pounds in a day, whereas in some weeks one barely makes enough to put food on the table. In the bad weeks family members help by providing credit. Ismail, like other *'urzuqīa*, was unable to join informal saving groups—*jam 'iyyāt*—among his neighbors, friends, and colleagues because he could not guarantee a steady income. He was excluded from the collective ways of saving that help regular workers plan their major life-cycle expenses and thereby control their lives.

Other members of Ismail's family cooperate with *tabābna* families specializing in more violent appropriations from the plant. For example, armed robbery of the plant's railway tracks is a recurrent phenomenon that intensified during the absence of state policing following the revolution. When a member of the security personnel was killed in such an attack in 2014, steelworkers called on the army (by then in power) to send tanks to protect them and the plant. Meanwhile, young men like Ismail are caught between living under the protection of big men like Ramy and being subject to police brutality. In one incident in 2013, the police razed a cemetery established on *al-tabābna* land, claiming it was previously empty land that was still owned by the plant as part of the property it had acquired around the company town. A mother had just buried her son, an *'urzuqī* who had died after an accident at work but whose family never received compensation for his death. On television, the minister announced that this was the state's land but the mother complained that the *'urzuqīa* had no rights in death or life.

'Ihab and Sha'lan are the eldest of eight siblings in a household similar to Ismail's. They have middle-school qualifications and work in a network set up as a *barrād* (he who does metal filings by cutting metal into various shapes). This is one of the better paid jobs in casual work. The brothers earned on average 40 Egyptian pounds (4.5 dollars) per day or 1,200 pounds (135 dollars) per month, which is double what a temporary worker their age makes at EISCO. They are married to two sisters with a slightly higher standard of living and education, whose father has a permanent job at EISCO. Their early marriage to 'Ihab and Sha'lan was enabled by the two brothers' relatively high incomes. Daughters in EISCO households are generally encouraged to study up to university and find a job afterwards; but those outside this enclave have very little control over their marital lives and financial matters. The brothers, however, would have been glad to work at EISCO for half their salary because of its greater *'istiqrār* (stability). Social insurance was particularly important: a younger brother had fallen off a scaffold at work and broken both legs and arms, but received no compensation from his private employer. Housing security was also an issue, as private landlords had become increasingly exploitative under the new tenancy law of 2006. In everyday life in Egypt, "stability" generally implies access to both tenured employment and the means to reproduce the conditions of "a good life" in the context of the family.

Al-Tabābna stress the importance of the extended family. Residents declare that "al-Tibbin [where *al-tabābna* live] is based on a family system while company housing is an individual system." *'amm* Zinhum, who resides among *al-tabābna*, told me, "we are dependent here on money and large family backing." Unlike EISCO offspring, who can rely on their stable fathers in a nuclear family setting oriented to intergenerational transmission of resources, the household economy of *al-tabābna* is vulnerable to the tensions, whims, and violence of powerful families (Makram-Ebeid 2012). Thus, even though EISCO workers have experienced a substantial retrenchment in their financial security, their conditions remain clearly better off than those of *al-tabābna*.

From Cosmology to Class

Islamic discourses and practices of piety shape industrial regimes across the Muslim world. Rudnyckyj (2010 and this volume) argues that problems of development in a public Indonesian steel factory, which in the past were cast in technical and infrastructural knowledge terms, are today increasingly situated as an ethical problem that can be solved by religious reform. His ethnography highlights the use of the proverb *al-ʾamal ʾibāda* (work is worship) to link efficiency to economic development by introducing a combination of entrepreneurial and religious arguments. In Turkey, Nichols and Sugur (2004) documented the use of the same proverb in car factories. Aware of their managers' secular orientation and their reluctance to allocate prayer breaks, workers use the expression strategically. Likewise, Shehata (2009) explains increased religiosity on the shop floor of two Egyptian textile factories as a reaction to white-collar workers' secular attitudes. I argue that discourses of *rizq* in the Helwan steel town express similar tensions and a potential class difference between workers with stable employment in the factory and those with less regular work on the margins of the town.

Rizq is God-given: "What we get in life is not in our hands," I was told by the sheikh who leads the prayers in a local mosque in al-Tibbin, a retired bus driver who acquired religious status through years of service in the mosque. He explained that one is born with one's *rizq*, which is unrelated to one's actions and work; hence the Arab proverb *ijrī jariy al-wuḥūsh ghir rizqak mahathūsh* (run like giants, you will get no nothing more than your *rizq*). *Rizq* is what God gives people, regardless of whether they are thieves or devout. Sustenance thus comes from God without reciprocation from man, which is why commentators often use *rizq* interchangeably with *hazz* (luck or fortune) (Bosworth and McAuliffe 1995). The term is used differently by people in Helwan, however. As noted, many *tabābna* refer to themselves as *ʾurzuqīā* to suggest their existential vulnerability, while steelworkers share the same beliefs about the universe and God's provision of sustenance without implying that their entire existence relies on *rizq*.

When I conducted my first survey on the shop floors of the steel plant, I asked, "What benefit did you get from working in the plant?" The answers ranged from "Everything," to "This plant is my mother, her generosity is endless." One permanent worker recalled that he had first arrived at the plant in plastic slippers and by working there had become a *bey* (person of high rank). Permanent workers stressed having acquired status (*makāna*) and high value (*qīma*) in the community. In the local markets, members of steel households are treated as financially able customers. Large houses in villages and well-furnished ones in the company town reflect this status. So do the advanced education and expensive marriage requirements of their children. Yet, rather than stress *rizq*, steelworkers envisioned the state as the main source of stability (*ʾistiqrār*) in their lives.

On the shop floor, they invoked the concept of *rizq* mostly in strategic ways. Upheavals took place when an engineer handed a worker notice of a pay cut.

Workers asserted that pay cuts would slash the *rizq* of not only the worker but also his or her children. This was a form of moral pressure on engineers—the shop-floor managers—not to implement cuts, because, as a crane operator put it, "nobody should cut what God has given." The engineers were indeed reluctant to do so, although some invoked *rizq* to render inequalities natural and God-given. When I mentioned daily workers' confrontation with hazardous tasks, a production engineer said the Quran stipulates that people are created in different classes and one's class position was dependent on his *rizq*. According to this argument, one should not complain about job conditions but accept what God has ordained. Religious workers rejected the engineer's interpretation. They said they worked hard so that their *rizq* would be *ḥalāl* (lawful by God). If their steel job was ordained by God, their religious duty was to "order the good and prevent the bad" (*al-'amr bi al-ma'rūf wa al-nahyi 'an al-munkar*). Each person should thus work to improve his or her lot in life, while accepting his or her *rizq*. Outside the shop floor, *rizq* was mentioned mostly in relation to marriage. *Rizq* together with *nasīb* (fate or one's lot in life) were considered the most crucial element in the culmination of a marriage. Workers and their families recounted how *rizq* and *nasīb* had helped family members find a matching partner.

In recent years, following significant cuts in their incomes and additional benefits, steelworkers have begun to talk about their work more often as *rizq*. Perpetual shortages in raw materials led many to fear that the plant might one day be liquidated. One of the popular chants during the occupation of 2013 was "with soul, with blood, the *rizq* of our children is more important." Workers considered their *rizq* to be that of their children and their households. In discussing their future prospects, they denoted the plant as their allotted *rizq*. Nevertheless, this increased reference to *rizq* did not lead steelworkers to call themselves *'urzuqīa*. They invoked *rizq* to express their vulnerability to the new economic conditions and their relative precarity compared to their past. But they never went as far as to call themselves *'urzuqīa* and continued making demands of the state, which they still considered a key player in their lives. Steelworkers thus began to talk about *rizq* in much the same way as *al-tabābna*, even though their precarity differs from that of those outside the company town. However, they never saw themselves as *'urzuqīa*, who are entirely dependent on God.

Precarity in Helwan is thus articulated in the language of religion. I argue that even when workers refer to the wider cosmological order, they are expressing their interpretations of class. Some consider themselves totally dependent on *rizq* by embodying it, while others are better described by their state job (the *muwaẓẓafīn*) in spite of increasingly acknowledging *rizq* in their lives. No account of labor politics in Egypt can fail to note the cleavage between workers who have a *waẓīfa* and those who have *shughl*. This reality corresponds to discourses about the *muwazzaf*'s superiority to the *'urzuqī*, emphasizing the stability of life versus the irregularity of *rizq*.

At the core of these binaries is an implicit notion of property relations. Those who have access to tenured employment (*wazīfa*) treat it as a right that distinguishes them from the rest of the working class. I take inspiration from Parry (2013), whose research at the Bhilai Steel Plant in India shows that permanent work contracts are treated as a quasi–property right marking the difference between public-sector workers as members of the middle class and contract workers as the unorganized sector of the working class. Jobs at EISCO were largely passed from fathers to sons, and sometimes to relatives and people from the same village. This understanding of *wazīfa* as a form of property resonates with historical debates on property relations in the Arab world, where property was delineated as *milkiya* (ownership) and *wazīfa* (office), respectively emphasizing claims to "things/objects" and "persons/individuals" (Mundy 2004). This view of property offers an alternative to teleological understandings of the relations between property and production that limit property to ownership of the means of production, which are generally understood as 'things/objects.' It makes sense, especially in plants like EISCO, which operated at losses for significant parts of its history, and thus complicates classical Marxist understandings of the relation between property, ownership of the means of production, and surplus extraction.

Given the successful transmission of jobs, the *muwazzafīn* can be considered to form not merely an "aristocracy of labor" but a middle class. As mentioned above, the precariousness of life conditions today has turned this "custom" into a "right." Access to permanent contracts gives the workers in such an aristocracy middle-class "potential," in the sense of Marilyn Strathern's explanation of property "as a capacity for development as yet unrealized" (1996: 17). Class is then a dynamic social relation developed in interaction with the locality. Who is a worker is contingent upon the intersection and overlap of multiple identities (Lockman 1994).

Some workers are unable to capitalize on a permanent job (e.g., by failing to bequeath it to their sons and daughters), buy a housing property in the privatized company town, or acquire agricultural land in the villages and towns where they reside. Hence they find themselves sliding down the labor hierarchy or at best remaining members of an "aristocracy of labor." Thus, in slight divergence from Parry's (2013) conclusion, I argue that access to permanent jobs as potential property, does not make workers a middle class, though it gives them the potential to be one. This potential is largely tied to workers' social reproduction and their intergenerational transmission of social entitlements. Whether or not a household succeeds in these tasks is crucial to its members' solid identity as members of one class or the other.

The differing invocations of *rizq* bring out the distinction between workers who have access to a potential property in their state jobs and workers who depend entirely on the benevolence of God. But the overt reference to God, especially by the *'urzuqīa*, downplays the state's role in reproducing inequalities in al-Tibbin. Indirectly, the state facilitates criminal activities run by men of capital from *al-tabābna* like Ramy Ragab and encourages what Galbraith (2006) calls "predatory capitalism" or what Sanchez (2015) calls "criminal capital" in the case of a similar industrial setting around a Tata factory in India. Thus the state continues to create inequalities between wealthy members of powerful families and the rest of *al-tabābna*. Although neoliberal doctrine implies a withdrawal of the state, the latter is in fact a resilient player in people's lives in al-Tibbin as well as inside EISCO. The state contributes further to the class politics between the *muwazzafin* and *'urzuqīa* by clandestinely empowering members of powerful families in al-Tibbin who cooperate with the plant over the dispossessed.

Conclusion

In Helwan, precarity abounds. Not even workers with permanent contracts are immune to serious indebtedness, and the future of their plant is no longer as certain as it used to be. Others are forced to rely on crime and face regular police brutality. The latter have less choice over the kind of life they lead. Cosmological reflections guide both groups, and the contexts in which they invoke *rizq* indicate how their vulnerabilities differ. Despite increasing resemblances in the degradation of their welfare, steelworkers still have more control over their everyday lives than do the rest, partly thanks to their indirect exploitation of *al-tabābna*, first when the latter were removed from their land to allow steelworkers from other places to resettle in the company town, and later when they were denied access to privileged jobs by steelworkers who demanded that the very few jobs available be passed on to their own children. Those at one end of the precarity continuum deepen the precarity of others, and all gradations of precarity depend on the state, directly or indirectly. To remain resilient before crushing realities and deeply uncertain futures, people in al-Tibbin meditate on their lot in life. Their religious and cosmological truths express the complexities of subjugation.

I have argued that narratives of *rizq* downplay the omnipresence of the state and its contribution to class politics in Helwan. Class formation involves violence and property as theft (Proudhon 1940 [1840]). Theft in Helwan takes many forms. The state steals the land of *al-tabābna* and they, in turn, appropriate its machinery and encroach on the land that they consider to be theirs. Other forms of theft require a deeper consideration of property, extending beyond Eurocentric traditions focused on things/objects to investigate the social relations constitutive of property relations. The steelworkers' aspirations have been aligned to those of the state: both want stability. Complex negotiations resulted in an unhappy alliance that entailed stealing the future of *al-tabābna*. Excluding al-*tabābna* from jobs in the plant is a predominant means of turning a *waẓīfa* into solid class status.

To study labor relations in Helwan without integrating the fringes of the steel plant would be to doubly exclude the victims of class exclusion. People's nuanced language of class, expressed through their different references to *rizq*, reveals crucial differences between workers inside and outside the steel factory that orthodox class language tends to overlook. It reveals the potentialities and violence of class struggle, which is key to the transfiguration of power over the *longue durée* in Egypt.

Acknowledgments

The ethnographic fieldwork for this research was conducted from October 2008 to August 2010 and August 2013 to May 2014. It was generously supported by the Wenner Gren Foundation for Anthropological Research, the Population Council West Asia and North Africa, and the Max Planck Institute for Social Anthropology. I wish to thank Massimiliano Mollona and Frances Pine for their very constructive remarks and contribution to this chapter.

Dina Makram-Ebeid is Assistant Professor at the Sociology, Egyptology and Anthropology Department of the American University in Cairo. After obtaining her doctorate from the London School of Economics and Political Science she held postdoctoral positions in Germany, including at the Max Planck Institute for Social Anthropology (2012–2015). Her research interests include the anthropology of work and labor, value, the state, social movements, gender, affect and confinement, and the anthropology of the Middle East and North Africa.

Notes

1. The labor force at EISCO was mostly reduced in the sixteen years from 1991 to 2007 by halting new employment without replacing retirees. A system of early retirement packages was introduced in 2001. Although 4,090 workers had opted for retirement

packages by 2009, the program soon became unpopular: 3,200 early retirements took place in 2001, compared to only 890 over the following eight years.

2. Daily workers were mostly hired through the plant's social club, which was treated as a separate financial entity and played the role of a labour contractor. Although not on the plant payroll, these workers were often listed as seasonal employees in the plant's social club records.

3. I refer to events since 2011 as "revolution" to reflect the parlance of the people I write about, whose terminology I adopt.

4. Residential saving groups are saving groups organized by members of the same building. Each household contributes a sum of money for a specific period of time, the total of which is collected by one household every month.

5. The annual bonus pay in 2013 was a significant sum equivalent to sixteen months' basic wage in the steel plant. This was workers' fixed pay without the additional incentive pay that make up the total salary. It constituted between one-fourth and one-eighth of a worker's actual monthly salary.

References

Breman, Jan. 2013. "A Bogus Concept?" *New Left Review* 84(November–December): 130–138. Retrieved 6 February 2015 from https://newleftreview.org/II/84/jan-breman-a-bogus-concept.

Bosworth, C.E., and Jane D. McAuliffe. 1995. "Rizḳ." In *The Encyclopedia of Islam*. New Edition, 567–568. Leiden: Brill.

Butler, Judith. 2009. *Frames of War: When Is Life Grievable?* New York: Verso.

da Col, Giovanni. 2007. "The View from Somewhen: Events, Bodies and the Perspective of Fortune Around Khawa Kapro, a Tibetan Sacred Mountain in Yunnan Province." *Inner Asia* 9(2): 215–235.

Galbraith, John Kenneth. 2006. "Taming Predatory Capitalism." *The Nation*, retrieved on 20 July 2015 from http://www.thenation.com/doc/2006041/forum/4.

Holmström, Mark. 1976. *South Indian Factory Workers: Their Life and Their World.* Cambridge: Cambridge University Press.

———. 1984. *Industry and Inequality: The Social Anthropology of Indian Labour.* Cambridge: Cambridge University Press.

Kotkin, Stephen. 1997 *Magnetic Mountain: Stalinism as Civilisation.* Berkley, CA: University of California Press.

Lockman, Zachary. 1994. "Introduction." In *Workers and Working Classes in the Middle East: Struggles, Histories, Historiographies*, ed. Zachary Lockman, xi–xxxi. Albany, NY: SUNY Press.

Makram-Ebeid, Dina. 2015a. "Labour Struggles and the Quest for Permanent Employment in Revolutionary Egypt." In *The Political Economy of the New Egyptian Republic*, ed. Nicholas S. Hopkins, 65–84. Cairo: American University in Cairo Press.

———. 2015b. *Old People Are Not Revolutionaries: Labour Struggles Between Precarity and 'Istiqrār in a Factory Occupation in Egypt, Jadaliyya*. Retrieved 25 January 2015 from http://www.jadaliyya.com/pages/index/20632/%E2%80%9Cold-people-are-not-revolutionaries%E2%80%9D-labor-struggl,.

————. 2012. "Manufacturing Stability: Everyday Politics of Work in an Industrial Steel Town in Helwan, Egypt." Ph.D. thesis, The London School of Economics and Political Science (LSE). Retrieved 7 February 2015 from http://etheses.lse. ac.uk/780/.

Mollona, Massimiliano. 2009. "Introduction." In *Industrial Work and Life: An Anthropological Reader (LSE Monographs on Social Anthropology)*, ed. Geert De Neve, Massimiliano Mollona, and Jonathan Parry, xi–xxviii. Oxford: Berg.

Mundy, Martha. 2004. "Property or Office? A Debate in Islamic Hanafite Jurisprudence over the Nature of the Military 'Fief,' From the Mamluks to the Ottomans." In *Law, Anthropology and the Constitution of the Social: Making Persons and Things*, ed. Alain Pottage and Martha Mundy, 142–165. Cambridge: Cambridge University Press.

Nichols, Theo, and Nadir Sugur. 2004. *Global Management, Local Labour: Turkish Workers and Modern Industry*. New York: Pelgrave Macmillan.

Parry, Jonathan. 2003. "Nehru's Dream and the Village 'waiting room': Long-distance Labour migrants to a Central Indian Steel Town." *Contributions to Indian Sociology*, 37(1–2): 217–249.

————. 2013. "Company and Contract Labor in a Central Indian Steel Plant." *Economy and Society*, 42 (3): 348–374.

Proudhon, Pierre-Joseph. 1940 [1840]. *What Is Property? An Inquiry into the Principle of Right and of Government*. Cambridge: Cambridge University Press.

Rogers, Joel et al. 2006. "Taming Predatory Capitalism." *The Nation*. Retrieved 7 February 2015 from http://economistsview.typepad.com/economistsview/2006/04/james_galbraith.html.

Rudnyckyj, Daromir. 2010. *Spiritual Economies: Islam, Globalization and the Afterlife of Development*. New York: Cornell University Press.

Sanchez, Andrew. 2015. *Criminal Capital: Violence, Corruption and the Making of Class in an Indian Steel Town*. London and New York: Routledge.

Shehata, Samer S. 2009. *Shop Floor Culture and Politics in Egypt*. Albany: SUNY Press.

Standing, Guy. 2011. *The Precariat: The New Dangerous Class*. London: Bloomsbury.

Strathern, Marilyn. 1996. "Potential Property: Intellectual Rights and Property in Persons." *Social Anthropology* 4(1): 17–32.

Strümpell, Christian. 2014. "The Politics of Dispossession in an Odishan Steel Town." *Contributions to Indian Sociology* 48(1): 45–72.

8

The (Un-)Making of Labor

*Capitalist Accelerations and Their Human Toll
at a South Korean Shipyard in the Philippines*

Elisabeth Schober

Introduction: The Price of a Ship

It looks as if they were hanging on to each other, during their fall toward their death. Two bodies embracing each other, young men in their twenties or thirties, from what can be seen on the grainy cellphone image taken hastily on a dark night. The puddles of blood where their heads hit the concrete floor have begun to stain their blue and white work uniforms. This haunting picture of two Filipino workers, taken shortly after their lives ended during an accident at the Korean shipyard in Subic, is featured prominently on a website called *Hanjinworkers' blog*.[1] The blog is run by a group called Samahan ng Manggagawa sa Hanjin Shipyard—Association of Workers at Hanjin's Shipyard, or Samahan for short—an unofficial union that is attempting to organize the tens of thousands of Filipino workers who have found employment in Subic Bay, Philippines, since the arrival of a South Korean shipbuilder in the mid 2000s.[2]

One afternoon in March 2014, I was sitting in the Samahan office located close to the public market of Subic Town, an urban agglomeration of about 90,000 people in Central Luzon. That afternoon, Lolo (Grandfather) Vincent, one of the activists I met at Samahan, told me the cost of a life in the Philippines: 20,000 pesos (ca. 400 dollars). This amount is the compensation relatives receive for a person's work-related death at the Korean shipyard. The money is paid out via a compensation system attached to the publicly run social security system, through which all workers are insured. In addition to this fixed, state-paid sum, Lolo says, the Koreans have on occasion added some extra compensation to appease relatives. Before we got to talking about the price of a worker's life, Lolo had listed recent casualties and serious accidents at the shipyard: three deaths and a number of serious, non-fatal accidents over the last five months. A metal plate had fallen onto one worker, crushing him to death; another man's head was pierced during a fall from scaffolding; a third died when a welding hose exploded. Lolo also took out his cellphone to show me a picture of a comatose worker who had fallen three meters and landed headfirst on the concrete. I glanced at the bruised, heavily swollen, nearly unrecognizable face of a man whose age I could not guess. He had been in a coma for over three months, and the doctors were preparing the family for the worst.

The workers' bodies, in contrast to the sturdy colossi they build, often prove fragile in this exceptionally dangerous work environment. At the website of Hanjin Heavy Industries and Construction, a subsidiary of the much larger Hanjin conglomerate (*chaebol*),[3] the entire production process is neatly laid out in a "cyber-tour." From the "design stations," represented by pictures of Filipino and Korean engineers working side by side, one is taken to "pre-treatment," then to "steel cutting," "assembly," "outfitting & installation," "painting," and "erection" to "launching," and finally to "inspection and sea-trial" and the "naming ceremony and delivery." The rhetoric about greater fuel efficiency, improved velocity, and perfected ship designs that one finds on such websites conceals the daunting task of bringing a ship from its conception on an engineer's drawing board to its christening. Within this production cycle, human sacrifices are too frequent for the workers to ignore.

Filipino labor activists, current and former employees of the Koreans, and various community members living nearby described the particularities of these deaths to the very last detail. But while ordinary people often focused on the specific circumstances of an accident, labor groups like Samahan were concerned with the bigger picture. They did not trust the Korean company or the Philippine Department of Labor to release accurate numbers about the health and safety records at the shipyard. Although the exact death toll is disputed, thirty-eight workers are known to have perished in work-related accidents between 2006 and 2014 (Datu 2014). Between 2006 and 2010 alone, more than five thousand accidents occurred (Robinson 2011).[4]

While numbers are a source of dispute, Filipino workers settle the question of responsibility for these accidents with sharp certainty, laying the blame firmly at the doorstep of the Korean employees. Besides Hanjin's own Korean managerial staff, which it brought to Subic, Hanjin employs several hundred South Korean citizens in foreman positions. They work alongside hundreds of Filipino and Romanian foremen. Meanwhile the rank-

and-file workers are all Filipino.[5] During a Samahan meeting I attended in April 2014, one former worker declared that "70 to 80% of the accidents happen under the supervision of the Koreans. Four Filipinos died while I was still working at Hanjin—they all had Korean foremen." Labor activists regard these dead workers as martyrs. To workers at the shipyard, they are reminders of the fate that may await them if they take one wrong step.

The online depictions of sudden, brutal deaths—of people flattened by tons of cement, of iron rods piercing bodies, of crushed skulls and severed limbs—have not ignited the kind of broad labor movement that Samahan aims to forge. The number of organized workers has declined in response to pressure exerted by the Korean conglomerate. Terminating the contracts of people suspected of being members of a union has been a frequent practice. Nowadays, only a handful of activists are left trying to organize their co-workers at Samahan.[6] However, news of casualties at the shipyard travels widely, contributing to Koreans' bad reputation in this part of the Philippines. Versions of these stories were told to me by hairdressers, waitresses, shop assistants, and taxi drivers. Rosalie, a 26-year-old teacher hailing from Olongapo (the nearest city), told me that "it was the talk of town a few years ago. That they pay 10,000 Pesos to the families to keep them quiet about the dead." For a while, Rosalie herself was considering applying for a job at Hanjin, but after rumors of unacknowledged deaths at the shipyard circulated in Olongapo, she changed her mind. "I wouldn't want to get involved in covering up accidents myself," she argues, shaking her head. The shipyard has been called a killing field (Fuller 2009; Jabola-Carolus 2010). Labor organizers have also used images of death, and used to unfurl banners proclaiming "Hanjin's shipyard, workers' graveyard."[7]

In this chapter I argue that Subic Bay's shipyard and its countless accidents have something to tell us about the workings of capitalism in the early twenty-first century. Fueled by dangerous contradictions amidst vast cultural gaps between Korean and Filipino understandings of how to work, this shipyard is a place that can alert us to the often deadly consequences of the "overheating" (Eriksen 2016) of accelerated global lifeworlds. Due to a unique historical trajectory that has turned South Korea into a major economic force in Southeast Asia, South Korean investors are in a privileged position vis-à-vis their Filipino workers, as they enforce a Korea-imported labor process geared to making ship production cheaper, faster, and more efficient. The relentless speedup of ship production needs to be read against the backdrop of a "capitalism of the barracks" (Schober 2016) that has enabled the spectacular rise of South Korean conglomerates like Hanjin both at home and abroad. Korean endeavors in the Philippines also exemplify a "spatio-temporal fix" (Harvey 2003), as the offshoring of much of Hanjin Heavy Industry's production from Korea to the Philippines was largely undertaken in order to tackle both technical insufficiencies and a combative unionized workforce at their older facility in Pusan.

From Pusan to Subic: The Story of One Offshoring Project

"Ninety percent of everything" that Western urban residents buy in stores these days has to move across our planet in container ships first (George 2013). Economist Marc Levinson (2006) has shown how the seemingly innocuous container, first used as a means for transporting goods in 1956, has revolutionized our world economy. After being used to supply US Forces in Vietnam, the standardization and increased efficiency of "the box" made it a significant factor in the integration of economies across the world. Although shipbuilding took a deep hit during the recent global recession, the market has made a recovery over the last few years (Y. Kim 2014). The pressure to make container ships even more cost-efficient has been passed on to the shipbuilders, who are now seeing significantly greater demand for ultra-large container ships, which East Asian shipbuilders produce for the major global players (the top three of which are European: Danish Maersk, Swiss MSC, and French CMA-CGM).

Shipyards are therefore key nodes in the global economic system. Shipyards necessarily need to expand their infrastructural basis—that is, their fixed capital—to cope with these demands, and Hanjin's shipyard in Subic is today the tenth largest in the world. Beyond the availability of large tracts of land on which the shipyard could be built, one arguable reason the conglomerate invested here was that labor was cheap and local labor laws could in practice be easily circumvented. Since the 1970s East Asia, and South Korea in particular, has completely replaced Northern Europe as the market leader. In Korea, this particular heavy industry was the decisive motor of a dynamic political economy (Nam 2009). In recent years, however, pressure from China has obliged the major players in the Korean shipbuilding industry to increase the number of workers hired through subcontractors. Within South Korea, more than 50 percent of jobs in shipbuilding, in which some hundred thousand people work, are now undertaken by precarious workers. Hanjin, however, has remained afloat using an additional strategy: offshoring much of its construction to the Philippines, which has enabled it to temporarily keep up with its Korean competitors, all deeply in the red following the recession. By taking most of its ship production to the Philippines, Hanjin became the Philippines' leading foreign direct investor, with a total investment of around two billion dollars. For now, the massive financial gamble behind this offshoring deal seems to have done the trick to keep Hanjin Heavy Industry in the running: the company has in the meantime also become the world's top producer of ultra-large container ships, having recently signed on to build three ships, each with a 20,600-container capacity, for the French shipping corporation CMA-CGM, to be delivered by mid 2017 (Schuler 2015).

Hanjin's success story in the Philippines is extraordinary because merely a decade earlier this company was only a minor player in the Korean shipbuilding scene, and handicapped by lengthy labor disputes at its relatively small, 27-hectare shipyard in Pusan, South Korea's second largest city. Hanjin Heavy Industries acquired the shipyard (built by Japanese colonizers in 1937) from the Korean state in the late 1980s. In the wake of the IMF crisis a decade later, the company began downsizing its workforce, which provoked a vigorous response from the heavily unionized Korean workforce. Conflicts culminated in a double suicide committed by protesting trade unionists in 2003. By 2011, the shipyard was again embroiled in extended labor unrest after an activist occupied a crane to protest against further mass dismissals (Robinson 2011). Following a dramatic standoff (for details, see Baca 2011; Robinson 2011), management compromised by agreeing to rehire some workers; still, the decline of the regular workforce in Pusan was halted only temporarily. As of late 2013, approximately 1,500 regular workers remained employed at Hanjin's old shipyard, and up to 5,000 temporary workers can be hired when warranted by new orders. Creditor-led restructuring plans announced in early 2016 indicate that the workforce left in Pusan will likely be reduced even more.

At the heart of the highly public controversies in Pusan was whether Hanjin's financial status at that time actually warranted the mass dismissals of unionized workers. Hanjin pointed out that not a single ship was commissioned at the Pusan shipyard between 2009 and 2011. However, new contracts to build large vessels in the Philippines raised suspicions that the company was intentionally relocating orders to a Philippine Special Economic Zone in order to justify its downsizing in Pusan (Lee 2011). Subic Bay was a uniquely suitable location for this offshoring project, as it had previously been home to the largest US naval base overseas. Subic Bay had already dealt with a crisis of its own when the US Navy departed in 1992, leaving tens of thousands jobless overnight. The region's urban centers seemed on the verge of becoming ghost towns, despite the proclamation of the Subic Bay Freeport Zone (Reyes 2015: 6ff.). After some unsuccessful years during which the Freeport managed to attract only a few minor investors, the big break came with the announcement that Hanjin Heavy Industries would build a new shipyard in 2006. The company's founders were already familiar with the area through their previous subcontracting experiences with the US military.

Thus, while workers at the Korean shipyard were steadily laid off, at its Subic site Hanjin was expanding its substantially cheaper Filipino workforce, which was required to work overtime and double shifts on a regular basis because business was booming. The number of workers declined briefly, from 20,000 workers in 2011 to about 16,000 workers in 2013, when Hanjin's Subic facility temporarily felt the last throes of the global economic crisis. With Hanjin's recent entry into the ultra-large container ship market, however, the workforce has again risen substantially; 34,000 people labored at the shipyard as of 2016. Hanjin has thus become one of the largest employers in the Philippines, a country with practically no home-grown heavy industry to speak of. Up to 77 percent of Filipinos work in the so-called informal sector (Ofreneo 2013: 424), a consequence of rapid population growth and the decline of traditional fishing and farming due to dispossession.[8] Corporate or state-driven land- and water-grabbing, low-level warfare in the south of the country, and the ever expanding effects of climate change combine to impair livelihoods (Schober in press). These conditions ensure a sizable local reserve army of labor for employers such as Hanjin (Grey 2015), and the "disciplining power of high unemployment" (McKay 2006: 42) has certainly played a key role in Hanjin's ability to keep its facility union-free up to this day.

Additionally, nearly all of Hanjin's Filipino workers are hired through a complicated network of subcontractors.[9] Initially, over 100 subcontractors divided virtually all of the non-Korean employees amongst themselves, but after much criticism from local labor groups their number fell to around 20.[10] The conflict over Hanjin's subcontracting system was primarily fought out over whether or not the conglomerate was compliant with local labor law. Filipino activists argued that most of these firms were illegal entities under the subcontracting law because they often seemed to lack the required sufficiency of capital and machinery. Underlying the row over whether or not Hanjin had built up a "real" or "illegitimate" subcontracting arrangement in the Philippines was the question of whether this system might actually be a veiled in-house arrangement. Activists both in South Korea and the Philippines have protested against the circumvention of social, health, and safety regulations that they believe is the actual primary motive behind the establishment of this vast network.

Philippine labor law allows unionization at the company level only, so organizers have not been able to form a union that would address the grievances of all workers at the shipyard;[11] instead they have been forced to organize workers at the level of the individual subcontracting companies that hire out workers to the shipbuilder. An activist from the National Union of Building and Construction Workers pointed to additional difficulties that disrupt attempts to organize workers at Hanjin—namely, the frequent shuffling of workers between subcontractors, which organizers suspect is a deliberate strategy to weaken labor's organizing capacities:

> The problem is really the system of subcons. You really have to run after the workers, to update the list of the workers for each particular subcon and try to find out where they are … The big problem is, for example, [if] I'm a worker in Hanjin, I was [initially] in this one subcon. Maybe a month or two later, I will be transferred to another subcon. So sometimes it's really hard to establish who are really the workers of a particular subcon. So if you want to form a union, you first have to establish who are the workers, and you have to ask them to sign up.[12] But what if they are [in the meantime] transferred to another one, and then to another one… So that's really a problem [when it comes to] organizing within each subcontractor.

Furthermore, if Hanjin's predominantly young and male Filipino workers, hired to perform physically demanding, dangerous, dirty work for the industrial minimum wage (around seven dollars a day), attempt to organize themselves to improve labor conditions, they are likely to be fired or see their career progression at the shipyard stalled, as the conglomerate can easily replace them. Forty workers were dismissed for trying to organize labor at the shipyard in just the three years from 2008 to 2011. And although complaints against perceived arbitrary terminations can be taken up with the Philippine Department of Labor, such contestations are de facto rather rare, as the nearest office where a complaint can be filed is located an expensive three-hour bus ride away from Subic Bay, and individual case processing times are notoriously long.

Korean investments in Southeast Asia and elsewhere challenge widespread understandings of globalization as a form of cultural and economic imperialism of "the West versus the Rest" (Keskülä, Lee, and Trevisani in this volume provide additional cases that point to similar "South-South" investments, complicating our picture of globalization). Such patterns can best be understood as part of the ongoing processes of the "hegemonic decline" of the West (Friedman 2004, see also Arrighi 2009). The export of a shipbuilding model from Korea to the Philippines—with all the social practices that accompany it—allows us to understand some marked continuities among putatively discontinuous developments. Subic Bay was drawn into the circuits of global modernity much earlier than other sites in the region. Subjected to a succession of imperial projects by Spain, Japan, and the United States over the last century, local economic networks underwent the prolonged and deep penetration of the foreign capital that arrived in the area together with large-scale foreign military installations. The history of Hanjin, too, is representative of big business's larger historical entanglements with militarism and war, which have played a fundamental role in Korea's economic ascent. Hanjin, nowadays amongst the ten largest *chaebol*s in South Korea, was founded during the Korean War as a shipping business catering to the US military—a little studied feature of the spectacular rise of these enterprises (Glassman and Choi 2014). Hanjin prospered during the Vietnam War when, together with other rising *chaebol*s, it was put in charge of much of the transportation of US material between Seoul and Saigon (Lie 1998: 64). This conglomerate thus became familiar with Subic Bay decades before its subsidiary entered the shipbuilding market.

South Korea's role as a sub-imperial force in the wider Asia-Pacific region enabled it to profit from the shared history of the "empire of bases" (Johnson 2004, cf. Lutz 2009) by building its new production site at a former US military installation in the Philippines. Hanjin is not alone in this strategy. With the onset of democratization and higher labor standards in the 1990s, wages in South Korea rose exponentially (Cumings 1997: 326ff., 342ff.; Koo 2000). The same *chaebol*s that profited massively from the authoritarian developmental state and its links to the US empire of bases have responded by gradually transferring their industrial sites overseas.

The Export of a Korean Capitalism of the Barracks

What does all of this mean for Filipino workers on the ground? The daily running of the shipyard involves a wide range of cultural negotiations, adaptations, and contestations between different actors. The hierarchies in place dictate who gets to impose what kind of practices on whom, a dynamic neatly summed up by a former Hanjin worker in the words "Because it's run by Koreans, according to them, we Filipinos need to follow the Korean culture, even if the shipyard is located in the Philippines." Korean labor practices are often unilaterally enforced from the top, leading to both increased conflict and the potential for lethal misunderstandings in a highly dangerous work environment.

The issue of time management has become a particular bone of contention, as Maribel, a Filipino woman[13] in her mid twenties who had worked for the shipbuilder for half a year, pointed out to me:

> That's one thing about Koreans … if they put (up) a time frame, they really have to stick to the time frame. Because Filipinos, they say, okay, *bahala na* (come what may) … go with the flow, like that. But when I worked with the Koreans—we had to finish this kind of project, and we had to meet the target, *really* meet the target, no matter what.

The extension of working hours has been pivotal to Hanjin's attempts to meet the increasingly tight deadlines set by overseas clients.[14] Although the tropical climate of the Philippines lends itself to relatively long breaks around noontime, such breaks have been largely eradicated at the shipyard, even on days when the temperature rises above 40 C° and people can literally grill eggs on the steel plates at the yard. The official nine-hour working day stipulated by Filipino labor law seems to be rarely observed. Ships are produced around the clock from Mondays to Saturdays in two shifts. Overtime and even double shifts are common, a fact that apparently has contributed to widespread drug usage. Many workers routinely take *shabu* (a cheap drug containing methamphetamine mixed in with caffeine) to stay awake and alert during long shifts.[15]

The long working hours, modeled after South Korean workdays, are an aspect of the quasi-authoritarian labor management practices that until very recently were widespread among Korean *chaebol*s. A human rights lawyer in Seoul alerted me to the export of a military-style workplace culture from Korea to the Philippines:

> We have an army culture [at our offices and factories], generally speaking. That's our Korean culture. Young generations don't like that, but the old generation says, "yes, that's natural." Hanjin has a very old history, in Pusan and other places. And their subcontractors, they also share a working culture. A kind of "order culture," an army culture.

The labor routines the Philippine work force is subjected to are reminiscent of the military-style drills that workers have practiced in South Korea since the Park Chung-hee era. A Filipino worker employed by one of Hanjin's subcontractors has first to go through one to three months of training at the Hanjin-run Skill Development Center, during which they receive only half of their pay. On the first day at the center, the worker's hair is shaved off. One former worker I spoke to, 27-year old Juan, noted: "They say, that's Korean style! That's why, when you are at Hanjin, you always know the new workers, by the hair." Another aspect of "Korean culture," according to Juan, was the use of physical punishment. "Some of the Koreans are physically violent toward their workers. They use … it's their culture to hit." Juan elaborated:

> I cannot tolerate being hit by anyone. It happened to me once. Some Korean foreman hit me on the head. I asked him not to do that again, or else … Because here in the Philippines, you are violating my rights. And … the foreman, he said, "I didn't know that's the culture here"…

The Al Jazeera documentary "Storm in Subic Bay" includes cell-phone footage secretly shot by a worker that documents the maltreatment of a Filipino employee by his Korean foreman. When I showed this video to a Korean labor activist, he immediately recognized the corporal punishment deployed by the foreman as a technique that is widely used in the South Korean military to control subordinates. He commented: "They are exporting the same pre-democracy conditions to the Philippines nowadays that we used to have in our own factories during the dictatorship of the 80s. They can no longer do it to us, but they're certainly trying with them."

In addition to physical punishment, yelling and swearing at workers are other widespread practices. Three Korean words are immediately recognized by most Filipino workers: *ppalli ppalli* (faster), *ssip'al* (fuck), and *kaesaekki* (son of a bitch). Filipino workers who have been with Hanjin for longer are familiar with another phrase that may seem odd at first: *chal sara pose!* (Let's live well!) It refers both to a famous South Korean idiom dating from Park's military regime, and to a physical routine that is a major technique of labor control at the shipyard. Every morning at 7:30 a.m., a siren goes off. Officially the shift starts at 8:00, but the workers must assemble earlier in their various departments. They line up and perform a number of exercises under the watchful eye of their Korean, Filipino or Romanian foremen, who yell various commands. The thirty-minute drill ends with the workers shouting in unison: *Hanjin!* In the recent past a song reverberated through the halls of the shipyard as the background music to this exercise: *chal sara pose!*—"Let's live well!" The original slogan, said to have been coined by none other than South Korean military dictator Park Chung-hee himself, is an idiom that sums up the belief at the heart of South Korean capitalism as Park imagined it: with hard work, the goods will be delivered to you one fine day. By promoting this and other such notions of development and sacrifice, President Park whipped his country into shape in the 1960s and 1970s, thereby enabling a progress that indeed demanded immense personal sacrifices from all who voluntarily subscribed to it (or were, more often than not, forcibly conscripted into it).

Although low labor costs in the Philippines help Hanjin to undercut Chinese competition, management is apparently still troubled by the "quality" of Filipino labor. During research in both Subic and Pusan, I repeatedly heard shipyard employees comment on how the Korean managers were quick to complain about Subic workers' commitment level, which they regarded as lower than that of Koreans. Hanjin's goal during its first years in Subic was to create a fast, efficient labor force based on the original Pusan model. Karen, a former shipyard employee who was on friendly terms with one of her Korean managers, told me how she had once asked him about Hanjin's long-term plans for the shipyard:

> And my manager told me: After 20 years, or 30 years, hypothetically, Hanjin could be run by Filipinos. Filipino managers, Filipino foremen. There will be no more Koreans. That's why they are so harsh to the Filipinos. They are training us to become

more diligent workers, be like the Koreans, something like that. That's what he said
to me, after I asked him.

If this judgment reflects a widespread standpoint amongst the Korean leadership of the shipyard, then Subic Bay can be viewed as an experiment in
how to create a cheap but "Koreanized" workforce.

There is a clear logic to what the foremen were doing by subjecting
their workers to the *chal sara pose* treatment. Beyond reducing the risk
of injury by "warming the workers up" before the day's work, it produces
an obvious physical display of power, evoking the ancient idea that bodies
that move synchronically to a catchy beat can be controlled more easily by
those in charge (e.g., Bücher 1899). Trade unionists in Korea told me that
in the ephemeral moments when the union had been strong at Hanjin, the
foremen had a much harder time getting workers to line up each morning.
From Filipino workers themselves I heard only of isolated individual protests. Lauren, who used to work in an administrative position, thought the
entire routine was so degrading to her as a woman that she regularly hid in
the toilet when the siren sounded. Others opted to subvert *chal sara pose*
in more subtle ways. It became a joke amongst the Filipino workers to greet
each other by uttering *chal sara pose* in order to confirm that they, too, had
been subjected to this ridiculous routine by their Korean managers.

When it became clear that the spirit of *chal sara pose*—the faith in better
days to come at the cost of hard work and self-sacrifice—could not be
inculcated into these Filipino workers as management had hoped, another
strategy was deployed. In place of a song that to older Koreans brought
back vivid memories of the sweatshops and difficult labor conditions of
the 1970s, the new spirit of Korean capitalism was introduced in the guise
of "Gangnam Style." This world hit by K-pop singer PSY is an ironic composition about a Korean protagonist who pretends to be part of the filthy
rich (who in Seoul are concentrated in the upscale district of Gangnam). At
first sight, a song that mocks wealth and its conspicuous display seems an
unlikely choice for Hanjin's Filipino workers, yet it was much more favor-
ably received by the shipyard's workers than *chal sara pose* had been. The
notion that better days are to come soon if only we all clench our fists and
work ourselves nearly to death today, has been replaced with a less glorious,
ironic message: no matter how destitute we may be, we can still partake
in wealth by becoming well-versed in the art of pretending. Fake it if you
cannot make it, or die trying along the way.

Even as these dramatic orchestrations pit Filipinos against Koreans,
some Filipinos benefit greatly from their incorporation into the shipyard
while some Koreans on the lower rungs of management face hardships
of their own. Many Korean foremen are housed in substandard barracks

inside the shipyard where they suffer from social isolation, having left their relatives behind in South Korea for the duration of their contracts. Senior managers, in contrast, are allowed to bring their families along. They are housed in luxurious condo units in a secluded part of the Subic Bay Freeport Zone and can send their children to private international schools in the area at company expense. I was told in Korea by union activists that a group of Korean foremen had grown so dissatisfied with working and living conditions in Subic Bay that they filed a request for membership in the local branch of the metalworkers' union at the shipyard in Pusan. The Subic-based foremen had been unable to unionize in the Philippines, since the Filipino labor code defines foremen as lower management rather than rank-and-file workers—a specificity of Philippine law that undermines the potential for forging associational ties between foremen and their workers.

To be able to recruit Korean foremen at all, the company has to pay them wages that are competitive by South Korean standards and allow them to support the families they have left back home. The Filipino foremen, however, are paid according to Philippine wage levels. Thus a local foreman might end up getting paid one-tenth of the wage that his Korean counterpart makes for performing the exact same tasks. Nonetheless, Filipino rank-and-file workers who acquiesce to the Korean labor regime do still have real prospects of promotion and increased benefits. One reason for this is the high turnover among workers. Unskilled workers from poor, rural areas of the Philippines, whose jobs at the shipyard were often their first experience of waged work, found even the minimal wage to be attractive but often had difficulty showing up to work on time, which usually led to the termination of their contracts. On the other hand, those who stayed long enough to learn skills were frequently lured away by new opportunities in regions such as the Middle East, or by better offers at another shipyard nearby. This high rate of turnover has forced managers to make more concessions toward certain sections of the workforce.

In the project of binding an unstable workforce, hired through subcontractors, to the shipyard, the strategy of providing housing has recently become central. Most of the workforce lives in substandard housing in the urban areas nearby, where as many as ten workers share a room and basic facilities in order to save money. Since 2012, though, even these workers can dream of better arrangements. The housing project dubbed Hanjin Village was launched in the town of Castillejos, nineteen kilometers away from the shipyard, where the company purchased a thirty-hectare plot and developed it in cooperation with the state-run Pag-IBIG fund (a home development fund that also offers cheap loans to workers who wish to buy themselves a unit). With its security guards, wide streets, and lush greenery, this settlement emulated upmarket gated communities nearby. Eligibility to purchase a unit of this "good life" (cf. Fischer 2014) is reserved for workers of long standing, thereby enticing them to make a long-term commitment to a company that is simultaneously keeping them at bay through the particular subcontracting system it has built up around its shipyard.

Precarious Fixes: Accelerations, Accidents, and the (Un-)Making of Labor

The most recent shipyard fatality was Jerwin Labajan, aged twenty-three. He had been working nonstop for 20 hours when he was pinned down and crushed by the mobile elevated platform on which he was working (Macatuno 2014). At a workplace where time is the scarcest of all resources and labor is cheap and abundant, Labajan's death confirmed the clash between the diverse temporal rhythms of Filipino workers and Korean management.

Capitalist temporality has long been of interest to social scientists and historians (Thompson 1967; Parry 1999). The speeding up of production and the space-time compression triggered by global economic processes are integral to contemporary capitalism (Harvey 1989). In recent contributions to the anthropology of time, Laura Bear (2014a, 2014b) has argued against seemingly uniform understandings of capitalist time as necessarily entailing compression and acceleration. She critiques David Harvey's notion of the spatio-temporal fix, claiming that in his understanding of the term, "fixes" are undertaken only on a large, often global scale, causing the contribution of individual workers disappear entirely. Instead, Bear sees capitalism (envisioned as an inherently heterogeneous force) as essentially held in place by manifold acts of labor, which she argues are mediations that stitch local workplaces together with the temporal and spatial demands that emerge from global levels. By focusing on river pilots who navigate container ships down the Hooghly River, and the kind of everyday knowledge they deploy to make their way safely through dangerous currents amidst ever increasing time pressures, her informants actively bring together diverse social rhythms and temporalities that are often at odds with the abstract time that capitalism promotes.

Bear's Harvey is a straw man, since his notion of the "fix" is an inherently temporary and unstable category. However, she is right to take him to task for neglecting the role of labor in the (un)making of capital accumulation. His oversight is certainly problematic. Silver (2003), while accepting Harvey's argument that capital seeks to escape recurrent crises by overcoming territorial barriers and relocating its production sites to ever new terrains, augments his analysis by showing how labor unrest, too, has hopped from location to location. In a similar vein, I have shown that the large-scale, crisis-ridden accumulative cycles of the shipbuilding sector have been a driving force in the making of this particular "fix" from Pusan to Subic Bay. Hanjin has deployed a strategy of relocation to escape from a pesky labor conflict in Pusan, South Korea, but in addition to the transfer of capital and managerial staff, it is instructive to note the export of a specific set of labor control techniques.

Spatio-temporal fixes that engage a global scale of accumulation simultaneously express themselves in contentious encounters on the ground. The specific "divide-and-rule" tactics that Hanjin has been deploying in Subic include different paychecks for people of different national backgrounds and disparate housing arrangements. Transportation policy is also discriminatory—Hanjin runs a fast ferry to transport Korean and Romanian commuters between the Special Economic Zone and the shipyard on the other side of the bay, but Filipinos are compelled to take slow commuter buses. And because Hanjin does not have an in-house hospital, workers who have sustained serious injuries are taken to the nearest public hospital (in Olongapo City) by bus, though it would be much faster to use the ferry. According to ex-employee Lauren, "they move [the Filipino] workers by land, not by ship, because it's [too] expensive (*laughs*). They only use the ship if a Korean has an accident." Thinking back on her years working at the shipyard, Lauren told me that working there

> … is like survival of the fittest. You go home, alive and complete. You are lucky! (*laughs*) … I would never want to return … because you cannot sit there and see … the real things that happen there. Because for the [people] outside, they can sugar-coat anything. They can spin it into good news. But if you're inside, you can see workers … receiving physical abuse from the Koreans. That's why I resigned.

Social distinctions drawn along ethnic lines on the shop floor and the discrimination resulting from such strategies have also been described by Kim Jaesok (2014) in his book *Chinese Labor in a Korean Factory*, some sections of which resonate strongly with Korean labor management tactics I learned about in Subic Bay. These tactics, Kim also argues, "had been formulated through the Korean historical experiences of the Cold War, oppressive military government, and authoritarian work culture as a result of the military regime" (ibid.: 11). Indeed, the fact that Korean capitalists nowadays quite often seem to be exporting militaristic labor disciplinary strategies to Southeast Asia and beyond is itself worth noting, but our vision on this matter can be broadened by taking into account that for the most part these methods are no longer deployed in South Korean factories themselves, as Korean labor has gained more rights in the decades since the military dictatorship of Park Chung-hee came to an end.

In propping up the fierce speedup of work processes at the shipyard by harking back to older times, the Koreans in charge of the acceleration were marking the Philippines and its workers as "less advanced" than the Korean working population. The "catching up" made necessary by this gap had to take place in a concentrated fashion within a few years. But instead of buying into the South Korean version of capitalism that is being promised to them, my Subic Bay informants focused on the high frequency of accidents as a sign that the Korean-Filipino encounter has been anything but frictionless.

Koreans working in Hanjin's orbit, whether in Korea or the Philippines, tend to have diverse views as to why accidents are such a frequent occurrence. Many of them put the blame on the laziness, ineffectiveness, and deceitfulness of their Filipino workers, thereby perpetuating a kind of "myth of the lazy native" (Alatas 1977). Such ideas featured prominently during colonial capitalism in this region in earlier periods (Li 2011). One Korean complained in an online forum that many accidents at the shipyard happened because the Filipinos had sold off the protective gear they were given. This commentator noted that on his way to the shipyard, he often saw farmers working their fields in Hanjin uniforms (see Im 2009). In Pusan I spoke with Mr. Kim, a Korean Hanjin worker who had often been to Subic. He too noted the problem of widespread theft of equipment and material there. Once, he told me, a worker had wrapped so much stolen cable around his body underneath his clothes that he could barely walk and had eventually fallen over, thus exposing his theft. This story became rather popular amongst the Pusan-based workforce, possibly because it assured them that Filipino workers would not be able to keep up with their own level of work performance. "They will never be able to build ships as quickly as us," Mr. Kim said.

Kim's statement illuminates some of the obstacles that prevent workers in Pusan and Subic from connecting their predicaments through a joint labor struggle. Korean workers, who have experienced the brutal dismantlement of their regular workforce over the last decade, find it hard not to think of the Filipinos as lower-cost competition and cling to the notion that they are more competent than their "cheaper" equivalents in Subic. In spite of numerous efforts, the two countries' labor histories have often proven too different to allow for the emergence of a more solid transnational movement that would connect workers of both countries in a meaningful way. In the case presented here, then, labor as a political force is simultaneously made and unmade by one and the same offshoring project, and it is the issue of speed, including the connection between accelerated labor processes and accidents, that lies at the very heart of contestations around this workplace in the Philippines.

Accidents at the Subic shipyard are frequently understood as the outcome of pushing workers too hard to meet impossible deadlines. They are deeply disruptive events whose perceived randomness and meaninglessness strikes fear into the hearts of witnesses. When yet another accident temporarily slows the shipbuilding process, workers are reminded that while the building of ships takes a significant share of their lifetime in exchange for wages, it also occasionally brings a young life to a sudden end. At the same time, accidents cause difficulties for the Korean management, as public scrutiny heightens with every new casualty. Internal investigations have to be undertaken, reports about the "unsafe act" that occurred have to be written and filed, the press and local administrators need to be placated. Both management and the workforce see accidents as reminders of how uneven, unpredictable, and risky the experiment of creating a "Koreanized" labor force has been, up to this point. In the long run, the outrage these accidents have provoked among the larger Filipino public, which has come to sense that workers' lives are sacrificed for a project that exploits their labor, may yet bolster workers' political capacity to unite.

Acknowledgments

As part of Thomas Hylland Eriksen's European Research CouncilAdvanced Grant project "Overheating," I conducted seven months of field research in Subic Bay, where from September 2013 to April 2014 I explored the impact of a South Korean shipyard on the communities nearby. I did not have access to the shipyard during my time in Subic, but I was able to collaborate with various labor groups and NGOs working in the area. Additionally, I spent two weeks in Seoul and Pusan, South Korea, where I interviewed labor and human rights activists. I would like to thank James Carrier and Michael Burawoy for their insightful comments on an earlier draft.

Elisabeth Schober is Associate Professor at the Department of Social Anthropology, University of Oslo. For her doctorate at the Central European University (Budapest) she investigated responses to the social impact of US bases in South Korea. Recently, she has focused on the manifold challenges emerging from the relocation of manufacturing from Korea to the Philippines. She is the author of *Base Encounters* (2016) and has co-edited (with Thomas Hylland Eriksen) a special issue of *Ethnos* entitled "Economies of Growth or Ecologies of Survival?"

Notes

1. See https://hanjinworkers.wordpress.com/.
2. Even though Samahan boasted a membership of several thousand workers in 2010, Hanjin has refused to acknowledge this union. Given the company-level collective bargaining system at work in the Philippines, the conglomerate can argue that it is the wrong address for these workers' claims as practically all of the Filipino workers are employed through subcontractors. The Filipino Department of Labor, faced with unionization requests, has argued similarly. Samahan therefore registered as an association instead, but Hanjin objects to the use of its name in the association's title. Behind Samahan, an affiliate of the MAKABAYAN trade union center, stands the Movement for National Democracy (Kilusan para sa Pambansang Demokrasya), a group that understands itself as a socialist alternative to the Philippine Maoist movement. Samahan, through its organizational embedding into the larger movement of the Nationalist Left in the country, is a typical example of the "social movement unionism" that the fragmentation of the Philippine labor movement has given rise to (see Lambert 1990 and McKay 2006; on the role of the Far Left in the Philippine labor movement, see also West 1997).
3. A *chaebol* is a South Korean business conglomerate. On this Korean business model and the labor control strategies deployed in *chaebol* affiliates in Korea and abroad, see Chang (2006), Janelli (1993), and Kwon and O'Donnell (2001).
4. Some workers have disputed these numbers, claiming that some deaths have been hidden (Rudin 2013). In addition to the 38 work-related deaths that labor groups can document, Samahan alleges that up to 50 workers may have died from a malaria epidemic triggered in the region after the shipyard was constructed. This is not counted as a work-related accident, even though the explosion of malaria cases in the area has been clearly linked to the construction of the shipyard (dela Cruz 2009).
5. The number of Romanian foremen at the shipyard was said to be about 200 in 2013/14. Filipino workers have consistently pointed out to me that the Romanians have a very good reputation at the shipyard, as they are understood to be less prone than their Korean counterparts to resort to verbal and physical abuse in case of a conflict. Romanians, being Caucasian, have apparently managed to tap into the positive standing still accorded to white males in this particular part of the Philippines due to the US Navy legacy. A Romanian foreman explained to me that in his view, the main source of conflict between Filipinos and Koreans had to do with many Korean foremen's lack of the English skills needed to communicate efficiently with their workers. Korean shipbuilding competitor Daewoo has been running a shipyard in Mangalia, Romania, since 1997, so Hanjin was able to recruit from a sizable pool of Romanians with experience working under Koreans in the shipbuilding sector.
6. As one Samahan activist explained: "They are all gone. We only have a few organizers left at Hanjin, brave ones. The other ones are all gone. Because they have all been terminated." Another (non-organized) former worker, who quit of her own accord after seeing too many accidents at the shipyard, said: "If you are going to

be a member [of the union], you are going to be terminated. Or no promotion at all. I think this is why Hanjin has that one year before they give you a permanent position. They test you."

7. See the *Al Jazeera* documentary *Storm in Subic Bay*. Retrieved 6 October 2017 from http://www.aljazeera.com/programmes/101east/2011/12/2011121391029605826.html.

8. More than half of the country's population lives on less than 100 pesos (2 dollars and 20 cents) a day ("Economy under the Aquino Administration" 2014).

9. This practice is increasingly widespread amongst South Korean shipbuilders at home as well.

10. This drastic reduction reflects the fact that most of these subcontractors, virtually all of which seem to be at least partially run by Korean businessmen who followed Hanjin from South Korea to the Philippines, were not properly licensed to run their businesses in the Philippines. For instance, Ernesto Arellano, National President of the National Union of Building and Construction Workers (Philippines) pointed out that "only 19 of these 101 subcontractors are legitimately registered with the Philippines' Department of Labor and Employment (DOLE) ... Based on our survey, none of these registered 19 subcontractors have sufficient capitalization or heavy machinery required to fulfill the scope of work required under contract filed with DOLE" (Robinson 2011).

11. An organizer of the construction union NUBCW explained this dilemma: "When we decided to register a union inside Hanjin Heavy Industries-Philippines, the Department of Labor rejected our application twice. Because they said, these people are not employees of Hanjin. They are employees of the different subcontractors. So if you want to have a union, you have to put a union in each subcontractor. And if you have twenty subcontractors, you have 20 local unions. It's really ridiculous, you know."

12. At least 20 percent of all workers in a subcontracting unit must sign up for union membership before an official application can be submitted at the Philippine Department of Labour.

13. Around 10 percent of shipyard employees are women working primarily in administrative positions, but also in ship construction.

14. South Koreans, according to the most recent per capita annual labor data compiled by the OECD, on average work 2,163 hours a year, which puts them second only to Mexico (2,237 hours) (cf. Koreans 2014).

15. In October 2014, a report on drug use stated that "sources within the shipyard and the local police said ... that the illegal drug problem within the shipyard has worsened. One factor they cited was Hanjin's alleged policy of making workers do 24-hour shifts. Some workers ... said these long shifts have 'forced' some of them to use drugs just to stay awake. Not being alert on the job could result in death" (Datu 2014).

References

Alatas, Syed Hussein. 1977. *The Myth of the Lazy Native: A Study of the Image of Malays, Filipino and Javanese from the 16th to the 20th Century and Its Function in the Ideology of Colonial Capitalism*. London: Routledge.

Arrighi, Giovanni. 2009. *Adam Smith in Beijing: Lineages of the Twenty-First Century*. London: Verso.

Baca, George. 2011. "Resentment of Neoliberals in South Korea: Kim Jin-Sook and the Bus of Hope Movement." *Journal of Eurasian Studies* 8(4): 125–140.

Bear, Laura. 2014a. "Doubt, Conflict, Mediation: The Anthropology of Modern Time." *Journal of the Royal Anthropological Institute* 20(S1): 3–30.

———. 2014b. "For Labour: Ajeet's Accident and the Ethics of Technological Fixes in Time." *Journal of the Royal Anthropological Institute* 20(S1): 71–88.

Bücher, Karl. 1899. *Arbeit und Rhythmus*. Leipzig: B.G. Teubner Verlag.

Chang, Dae-oup. 2006. "Samsung Moves: A Portrait of Struggles." In *Labour in Globalising Asian Corporations: A Portrait of Struggle*, ed. Dae-oup Chang, 3–64. Hong Kong: Asia Monitor Resource Centre.

Cumings, Bruce. 1997. *Korea's Place in the Sun: A Modern History*. New York and London: W.W. Norton.

Datu, Randy. V. 2014. "Security Tightens at Hanjin Shipyard Over Workers' Drug Use." *Rappler*. Retrieved 6 October 2014 from http://www.rappler.com/nation/71234-security-tightens-hanjin-shipyard-workers-drug-use.

dela Cruz, Gil. 2009. "Malaria Epidemic in Subic, Zambales, Philippines." *Malaria Elimination* (blog). Retrieved from http://malariaelimination.blogspot.no/2009/04/malaria-epidemic-in-subic-zambales.html.

"Economy under the Aquino Administration: Worsening Exclusivity." *Ibon News*. Retrieved 28 July 2014 from http://ibon.org/ibon_articles.php?id=424.

Eriksen, Thomas Hylland. 2016. *Overheating: An Anthropology of Accelerated Change*. London: Pluto Press.

Fischer, Edward. 2014. *The Good Life: Aspiration, Dignity, and the Anthropology of Wellbeing*. Stanford, CA: Stanford University Press.

Friedman, Jonathan. 2004. *Hegemonic Decline: Past and Present*. Boulder, CO, and London: Paradigm.

Fuller, Ken. 2009. "Korean Owned Shipyard a 'Killing Field.'" *Tribune Magazine*. Retrieved 23 February 2009 from http://www.tribunemagazine.org/2009/02/ken-fuller-korean-owned-shipyard-%E2%80%98a-killing-field%E2%80%99/.

George, Rose. 2013. *Ninety Percent of Everything: Inside Shipping, the Invisible Industry that Puts Clothes on Your Back, Gas in Your Car, Food on Your Plate*. New York: Metropolitan Books.

Glassman, Jim and Young-Jin Choi. 2014. "The Chaebol and the US Military-Industrial Complex: Cold War Geopolitical Economy and South Korean Industrialization." *Environment and Planning* 46: 1160–1180.

Grey, Eva. 2015. "Southeast Asia's Shipbuilding Solution." *Ship-technology.com*. Retrieved 29 May 2015 from http://www.ship-technology.com/features/feature southeast-asias-shipbuilding-evolution-4572766/.

Harvey, David. 1989. *The Condition of Post-Modernity*. Oxford: Blackwell.

———. 2003. *The New Imperialism*. Oxford: Oxford University Press.

Im, Shi-Yeon. 2009. "Subicchosŏnso algo chom jaegi hapshida". *IMBC*. Retrieved 06 October 2017 from http://imbbs.imbc.com/view.mbc?list_id=1708973&pre_list_id=1&next_list_id=1709003&page=1&bid=pd_bbs&sk=user_name&sv=%C0%D3%B-D%C3%C7%F6.

Jabola-Carolus, Khara. 2010. "A Killing Field in the Philippines." *Labor Is Not a Commodity* (blog). Retrieved 5 April 2010 from http://laborrightsblog.typepad.com/international_labor_right/2010/04/a-killing-field-in-the-philippines.html.

Janelli, Roger. 1993. *Making Capitalism: The Social and Cultural Construction of a South Korean Conglomerate*. Stanford, CA: Stanford University Press.

Johnson, Chalmer. 2004. *The Sorrows of Empire: Militarism, Secrecy, and the End of the Republic*. New York: Metropolitan Books.

Kim, Jaesok. 2013. *Chinese Labor in a Korean Factory: Class, Ethnicity, and Productivity on the Shop Floor in Globalizing China*. Stanford, CA: Stanford University Press.

Kim, Young-Hak. 2014. "The Resurgence of Shipping." *Txf News*. Retrieved 1 May 2014 from http://www.txfnews.com/News/Article/2772/The-resurgence-of-shipping.

Koo, Hagen. 2000. *Korean Workers: The Culture and Politics of Class Formation*. Ithaca, NY: Cornell University Press.

"Koreans Work 2nd Longest Hours in OECD". 2014. *Korea Herald*. Retrieved 06 October 2017 from http://www.koreaherald.com/view.php?ud=20140825000723.

Kwon, Seung-ho and Michael O'Donnell. 2001. *The Chaebol and Labour in Korea: The Development of Management Strategy in Hyundai*. London: Routledge.

Lambert, Rob. 1990. "Kilusan Mayo Uno and the Rise of Social Movement Unionism in the Philippines." *Labor & Industry* 3(2–3): 258–280.

Levinson, Michael. 2006. *The Box: How the Shipping Container Made the World Smaller and the World Economy Bigger*. Princeton, NJ: Princeton University Press.

Lee, Sun-young. 2011. "Hanjin Boss Apologizes for Dispute". *Korea Herald*. Retrieved 06 October 2016 from http://www.koreaherald.com/national/Detail.jsp?news MLId=20110818000777.

Li, Tania Murray. 2011. "Centering Labor in the Land Grab Debate." *Journal of Peasant Studies* 38(2): 281–298.

Lie, John. 1998. *Han Unbound: The Political Economy of South Korea*. Stanford, CA: Stanford University Press.

Lutz, Catherine. ed. 2009. *The Bases of Empire: The Global Struggle against U.S. Military Posts*. New York: New York University Press.

Macatuno, Allan. 2014. "Extended Work Hours Cited in Death in Hanjin." *Inquirer*. Retrieved 6 October 2016 from http://newsinfo.inquirer.net/639624/extended-work-hours-cited-in-death-in-hanjin.

McKay, Steven C. 2006. "The Squeaky Wheel's Dilemma: New Forms of Labor Organizing in the Philippines." *Labor Studies Journal* 30(4): 41–63.

Nam, Hwasook. 2009. *Building Ships, Building a Nation: Korea's Democratic Unionism under Park Chung Hee*. Seattle, WA: University of Washington Press.

Ofreneo, Rene E. 2013. "Precarious Philippines: Expanding Informal Sector, Flexibilizing Labor Market." *American Behavioral Scientist* 57(4): 420–443.

Parry, Jonathan. 1999. "Lords of Labour: Working and Shirking in Bhilai." *Contributions to Indian Sociology* 33: 107–140.

Reyes, Victoria. 2015. "Legacies of Place and Power: From Military Base to Freeport Zone." *City and Community* 14(1): 1–26.

Robinson, tammy ko. 2011. "South Korea's 300 Day Aerial Sit-in Strike Highlights Plight of Precarious Workers in Korea and the Philippines." *Asia-Pacific Journal* (9)45. Retrieved 6 October 2017 from http://www.japanfocus. org/-tammy_ko-Robinson/3644.

Rudin, Daniel. 2013. "Workers Find Ways: The Ship Builder." *Rappler*. Retrieved 15 September 2013 from http://www.rappler.com/business/26562-workers-find-ways-graveyard-shipyard.

Schober, Elisabeth. 2016. *Base Encounters: The U.S. Armed Forces in South Korea*. London: Pluto Press.

———. In press. "Between a Rock and a Stormy Place: From Overheating to Expulsion in Subic Bay (Philippines)." *Ethnos*.

Schuler, Mike. 2015. "Hanjin Heavy Industries Confirms 20,600 TEU Container Ship Orders." *GCaptain*. Retrieved 6 April 2015 from https://gcaptain.com/hanjin-heavy-industries-confirms-20600-teu-container-ship-orders/.

Silver, Beverly. 2003. *Forces of Labor. Workers' Movements and Globalization Since 1870*. Cambridge: Cambridge University Press.

Thompson, E.P. 1967. "Time, Work-Discipline, and Industrial Capitalism." *Past & Present* 38: 56–97.

West, Lois. 1997. *Militant Labor in the Philippines*. Philadelphia, PA: Temple University Press.

9

Relative Precarity
Decline, Hope, and the Politics of Work

Andrew Sanchez

Introduction

On the morning after India's general election of 2014, the streets of Jamshedpur were littered with discarded political banners and leaflets. The election had dominated the Indian media for several months as politicians pledged solutions to the endemic national concerns of poverty and corruption. For the past two weeks, Jamshedpur was filled with convoys of jeeps and motorcycles that circled the city proclaiming a brighter future through distorted PA systems. But the streets were quiet that morning as I made my way across town in a shared rickshaw to begin a day's fieldwork at a local scrap metal yard called Lohar Enterprises. My fellow passengers were a cross-section of the usual rush hour traffic. An elderly man carried a set of iron scales and a large sack filled with vegetables, another wore the faded white shirt and safety shoes of a foreman in the nearby Tata Steel plant, and the third was a young businessman carrying a smart leather satchel. The nail of each man's right index finger was dyed black with indelible ink, proving that they had voted in the election the day before.

At Lohar Enterprises the day was much like any other. Two cycle rickshaws stood piled with loads of iron rods while their drivers waited for 32-year-old Jivesh to weigh them on the large balance scale in the center of the yard. Jivesh called the weight to Manoj and Ranjit, the uncle and nephew who own the business. While 66-year-old Ranjit noted the weight and value of the material in a ledger, his nephew, 63-year-old Manoj, paid the rickshaw drivers from a leather purse stuffed with rupee notes. Seated under the corrugated iron lean-to that served as the yard office, Manoj and Ranjit drank cups of hot tea and argued with customers over the constant sound of hammering from the yard. At its back, three men used axes and cudgels to flatten steel oil cans into bundles of metal that were tightly bound with wire. At the front of the yard, another two men and a woman sat on upturned paint tins, using chisels and heavy hammers to disassemble bicycle wheels and electric motors. With the exception of Manoj and Ranjit, none of the yard's workers had had a fingernail dyed at a pollingxbooth.

That day, I squatted on the ground beside Rakesh, Dipesh, and Sapna. We chatted as their tools reduced a heap of bicycle wheels into piles of chopped metal. Seeing that all three of them lacked the telltale black finger of a recent voter, I asked whether they had visited their local polling booth the day before. Forty-year-old Sapna shrugged and simply shook her head, while 32-year-old Rakesh looked sheepish and said there was a "problem" at the polling station. When asked to elaborate, he explained that he had not wanted to wait in the long line to vote and had gone home instead. Dipesh, who was thirty-three, was more expansive:

What is the point in voting? All of the candidates are the same. All of the parties are the same. Whoever wins, after the election everything will be the same.

Dipesh's colleagues nodded that he was right and agreed that elections were essentially pointless. The men and women I was speaking with enjoyed the benefits of regular work and were therefore more fortunate than the unemployed masses in India's villages. Nonetheless, the workers of Lohar Enterprises regarded themselves as precarious persons whose lives thus far had been defined by strife and personal tragedy. Mostly in their thirties and forties, they had migrated to Jamshedpur from impoverished villages in neighboring states as young children when a parent's death or illness forced them to seek their fortune in the nearest prosperous town. Sapna had become destitute following her husband's premature death from stomach cancer many years earlier, and now relied on her 200-rupee (2 pounds sterling) daily wage to survive. The labor force of Lohar Enterprises was drawn from the disparate demographic of rural Indians who have been pushed and pulled across the subcontinent by drought, famine, disease, unemployment, and communal violence for centuries. The day after the Indian general election, the dominant opinion among the employees of Lohar Enterprises was that whoever won, the issues that affected their lives were unlikely to change.

I initially found this perspective surprising. In the days leading up to the election, Lohar workers and I had discussed topics as varied as poverty, the labor market, and corruption in some detail. However, what the election revealed was that despite having a critical outlook on the key issues of the national campaign, scrap yard workers doubted the possibility that positive change could take place through collective political action and were therefore skeptical of the parliamentary process. Regional literature suggests that poorer Indians are more politically engaged than the middle classes (Chatterjee 2004), and that voter turnout is higher in India than in almost any other industrialized nation (Banerjee 2014). However, it would be simplistic to assume that a lack of electoral participation infers an absence of political opinion in the case described here. In fact the workers of Lohar Enterprises held well-informed opinions about key election issues—they just felt that the results of the election would be unlikely to impact upon those issues in a way that was relevant to them. This type of engagement with electoral politics sets Dipesh, Sapna, and Rakesh apart from the majority of their countrymen, and their experiences should not be read as a case study about the political dispositions of the "Indian poor" per se. Rather, Lohar workers articulate the political consciousness of a disparate swathe of global persons whose experiences of marginality have led them to lack faith in political institutions. These are not the anomic actions of people who feel they have nothing to lose. Rather, they are the reasonable responses of people who feel that they have nothing to gain.

Unlike most members of the "political society" of subaltern India (Chatterjee 2004), Lohar workers are largely alienated from the traditional networks of kinship, caste, and place that embed electoral politics within collective entitlements. As marginal persons who lack an inalienable identity even with one another, their precarity is a characteristic of life that extends far beyond the domain of wages and employment contracts, and has continuing effects upon the nature of political action. Over the next few days, it became clear that Lohar workers' perspectives on the Indian general election extended to most forms of institutionalized politics, including trade unionism, which was generally regarded as ineffectual. This cynical reading of political institutions was a wholly different type of engagement with the experience of precarity from that found among precariously employed workers in the city's larger industrial workplaces (Sanchez 2016).

Since the 1990s, precarity and uncertainty are no longer restricted to Jamshedpur's rural migrants in scrap yards, construction sites, and small factories. Over the course of the previous two decades, the labor forces of the city's Tata Steel and Tata Motors plants suffered a dramatic decline in their standard of living as well-paid, lifetime employment was replaced by a complex system of short-term contracts that routinely pay even less than Sapna's daily wage of 200 rupees (2 pounds). So while the city's traditional "aristocracy of labor" once benefited from the security of Tata company pensions, housing, and the knowledge that one's children could effectively inherit one's job, younger Tata workers today negotiate their daily lives with little certainty regarding their employment. As the Tata workforce now enters its second generation of casual labor, even the economic security that derives from being the precariously employed child of a well-paid worker has begun to erode. Casual employees' precarity used to be mediated by secure residence in the company homes of their parents, but this resource is now slowly declining. Meanwhile, though the standard of living in the contrasting economic environments I describe may be increasingly similar, the subjective political experience of precarity is different in important ways. While Lohar workers experience precarity as a constant condition of vulnerability, Tata workers engage their present in historically dynamic terms that invoke labor struggle and the formal structures of promotion, to stress the possibility for advancement.

A popular discourse among Jamshedpur's casual Tata workers claimed that corrupt and violent relations between corporate capitalism and trade unions had facilitated the erosion of their employment security (Sanchez 2010, 2012a, 2012b, 2015b). But though it was deeply critical of the practices and motives of contemporary political elites, this discourse nonetheless used a language of corruption to restate the value of the *ideal practices* from which they deviated. Despite experiencing the negative effects of pervasive trade union corruption, the increasingly precarious employees of the Tata Motors plant believe strongly in the feasibility of positive political change and assume that uncorrupted forms of representative democracy have the capacity to improve their lives. By comparison, the workers of Lohar Enterprises regard institutional forms of politics such as parliamentary democracy and trade unionism as inherently incapable of alleviating the suffering of their everyday lives. A striking characteristic of this perspective is that although it speaks critically about contemporary political structures, it neither engages with nor suggests alternatives to them.

A large body of current research demonstrates that precarity characterizes an increasingly broad swathe of the globe's working lives. This volume' focus is on industrial labor, however insecure employment is also a recurrent theme in the modern service sector, care work, administration, creative industries, education, and consultancy. This development is consistent with the processes of accumulation by dispossession, and one can theorize the global attack on employment security as an act of elite class struggle (Sanchez 2016: 26). On this basis, it is tempting to view precariously employed persons as a newly emergent class that enjoys economic and ideological coherence. However, this chapter demonstrates two ways in which the model of "precarity-as-class" is not well substantiated. First, by comparing precarious industrial employment in two different sectors in the same city, I show that the experience of precarity is heavily informed by peoples' history and expectations. One can identify diverse workforces with similar wage levels and welfare packages, but people's response to the facts of their situation depends upon whether their current condition is perceived to be new or subject to further change. Second, I demonstrate why a precarious workforce in any given instance is not *necessarily* distinct from a coherent class of "labor aristocrats," especially within sectors that have undergone a significant decline in working conditions. These two points show why precarity cannot be deployed as a blunt analytic of class, and why class itself is something more than a static index of employment conditions.

I argue that although employees in Tata industry are currently experiencing a casualization of their employment, they nonetheless understand this process in reference to a long, shared history of successful labor struggle and secure family employment that provides a tangible model of what the "good life" looks like and how one attains it. Accordingly, Tata workers continue to believe in their ability to effect positive change on their lives via uncorrupted forms of collective political action. Classic sociological analyses have similarly claimed that "affluent" industrial labor forces place their faith in collective rather than individualized politics as a means of realizing ambitions (Goldthorpe et al. 1969: 153). However, Goldthorpe and colleagues' research subjects lived and worked in secure environments and were optimistic that their ambitions would be fulfilled, whereas the emphasis in the Tata workplace is instead on the presence of structures that would make such fulfillment possible. For their part, scrap yard workers regard their poverty and lack of security as perennial conditions of life that are essentially personal rather than collective experiences. Based on a comparison of these cases, I conclude that conceptual models of the "precariat," notably that of Standing (2011), fail to grasp class as a dynamic historical object that intersects with experiences of struggle, decline, hope, and fatalism.

Jamshedpur and the Tata Political Imagination

Jamshedpur is the site of the Tata Motors and Tata Steel plant, which was built in 1907 by the industrialist Jamshed Tata, after whom the city is named (Bahl 1995; Fraser 1919; Pillai 1923). Today, Jamshedpur is a prosperous industrial city of 1.3 million people, many of them descended from labor migrants who arrived from the Indian states of Bihar, Bengal, Uttar Pradesh, Chhattisgarh, and Orissa in the early twentieth century (Weiner 1978: 161). Tata industrialization in the early twentieth century was based on the North American "company town" model, in which settled workers lived in company homes, were cared for in company hospitals, and had their children educated at company schools (Keenan and Sorsby 1945: 33). Throughout the 1900s, the company built townships where tens of thousands of steelworkers lived in houses and apartment blocks. Between these industrial townships, eclectic non-company neighborhoods gradually emerged on land leased from the Tata company. Here, in various states of poverty and prosperity, there currently live hundreds of thousands of merchants, entrepreneurs, service-sector workers, and laborers such as those employed by Lohar Enterprises.

Throughout much of the twentieth century, Indian taxes on imports were high, foreign investment tightly controlled, and foreign ownership of Indian companies all but prohibited. The older national corporations flourished in this environment, and the company town model provided Tata with a stable, well-supported labor force. However, once India's economy was liberalized in 1991, Tata's monopoly in the production of trucks and private-sector steel began to collapse. Cheap imports flooded the domestic market, and Tata's ailing rivals in the manufacture of automobiles were reinvigorated by investment from Japan, Europe, and North America. Faced with declining profits, Tata proposed early retirement for large numbers of employees in Jamshedpur, whose jobs could then be filled by cheaper casual workers. This new, flexible labor force would receive lower wages and none of the employment benefits that had characterized Tata work for decades. Families that had worked in the same plant and lived in the same townships for generations now faced a future where children's standard of living would be lower than their parents'.

When Tata redundancies were first proposed in the early 1990s, much of the Tata Workers' Union leadership took pride in harmonious relationship with the company, which had not seen its members strike since the 1920s. To maintain this harmony, the union refused membership to thousands of disgruntled maintenance staff and seasonal laborers, and had been beset by popular allegations of corruption for decades. In 1993, when the union's president, V.G. Gopal, proposed a general strike to resist the casualization of permanent jobs, the strongest opposition came from within his own organization. That same year, two gunmen hired by members of Gopal's own union committee assassinated him outside his office.[1] After Gopal's death, the casualization of Tata labor met with no further resistance from the Tata Workers' Union. By the time I began research on the shop floor of the Tata Motors plant in 2006, more than three-quarters of all company workers were employed on fixed-term contracts that could be terminated without notice. They were barred from membership in the plant's only trade union, took home as little as one-fifth of the wages paid to their permanent colleagues, and were not entitled to sick pay, pensions, or company health care, homes, or schooling for their children. Such "casual" workers, recruited from company families, accumulated years of continuous service on a single shop floor as they were shifted back and forth between different job categories of employment. Many claimed that corrupt and violent trade union leaders were complicit in the casualization process, a charge leveled by both the casually employed majority and their permanently employed fathers (Sanchez 2016).

Despite the pervasive discourse of corruption among Tata workers, company employees today are generally proud of their union's illustrious early history, in which a series of iconic strikes in the 1920s secured minimum wages, maximum working hours, and maternity pay for union members (Bahl 1995; Keenan and Sorsby 1945: 133–136). Tata employees viewed the collective actions of their shop-floor ancestors as having laid the foundation for several generations of prosperity. Throughout much of the early twentieth century, the securely employed Tata workforce presented a stark contrast to the insecure urban proletariat elsewhere in India (Chandavarkar 1985, 1994, 1999; Gooptu 2001). Even after the establishment of Nehru's public-sector steel towns in the 1950s and 1960s, Tata workers remained the national archetype of a secure, well-compensated labor force (cf. Parry 1999a, 1999b; Parry and Strümpell 2008). The notion that this status was at least partly fought and won through trade unionism is integral to the workforce's political consciousness as an industrial elite. Furthermore, even the most critical workers express a positive identification with an unbroken line of family employment within the company, which often stretches back a century.

The principle of the heritability of Tata employment effectively stabilized a migrant labor force in a private-sector industry that called for continuous year-round production. By 1938, less than 3 percent of Tata workers engaged in agricultural production in their home regions, while a quarter claimed to have severed relations with their "native place" entirely (Bahl 1982: 34). For four generations thereafter, Tata offered an effective guarantee of lifetime employment to the children of its workers, with all employees entitled to nominate a "ward" for preference in recruitment. A ward is typically an employee's eldest son, who graduates from school or university and then joins Tata in anticipation of a company home and health care plan, with a lifetime of employment thereafter.

However, ever since India's economic liberalization Tata wards have entered the labor force under an array of short-term contracts offering lower wages than those received by employees in the Lohar Enterprises scrap yard (Sanchez 2012a: 813).[2] As outlined in Table 9.1, in 2006, although the gross monthly pay packet of a permanent Tata employee could be as

Table 9.1 Summary of Tata Motors work grades and salaries (2006)

Employment Grade and Description	Union Membership	Monthly Salary (rupees)	Monthly Allowances (rupees)*
Tata Motors Full-Time Apprentice • Worker in a 3-year training program. • Usually the ward of a permanent employee. • To sit government exam.	Ineligible	1,500 Year 1 2,000 Year 2 2,400 Year 3	None
Tata Motors Skilled Trainee • Worker in a 3-year training program. • Usually the ward of a permanent employee. • To sit company exam. • Identified as "skilled."	Ineligible	2,400	None
Temporary Worker • Usually previously failed Tata Motors training or • Not a ward of a permanent employee.	Ineligible	5,000	None
Contract Worker • Usually the ward of a permanent employee and either: • A graduated apprentice or trainee or • A previous recipient of discontinued "temporary" work through a labour bureau under 3- to 5-week contracts.	Ineligible	6,000	None
Basic Worker (i.e., permanent) • Usually the ward of a permanent employee.	Eligible	8,000–12,000	2,701–2,759

*Dearness allowance (1,235–1,293 per calendar month (pcm)); travel allowance (685 pcm); house maintenance allowance (276 pcm); uniform maintenance allowance (455 pcm); sanitation allowance (50 pcm).
Source: Tata Motors Company, Jamshedpur.

high as 14,759 rupees, a third of workers earned less than the 50-rupee legal minimum daily wage by virtue of being classified as "apprentices." Apprentices and trainees are the only Indian workers formally denied a minimum wage or maximum working hours.[3] However, because Tata casual labor is structured as an uncertain process of regularization—by which one ostensibly progresses from trainee to temporary worker to contract worker before possibly entering permanent employment in the distant future—the popular sense is that there exists an institutional mechanism by which advancement out of precarity is theoretically possible (Sanchez 2012a). Furthermore, the experience of sudden decline in one's entitlement to secure employment has led casual Tata workers to regard their current status as a betrayal of older forms of corporate industrialism.

The working poor of India's scrap yards may never have expected to attain formal job security, but in casualized corporate environments the recent loss of people's former status informed a strongly collective sense of injustice on the shop floor. Tata's casual labor force in Jamshedpur is largely comprised of people from company families whose adolescence was defined by anticipation of a career in a corporation internationally renowned for its employment benefits. But in contrast to earlier generations of Tata employees that could expect to have a secure home and a good deal of disposable income by their mid twenties, the experience of today's casual workers is radically different from that of their parents. The situation is particularly acute for young apprentices. Their salaries are usually too low to allow them to leave their parents' homes, and their long-term prospects are unappealing to marriage partners. Many still live in their childhood bedrooms well into their late twenties while they consider the origins of, and solutions to, their current predicament (Sanchez 2012b). As a result, the current generation of Tata wards engages very assertively with the experience of precarity, using a language of disappointment and betrayal to state that one's current position is not only unpleasant, but unjust. This perspective is further solidified when current experience is judged against the successful trade union struggles of the 1920s that loom so large in the workforce's self-understanding.

While the global decline of the company town model poses serious problems for the industrial family as the elder generation shifts to a potentially rather different class position (Narotzsky 2010), interpreting the current struggle within such a family history fosters development of the conceptual tools needed to view political-economic problems of this kind as collective concerns (Narotzsky 2015). For example, in a conversation much like many others I had on the shop floor of the Tata Motors plant, a middle-aged man asked me to look across his workplace to see where the union was "right now" and whether it was doing anything useful. Using his own predicament as an illustration, he explained that he had been continuously employed as a contract laborer in the Tata Motors plant, earning significantly less than others performing the same work, for twelve years. He considered himself adept at the relatively low-skilled tasks he had performed for more than a decade, but only a month earlier, his foreman had selected him to undergo a compulsory six months of "refresher training" that entailed a pay cut of 1,000 rupees (£10) per month, even though his daily work remained unchanged in practice. This nominal reclassification scuppered his hopes of petitioning for regularization in the near future. The union was indifferent to his complaint, since he (like three-quarters of his colleagues) was not allowed to become a member.

Popular corruption discourses on the Tata shop floor explain casual labor with reference to the failures of political institutions. What is more telling, however, is that workers' attempts to negotiate these failings implicitly support the ideals on which those institutions are based. For example, in September 2006 the Tata Motors apprentices began to agitate for a bonus during the religious holiday of Durga Puja, ostensibly because the occasion called for personal expenditure that other employees were compensated for.[4] In the plant's hierarchy of payments, permanent workers received a 17.99 percent bonus during the month of Durga Puja, whereas casual workers received only 7.9 percent and apprentices receive nothing at all. Although the apprentices' bonus complaints were real enough, the issue articulated a broader dissatisfaction with current Tata employment practice. In the days leading up to the holiday, apprentices throughout the plant began to voice their discontent in increasingly vocal and indignant terms, questioning the legality of their employment:

> We [the apprentices] are supposed to only do four hours' work a day, the rest is supposed to be training, but this is a big company and gives a lot of money to the government, so they [the government] will do nothing for us. The company even claims back money for our wages under the Apprentices Act. Tata Motors are making two profits; they are using us for work and production and are claiming back our wages also.

Led by a small group of charismatic agitators, the apprentices of the Tata Motors Chassis Division followed the example of a famous 1928 Tata labor dispute by staging a sit-down to halt production. However, key provisions of the Apprentices Act disenfranchise trainees from legislative protection, and several strikers were summarily sacked that same day (Sanchez 2012b: 444). For those who remained on the shop floor, further unrest was forestalled by the threat of redundancies and the refusal, by the plant's only trade union, to oppose them.[5]

Despite such events, the Tata discourse on precarity and civic decline is still grounded in the same language of localized class struggle that defined

Tata labor politics throughout the twentieth century (Sanchez 2016)—hence the popular belief that the injustices and inequalities of daily life can be explained with reference to the corruption of political structures. Here "corruption" implies that the principles and ideal practices of institutions such as parliament and trade unions are essentially sound, even if they are presently undermined by systemic criminality. By comparison, the explanatory political models of Lohar Enterprises workers posit poverty and suffering as perennial conditions of life for India's poorest citizens, and claim that these conditions are resistant to political change. For employees in such workplaces, faith in the efficacy of political change is undermined by the lack of any clear examples of this type of change having actually occurred. Working within a horizontal labor regime that lacks promotional structures and intergenerational security, where employees define their misfortune through highly personal experiences of tragedy, precarity cannot be confined to the politics and conditions of labor.

Work, Suffering, and the Lohar Political Imagination

Lohar Enterprises was founded in 1977 by a family of Hindu migrants who had escaped communal violence in the Pakistani Punjab in 1947 by fleeing to India with their six sons. The family carried liquid assets in the form of gold and cash, which they shrewdly invested in a detergent factory, and later a civil engineering firm. When Manoj (the eldest of the six brothers' children) married in 1977, his father gave him the considerable sum of 50,000 rupees (500 pounds) to start his own business. With the support of his youngest uncle, Manoj founded the Lohar Enterprises scrap yard and began buying mild-steel waste from a fleet of cycle rickshaw drivers and selling it to one of several large melting plants. Today the yard employs a foreman who earns 8,000 rupees (80 pounds) per month and is responsible for the day-to-day operation of the business; four daily wage workers who earn 200 rupees (2 pounds) per day to collect, weigh, and process material brought in by rickshaw drivers and other sellers; and three piece-rate workers with an average daily income of 300 rupees (3 pounds) who are responsible for the greater part of skilled disassembly work and the compacting of processed metal into 50-kilogram bundles.

The thirty rickshaw drivers who supply a large proportion of the yard's raw materials are male, Muslim seasonal migrants from impoverished villages in the neighboring state of Bihar. The drivers hire their vehicles from the yard for 10 rupees (0.10 pounds) per day and regard themselves as self-employed entrepreneurs. Though they are frequently members of the same extended families, they compete fiercely with one another for access to the city garbage dumps, neighborhoods, and industrial workplaces where they find their material. Most also use the Lohar vehicles to collect plastic, glass, and paper waste for sale to other specialist yards across the city. The majority have worked intermittently for Lohar enterprises for many years. The three piece-rate workers who transform disorderly mounds of waste into regularly shaped cubes of metal are closely related Adivasi tribal men who cycle to work every day from a nearby village. All three began work in the yard as children in the early 1980s, and there has been little change since in either the size and composition of the labor force, or the form and extent of the yard's business. The yard's four daily-wage workers, who are based at the front of the yard and charged with handling the scales, collections, deliveries, and lighter disassembly, are also long-term employees. Three are men aged 32–33, while the woman worker Sapna, as mentioned above, is forty. All the men have worked in the yard for 20–25 years. Sapna, started work in the yard nine years ago. All of the daily-wage workers are Hindu migrants from the neighboring states of West Bengal, Chhattisgarh, and Orissa.

Lohar Enterprises lacks any formal employment security and certainly makes no provision for pensions, yet a measure of stability is nonetheless afforded by the personal relationships that workers enjoy with their bosses. The owners of the scrap yard are present every day at the workplace, where they perform the entrepreneurial work of negotiating contracts for waste collection and haulage, and the difficult task of managing corrupt law enforcement officers' demands for protection money. But although they play an active role in the business negotiations of the yard, Manoj and Ranjit favor a hands-off approach to its tactile labor. Both men place a great deal of trust in their employees, whom they have generally known for much of their lives, and make ad hoc concessions to the demands of their personal circumstances. Although the yard is formally closed only one day per year, workers are permitted to take occasional unpaid vacations and sick days without jeopardizing their position. The yard will also tolerate sporadic non-attendance during alcoholic binges, providing that the employee in question is an otherwise competent worker. Daily work is subject to little overt instruction on the part of Manoj, Ranjit, or their elderly foreman, so workers are largely left to complete tasks under their own initiative. In this environment, employees who have proven themselves willing and capable of working well without supervision are regarded as an important resource. As such, the current cohort of employees has managed to acquire a good deal of informal stability in their work.

Even though employment in Lohar Enterprises is informally secure over many years, employees nonetheless experience their lives as a daily struggle against economic precarity and all find it difficult to support their families on the wages they earn. With the exception of Sapna, who is a widow raising a teenage daughter, all of the workers belong to families in which the household income must be supplemented by the labor of a spouse. The wives of Lohar employees work at sewing machines in their home, stitching clothes to sell in the marketplace, operate tea stalls, or take on work as cleaners and construction site laborers. However, Lohar workers still struggle to pay their rent, provide food for their families, and replace their work clothes, which degenerate at an alarming rate under the trying conditions of their labor. In this sense, scrap metal workers share some affinity with the current generation of young Tata workers, whose wage levels are frequently far lower, and who are unable to depend upon a future of secure company employment (Sanchez 2012b).

However, in contrast to the Tata case, economically precarious workers in Lohar Enterprises do not understand their current condition as a decline from any particular historical standard, since most hail from impoverished families that have never known security of any kind. The workplace has no history of emotive and successful labor disputes, and no evidence of any clear, positive improvement can be seen over the course of a single career in the yard. The yard's foreman, for example, a congenial 65-year-old man who migrated to Jamshedpur from the Punjab in 1972, was not forced from his home by any specific family tragedy as his subordinates were. Rather, as a bored and restless young man, he simply decided to work his way across the country in search of a new life elsewhere. Upon arriving in Jamshedpur, he spent four months working as a laborer on a building site, after which he became a supervisor on a road crew operated by a contractor. Shortly after Lohar Enterprises was founded, he was recruited as the yard's foreman. Conspicuously, his career advancement had not taken place within the yard itself, which he joined in the supervisory capacity that he still holds to this day. The men and women whose work he oversees likewise hold the very same posts that they were recruited for as children and young adults. One might expect that belief in the capacity for political change requires engagement with a precedent for that change taking place. I suggest that in workplaces like Lohar Enterprises, political fatalism coincides with political cynicism partly because of the shape of the employment regime itself. Most notably, the horizontal structure of the workforce and the lack of any clear career trajectory inspire a belief that life-altering changes are unlikely to arise from within the workplace.

The bulk of Lohar Enterprises' employees were between the ages of seven and twelve when they began working in the yard. Long-term career prospects are limited in a small, family-run business of this kind. A child that enters employment in the yard can expect to learn many specialized skills such as accurately identifying a wide variety of metals, dismantling complex items of machinery, collecting waste materials from workshops, and defusing tensions with customers. However, although a worker might be expected to become more competent at these tasks over time and accordingly attain the respect of colleagues, neither the work itself nor the level of remuneration is subject to change throughout a career. As Lohar Enterprises' workers progressed from childhood to adulthood, they acquired families of their own and underwent profound changes in their personal lives. In the workplace, the only discernible change associated with maturation is the ability to perform larger volumes of the same work. For employees in this environment, despite length of service and depth of skill, there is no clear place to which one *could* progress over time. As the yard employs only eight people, there is no formal hierarchy among workers, nor any structure that rewards lengthy employment with pay increases or pensions. Such structures are popularly regarded as characteristic of large workplaces with specialized bureaucracies (e.g., corporate shop floors, the railways, or civil service). Lohar workers therefore consider the poverty of everyday life to be impervious to change via the workplace, and their engagement with the notion of progress and historical change differs fundamentally from cases such as Tata. With regard to industrial attitudes and behaviors, Goldthorpe et al. (1968: 118) suggested that fatalism is a traditional defense marshaled by the working poor. I argue that such attitudes are best conceived not as reactive defenses against precarity, but rather as reasonable appraisals of actual economic and political conditions.

This sensation that one's life is decoupled from advancement seems particularly alienating in modern industrial environments, since it conflicts with capitalism's own temporal registers of progress (Negri 2004). Guyer's (2007) contention that this decline of the mid-term future is epiphenomenal to neoliberalism is an intriguing suggestion that potentially explains the temporal register of precarity. But although the types of precarity emerging among global corporate workforces are expressions of the logics of modern neoliberal capitalism (Freeman 1998; Genda 2005; Gill 2000; Harvey 1987; Kosugi 2008; Mathur 1998), very large sections of the global labor force experience precarity as a decidedly older phenomenon and engage with it in rather different ways. Post-Fordist precarity is a politically important and analytically productive field, yet when judged against the global experience of labor, it is still an exceptional process (Allison 2012; Muehlebach and Shoshan 2012; Neilson and Rossiter 2008). For much of the working poor in the Global South, precarious working conditions have always been a characteristic of life (Millar 2014: 34; Munck 2013).

For example, 32-year-old Rakesh came to the scrap yard from the state of Chhattisgarh as a child of seven after his father's death from cancer. His father, a rickshaw driver, had supported the entire family on his meager earnings, and his death left them destitute. Rakesh, his mother, and three younger sisters moved to Jamshedpur, where Rakesh became the family's primary breadwinner. In contrast to the young Tata Motors workers who shared his wage levels, Rakesh did not craft his grievances in terms of a modern global corruption that conspired to alienate him and his colleagues from their birthright. Rather, he saw his own trials as rooted in a life of tragedy and vulnerability that he felt had been reproduced among India's poor for generations. Unlike the Tata worker, whose political imagination describes a class of antagonists in the shape of corrupt trade unionists and corporate capitalists, Rakesh perceived the sources of his problems as far more diffuse. He has been disenfranchised by the Indian caste system, the unequal distribution of agricultural land in his native village, the education system, the lack of state welfare support, and his employer. Rakesh's problems are bigger than the politics of labor.

Rakesh rents a house in the Jamshedpur district of Bagbera, in a slum settlement without access to reliable utilities. His most costly possessions are a small television set and a bicycle that he uses to travel to and from work. Every lunch hour after he has eaten with his family, he takes a brief detour to a makeshift liquor stall, where he pays 15 rupees to quickly swallow three cups of the homemade Indian alcohol called Mahua. He is invariably drunk by the time he arrives back at the yard. On many an afternoon Rakesh is in higher spirits than he was in the morning and becomes liable to joke with his colleagues. Other times, he arrives late and belligerent, whereupon the yard's staff and customers avoid speaking with him. He has very little formal education and claims to be able to read nothing more than the family names tattooed on his forearms. He lives in a cramped house with his wife, son, daughter, mother, sister, and his sister's two young sons. Their home comprises five small rooms arranged around a central patio with a hand pump that provides all of the family's water. In two of the rooms the female members of the household sit commercially sewing women's garments from rolls of cloth. Rakesh's room contains the family kitchen, television, wardrobe, and a small double bed where he sleeps with his wife and two young children.

In the workplace Rakesh is valued by his colleagues for his ability to identify obscure types of metal using a set of tools that he keeps in his wallet: a small magnet for testing their iron content, and a tungsten drill bit for determining their hardness.[6] Rakesh is at his best when he is tasked with appraising a sample of metal. The yard's staff and visitors stop to stand around watching him while he squats on the floor to investigate the material. Nobody comments on or interrupts his work, and his expert opinion is never contradicted. Despite these skills, Rakesh receives the same daily wages as Sapna, who arrived comparatively recently, only nine years earlier.

Like her, he can anticipate no likely improvement in his situation, since there is no role to which he could be effectively promoted. The notion of positive change entering Rakesh's life through the politics of labor is not supportable by any observable historical example. He is illiterate, comes from a cripplingly poor family, and is employed in one of the few steady jobs that a local man in his position can hope to acquire. The likelihood of his finding better paid work outside of Lohar is not high, so he is bound to a job that had already given him everything it had to give before he was eight years old.

For Rakesh and his colleagues, the "suffering" that is said to afflict the lives of the poor is referred to as *tang*. It describes the mental anguish of being unable to pay one's bills, the fear for the future of one's children, and the gradually declining health associated with hard manual labor. *Tang* also implies harassment and stress, but not the sense of "injustice" articulated by the Tata corruption discourse. Rooted in experiences of deep and unchanging marginality, the affect of *tang* is one of weary and unhappy resolve that locates one's self in a perpetual present. Comparative ethnographic studies have shown that marginal people may practice a willful disregard for any time but the present, and gone on to claim that these are "people who live resolutely in the short term, and, in privileged moments, they transform this short term into a transcendent escape from time itself" (Day, Papataxiarchis, and Stewart 1999: 2). Such marginalized persons subvert the dominant notion of the present as a site of suffering to be overcome through careful planning, by performatively stating that the true domain of suffering is the future, mitigated by the impulsive act of living for the "now" (ibid.). However, a fatalistic assessment of the future does not necessarily correlate with willful impetuousness regarding the present. Not all suffering people identify a particular temporality as the domain of release and freedom, and Rakesh's perpetual "now" is not one of happy disregard. A marginal and fractured community's view that the past, present, and future are equally informed by suffering and insecurity has consequences for its political consciousness and action.

For the people who voice the language of suffering at Lohar Enterprises, the material concerns of poverty bleed out of the workplace and into the business of everyday life, where they are experienced as a slow, painful erosion of dignity. For Rakesh, the stresses of precarity follow him everywhere he goes. Walking on the street outside his workplace, he passes groups of boisterous, wealthy older men who gather outside their prosperous businesses to smoke cigarettes. These men have known Rakesh since he was a child and are well acquainted with his family history, his employment, and his problems with alcoholism. Several times a week one of these groups would beckon Rakesh, ask him to fetch *chai* from a nearby stall, tease him about his drinking, call him "boy," and manhandle him with playful slaps to the face.

Despite being a grown man with a twenty-five-year history of employ-ment, a home, a wife, and a family, Rakesh is unable to work his way out of the social and economic status he had when he first arrived in Jamshedpur as a seven-year-old boy. He has acquired many practical skills over the years, made friends and affines, adorned his arms with cheap tattoos, and learned to drink and chew betel nut as a local man should. However, a life-time of work has not made him any less poor, and in broader city society there were definite limits to the respect that he could aspire to demand. He is continuously reminded of these facts by the emptiness of his pockets, the sparse furnishings of his home, and the jeers of his betters. These are questions of dignity and hope that strict analyses of labor conditions and employment security cannot fully account for. As Cannell (1999: 18) notes, objective aspects of poverty are felt in reference to the conditions and agency of other people, and are reinforced by feelings of shame and humiliation. Even the lowest paid casual Tata workers are unlikely, while walking in their neighborhoods, to endure the same disrespect as Rakesh, because whereas they may enjoy similar wages and a lack of employment permanence, they nonetheless possess social capital, derived from their status as company people, their residence in company townships, and their education in company schools. For the time being, these combined resources offer some level of hope in conditions of precarity, and recogni-tion by others that their current role is somehow undeserved. By compari-son, Rakesh is widely reckoned to be exactly where he belongs.

Conclusion: Precarity, Class, and Hope

More of the world's working population is employed in precarious con-ditions now than they were a generation ago. Whether the mechanics of this process involve the corruption of trade unions, the weakening of labor legislation, the growth of unpaid internships, or surplus labor markets, the development seems to be pervasive. The political fact of increasing pre-carity requires an analytic response that is sensitive to the new contradic-tions and tensions that the development engenders. For this reason, I argue that a class modeling of precarity must account for the basic distinction between persons who find themselves suddenly poor and vulnerable (and believe they are able to change this condition), and people who feel that they always have been precarious and always will be. Influential attempts to model the class structures of precarity tend to miss this distinction entirely. This is problematic because it is the expansion of precarity into new areas of working life that makes the phenomenon significant and truly embodies the logics of modern capitalism.

Standing's (2011) concept of the "precariat" describes a growing segment of the global working population that is insecurely engaged under part-time or short-term contracts, and lacks access to pensions and holiday pay. While Standing's observation of increasing global employment precarity is timely, his broader conclusions about class politics are problematic. The central analytic thrust of Standing's work is that the precariat constitutes a class that is empirically and politically separate from the unionized, permanently employed working class. However, Standing's "precariat" concept fails to account for two important characteristics of insecure modern employment.

First, the erosion of job security is such a pervasive tendency in almost all areas of modern capitalism that precarization breaks down distinctions between permanently and temporarily employed persons within the same sector, as traditionally secure labor forces begin to share their homes and workplaces with casually employed younger colleagues. In the Tata company town of Jamshedpur, a casual employee at Tata Motors is invariably the son or nephew of a permanently employed worker on the very same shop floor. Since these sections of the workforce routinely participate in the same household economy and are also united by a shared critical perspective on the operation of corporate capital, the suggestion that they constitute distinct classes is not tenable in terms of either their economic position or political consciousness. While such enduring relationships between casual and permanent employees may presently be exceptional in comparison to similar industrial workplaces, the trend nonetheless represents the far broader decline of global employment security. On many industrial shop floors, permanently employed workers may see themselves as wholly distinct from their casual counterparts (Parry 2013). However, the same cannot be said of the vast numbers of people employed in offices, shops, care homes, schools, and universities, where casual employment is rapidly becoming the preserve of persons with social capital similar to that of their permanently employed colleagues. The Tata case represents this trend and suggests a fundamental flaw in the "precariat-as-class" model, by showing that there is no *necessary* class distinction between the salariat and precariat in any given instance. In fact, the notion that there should be fails to grasp the true character and intent of casualization initiatives, which is to ultimately erode the working conditions of all waged persons.

Second, and more important to this analysis, Standing's model does not account for the fact that the subjective experience of precarity between sectors depends upon history and expectations, so the model of class that he presents is reductive and ahistorical. In this chapter I have argued that the degree to which persons and communities are able to construct hopeful visions of the future by drawing upon their experiences of the past is crucial to political consciousness and behavior.

"Hope" is a difficult concept that encompasses a variety of distinct processes. In one sense, hope may be an expression of a desired outcome that does not comment on the feasibility of that outcome's occurrence. This is the case in the passive hope to see one's friends again, or the hope that it does not rain. However, hope also has an active form that expresses the extent to which one believes it is possible to determine the course of the future—a form that thus has political applications, as when a person is "hopeful" that a specific development will occur. Even if the specific shape of one's hope is that the future stays the same, this nonetheless implies the ability to use political tools to force change if the future does not in fact turn out as one wished. This type of active, applied hope is different from the passive form that merely wishes for something, and corresponds to the Hindi *aasha*, which implies expectance and promise. Hope of this form is absent when people are unaware of the political tools by which social change can be forced, when they know that those tools are inaccessible, or when the available tools have been seen to fail. Following Crapanzano's definition of hope as a temporal orientation toward a future goal, hope should not be regarded as a naïve political orientation that is oblivious to obstacles. Hope is rather an empowering orientation that collectivizes suffering and underpins the will to struggle (Crapanzano 2004: 100–101).

Seen in this way, the systemic corruption discourse of the Tata shop floor is a politically potent engagement with the collective experience of precarity. Such a discourse seeks the reinstatement of an earlier, paternalistic employment regime that afforded a position of relative privilege for Tata workers. As I have argued elsewhere, while this political consciousness is critical, it is by no means radical, since it restates the essential legitimacy of the company town model and largely excludes the class interests of outsiders like Rakesh (Sanchez 2016: 148–150). However, by identifying a common history, grievance, and antagonist for precarious Tata workers, the discourse implicitly, and somewhat hopefully, states a remedy for the problems of everyday life. The interplay between uncertainty and hope raises important questions for the study of social decline and precarization, since idealized perceptions of the past structure engagements with the political life of the future (Pelkmans 2013a, 2013b: 20; Stewart 2008).

If social classes become political actors through recognition of their shared history, then the very notion of a precariat has great discursive salience for communities of people who define their insecurity in temporal terms, distinguishing it from experiences of decline and the potential for progress. For Fordist labor forces like that of the Tata Motors plant, precarization is a novel collective experience that destabilizes identity, family structure, and ways of life (Allison 2012: 349; Muehlebach 2011). The political discourses that emerge from these environments are collective ones that build continuities with older languages of collective struggle and paternalistic entitlement. By comparison, workers like Rakesh, Dipesh and Sapna do not regard precarity as new or as grounded in any type of collective labor history. In the scrap yard of Lohar Enterprises, the critical language of suffering is essentially personalizing: it refers primarily to individual experiences of illness, migration, and bereavement. While these workers may regard themselves as sharing similar types of experiences, the origins of their misfortune are believed to be particular to each individual and are resistant to the class-based technologies of trade unionism. This difference in perspectives suggests that the class modeling of the "precariat" concept is ill equipped to engage with the complex political life of insecure labor in modern workplaces.

Acknowledgments

This chapter is based on two periods of fieldwork. The first, conducted in 2006/07, was funded by the Economic and Social Research Council. The second, conducted in 2014, was funded by the Max Planck Society as part of the "Industry and Inequality" project group based at the Max Planck Institute for Social Anthropology.

Andrew Sanchez is Lecturer in Social Anthropology at the University of Cambridge. After earning his Ph.D. from the London School of Economics and Political Science in 2009, he held teaching and research positions at the LSE, the Max Planck Institute for Social Anthropology, and the University of Kent. Sanchez has published a monograph titled *Criminal Capital: Violence, Corruption and Class in Industrial India* (2016) and numerous journal articles. Specializing in the anthropology of class, corruption, labor, and value, he has conducted fieldwork in urban India among industrial workers, trade unionists, and entrepreneurs.

Notes

1. Gopal's assassination was orchestrated by a Tata Workers' Union official named Amrendra Kumar Singh, who was convicted of his murder in 2006.
2. Apprentices and trainees, who make up one-third of the entire labor force of the Tata Motors plant in Jamshedpur, earn between 1,500 and 2,400 rupees (15–24

pounds) a month for working a six-day week, while casual Tata workers' monthly pay ranges from 5,000 to 6,000 rupees (50–60 pounds) per month, likewise for a six-day week. By comparison, employees at Lohar Enterprises earn between 6,000 and 9,000 rupees (£60–90) per month, for a seven-day week.

3. The Apprentices Act (1961), Section 15, states: "The weekly and daily hours of work of an Apprentice while undergoing practical training in a workshop shall be as such as may be prescribed." The act goes on to stipulate, in Section 18: "a) every Apprentice undergoing Apprenticeship training in an establishment shall be a trainee and not a worker; b) the provisions of any law with respect to labour shall not apply to or in relation to such Apprenticeship."

4. The festival honors the Hindu goddess Durga.

5. The conservative Tata Workers' Union has an effective monopoly on representation in Jamshedpur's largest industries, so alternative unions struggle to gain employer recognition in Tata workplaces. All of Jamshedpur's Tata industries have an explicit policy of negotiation with unions affiliated to the Indian National Trade Union Congress, of which the Tata Workers' Union is a founding member (Tata Motors Ltd. 2001).

6. For a discussion of skill and job satisfaction in scrap work, see Sanchez (n.d.).

References

Allison, Anne. 2012. "Ordinary Refugees: Social Precarity and Soul in 21st Century Japan." *Anthropological Quarterly* 85(2): 345–370.

Bahl, Vinay. 1982. "TISCO Workers' Struggles: 1920–1928." *Social Scientist* 10(8): 32–44.

———. 1995. *The Making of the Indian Working Class: The Case of the Tata Iron and Steel Co., 1880–1946.* New Delhi and Thousand Oaks, CA: Sage.

Banerjee, Mukulika. 2014 *Why India Votes*. Delhi, London, Oxford: Routledge.

Cannell, Fenella. 1999. *Power and Intimacy in the Christian Philippines*. Cambridge: Cambridge University Press.

Chandavarkar, Rajnarayan. 1985. "Industrialization in India before 1947: Conventional Approaches and Alternative Perspectives." *Modern Asian Studies* 19(3): 623–668.

———. 1994. *The Origins of Industrial Capitalism in India: Business Strategies and the Working Classes in Bombay, 1900–40.* Cambridge: Cambridge University Press.

———. 1999. "Questions of Class: The General Strikes in Bombay, 1928–29." In *The Worlds of Indian Industrial Labour: Contributions to Indian Sociology; Occasional Studies 9*, eds. J. Breman, K. Kapadia, J.P. Parry, 205–237. New Delhi, Thousand Oaks, London: Sage.

Chatterjee Partha. 2004. *The Politics of the Governed: Reflections on Political Society in Most of the World.* New York: Columbia University Press.

Crapanzano, Vincent. 2004. *Imaginative Horizons: An Essay in Literary Philosophical Anthropology.* Chicago, IL: University of Chicago Press.

Day, Sophie, Evthymios Papataxiarchis, and Michael Stewart, eds. 1999. *Lilies of the Field: Marginal People Who Live for the Moment.* Boulder, CO: Westview Press.

Fraser, Lovat. 1919. *Iron and Steel in India: A Chapter from the Life of Jamshedji N. Tata.* Bombay: The Times Press.

Freeman, Carla. 1998. "Femininity and Flexible Labor: Fashioning Class through Gender on the Global Assembly Line." *Critique of Anthropology* 18(3): 245–263.

Genda, Yuji. 2005. *A Nagging Sense of Job Insecurity: The New Reality Facing Japanese Youth.* Tokyo: International House of Japan.

Gill, Thomas. 2000. "Yoseba and Ninpudashi: Changing Patterns of Employment on the Fringes of Japanese Economy." In *Globalization and Social Change in Contemporary Japan*, ed. J.S. Eades, T. Gill, and H. Befu, 123–143. Melbourne: Trans Pacific Press.

Goldthorpe, John., David Lockwood, Frank Bechhofer, and Jenifer Platt. 1968. *The Affluent Worker: Industrial Attitudes and Behaviour.* London: Cambridge University Press.

———. 1969. *The Affluent Worker in the Class Structure.* London: Cambridge University Press.

Gooptu, Nandini. 2001. *The Politics of the Urban Poor in Early Twentieth-Century India.* Cambridge, New York: Cambridge University Press.

Guyer, Jane. 2007. "Prophecy and the Near Future: Thoughts on Macroeconomic, Evangelical, and Punctuated Time." *American Ethnologist* 34(3): 409–421.

Harvey, David. 1987. "Flexible Accumulation Through Urbanization: Reflections on 'Post-Modernism' in the American City." *Antipode* 19(3): 260–286.

Keenan, John. L., with Lenore Sorsby. 1945. *A Steel Man in India.* Introduction by L. Bromfield. London: Victor Gollancz.

Kosugi, Reiko. 2008. *Escape from Work: Freelancing Youth and the Challenge to Corporate Japan*, trans. R. Mouer. Melbourne: Trans Pacific Press.

Mathur, Chandana. 1998. "Transformation as Usual? The Meanings of a Changing Labour Process for Indiana Aluminium Workers." *Critique of Anthropology* 18(3): 263–277.

Millar, Kathleen. 2014. "The Precarious Present: Wageless Labor and Disrupted Life in Rio de Janeiro, Brazil." *Cultural Anthropology* 29(1): 32–53.

Muehlebach, Andrea. 2011. "On Affective Labor in Post-Fordist Italy." *Cultural Anthropology* 26(1): 59–82.

Muehlebach, Andrea., and Nitzan Shoshan. 2012. "Post-Fordist Affect: An Introduction." *Anthropological Quarterly* 85(2): 317–343.

Munck, Ronaldo. 2013. "The Precariat: A View from the South." *Third World Quarterly* 34(5): 747–762.

Narotzky, Susana. 2010. "Gender, History and Political Activism in Spain." In *Class, Contention and a World in Motion*, ed. W. Lem and P.G. Barber, 125–137. New York: Berghahn Books.

———. 2015. "The Organic Intellectual and the Production of Class in Spain." In *Anthropologies of Class: Power, Practice and Inequality*, ed. J. Carrier and D. Kalb, 53–71. Cambridge: Cambridge University Press.

Negri, Antonio. 2004. "The Constitution of Time." In *Time for Revolution.* London, New York: Continuum Books.

Neilson, Brett, and Ned Rossiter. 2008. "Precarity as a Political Concept, or, Fordism as Exception." *Theory, Culture & Society* 25(7–8): 51–72.

Parry, Jonathan. 1999a. "Lords of Labour: Working and Shirking in Bhilai." *Contributions to Indian Sociology* 33(1): 107–140.

———. 1999b. "Two Cheers for Reservation: The Satnamis and the Steel Plant." In *Institutions and Inequalities: Essays in Honour of Andre Beteille*, ed. R. Guha and J. Parry, 128–170. New Delhi: Oxford.

———. 2013. "The Embourgeoisement of a Proletarian Vanguard?" In *Interrogating India's Modernity: Democracy, Identity and Citizenship*, ed. S. Jodhka. Delhi: Oxford University Press.

Parry, Jonathan, and Christian Strümpell. 2008. "On the Desecration of Nehru's 'Temples': Bhilai and Rourkela Compared." *Economic and Political Weekly* 43(19): 47–57.

Pelkmans, Mathijs. 2013a. "Outline for an Ethnography of Doubt." In *Ethnographies of Doubt: Faith and Uncertainty in Contemporary Societies*, ed. M. Pelkmans, 1–43. London and New York: I.B. Tauris.

———. 2013b. "Ruins of Hope in a Kyrgyz Post-Industrial Wasteland." *Anthropology Today* 29(5): 16–20.

Pillai, P. P. 1923. "Iron and Steel Production in India." *Economica* 7(January): 55–66.

Sanchez, Andrew. 2010. "Capitalism, Violence and the State: Crime, Corruption and Entrepreneurship in an Indian Company Town." *Journal of Legal Anthropology* 1(2): 165–188.

———. 2012a. "Deadwood and Paternalism: Rationalising Casual Labour in an Indian Company Town." *Journal of the Royal Anthropological Institute* 18(4): 808–827.

———. 2012b. "Questioning Success: Dispossession and the Criminal Entrepreneur in Urban India." *Critique of Anthropology* 32(4): 435–457.

———. 2016. *Criminal Capital: Violence, Corruption and Class in Industrial India*. Oxford and New York: Routledge.

———. n.d. *Creation and Transformation: Work, Skill and Value in an Indian Scrap Yard*. Unpublished manuscript.

Standing, Guy. 2011. *The Precariat: The New Dangerous Class*. London: Bloomsbury Academic.

Stewart, Kathleen. 2008. "Nostalgia—A Polemic." *Cultural Anthropology* 3(3): 227–241.

Tata Motors Limited. Jamshedpur. 2001. *Managers' handbook*. Jamshedpur: Tata Motors

Weiner, Myron. 1978. *Sons of the Soil: Migration and Ethnic Conflict in India*. Princeton: Guildford.

10

From *Avtoritet* and Autonomy to Self-Exploitation in the Russian Automotive Industry

JEREMY MORRIS AND SARAH HINZ

Introduction: Labor Landscapes in Russia Today

As transnational corporations (TNCs) have appeared southeast of Moscow in Kaluga Region, particularly in the automotive industry and the plants supplying it, younger Russian workers are for the first time presented with a choice other than the risky informal economy or work in surviving factories from the Soviet era, most of which offer poor conditions and very low pay. However, workers in both the "new" high-tech, foreign-owned automotive assembly, and "old" low-tech "Soviet" production contexts articulate similar interpretive understandings of what makes work "precarious"— here understood as a sense of insecurity relating to degrees of alienation that workers experience in these different contexts. They respond to a general intensification of work associated with neoliberal transformation by stressing the "good" aspects of work associated with socialist-era labor "autonomy" and the "social wage" generally (in-kind enterprise benefits). A generalized and emic understanding of "bad," insecure work has little to do with the literal precarity of work or poor pay. In both contexts insecurity of work tenure and poverty wages are widely understood as "normal"—and this is little changed since 1991. What really sets old and new work apart is the degree to which pace, intensity, and autonomy in task fulfillment are under the control of the worker, or at least subject to some kind of informal negotiation or mitigation through personalized production relations. While workers everywhere are subject to intensification, the loss of these socialist-era mitigations is most keenly felt by those in new TNCs. Many informants consider the old style of enterprise the "least worse" for those conditioned by the rhythms of the Soviet factory.[1]

In this chapter we explore these understandings through in-depth interviews with workers in this sector and other industries locally. We document a divide between "entrepreneurial" workers who go to work for the car plants, and those who reject the labor relations model that it offers, contrasting it to a traditional "paternalistic" Russian model that remains the object of nostalgia, even as it has largely "decayed" into a purely symbolic form (Clarke 1995: 128). We do not interrogate the veracity of these interpretations but focus on how workers position themselves in Russian society as "losers" of global processes of transition and as the social group most exposed to precarity. These interpretations hold regardless of whether workers "stay" in traditional Russian industrial firms or "go" to TNCs. Overall precariousness has subjective as well as objective facets (International Labour Office 2012: 5). Both structural and perceived insecurities often hinge on the extension of new forms of labor discipline to securely and formally employed persons (Bourdieu 1998). Precariousness is thus a relational category that fundamentally depends upon the definition of societal standards of normality (Castel and Dörre 2009: 17). In most Global North contexts, precarious work is understood as a generational erosion of the Fordist standard employment relationship (Rodgers 1989; Dörre 2010; Brinkmann et al. 2006: 17). Precariousness means "return of social insecurity" (Castel 2011), and the expansion of the precariat is driven by financial capitalism (Dörre 2009).

For most industrial workers in the Soviet Union and elsewhere in Eastern Europe, the socialist period was generally marked by secure, formalized jobs and an extensive system of social benefits for workers and their families that implicitly compensated for often poor working conditions and the lack of political representation (Cook 1993; Kotkin 1995). A hybrid form of flexibility between Fordism and individual craftwork emerged in many industrial contexts. The Soviet Union's adoption of Taylorist/Fordist production techniques was less than successful (Wren 1980; Van Atta 1986). Production bottlenecks and the bureaucratic institutions of socialism allowed for a considerable degree of self-management on the shop floor in "unit clusters" of autonomous task fulfillment (Prokhorov 2002: 49–72).

Comparing the relative alienation of workers under postwar capitalism and socialism, Chris Hann (2006: 105–107) points to the significance of consumption in the West. Whereas Fordism contributed to the stability of the capitalist social order by creating "satisfied" consumers at the expense of "satisfied" workers, the legitimacy of the socialist system rested on a more general social contract—a sense of security not tied to consumption norms resulting *from* labor (the ability to consume production), but tightly connected to security *in* labor, and certain basic social guarantees. As a consequence, understandings of security and its lack—precarity—remain infused with particular mnemonic resources of class position as propagated in the socialist era, even if these may be, in part, "false" memories (Morris 2014a).

The scope of the paternalistic-bureaucratic system of central planning occasionally extended to severe disciplinary practices of "worker optimization," but insecurity was rare and persistent unemployment unknown. Since the onset of post-Soviet market deregulation, by contrast, standard employment has been continually eroded and replaced by growing underemployment, sporadic wage arrears, increasing numbers of informal and semi-formal jobs, less secure jobs, the lack of legal development of workers' social rights, wage arbitrariness, and a steep decline in social benefits (Hauslohner 1987; Clarke 1995; Stenning et al. 2010). Thus in Russia too, "precarity is everywhere" (Bourdieu 1998). But the response of workers to the new positioning of labor and production regimes in the global economy varies depending on workers' inherited norms and prior experiences of socially embedded work.

Methods and Fieldsites

This chapter comprises materials collected in two distinct modes of research. Jeremy Morris has conducted long-term ethnographic fieldwork with blue-collar workers in an ex-monotown near Kaluga about an hour's drive from the regional capital, site of the new TNC car plant. About 15,000 people live in Izluchino, an urban space that developed as the result of a "town-forming enterprise" in the postwar era.[2] Local manufacturing includes aggregate extraction and processing (into bricks, lime, powders, and other construction materials), steel, and plastic fabrication (including tubing and cables for the domestic plumbing market and extractive gas industry). In addition, Izluchino has a linoleum rolling mill (foreign owned), small-scale manufacture of industrial filters, plastic window production shops, and a small rolling-stock repair workshop. The extractive and steel/plastic processes date from the Soviet period, as do the gravel aggregates. The other, post-USSR processes developed out of the extractive economic base. We refer to all enterprises that existed as of the Soviet period or early 1990s as "inheritors" of plant, personnel, and production "culture." Many of those laid off in the 1990s never returned to blue-collar work—they either died off in the massive demographic collapse, survived on meager pensions, or disappeared into the informal economy, typically driving unregistered cabs, working on construction sites in Moscow, or engaging in petty trades. Since 2010 some younger workers have started to commute from this town to the Frunzensky auto-motive plant and two other TNCs based in Kaluga. The chapter also draws on semi-structured interviews with union representatives and activists, mainly conducted by Sarah Hinz in 2013. Starting with gatekeepers working in blue-collar work in and near Kaluga city, we have established a group of key informants that includes union activists, "ordinary" assembly workers, and ex-workers.

Izluchino is set amidst a sea of surface quarries (most still exploitable) and is officially an "ex-monotown," as it is no longer dominated by a single employer. Survivor production shops have disaggregated from the origi-nal plant, which was affiliated to a single powerful ministry. In the 1950s, when this ministry needed raw materials for vast military building projects throughout European Russia, the town was set to work. A few individually owned wooden houses, rebuilt after World War II, were surrounded by wooden barrack-houses for the new workers. New quarries were opened up. As lime kilns poured out their smoke, the skyline of the industrial zone filled with chimneys. After the 1960s, machine factories under the ministry also arrived, and Izluchino grew rapidly right up to the end of the Soviet period, as evidenced by the gradual change in housing stock as one moves away from the river's edge: wooden houses from the 1940s, then 1950s wooden barracks, the low-rise panel buildings of the 1960s and 1970s, and finally, at the edge of the forest, the "best" five-story flats, built from brick in the 1980s and spacious by Soviet standards. The settlement functioned as the fiefdom of a single state employer. The "one-company city" gave the enterprise an exceptionally important role in the provision of para-state systems of welfare and patronage. Housing was built and maintained by the factory organization, and leisure, health, and other amenities were partly funded from the same source (Alexander and Buchli 2007). Many monotown enterprises acted almost as "total social institutions" and "states within states" (Clarke 1993: 26). The economy of the town was 'the nexus of need fulfillment' (Collier 2011: 83).

After the collapse of the USSR, the need for the quarries' raw mate-rial diminished rapidly. Like many other Russian towns, Izluchino suffered significant loss of employment and services in the 1990s. Nonetheless, a number of successor employers and inheritor firms employ around 3,000 people in extractive industry. After 1998, following a major devaluation of the currency and the beginning of a building boom in Moscow, the town recovered economically. Before turning to the present situation, it is important for our argument to appreciate the nature of work on the shop floor and the social wage in the socialist past.

Soviet Industrial Work Remembered

Three themes emerge strongly from conversations with workers old enough to have experienced life in Izluchino's factories and quarries in socialist days: labor mobility, personalized and flexible shop-floor relations, and the social wage. Although the inhabitants of Izluchino have a palpable sense of their "rootlessness," as many were born elsewhere, they simultaneously express feelings of placeness, if not local patriotism.[3] In the 1970s migrants from neighboring regions and further afield were attracted to the town's well-paid industrial blue-collar jobs. As the housing queue was relatively short in this privileged location, men and women started families, many relatively large by Soviet Russian standards (three children). Izluchino bore witness to the high level of Soviet and post-Soviet Russian interregional labor mobility (Clarke 1999 and White 2007, both in Walker 2010: 649). As the director of the surviving factory Steelpipe recalls:

> Izluchino was just *Sredmash* [an acronym for the industrial-defense complex tasked with ensuring a supply of fissile material] and the gravel pits. The mechanical factories were just a few particular cogs in the machinery of the ministry—the ministry had one aim: turning nuclear fissile material into warheads and pointing them at the West. But that aim was a million miles away from us here. We were a state within a state within a state. Each responsible for sourcing its own material and delivering it. The *Sredmash* director here was Tsar, or at least it was his personal fiefdom. The ministry had its own building directorate which alone built complexes for the military—the town-forming concern worked like a pump, churning out the material for that. It also sucked up labor from surrounding regions.

The almost universal experience of labor migration in the past continues to characterize people's understanding of precarity and their response to it. Blue-collar workers in Izluchino occupied a particularly privileged space in the Soviet labor hierarchy, and memories of labor conditions idealize the past accordingly. They must be interpreted alongside other observations about state-labor compacts in the Soviet period. Practices of incentive and discipline in Soviet factories were "personalized" (Morrison 2008: 135; cf. Collier 2011: 106) but not "individualized." Negotiations and bargaining on issues that materially affected workers, such as bonuses, piecework rates (only "loosely" set in late Soviet times) or overtime allowed brigade leaders and managers to exercise a large degree of discretion (Van Atta 1986; Morrison 2008: 139) based on personal relations of favor and "prestige" (*avtoritet*) within teams, rather than management's assessment of an individual's output or objective measures of value (Morris 2012a). This was largely due to the high ineffectuality of trade union organization: unions were effectively a part of management and did not engage in promoting the interests of workers. Many unions of this type remain embedded in the management of Russian firms, relegated to the role of distributing minor social benefits. In some contexts, including the car industry, they are subject to increasing competition from "free" unions, as we discuss below.

One unintended outcome of discretion and other production issues was the high degree of autonomy practiced among work teams on the shop floor (Alasheev 1995; cf. Burawoy 1992). Aleksandr Prokhorov (2002: 155) identified a strong form of "grassroots solidarity" where management is at the mercy of workers who are united in feelings of alienation and subordination. Workers, it was said, were often willing to cover for each other within a team and were not subject to the surveillance and subordinating imperatives of today's workplace. At least, this is the dominant narrative of workers in Izluchino two decades after this system's disintegration.

Middle-aged and older Izluchino workers speak nostalgically about team-level solidarity in Soviet days. Solidarity here does not mean a sense of standing together in opposing exploitation (they often quip that state socialism and capitalism are equally exploitative; see Burawoy 1992). Rather, workers feel that the labor relations in the late Soviet period enabled them to develop a particular kind of work- and skill-based respect among other workers and management. This *avtoritet* (authority or prestige) was the basis of a personhood in which their labor was valued both for its own sake and socially (Morris 2012a). Workers associate their *avtoritet* with monetary and in-kind rewards from the enterprise, and with dignity in labor. As a feeder to the high-priority defense sector and a "closed" town, Izluchino remunerated its workers relatively well, not in terms of wages or easy working conditions but with provisions and other benefits. Blue-collar work was a route to social mobility and to "security ... education, training, childcare, housing, recreation and leisure, health facilities, retail and consumption, and heating and energy" (Stenning et al. 2010: 86; see also Keskülä 2014: 62). This "social wage"—social amenities in kind linked to employment—was fundamental to an implicit social contract (Smith et al. 2008: 288).[4] The solidaristic community noted above was a further intangible component of this social wage. Thus Izluchino workers recall being able to articulate rights and expectations of certain benefits, even in person to the director of the enterprise, known to everyone by his first name and patronymic (see Collier 2011: 107). Younger male workers, the main focus of our research, access these narratives through parents and older peers.

Laboring Personhoods after 1991

The period 1993–1998, when most of the newly privatized and disaggregated inheritor businesses became insolvent, is perceived as one of crisis. Izluchino's main enterprise was split up in 1998, and for a time everyone suffered real privations. However, the town showed resilience, and major losses in core employment are understood not only as displacements and "dislocations" (Burawoy, Krotov, and Lytkina 2000: 61) but also as shifts in patterns of employment and labor. People made do with their garden plots and petty trade, and by simply not engaging with the emerging consumer economy. From the late 1980s, the inheritor businesses, sometimes technically insolvent for over five years at a time, slowly but surely shed four thousand jobs before the 1998 financial crisis and default ushered in a turnaround, at least of sorts (Clarke 2007: 61–63[5]). The devaluation of the ruble led to some respite for domestic industry, so that 1998 is the local mnemonic marker for the return to hiring. The smaller enterprises were bought out by managers or taken over by Moscow concerns.

In the early 2000s a number of pioneering multinational corporations—brewers, confectioners, and others—came to Kaluga Region because of its good transport links to Moscow, lower production costs, and geographical proximity to Europe. In 2012 the "border" with Moscow city suddenly became closer still when a large corridor along the Moscow-Kiev highway was incorporated into the city (having formerly belonged to Moscow Region). Kaluga Region now borders Moscow. A sizeable cohort of workers had exploited opportunities in informal construction work in Moscow after 1991.[6] From the mid 2000s, however, the TNCs now present in the region created very different employment opportunities that, though outside the immediate vicinity of the town, were still much closer than Moscow—just an hour's drive away, on the outskirts of Kaluga city. Younger workers were thus presented with an alternative to local employment or informal work in construction. The TNC vehicle factories offered better pay, but besides the long commute the jobs also entailed new, untested models of shop-floor relations.

Scholars of neoliberal production regimes in Russia have emphasized that a trend of increased control over workers, intensification of the work burden, and a general tightening of the workday's regime (or timetable) has resulted in a loss of autonomy, reflected in increasing monitoring of how workers complete tasks (Kagarlitsky 2008; Levinson 2007). Both younger and older workers in Izluchino, including those who stayed the course with the TNC conveyor work assembling automobiles and those who quit, support those findings (Morris 2012a). Simon Clarke (2007) has argued that the subordination of production to the new law of value has caused line managers to change from patriarchal representatives of collectives (the traditional Soviet role) into agents of management. The enterprise social wage has been reduced to a symbolic level, even as state welfare provision has retreated. In addition, job opportunities were no longer "inheritable" through personal connections of relatives at the plant as they had been in the socialist period, so this sense of a secure pathway for youth has also disappeared. Though "connections" (*blat*) are important in well-paid white-collar jobs, this kind of hiring process is less common in industrial work.

Those who continue to work for plastic, steel, or extraction enterprises in the town complain about changes in production relations and diminishing social protection. Nonetheless, traditional roles and "echoes" of the perceived social benefits of Soviet shop-floor relations persist in these workplaces (Morris 2016). Thus the meanings of "precarious work" are inflected by place and the (sometimes idealized) past. Blue-collar workers understand bad work in terms of specific micro-processes of labor: a lack of autonomy in task solving, flexibility in time management, unmediated oversight by the managers—all symptoms of intensification processes. Thus when workers complain about bad jobs and understand the new position of their labor as insecure, marginalized, and inequitable, they tell a wider story about the expansion of capitalist relations into the "hidden abode of production"—particularly considering that throughout the postsocialist economic transformation, many scholars observed the stubborn persistence of a Soviet shop-floor culture where paternalism, personalized relations, worker autonomy, and flexible use of the workday continue.

New Blood at the Car Plant

It is 2010, and a new cohort of workers has just been taken on at Frunzensky and other car plants near Kaluga as production of cars for the domestic market ramps up. This intake includes Slava, who at twenty-four is leaving a blue-collar job in town to commute to the TNC and make mid-priced cars for the Russian market. In our first few encounters, Slava and his future wife are very guarded. Perhaps they are worried about envy; after all, Slava now has a prestigious, relatively well-paid blue-collar job. But jealousy could hardly be over money alone. After a relatively lengthy probationary period, Slava earns no more than 18,000 rubles (800 US dollars) a month, while his former mates at the old-style factories earn around 14,000 rubles (470 dollars). Later, after union action in 2012 raises the wages of car plant workers to significantly higher levels than those paid in Izluchino, they are still not much higher than the Kaluga city average for blue-collar work.

Slava was previously a core member of a dense social network of male workers, many of them former school friends with whom he worked at a cement factory as well as in the informal economy in an unlicensed (i.e., unregistered for tax and insurance) enterprise making plastic window frames. For him and his best friend Petr, the new plant had presented an opportunity for stabler conditions and the hope of higher wages in the long term. It was an exciting, if hazy, "prospect." For both young men, the perceived flexibility, autonomy, and paternalism of the inheritor enterprises did not mitigate the risk that they would soon go out of business. They saw the TNC as holding the possibility of entry into a kind of aristocracy of labor that would offer them long-term social mobility.

Slava's initial job status as an external "agency" worker at Frunzensky puts him on a waiting list. Numerous hoops have to be jumped through before there can be any hope of transfer to permanent worker status with legal rights, benefits, and pay. Sickness time off is one such issue to overcome, particularly as Slava's wife gave birth a year after he started there. When the child was sick Slava felt pressure to care for the child at home, as his wife also worked. Meanwhile, one has to have the "right attitude" and get in with the "right" people to make sure one's name progresses up the list toward the coveted status of permanent employment instead of agency worker. Other workers underline the "harsh physical demands." Here a lack of "flexibility" and intensification are linked in workers' minds. Unlike in local Russian companies, where moves toward intensification were gradual and the history of flexible working is long, there is no conception of "optimization" of labor, by which informants mean that a person who is unable to cope with the conveyor work (including heavy labor lifting car parts) can be redeployed in a different part of plant. The attitude at the TNCs is that weaker workers are "disposable."

With this knowledge, it is easy to see why Slava is guarded. Even in a friendly group, the sense of "getting above one's station" is keenly felt. In 2014, after Petr too has been working at the car plant for a few years, he says of another friend, Nikita, who has no overt ambitions to try work at Frunzensky: "He has to work, but doesn't know why, certainly not towards a directed aim. That's just the way he is and he is happy with himself. Nikita just has to spend all his pay even before he gets it." This comes in response to Slava talking about feeling "trapped" by his well-paid conveyor job at Frunzensky (having taken on a mortgage and started to climb the career ladder). But it is almost as if now, with the benefit of hindsight, Petr (the other conveyor worker) and Slava have some secret admiration, as much as scorn, for their friend Nikita's "easy-come-easy-go" attitude. And this is related to Slava's (and to a lesser extent Petr's) anxiety in talking about the car plant work. The feeling of being trapped by the work at the TNC results from prior expectations of a significantly better working environment with the ability to earn more in the long term. These expectations are not met, and after a short "honeymoon" period most workers feel significant disillusionment.

Such disillusionment results in labor turnover at the plant that is high even by Russian standards and a source of some embarrassment for the firm. Slava's entry into the plant coincided with a remarkable period of new, "free" trade union activity, itself spurred on by this general feeling of dissatisfaction with conditions and pay at the plant. The union sees this high turnover (Russian *tekuchka*, churning) as evidence that the plant was fertile ground for labor agitation, and the activists' hunch proved to be correct. Along with "standard" issues such increasing pay and reducing hours, they see the issue of agency workers' status and rights as a key element of their militancy.

Approximately 12 percent of the workforce—about 540 people—are agency workers. The plant uses agency work explicitly as a recruiting method—the most loyal workers have a realistic chance of being "transferred" to permanent staff. Agency workers are paid at least 13 percent less than permanent staff and do not have access to benefits like enhanced medical insurance and long, paid vacations. As churn is also quite high among the permanent personnel, the Frunzensky management can immediately compensate by replacing the vacant position with a suitable worker from the extensive pool of agency workers already employed, instead of having to turn to the labor market. This is how Slava and Petr, luckily, will find themselves permanent contracts. They will also benefit from the union's successful fight in the other areas, for in 2013 the union will sign a collective bargaining agreement with management—the firm's acknowledgement of the union's success and its dislocation of the "traditional" Soviet-style union also operating at the plant.

Another factor contributing to workers' anxiety is the absolute novelty of foreign employers, managers, and relatively high-tech production lines. The car plants symbolize the shock to the individual in these new times, as productivity demands are imposed on Russian workers used to Soviet-style production regimes and practices. Coupled with more general cultural differences, Slava and Petr feel perpetually tested by the new plant and therefore reluctant to discuss it, even with close friends. After taking a risk as great as that taken by those who escape into the informal economy, what if those going to work for the foreigners come back as failures?

Along with an ongoing sense of novelty, strangeness, and the sense of being tested is the endemic suspicion and distrust of all things foreign among the Russian men, young and old alike. The influence of the closed Soviet society and the experience of growing up in the semi-closed defense ministry town live on. The watchfulness appears mutual. The first chink in Slava's armor was his surprise at the cultural difference of management. Instead of shouting and swearing, the foreign supervisors were always calm, if insistent and demanding. The usual stereotype of Russian inscrutability was reversed and projected onto the Germans and others (such as Slovak lower-level supervisors). Working for and with foreigners was a major milestone, not only in Slava's working life, but also in terms of his and his family's life experience. It was "weird" in a way he struggled to articulate, but given the former status of Izluchino, not difficult to understand. Added to this was the sense that this shiny and relatively promising work might disappear as soon as it had magically arrived. Given the sense of generalized insecurity in the labor market that has become part of the "normal" backdrop of workers' lives since 1991, workers have learned wariness, patience, and above all cynicism. This also added to Slava's and Petr's reticence. 'Don't look a gift horse in the mouth' is a Russian saying too.

Slava soon admits that one reason for his wariness is the overly formal way that his work contract has been set up: even as a probationer he had to sign an agreement not to disclose to third parties any business practices at the plant. He takes this seriously when being questioned by a foreign researcher. Also, for the first year or so, Slava's pay is not very much higher than that in the town, therefore he feels it is imprudent to talk too much about the work, given the possibility that the "risk" he has taken will turn out to be "not worth it." Just as elsewhere—in the local, "old style" factories in Izluchino, a significant proportion of salary is paid as a "bonus." But in contrast to his previous experience in the town in "Soviet-style" factories, the supervisors at the car plant, whether Russian or foreign, have no qualms about withholding or "fining" workers' bonuses for what would be considered relatively minor infractions elsewhere.

In another conversation, Slava and others discuss the lack of self-realization and satisfaction in work. There is little specialized work on the shop floor, so highly qualified workers are not needed. Those like Slava who are able to compare the more traditional working environment in the town with the Kaluga assembly line's repetitive, monotonous tasks day in and day out, explain that many workers quit because they have the feeling there is no way out. The paucity of possibilities for "ordinary" workers to develop themselves in the workplace is mirrored in the low level of the wages at the plant—between 26,000 and 40,000 rubles (in 2013, 800–1250 US dollars)—and good workers reach the higher end of the scale after only a couple of years. This means that human capital is not bound to the plant. Naturally, this is an issue for both the independent union at the plant and individuals, despite considerable successes in collective bargaining that have already been achieved through struggles and negotiations with management. The plant has a very high market share, and although the wage at AvtoVAZ (the "standard" Russian car plant making the lion's share of domestic autos) is about 2.5 times lower than that at Frunzensky, the latter is only a little higher than the average wage paid in the Kaluga region. For the union and many workers, the calculation is simple: if Ford near St. Petersburg is able to pay more—up to twice as much as Frunzensky—why can't Frunzensky do the same? But for Frunzensky management, the slogan seems to be: Why pay more when you can pay less? It was the union that drew attention to these disparities, but such comparisons are an effective articulation of general disillusionment after the initial period of employment for many workers. Their articulations follow an arc of growing self-realization about the positioning of their labor in this new context.

Even more of an issue in terms of disillusionment, and sometimes of explicit comparison to more traditional production relations, is the shift system at the car plant and the lack of spare time for workers that comes with it. Working long hours and weekends is less an exception than an actual rule. Added to this is the long commute many make from outlying areas. Because of these time constraints, a place at the plant precludes the secondary employment and informal work that are extremely common and often lucrative for other blue-collar workers in Russia, including those in the "old" plants in Izluchino. So depending on an employer with an all-consuming job that leaves neither enough spare time to recover from long shifts nor sufficient time for a further informal job, adds to the perceived insecurity of many workers at the plant. Anxiety is also heightened by the disparity in production relations between the foreign plant and the inheritor businesses like the cement and steel pipe enterprises in the town. Petr and Slava were experiencing coercion in a completely "new" and unnerving way. They are fundamentally disturbed by the "indirect" nature of the more Taylorist, compartmentalized, highly organized production regime. This takes time to get used to, and with time Slava and Petr become able to articulate more and more of what they feel is "weird," for instance, the conspicuous absence at the European and Asian plants of normal Russian management practices: minimal oversight, lack of forward planning, and a lot of slack followed by "storming" to meet deadlines, with a bonus for the whole team at the end regardless of quality. At Frunzensky the benchmark is global competitiveness, but Russian car producers are less subject to pressure to maximize profits because the Russian government subsidizes them, supporting a key employment sector. As Slava sheepishly admits, "they really know how to get every ounce out of you all the time, every day, from the start to the end of the shift." It turned out, as his soon-to-be-wife Marina articulates, that "he's not trying to avoid talking about the conveyor; he's just completely exhausted!" A fit young man of twenty-four, Slava collapses into bed at home after his shift and falls asleep in front of the television.

It is a long time before I see Slava again. It seems he has disappeared from the social group entirely. But at the end of summer, all the car plants have a furlough period when they retool. In late August 2012, Slava and his wife, along with Petr and others, have a barbeque at a village plot outside town. By this time, Petr too works for Frunzensky, having become a permanent worker after a period as an agency contractor. This social occasion is where Slava's feeling of being hemmed in really comes to the fore. Slava has been promoted to foreman on the conveyor, and the independent trade union, after instigating industrial action at the plant and in supplier plants, has signed a collective wage agreement resulting in better wages and conditions. Yet Slava looks ever more like a haunted man. As the women busy themselves putting children to bed and cleaning up after the meal, a group of men gather round the fire some distance away. Stumbling over his words, and with a pained look into the fire, Slava keeps talking—somewhat in awe—of the mortgage he has taken out on a new-build Kaluga flat and his new, "physical" realization that he is now "tied" to the foreman's job permanently. Petr, just a conveyor worker but also destined for a more specialized role, uses the word "trap," but leaves it unclear whether he is referring to the mortgage or to the higher-paid foreman's role, although arguably they arc connected.

Slava continues: "It's difficult to swallow. I took on the foreman's job, but I just can't really push people around like I am supposed to. I needed the promotion to get the mortgage—Marina isn't working while the kid is small. But now, it's kind of like I am surprised that I can't give it up."

Shortly afterward, Slava and his family leave the village for their long journey home, leaving Nikita and Petr to ponder on their friend's predicament. While Petr is sympathetic, he criticizes Slava's choice of taking on a burdensome mortgage so soon. Petr himself had saved up for years to buy a very modest local apartment before taking the "risk" of working for Frunzensky. Nikita is visibly angry at Petr's balanced and calculating response:

> You clearly didn't see the weld burns on Slava's arms and face. Everyone's talking about how poor the conditions really are at the plant. No better than anywhere else in reality. And yes, I was tempted by the extra 5-10k pay a month, but then there is the commute. You look tired yourself, mate. How long do you spend on the road behind the wheel of your Lada?

Nikita cannot let it lie, and the following exchange results:

Nikita: Ok, the lad will have a flat in Kaluga. And a discount or credit on a Škoda that will fall apart on our roads. So fucking what? To break his back for the "new deal" at the plant that they only won after the strikes? Physically that job, despite the shiny German plant and showers and clean overalls, is no different from mine at the Cement. And we have showers too you know. And there's no sitting around or smoking in the back there. That's the only plant that'll sack you for coming in smelling of booze too!

Petr: Well, that would be you out on your ear after the second shift, then [good-naturedly laughing]! At the end of the day, I still don't know yet whether it was worth buying my flat here or in Kaluga. Both are extortionate. The prices are almost like Moscow. That's the problem. If you live with your mum then the pay is amazing. If you have responsibilities it is no different from the Cement.

You are right about the physicality. I've been off sick for most of August due to my back. And the travel time, well, yes, that's dead time regardless of whether you are in your own car or the works bus—the cost of which they take out of your pay, by the way.

Clearly, Nikita's talk is significantly inflected by resentment, possibly envy, and some second-hand, if not inaccurate, information about conditions at the plant. On the other hand, his practical reasoning about the risks associated with work at Frunzensky and other plants is firmly shared by many others. Petr's considered position frankly acknowledges some of Nikita's points. In fact, as time goes on, Petr's pre-existing health problems get worse at the plant, necessitating long and involved medical intervention. Petr's "worth" to Frunzensky does not amount to his employer paying for the necessary medical care beyond the absolute legal minimum—whereas in the "old" factories, rightly or wrongly, a more paternalist attitude (including personalized treatment by management) is perceived to still prevail.

Locally in Izluchino, the arrival of the car plants and other enterprise facilities is a major source of bitterness, because it is the best and youngest workers who are most likely to leave the town's struggling enterprises. The anxieties Slava expresses about his new work are replicated by local businesses: it is all some trick, a sleight of hand by the regional governor to please Putin. The Germans, French, Swedes, and Japanese will suck out what marrow is left here and then relocate back to their homelands. "We're the blacks of Europe alright," says one worker. "Do you know how much the Slovak Frunzensky workers building the cars in Bratislava get paid? Twice as much as even our specialist workers! Are they any more productive? Of course not!"[7] This is not accurate—Slovak workers' wages are perhaps 30 per cent higher— however, the Slovakian cost of living may well be lower due to the higher cost of food in Russia.

While many locals are genuinely concerned for their town because of the competition for labor, many more articulate politically aware cynicism about the companies and their government. They talk of Kaluga becoming a low-wage global outsourcing site of blue-collar labor. Now that the "honeymoon" period of workers like Slava at the plants is over, people are not surprised by the labor turnover in the foreign plants and their workers' militancy, which is supposed to be even stronger than it is in the Russian and "Soviet" plants.

Two related articulations of dissatisfaction are noteworthy. First, even relatively young workers often cannot reconcile themselves to the increasing imperatives to "self-exploit." This term denotes the coercion of labor regimes that "produce" the entrepreneurial individual in a way that appears to relate to intrinsic motivation, but is actually an effect of the biopolitics at the heart of neoliberal intensification and disciplining regimes (Hamann 2009). The blue-collar work at the car plants that exemplifies this regime is rejected by those in the informal economy and those who opt to stay in "old" factories with slower, more predictable rhythms, even if here too postsocialist dispossession is acutely felt. The search for alternative autonomist values can be observed in different global contexts very different from that in Russia (Skeggs 2011; De Neve 2014). However, even those who develop more enterprising selves, like Slava and Petr, articulate frustration at the lack of autonomy in regulating their own pace and approach to solving tasks and meeting production targets. Second, locals are aware of the "offshoring" and state-within-a-state nature of many of the industrial parks, one of which is dominated by Frunzensky and its most important suppliers. In some ways they ironically resemble "closed" factory towns of the Soviet period like Izluchino: gated entry; only works buses allowed in and out; significant monitoring and searching of staff entering and leaving (workplace theft was immediately a problem at Frunzensky); heightened labor discipline (e.g., concerning alcohol use). In comparison, old-style factories are more lenient, as they want to keep the workers they have and are willing to overlook some absences as long as the individual has skills in demand.

Those of a more reflective nature go further: aren't these little fiefdoms of Germany, France, and Japan, like colonies in the third world? Extracting surplus value to be shipped back home? "And we're not even up to the standard of Brazil!" said another worker. "They even get better pay in the Anchieta factory that makes saloon cars near Sao Paolo." Multiple generations of Marxist-Leninist education have not gone entirely to waste—even the less educated can readily connect the dots to spell "exploitation" and "proletariat." The resulting problem of labor churn (*tekuchka*) is bemoaned by entrepreneurs at every turn, and it is especially bad at Frunzensky. A candid, relatively balanced local news report highlights this after a third shift is taken on and union activity increases in response to the large numbers of agency contract workers. A human resources manager comments:

> I have never seen such churning of labor as in that factory. Since I arrived we've lost 600 workers in six months. And of these around 60% left of their own accord. The ones forced to leave were due to infractions of labor discipline, alcohol. At first I was surprised but now I get it. Many people who come to work from the edges of Kaluga and worked previously in agriculture or construction. Many were unaccustomed to work in three shifts and on the conveyor. Therefore the majority of those quitting left in the first two months. (Gusev 2011)

Although the foreign HR manager's account is partial (his reference to the lack of worker experience in factory work is disingenuous at best), it is revealing of the problems of churn and their rootedness in differing cultural and moral norms of production. A more polemical piece entitled "The Path of the Blue-Collars" appears in the national business weekly magazine *Expert* that year (Rytsareva 2011). Its main message is the familiar line that Russians are unsuited to the disciplined demands of the "shiny" globalized factory. The journalist, who has found "sad-faced," downtrodden workers there, implied that they are ungrateful for the opportunity the benevolent foreigners have provided in this provincial city. The author bemoans the lack of technical preparation of young people in the vocational education sector as well as the inability of Russian firms to act as suppliers to the factory. Nowhere does the author address the issue of labor turnover. Interestingly, a representative of the International Metalworkers' Federation associated with the local independent union at the Kaluga plant takes the time to respond substantively to the article: "I don't really get this position: creatively describing the glum, gloomy people without even trying to find out what is actually happening at their workplace." After describing some issues with safety at the plant that the union has highlighted (including the burns Slava suffered), the metalworkers' representative continues:

> So, the main problem is as always, the [quality of the] "people"? … I will make no mention of the fact that the huge pay of the workers (about 20,000 rubles) is lower than the average for Kaluga Region in large and medium sized enterprises. That's not the problem, the people are. How many times can the liberal cliché of undisciplined Russian workers be repeated at the same time as refusing to even ask about how things are at the factory? (Matveev 2011)

The undeniable fact of relatively uncompetitive, or, as informants sometimes say, "stingy" wages, especially when deductions for work clothes, transport, and canteens are taken into account, no doubt adds to workers' attraction to the new union at the car plants. Slava and Petr have not joined the union yet but have benefited from its work. Their paternalistic expectations of a union echo the older generation's understanding of industrial relations and are a source of frustration to the new union. Elsewhere we tell the story of union activism at the plant (Morris and Hinz 2016), which is beyond the scope of this chapter. A major issue for unions trying to gain critical mass at plants is the problem of the "free rider," represented here by our informants. Slava and Petr are wary of the union, but grudgingly acknowledge its effectiveness, despite only around 20 percent of the workforce being members at any one time. In a sense they exhibit a neoliberal entrepreneurialism of self that is different from that of their peers who reject work in the factory (cf. Morris 2012a).

Concluding Remarks

To grasp the transformative power of neoliberalism, it is essential to investigate how workers "understand, reflect, and act collectively upon subordination to increasingly precarious positions" within a global economy (Krinsky 2007: 344), even if they remain in a "normative" model of permanent employment. Precarity in Russian industrial work is less about job insecurity, although even for permanent plant workers the threat of dismissal—for not keeping up the pace, for disciplinary infractions, or simply because of the geopolitical risks of global business in Russia—is real. The objective evaluation of what is "bad" versus "good" work is tied to a sense of what a proper person *qua* worker should be—as are dreams of elevation into an increasingly unreachable labor aristocracy and fears of descent into the reserve labor pool. This is indivisible from the sense of self- and objective "worth" and "value" developed in the socialist period. The sense of what makes the present precarious comes to take on a psycho-social articulation in classed personhood.

Any reading of the impact of neoliberalism on workers in Russia must take account of past narratives of labor that continue to influence contemporary lived experience. We must be careful not to construct a one-dimensional perspective of workers as merely passive in their reception of global processes and reshapings of space, and instead seek to reveal more nuanced and differentiated meanings and narratives of work, and the negotiation of work relationships under post-socialism (Crowley and Ost 2001).

The meaning of precarious work in the Global North remains firmly anchored to workers' fears about loss of permanent work and underemployment (Kalleberg 2009: 7–8). It is essentially related to the post-Fordist period since the 1970s in the West, which is problematic to transplant to other contexts (Munck 2013). Workers in Russia may not be frightened of losing "bad" jobs, as there is no shortage of alternatives in both traditional factories and the informal economy.

This chapter ends with the contradictory yet resolutely moral perspectives of the main informants as, to different degrees, they make efforts to "adapt" to the ever changing demands of production in the globalized labor market of Kaluga Region. The differences between those who go to the car plant and others who stubbornly resist the chance to earn better wages there cannot be explained easily by any one factor. But one thing is clear: informants unambiguously interpret TNC conveyor work and other such jobs as a kind of metastasis of processes of intensification in, and alienation of, labor—processes that are emblematic of what makes jobs "bad" and work life "precarious."

Meanwhile, some workers (like Petr in his labor at Frunzensky), who equally well articulate the sense of unfair exploitation and inadequate remuneration, are nonetheless more accommodating, more accepting of their lot. In the most positive light, such a life strategy can be seen as striving for betterment, for mobility, for the long-term sustainability of his household. Certainly that is the moral justification that is internalized. But it remains to be seen how sustainable such a position is, given ongoing health and other "contingent" risks to these workers. In 2014, as the economic downturn intensified due to new international sanctions against Russia, Frunzensky experienced its third period of shutdown due to low demand. In the autumn and winter of that year, permanent workers lost nearly seven weeks of work but still received two-thirds pay during the stoppages.

This chapter has highlighted Russian workers' particularistic interpretations of the positioning of their labor in the globalizing blue-collar work of Kaluga Region. These encompass subjective and objective understandings of a loss of autonomy in task completion, increased surveillance, and the erasure of a buffering of work relations by team structure. While these effects of the neoliberalization of work are felt in the surviving Russian industrial contexts in the town of Izluchino, they are even more keenly experienced in the Frunzensky TNC auto plant. There, even the compressed wage structure (largely beyond the scope of this chapter) is experienced as a symptom of work intensification. Even when the union won a significant increase in wages after 2012, a widespread interpretation in the plant and beyond held that such physically intensive work *and* monitoring meant that wages were not adequate compensation in comparison to lower-paid, less demanding blue-collar employment elsewhere.

People's talk continually references the community-level memory of the socialist-era social contract and the perceived affordances of labor prior to the present period. They refer especially to the loss, over the last quarter century, of the social wages and the modest autonomy and flexibility in work/shop-floor relations that once compensated for poor conditions and wages. Lastly, labor mobility remains a paradoxical element in workers' response to insecurity. Large-scale mobility in the Soviet period gave the working class an opportunity to access real social mobility. At the same time, demand for labor led the socialist state to make concessions to workers in the form of a commitment to increase the social wage over time. This process broke down from the 1990s on. However, mobility— whether exercised by turning to even more precarious work in the local informal economy, or by taking up construction work, shuttle trading, or other activities further afield—was a key way in which blue-collar workers dealt with the postsocialist transition. Labor mobility in response to precarity has been a central object of study in labor economics of postsocialist transition generally (Friebel and Guriev 1999).

Albert Hirschman's (1970) hermeneutic framework of responses to insecurity in organizations faced with crisis has been used elsewhere to analyze choices facing ordinary people after socialism, particularly as an apt metaphor for the "non"-choices facing workers during the 1990s transition (e.g., Bohle and Greskovits 2007; Sippola 2014). Stephen Crowley (2004) proposes "exit" into the informal economy for workers who have no "voice" (cf. Greskovits 1998; Morris 2016).

In the present, workers in turn are leaving informal work and local employment swayed by the promises of the TNC conveyor in the regional capital of Kaluga. However, labor turnover at the German plant is higher than in the surviving Russian businesses, and labor unrest is significant. It is no longer TNCs that confront postsocialist workers with the non-choice of accepting neoliberalized workspaces, but workers who increasingly confront the globalization of their labor through TNCs by questioning the value the companies ascribe to it. They do this by accessing enduring moral understandings about autonomy, reward, dignity in labor, and ultimately localized, socially embedded understandings of what "bad" and "worse" work is. This is apparent in their choices: sticking with the TNCs, retreating to the remaining Soviet-style enterprises, or taking a risk to pursue even more insecure work as taxi drivers, tradespersons, and seasonal construction workers in the informal economy (Morris 2012a, 2014b).

Acknowledgments

Fieldwork for this research was carried out between 2009 and 2015. Most of the material used for this chapter is from 2012. A core of about fifty informants were involved in the research, which focused particularly on four households. We owe many insights that improved this chapter to the editors and to Sarah Ashwin, who commented on an earlier version of the essay.

Jeremy Morris is Associate Professor of Global Studies at Aarhus University. He was previously based at the University of Birmingham, where he co-directed the Centre for Russian, European and Eurasian Studies As an ethnographer of postsocialist societies, Morris's research focuses on "actually lived experience" in relation to work, class, and the informal economy. He is the author of *Everyday Postsocialism: Working-class Life Strategies in the Russian Margins* (2016), *The Informal Postsocialist Economy: Embedded Practices and Livelihoods* (2014), and numerous journal articles.

Sarah Hinz is a labour sociologist, doctoral student, and Research Associate at the University of Jena. In her research she focuses on transnational companies, employment relations, and precarious work, together with social policy. She has carried out a number of industrial case studies in Germany and Russia. Her work has appeared in edited volumes and journals on trade union revitalization, as well as in the *European Journal of Industrial Relations*.

Notes

1. While it is overly simplistic to contrast old Soviet-style firms with TNCs—both are subject to the imperatives of "streamlining" labor, extracting greater value, and intensifying production—we highlight the culture of production in TNCs in particular as emblematic of more general neoliberalizing processes. Though we are at pains to stress that remaining in "Soviet-style" production-scapes is no bed of roses, it does offer measurable affordances—be they economistic rational ones to do with use of free time (for earning money in the informal economy and self-provisioning) and access to family, tangible social benefits, or token psychological ones (Morris 2014b). Similarly, while 'Soviet-style' is a necessary simplification of the diversity of production-scapes, in terms of shopfloor cultures they resemble each other and this is important for worker's interpretations of 'bad' and 'less bad' work. See Morris (2016).
2. Izluchino is a pseudonym. It is not officially a town, but an "urban settlement" (*poselek gorodskogo tipa*), reflecting its connection to rapid industrialization after World War II. Locally, the town is emblematic of the proliferation of small and medium-sized towns, a process that occurred throughout the Soviet Union. By the end of the Soviet period, nearly 30 percent of Russia's population lived in industrial cities with fewer than 100,000 inhabitants (Collier 2011:111).

3. A sense of belonging to the locality was sometimes expressed using the common phrase *malaia rodina,* or "little motherland."
4. Clarke and Soulsby (1998: 36, in Stenning *et al.* 2010: 87) calculated that the social wage was worth up to 20 percent of the value of the money wage in industrial enterprises in 1980s Czechoslovakia. On the expansion of the social wage among workers and others in the period up to 1991 see Hauslohner (1987). For a broad comparison of case studies of changes to social wages in postsocialist countries see Rein, Friedman, and Wörgötter (1997); on the social wage as a mechanism of social control see Domański (1997).
5. For industrial contexts similar to Izluchino, Clarke identified several particularly relevant features of the period: the lag in salary increases, consolidation of ownership, a new impetus for hands-on management, and strong recovery for strategically located firms and those with flexibility in use of space and resources.
6. Informal refers here to work paid off the books, often seasonal and without any legal protection. See Morris (2014b) and Morris and Polese (2014).
7. It should be noted that the cars produced for the TNC in Russia are for the domestic market. However, this does not negate the point workers make about exploitation.

References

Alasheev, Sergei. 1995. "On a Particular Kind of Love and the Specificity of Soviet Production." In *Management and Industry in Russia: Formal and Informal Relations in the Period of Transition,* ed. Simon Clarke, 72–98. Cheltenham: Edward Elgar.

Alexander, Catherine, and Buchli, Victor. 2007. "Introduction." In Catherine Alexander, Victor
Buchli and Caroline Humphrey, eds, *Urban Life in Post-Soviet Asia,* 1–40. London and New York: Routledge.

Bohle, Dorothee, and Béla Greskovits. 2007. "Neoliberalism, Embedded Neoliberalism and Neocorporatism: Towards Transnational Capitalism in Central-Eastern Europe." *West European Politics* 30(3): 443–466.

Bourdieu, Pierre. 1998. "Prekarität ist überall." In *Gegenfeuer: Wort-Meldungen im Dienste des Widerstands gegen die neoliberale Invasion,* ed. Pierre Bourdieu, 96–102. Constance: UvK.

Brinkmann, Ulrich, Klaus Dörre, Silke Röbenack, Klaus Kraemer, and Friedric Speidel. 2006. *Prekäre Arbeit: Ursachen, Ausmaß, soziale Folgen und subjektive Verarbeitungsformen unsicherer Beschäftigungsverhältnisse.* Bonn: Friedrich-Ebert-Stiftung.

Burawoy, Michael, with János Lukács. 1992. *The Radiant Past: Ideology and Reality in Hungary's Road to Capitalism.* Chicago, IL: Chicago University Press.

Burawoy, Michael, Pavel Krotov, and Tatyana Lytkina. 2000. "Involution and Destitution in Capitalist Russia." *Ethnography* 1(1): 43–65.

Castel, Robert. 2011. *Die Krise der Arbeit: Neue Unsicherheiten und die Zukunft des Individuums.* Hamburg: Hamburger Ed.

Castel, Robert, and Klaus Dörre, ed. 2009. *Prekarität, Abstieg, Ausgrenzung: Die soziale Frage am Beginn des 21. Jahrhunderts*. Frankfurt am Main: Campus.

Clarke, Simon. 1993. "The Contradictions of 'State Socialism.'" In *What About the Workers? Workers and the Transition to Capitalism in Russia*, ed. Simon Clarke, Peter Fairbrother, Michael Burawoy, and Pavel Krotov. London and New York: Verso.

———. 1995. *Management and Industry in Russia: Formal and Informal Relations in the Period of Transition*. Cheltenham: Edward Elgar.

———. 2007. *The Development of Capitalism in Russia*. London: Routledge.

Clarke, Ed, and Anna Soulsby. 1998. "Organization-Community Embeddedness: The Social Impact of Enterprise Restructuring in the Post-Communist Czech Republic." *Human Relations* 51(1): 25–50.

Collier, Stephen J. 2011. *Post-Soviet Social: Neoliberalism, Social Modernity, Biopolitics*. Princeton, NJ: Princeton University Press.

Cook, Linda. 1993. *The Soviet Social Contract and Why It Failed: Welfare Policy and Workers' Politics from Brezhnev to Yeltsin*. London and Cambridge, MA: Harvard University Press.

Crowley, Stephen. 2004. "Explaining Labor Weakness in Post-Communist Europe: Historical Legacies and Comparative Perspective." *East European Politics & Societies* 18(3): 394–429.

Crowley, Stephen, and David Ost, eds. 2001. *Workers After Workers' States: Labor and Politics in Postcommunist Eastern Europe*. Lanham, MD: Rowman & Littlefield.

De Neve, Geert. 2014. "Fordism, Flexible Specialization and CSR: How Indian Garment Workers Critique Neoliberal Labour Regimes." *Ethnography* 15(2): 184–207.

Domański, Boleslaw. 1997. *Industrial Control Over the Socialist Town*. Westport: Praeger.

Dörre, Klaus. 2009. "Prekarität im Finanzmarkt-Kapitalismus." In *Prekarität, Abstieg, Ausgrenzung: Die soziale Frage am Beginn des 21. Jahrhunderts*, ed. Robert Castel and Klaus Dörre, 35–64. Frankfurt am Main: Campus.

———. 2010. "Génération Précaire – Ein europäisches Phänomen?" In *Zwischen Prekarisierung und Protest: Die Lebenslagen und Generationsbilder von Jugendlichen in Ost und West*, ed. Michael Busch, Jan Jeskow, and Rüdiger Stutz, 41–76. Bielefeld: transcript.

Friebel, Guido, and Sergei Guriev. 1999. "Should I Stay or Can I Go? Attaching Workers through In-Kind Payments." Stockholm Institute of Transition Economics, Staff Paper No. 00/07.

Greskovits, Béla. 1998. *The Political Economy of Protest and Patience: East European and Latin American Transformations Compared*. Budapest: Central European University Press.

Gusev, Andrei. 2011. "Fol'ksvagen otkryl tret'iu smenu i prinial na rabotu 2000 chelovek" [Volkswagen opened a third shift and took on 2000 extra workers]. Interview with VW HR Director Henri Menert, *Komsomolskaia Pravda Kaluga* online newspaper, 19 October. Retrieved 24 September 2017 from http://www.kp40.ru/news/kp/14731/.

Hamann, Trent H. 2009. "Neoliberalism, Governmentality, and Ethics." *Foucault Studies* 6: 37–59.

Hann, Chris. 2006. *"Not the Horse We Wanted!" Postsocialism, Neoliberalism, and Eurasia.* Münster: Lit Verlag.

Hauslohner, Peter. 1987. "Gorbachev's Social Contract." *Soviet Economy* 3(1): 54–89.

Hirschman, Albert O. 1971. *Exit, Voice, and Loyalty: Responses to Decline in Firms, Organizations, and States.* Cambridge, MA: Harvard University Press.

International Labour Office. 2012. *From Precarious Work to Decent Work: Outcome Document to the Workers' Symposium on Policies and Regulations to Combat Precarious Employment.* Geneva: International Labour Office, Bureau for Workers' Activities.

Kagarlitsky, Boris 2008. "Nevroz v ofise." *Vzgliad: delovaia gazeta*, 7 April 2008. Retrieved 24 September 2017 from http://www.vz.ru/columns/2008/4/7/157651.html.

Kalleberg, Arne L. 2009. "Precarious Work, Insecure Workers: Employment Relations in Transition." *American Sociological Review* 74: 1–22.

Kesküla, Eeva. 2014. "Disembedding the Company from Kinship: Unethical Families and Atomized Labor in an Estonian Mine." *Laboratorium: Russian Review of Social Research* 2: 58–76.

Kotkin. Stephen. 1995. *Magnetic Mountain: Stalinism as Civilisation.* Berkeley, CA: University of California Press.

Krinsky, John. 2007. "Constructing Workers: Working-Class Formation under Neoliberalism." *Qualitative Sociology* 30: 343–360.

Levinson, Aleksei. 2007. "O tom, kak rabochie na nashikh zapadnykh zavodakh mechtaiut vernut'sia v VPK." *Otechestvennye zapiski* 4. Retrieved 24 September 2017 from http://demoscope.ru/weekly/2008/0337/analit03.php.

Matveev, Ilya. 2011. "Uvazhamaia Elena" [Dear Elena] – [online comment in response to Rytsareva, E. (2011). "Tropoi sinikh vorotnichkov" [On the trail of the blue collar]. *Ekspert*, 2(736). Retrieved 24 September 2017 from http://expert.ru/expert/2011/02/tropoj-sinih-vorotnichkov/.

Morris, Jeremy. 2012a. "Unruly Entrepreneurs: Russian Worker Responses to Insecure Formal Employment." *Global Labour Journal* 3(2): 217–236.

———. 2012b. "Beyond Coping? Alternatives to Consumption within Russian Worker Networks." *Ethnography* 14(1): 85–103.

———. 2014a. "The Warm Home of Cacti and Other Soviet Memories: Russian Workers Reflect on the Socialist Period." *Central Europe* 12(1): 16–31.

———. 2014b. "Moonlighting Strangers Met on the Way: The Nexus of Informality and Blue-Collar Sociality in Russia." In *The Informal Post-Socialist Economy: Embedded Practices and Livelihoods*, ed. J. Morris and A. Polese, 51–66. London and New York: Routledge.

———. 2016. *Everyday Postsocialism: Working-Class Communities in the Russian Margins.* Aldershot, Palgrave.

Morris, Jeremy, and Sarah Hinz. 2016. "Trade Unions in Transnational Automotive Companies in Russia and Slovakia: Prospects for Working Class Power." *European Journal of Industrial Relations* 23(1): 97–112.

Morris, Jeremy, and Abel Polese, eds. 2014. *The Informal Post-Socialist Economy: Embedded Practices and Livelihoods*. London and New York: Routledge.

Morrison, Claudio. 2008. *A Russian Factory Enters the Market Economy*. London: Routledge.

Munck, Ronaldo. 2013. "The Precariat: A View from the South." *Third World Quarterly* 34(5): 747–762.

Prokhorov, Aleksandr. 2002. *Russkaia model' upravleniia*. Moscow: Zhurnal Ekspert.

Rein, Martin, Barry L. Friedman, and Andreas Wörgötter, eds. 1997. *Enterprise and Social Benefits After Communism*. Cambridge: Cambridge University Press.

Rodgers, Gerry. 1989. "Precarious Work in Western Europe: The State of Debate." In *Precarious Jobs in Labour Market Regulation: The Growth of Atypical Employment in Western Europe*, ed. G. Rodgers and J. Rodgers. Geneva: ILO.

Rytsareva, Elena. 2011. "Tropoi sinikh vorotnichkov" [On the trail of the blue-collars] *Ekspert,*

2(736). Retrieved 24 September from http://expert.ru/expert/2011/02/tropoj-sinih-vorotnichkov/.

Sippola, Markku. 2014. "Balancing between Exit, Voice and Loyalty: Labour Market Policy Choices in Estonia." In *The Contradictions of Austerity: The Socio-Economic Costs of the Neoliberal Baltic Model*, ed. Jeffrey Sommers and Charles Woolfson, 118–137. London and New York: Routledge

Skeggs, Bev. 2011."Imagining Personhood Differently: Person Value and Autonomist Working-Class Practices." *Sociological Review* 59(3): 496–513.

Smith, Adrian, Alison Stenning, Alena Rochovská, and Dariusz Świątek. 2008. "The Emergence of a Working Poor: Labour Markets, Neoliberalisation and Diverse Economies in Post-Socialist Cities." *Antipode* 40(2): 283–311.

Stenning, Alison, Adrian Smith, Alena Rochovská and Dariusz Swiatek. 2010. *Domesticating Neo-Liberalism: Spaces of Economic Practice and Social Reproduction in Post-Socialist Cities*. Malden, MA: Wiley-Blackwell.

Van Atta, Don. 1986. "Why Is There No Taylorism in the Soviet Union?" *Comparative Politics* 18(3): 327–337.

Walker, Charles. 2010. "Space, Kinship Networks and Youth Transition in Provincial Russia:

Negotiating Urban-Rural and Inter-Regional Migration" *Europe-Asia Studies* 62(4): 647–669.

Wren, Daniel A. 1980. "Scientific Management in the U.S.S.R., with Particular Reference to the Contribution of Walter N. Polakov." *The Academy of Management Review* 5(1): 1–11.

11

Precarity, *Guanxi*, and the Informal Economy of Peasant Workers in Contemporary China

I-Chieh Fang

Introduction: *Guanxi* Matters, Even in Factories

The Chinese working class (*gongren jieji*) has collapsed. The factory labor force is no longer made up of the urban proletariat, as those workers have mostly been replaced by peasants from the countryside. Under the *hukou* system, the state still denies urban resident status to rural migrants, who are obliged to return to the countryside when the labor market has no further need of them (Murphy 2002; Pun 2005; H. Yan 2003). As peasant workers (*nonminggong*), they are still officially rural dwellers even though they are physically working in urban settings. A discourse of quality (*suzhi*) has marked rural migrants as "low quality" against the higher standard of civility and self-discipline of urbanites. This circumstance makes migrant workers "expendable" (Anagnost 2006: 514). This "expendability" forces young migrant workers to endure harder working conditions and lower pay than their urban counterparts. It also deprives migrants of bargaining power. Many scholars have tried to capture the subjectivities of these "new workers" (Lu 2013; Wang 2014; X. Yan 2015). This chapter argues that they are better understood as a precariat, albeit a precariat with distinctive Chinese characteristics.

China's precariat is not the precariat of South Asia, where the term refers primarily to workers without regular employment (Parry 2013). Chinese peasant workers also lack stable employment, but their life experiences differ greatly from those of workers resident in the city. In their daily lives, precariat peasant workers struggle constantly with ruptures of social relations, including intergenerational relations. They flood into factories to become workers, enduring hardship and exploitative working conditions while trying to transcend these ruptures. They invest enormous time and energy in cultivating social relationships in the factory settings, since this is the strategy they have learned to combat precarity. During my fieldwork I was struck by how *guanxi*—informal exchange and commitment to mutuality—flourished in the factory setting. Not only during their highly constrained personal time but also during working hours, workers and managers are busy establishing and maintaining relationships. At first glance, the Shenzhen factory I discuss below appeared to be organized according to the principle of *gongsifenming*, "business is business," but I soon learned that a more appropriate description was *gongsibufen*, "business mingles with personal relationships." The confirmation of social relations seems to help migrant workers overcome uncertainty and the sense of crisis in precarious, informal employment. Although they fit the definition of a precariat, their consciousness is quite different due to the persistence of the traditional peasant world of *guanxi*.[1] I shall show how workers define precarity differently in two factories with very different histories, as well as how generational and life course factors come into play. I shall focus on three dimensions: (1) subjective experiences and perceptions of precarity, (2) the moral economy (questions of what is fair, what is exploitation, and the extent to which exploitation can be made tolerable and compensated by caring paternalism), and (3) the meaning and value of work (how, in spite of their dispossession, workers create their own value through social reproduction).

Perceptions of Precarity: Generations, Life Course, and Economic Reform

In her studies of Chinese textile workers, Lisa Rofel (1992; 1999) showed that generational difference was the key to understanding the behavior of textile workers in Hangzhou. Differing perceptions of discipline and imaginings of order among female workers of different generations led to different strategies of resistance to the spatial disciplinary regime. The oldest generation displayed a "lack of industriousness," but the "only partially effective" nature of their work was their way of indicating that they were "good workers" in the sense of having an enlightened class consciousness (Rofel 1992: 92). Resting rather than working formed an important part of their identity (ibid.: 101). The next generation, those born during the Cultural Revolution, showed contempt for authority. However, the youngest generation of workers, comprising teenagers who had just arrived from rural areas, resisted through their unwillingness to settle down in one place. They moved back and forth between village and factory and admitted that they would never be like the city girls. This youngest generation of female migrant workers thus subverted the gendered space control regime system (ibid.: 103). In my terms, they were subjectively aware of their precarity, but their "freedom to come and go" (*laiquziru*), previously unthinkable under the socialist regime, was their way of exercising agency.

A generation after the pioneering research of Rofel, I conducted field-work primarily at the THS electronics factory in the Shenzhen Special Economic Zone (SEZ) on the Pearl River delta, and supplemented this with further research at the KS1 factory in Kunshan, near Shanghai (on the Yangtze River delta). KS1 and THS offered significant contrasts: one was a large, formerly state-owned electroplate factory with a mainly middle-aged labor force; the other, a new electronics firm owned and managed by Taiwanese, with a much younger labor force one-tenth the size of KS1's, composed mainly of migrant workers.

The electroplate factory was less attractive to migrant workers due to heavy levels of pollution and the fact that the majority of workers at KS1 were middle-aged, that is, the generation of the Cultural Revolution. They had grown up at the apex of party-state power, which mobilized people "up to the mountain and down to the village" (Bernstein 1993 [1977]). As the younger generation at that time, they had been empowered to fight against their elders and challenge authority in general. The party-state had arranged all the details of their lives, including their jobs. KS1 was owned by the state in this era, and many workers were initially taken on through "allocation" (*fenpei*) and then remained in their jobs after economic reform and privat-ization. In the perceptions of workers at KS1, their work is a gift from the state and, even in the new century, a "privilege" (*rongyu*) for which they are legally eligible thanks to the *hukou* system. Their work status is granted by the party-state, to which loyalty is expected. In this sense, workers of this generation, locals and migrants alike, see their work status as confirm-ing the encompassing social order of the party-state. Migrant workers, by contrast, are peasants. They come to work in the factory because this is strategically necessary for China's development, but if they were to stay forever, they would threaten the existing social(ist) order. The KS1 precar-iat is thus a product of a temporary bending of state development policies. The work one does is inconsistent with the work status one has, and this precarity leaves room for flexibility and ambiguity. Employers do not ask for full loyalty from employees, and employees do not ask for full respon-sibility from employers. Both parties have only a half-commitment. This is conducive to the rapid development of the Chinese economy, as it allows peasant workers to earn extra money without giving up their land and rural status. This precarity is the crucial means by which the state continues ideologically to proclaim a socialist order, while in actual fact the market economy has become thoroughly entrenched. The party-state retains its supreme role because the *hukou* system prevents the emergence of a "free" labor market.

Precarity is perceived and experienced differently in THS, Shenzhen, which came into existence only after marketization. The socialist legacy and ideology has had little impact here. Most workers are teenagers or in their early twenties, and turnover is high. Young villagers want to "see the world" (*jian shimian*). Job-hopping between factories, with travel expenses covered by wages, enables them to do so. For some of the more ambitious, factory work can be a kind of stepping stone toward an entrepreneurial engagement with the market economy: accumulating some money, knowledge, experience, and potential customers. In short, this aspirational minority does not perceive its precarity as a problem but more as a flexible arrangement as it progresses toward better opportunities. None of these villagers have the same respect for order as the workers at KS1. On the contrary, they want to escape from it, and seeking precarious work in Shenzhen is one of the most convenient ways to do so (cf. Shah 2006). Young migrant workers at THS perceive precarity as a transition to an alternative adulthood and a better future, rather than a threat to the social order.

Apart from generational differences, I also want to emphasize how the life course shapes subjective perceptions of precarity. The KS1 workers are mostly middle-aged and married. For them, work is what they must do to support their families. But for young migrant workers in THS, work is about "seeing the world" (*jian shimian*), "opportunities of meeting love interest" (*zhao duixiang*) and "being independent" (*duli*). Whereas the ageing work force at KS1 sees precarity as a kind of suffering and threat, young migrants at THS see it as a space where they can pursue their own agendas outside the order of the countryside.

Given these differences in subjective perceptions, workers' response to precarity in the two factories is also completely different. In the ethnographic sections below I will show how workers in KS1 *accept* whatever precarity brings, with a particular generational attitude to an allocation made by the socialist state. I will also elaborate on how THS workers utilize the ambiguity and flexibility of their precarity to strategize in the market economy. Before turning to this ethnography, however, it is necessary to consider the nature of social relations in Chinese economic life historically, in order to grasp the ways in which new moral economies are emerging today.

Rethinking Chinese Migrant Workers: *Guanxi* and Class Consciousness?

Peasant workers have dual identities and subjectivities shaped by both countryside and factories. This complicates the process of class formation and requires serious attention to how the "peasantry" has been shaped historically by kinship structure, hierarchy, division of labor, belief and rituals, gift exchange, cosmologies, filial piety, and morality. The situation in China has not changed fundamentally since Honig studied the female workers who constituted two-thirds of the industrial labor force in Shanghai in the Republican era. She expected to find workers with a strong class consciousness, but concluded that "at their most class-conscious, female cotton mill workers in Shanghai did not see themselves exclusively, or even primarily, as members of a working class" (Honig 1986: 249). Workers differed according to their regional backgrounds, accents, lifestyles, beliefs, and values. Their social organization and loyalties inhibited the development of a proletarian consciousness. The labor movement was organized through traditional sisterhoods and mutual-help groups, with which the Chinese Communist Party (CCP) eventually came to terms. Perry (1993) confirms this analysis in her study of workers' demonstrations in the same period, which shows class consciousness to be less significant than other social relations, such as those based on gender, education, and place of origin.

After the revolution, the category "workers" came to refer mostly to communist cadres rather than manual workers (Huang 2013). Propaganda and legal definitions also complicate the term *nonming* (peasant), another concept constructed after the liberation. The "peasant" is constructed in contrast to the urbanite, as backward and feudal. Yet Chinese rural people were not classified this way historically: a big family could have both urban and rural residences, owning land in both city and countryside (Cohen 1993).

Once the social engineering imposed by the party-state was lifted following the death of Chairman Mao, the "revival" or "recovery" of traditions permeated every aspect of life (Bruun 1995; Harrell 2001; Wolf 1985). Arguably, in attempting to move China to socialism, the CCP failed entirely to destroy the pre-existing local social networks and personally based forms of rule among the peasantry (Shue 1980).

Studies of migrant workers cannot ignore the agency left residing within the peasantry by these continuities, the most important forms of which are gift economy and *guanxi* (Y. Yan 2005). In Yang's (1994: 6) definition, "*guanxixue* involves the exchange of gifts, favors, and banquets; the cultivation of personal relationships and networks of mutual dependence; and the manufacturing of obligation and indebtedness." She argues that social actors meet their everyday needs and desires through a close-knit network of personal relations embedded in the gift economy, and in this way are even able to undermine the state's overwhelming power and form a civil society (albeit a Chinese version).

Previous researchers into Chinese factory life have noted that relationships, like regional origins, ethnicity, gender, and dialects, can function to differentiate the labor force. However, they have not paid sufficient attention to the ways in which relationships are deliberately created in order to undermine formal structures and thereby serve personal interests (cf. De Neve 2003, for India). I argue that *guanxi* is central to understanding the mindset of Chinese migrant workers in post-Mao China, particularly what they consider fair, whom one can trust, what one can exchange, and how one can organize and cooperate. Workers act upon their firm belief that *"guanxixue* will get a person much further in the world than formal learning ever can"* (Yang 1994: 8) by striving constantly to enlarge their *guanxi* networks.[2]

Yang found that *guanxi* is ubiquitous in the factory and present in both traditional apprenticeships and modern leader-subordinate relationships. The relationship between *shifu* (master) and *xuetu* (apprentice) is "often a deep, lifetime relationship involving both emotional bounding as well as *guanxi* exchange" (ibid.: 118) and often forms the basis of "factions" (*bangpai*) that persist across several generations of masters. By contrast, "the *guanxi* between work-unit leader and subordinate is less often suffused with affective elements as strong as those found in between manager and workers ... *guanxi* exchanges in these relationships tend to be motivated by more instrumental and politicized considerations" (ibid.: 119).

Yang goes on to draw attention to other elements of *guanxi*:

> This is the element of coerciveness, aggressiveness, and threat. Sometimes the art of *guanxi* involves the exercise of aggressive humility and coercive generosity ... the skilful deployment of *guanxi* tactics can reverse the power relations between officials and those whom they rule ... without resorting to revolution, *guanxixue* provides a leverage for control by those in weak social positions. Much like the Malaysian peasants described by James Scott (1985), who appeal to the precapitalist noblesse oblige or notions of virtuous charity to manipulate their employers, *guanxi* tacticians also make use of ethics, rather than just conform to them. (Yang 1994: 133–134)

While many factors inhibit migrant workers from developing class consciousness, the creation through *guanxi* of an entire informal sector, coexisting with and compensating for the formal structure, enables workers to renegotiate the latter. *Guanxi* provides a set of values and rules for workers to calculate what is fair, what is freedom, what is exploitation. This informal sector is the basis of the factory's moral economy.

The Two Factories Compared

The SEZ of Shenzhen and the town of Kunshan are adjacent to the big cities of Shenzhen and Shanghai respectively, not within the cities proper. In each case the trip to the big city takes around one hour by car. Migrant workers make up a large proportion of the population of Shenzhen and Kunshan, and can be seen wearing their factory uniforms even during their leisure time. In addition to the many factories clustered there, Shenzhen and Kunshan contain markets, shopping malls, restaurants, and large luxury hotels for business meetings. Trade unions are weak and neither of the factories I studied had any union organization.

KS1, Kunshan

In the course of doing research among KS1 workers, I heard of numerous inequities and complexities in the way work is organized at the factory. KS1 was an electroplate factory that had been privatized in 1997 and at the time of my fieldwork was owned by a mainlander. It was founded in 1976 as a small-scale state-owned enterprise. My flatmate in Jianyuan (a residential compound near KS1) told me that before the entry of Foxconn in 1994, Kunshan had been a very poor area, all wasteland around the roads from Jiayuan to KS1. There was no development at all, and the roads were unpaved. Later, thanks to a successful policy of attracting foreign investment, the town started to develop. The infrastructure was improved, roads were paved, and more foreign investment followed. Because the local government offered foreign companies considerable concessions, and also because of Kunshan's convenient proximity to Shanghai, the Taiwanese technology concern Foxconn (best known as a major supplier of components for Apple) decided to set up a factory here in 1994. Since then, economic and social change has been rapid.

KS1 is the name of both the factory and the village itself. For local men, working in the factory is the only way to earn any money. The women prefer not to marry local men, because they know how hard their lives will be. Due to policy changes effected in several rounds of administrative reform, the township re-categorized KS1 from *gongshe* (commune) to *jiedao* (literally "streets") and then to *shequ* (community). Residence in KS1 was no longer categorized as *nonming* (peasant). After the reform and opening up, when foreign capital entered and factories were established, the government began acquiring land for the expansion of plants. Residents around who lost land and received compensation said their living conditions had improved steadily.

However, the crucial reason for KS1's rapid development was not economic, but political. The original director of the factory was promoted to become a high-ranking official of the township. When he left his position in the factory, his son and son-in-law stepped in and took over. Because of these personal connections and the resulting *guanxi*, policies taken under his leadership of the township favored KS1. People told me, "He made it very convenient for KS1 (*ta geile henduo fangbian*)." My flatmates told me that collusion, corruption, and nepotism were the true reasons KS1 developed so fast. Even today, the nearby factories spread the word that KS1 is still entitled to many *fangbian* (favors) that are never extended to other factories. For example, KS1 has for some time been a titular social welfare institution, which means that it hires a certain percentage of people with disabilities in order to lower its tax rate. But in fact, there are no disabled workers in KS1; instead, it "borrows" the names of disabled people to fulfill the paperwork requirements. In short, *guanxi* persists, regardless of the economic framework's shift from socialism to capitalism. Thanks to the party-state, the farmers have become workers and are able to obtain stabler jobs and incomes than migrant workers.

At the time of my field research KS1 had two main leaders: Mr Chen, chairman and general manager, and Mr Ann, his deputy in both positions. Both had been basic workers in KS1 during the period of state ownership. They were born in the village and started to work at KS1 at the age of sixteen when they were allocated jobs there through the socialist distribution system. They entered the shop floor and started at the bottom. In time the then director was promoted to mayor, and when Mr Chen succeeded him, he married the daughter of the original director. Mr Chen's good friend, Mr Ann, became his deputy. The names of positions changed after privatization, but the people remained the same. Some people called the chairman and general manager CEO Chen. Under his leadership, KS1 continues to maintain good vertical *guanxi* with senior government officials. This kind of relationship is not formal and structural but subtle and implicit; still, everyone knows and talks about it. Local workers too cultivate informal relationships with representatives and agents of the local state, who might be their classmates, co-workers, in-laws, and relatives. However, migrant workers are largely excluded from such relationships.

The factory had a large parking lot near the entrance. The main building facing the gate was for managers and clerical workers. Besides the main building, there were two long workshop buildings and one small building housing the canteen. Altogether around 1,253 workers were employed here (803 male and 450 female). The majority of the workers (565) came from Jiangsu province. Workers from Sichuan (181) and Anhui (178) were the second most numerous. In total, the workers came from twenty different provinces. The popular distinction between "northerners versus south-erners" (Lee 1998: 118–119) was prevalent here, as elsewhere in China. But what functioned most powerfully in the managerial structure was the "local" versus "outsiders" distinction. Unlike outsiders, the locals got long-term contracts. Their local *hukou* status, rather than their work perfor-mance, was what helped them secure their jobs. Their wage was higher than outsiders'. The leaders of the factory were primarily from Kunshan and spoke Kunshan dialect to each other. When they gave an order to subor-dinates, they spoke strongly accented Mandarin. Since most workers from other provinces could not understand the Kunshan dialect, it was a very direct way to construct "localistic otherness" (ibid.: 117).

Even though many of its workers were not Kunshan locals, this factory did not provide dormitory accommodation. Local workers traveled to work by bicycle, going home every day. Migrant workers rented houses in the adjacent villages. The rent was a huge expense for them. Even if they squeezed in as many residents as possible (spouse, family members, relatives, or people from the same native place), the rent still amounted to almost one-third of their income (around 300 renminbi). This made migrant workers highly conscious of their status and produced a sense of envy toward "locals," whom migrants saw as the real beneficiaries of the development of Kunshan: locals got a stable job, a normal life, and extra income by renting out their houses, had no transportation costs, and prof-ited from the development of their hometown as a consequence of the fac-tory's being there. Migrant workers had to pay for their meals in the factory. Many told me they wanted to return home and never come back again. At home, they said, they were not forced to work hard every day to earn only enough money to cover basic expenses like food and housing.

Most workers at KS1 were middle-aged. The chemicals in the air were believed to be a significant health risk, workers told me, so younger skilled workers tended to move on quickly. The division of labor was mainly by gender. Male workers toiled on the assembly line; female workers were concentrated in quality control. The general educational background was a junior high school certificate. Those with a senior high school degree were considered eligible to become a group leader or clerical worker. Most workers had been in the factory for ten years or more. Job-hopping options were discussed only among the temporary workers in the quality control section, who were paid on a piecework basis.

Apart from job titles, the factory categorized its workers into two groups: *zigong* and *yuangong*. The difference lay in whether or not the person was a regular worker or a temporary worker. At KS1, the regular workers were known as *zigong* (regular worker). Workers who were hired temporarily were known as *yuangong* (temporary worker). For doing the same work

Table 11.1 Staff workers and employees at KS1

	Total numbers	Kunshan locals	Migrant workers
Numbers of employees	1,355	272	1,083
Zigong (regular workers)	467	262	205
Yuangong (temporary workers)	888	10	878

on the assembly line, *zigong* were paid more than *yuangong*, who were paid an hourly rate or a piece rate. Only *zigong* were entitled to bonuses and benefits. Thus *zigong* got money at the holidays (Chinese New Year, Moon Festival, and Dragon Boat Festival), but the *yuangong* did not. As can be seen in Table 11.1, the division between *zigong* and *yuangong* was strongly correlated with that between locals and migrants. Only a very small number of locals were *yuangong*.

Because most peasant workers are not regular workers, they do not expect to have a long career in the factory. Therefore, they very often leave the factory right after they are paid. To prevent their sudden departure, the factory deliberately delays the payment of wages, so that workers are paid a month in arrears. The Chinese New Year is the most "dangerous" season for factory managers, who frequently cannot find enough workers after the holiday, for two reasons. First, because of the long distance and high transportation costs, migrant workers who have returned home for family reunion during Chinese New Year often opt to stay longer rather than rush back to the factory to work. Second, reunited relatives working at different factories exchange information about wages and working conditions, and peasant workers who hear about better pay and working conditions at other enterprises tend to follow their relatives and neighbors to those factories. To get their wages for January, workers at KS1 have to return to the factory after the New Year and receive three months' wages at the end of March. Other factories around have adopted similar strategies. Managers explain that this costs less than paying higher wages to local workers.

Yuangong do not sign a contract, so the factory can dismiss them at any time. But until now, KS1 has been short of workers, so Subei Mama has stayed on for several years. She said that peasant workers like her actually do not want to sign long-term contracts, as without one it is easier to hop to other factories that might offer better pay and conditions. Relatives and people from the same hometown compare wage and working conditions among factories and decide where to go after the holiday. People in the vicinity of Subei Mama's hometown used to go to work in Shenzhen, but now they prefer Kunshan, Shanghai, and Suzhou.

In KS1, the gulf between the two categories of worker, *yuangong* and *zigong*, is vividly illustrated in the quality-check room, which is the unit with the most peasant workers. Female migrant workers frequently discuss the topic of "redoing work," chatting about who is being asked to repeat their task, how many times they have done it, and whether it is fair or not. The most pressing reason for their interest is that having to redo too much work means that they will not earn enough money to cover their daily expenses. Sometimes they have to work until ten o'clock at night in order to check all the products.

These peasant workers are managed by a female supervisor with the nickname *laoda* (boss), the leader in charge of the quality-check room, and a team of inspectors. The inspectors are all local workers who are no more skilled than the peasant workers. Their job is to double-check the work of the latter and decide whether it meets the standard. If they judge that a basket still contains too many flawed products, they ask the peasant workers to repeat it (*fan gong*). If the inspectors pass the basket of products, then it is counted as one piece towards the peasant worker's wage. Female peasant workers sit at the rear of the quality-check room, still working, as they wait for the "results release." If their work remains below expectations, they are put on "probation" and asked to sit next to the inspectors to repeat the task. The *laoda* often points at peasant workers, scolds them, or yells their names loudly. One peasant worker remarks to me: "The sound when she calls your name is like thunder. It's scary!"

The *laoda* and the team of inspectors finish work at four o'clock every day. Before the inspectors leave work, they check the products once again and decide which baskets need to be reworked. Then they depart, leaving the female peasant workers to carry on by themselves to finish the rest of the work. As soon as the *laoda* and her inspectors are gone, the atmosphere in the quality-check room relaxes. Young women stand up and walk around the tables, chatting loudly with each other and calling each other by nicknames. They discuss shopping and show each other new goods such as handbags or shoes, comparing the quality and price. People contribute opinions and advice on how to be a smart consumer. As one young woman said to me, "It is like a little market here!"

Apart from chatting and socializing, the peasant workers also seize the chance to resist. Most of the time, they simply ignore the inspectors' instructions to rework items and instead spend their time networking and establishing social relationships with co-workers, leaving the basket of products marked "rework" intact on the inspectors' tables to be rechecked the next morning. Sometimes the basket passes the second inspection, leading one Hubei migrant to comment ironically, "The boss and inspectors think they are shrewd!" These peasant workers are all *yuangong*, paid by piece rate, with a high turnover rate and longer working hours than those of the "boss" and the inspectors, who are all local people categorized as *zigong*.

Local *zigong* workers' social relations outside the factory are closely intertwined with their relations inside the factory, but this is not the case for migrant workers. Meijuan, now fifty-two years old, has been working in KS1 for twenty-five years altogether. She first began working there when she was twenty. The youngest of eight siblings in her natal family, she obtained only a primary school diploma. All of her siblings are now in Kunshan, and she is married to a Kunshan local. They have a son, now twenty-one years old, who still lives with them in Kunshan. Her husband also works at KS1. He has seven siblings who all live in Kunshan too. Both spouses' family connections remain intact, and they have stayed close in spite of the social and economic changes. Meijuan left the factory and became self-employed for seven years, selling clothes in a shop. She says she made more money selling clothes than working in the factory, but business in the shop required constant movement, which often made it difficult for her to shoulder her duties as a mother and a wife; thus, she decided to return to the factory. Because she is a Kunshan local and her husband, old classmates, neighbors, and friends were all working at KS1, she had no difficulty re-entering KS1 after seven years away.

Fengying is a local high school graduate who married a local and has one daughter. When she was about thirty-three, she finally got a job at KS1, where she has now worked for thirteen years. She tells me about the process through which factory positions were assigned in her household:

> When I graduated from high school, it happened that KS1 was setting up factories in the village. One job was promised to every household as part of the compensation for its land. At that time I had just graduated from high school, so people said I was the most suitable person to enter KS1. My brother was still in high school, a little bit younger than me, there were still a few years to go before he graduated. At that time my father said, "It doesn't matter whether a daughter is assigned a job or not. The post should be reserved for my son." So I had no chance to enter the KS1. Later, KS1 held a recruitment exam. I took the exam and passed: I ranked first. So I became a KS1 worker.

Although she was recruited by exam and had waited for many years, Fengying still emphasizes that *guanxi* is crucial in terms of career development. She says, "Just at the beginning, qualifications [like passing the exam] are important. Then we should look at the *guanxi*. Besides, it also depends

on how the boss feels about you. Everything is judged by their feeling."[3]
Fengying has five siblings. Like Meijuan, she has many relatives working in
the same factory and her social networks are rooted in Kunshan. Her eldest
sister is six years older than her. Although not categorized as *nonming*
(peasant), she raised geese and chickens at home to increase the household
income. After her daughter was grown, she left home to become a house-
maid in Shanghai. Since her own sister's behavior is very similar to that
of the so-called peasant workers, I ask Fengying about her feelings about
peasant workers. She answers as follows:

> The phenomenon of migrants flooding into Kunshan is both good and bad. Looking
> on the bright side, they come, you get rent. So they come with the capacity to
> promote the economy. The bad thing is they worsen the living environment. Now
> we don't dare to open the door and windows. Too many thieves. Three vehicles have
> been stolen from my house: two battery scooters, and a motorcycle. One night, we
> slept inside the house. The thief still broke in and stole from us. How dare they? It
> wouldn't happen before these migrants flooded in. At that time, at night you didn't
> need to close windows and doors.

Fengying, sees the peasant workers' broken social relations as the fundamental reason that they are "dangerous" and threatening for local society.
Peasant workers do not form any durable social relations in Kunshan.
They have no stable working relations, no stable family relations, and no
friendship networks to tie them in to social orders. All these instabilities
make them potentially dangerous, while local workers are rooted in dense
social relations.

In short, Meijuan and Fengying both have tight connections to Kunshan.
They live with their families and most of their relatives are close by. The
networks they have built through family, school, and work remain intact.
On the basis of these networks, they secure jobs and support each other
continuously. In contrast, peasant workers have almost no connections
to Kunshan, and their pre-existing social networks are endangered by
migration. Yet they themselves often say that migration is the cure for
broken social relations in the countryside, altered beyond recognition by
the market economy. From this point of view, the migrant workers can be
considered dispossessed. Only old people and children are left behind in
the countryside. Adults of working age migrate to coastal factories to earn
money to pay children's tuition fees, to save up a brideprice for sons, to find
prospective partners, to seize opportunities for upward mobility, and to
adopt forms of adulthood that differ from those of their parents.

The continued significance of family relations even among young
workers becomes clear to me one day after lunch when I take a stroll
around the factory. Near the factory gate, across the street, are three street

vendors. One of them sells oranges; the second stall sells all kinds of snacks: cans of juice, candied fruit, apple cakes. These two stalls have no customers. Three workers—two boys and a girl—are looking excitedly at the third booth. The boys are wearing the uniforms of Wing Yip Electronics, and the girl is in a KS1 uniform. Before I can approach to see what the stall is selling, I catch sight of sparkling light reflecting from the booth. It is selling earrings, rings, and other small items of jewelry. Although most workers (local and migrants alike) in KS1 are married, it is not unusual to hear of young, unmarried workers who try to find partners here. The two boys are selecting earrings to please their girlfriends.[4]

Middle-aged peasant workers' motivations for seeking work at KS1 are primarily financial. If factory jobs are available at all in their hometowns, they are very badly paid. For example, Subei Mama and her husband have a twelve-year-old son who is being brought up by her mother back home. This arrangement leaves her family "broken" and precarious. Her son behaves as though his mother is a stranger when she goes back to visit him, which she finds very painful. For years their son lived with them in Kunshan, but this became increasingly difficult due to the different schedules of schools and factories. Both parents worked long hours, especially Subei's husband, who was a laborer on a building site. Her son had to wait alone for her to return at 8:00 p.m. and cook for him. She herself ate her own dinner at the factory, while her husband ate whenever he could. She says, "My family didn't feel like a family. We're helpless (*mei banfa*)." Subei says she has no plans to settle in Kunshan, and even if they want to, it is impossible because they have no money and cannot afford a house there. Yet she hopes that one day her son will be able to migrate to this township, and her sole goal in working here is to create a better environment for him. Peasants, even when they temporarily become migrant workers, try to fight for the social order they believe they can always rely on, which is "home" and "household." They are willing to endure hardship if it will bring their families a better life. They would rather remain a "precariat" and enjoy the freedom to go home anytime than become "workers" in a foreign town.

In short, "socialist order" is not challenged in KS1 because the peasant-worker precariat remains basically rural, allowing workers to remain workers. The precariat in KS1 reaffirms the peculiarities of "socialism with Chinese characteristics" in an increasingly marketized state that remains under party control.

The THS Factory, Shenzhen

The THS factory in Shenzhen is owned by a middle-aged Taiwanese businessman who grew up in Taiwan and obtained a master's degree in engineering in Japan. He still maintains close connections with Japanese experts who are invited to THS to conduct training from time to time. The owner's family and his main business partners are in Taiwan, and the owner himself moves back and forth several times a year. To achieve efficient management, he expects all clerical workers and managers to install Skype on their computers and stay online during working hours so that he can give them orders if necessary.

The THS factory has a courtyard surrounded by three buildings and a main gate. One building houses the office and shop floor, one is the site of the kitchen and canteen, and the third is the dormitory. There are around 122 workers in total, 52 male and 70 female. Workers from Henan form the largest group of origin (25 people, 13 males and 12 females). The second largest group comprises workers from Hubei (19 people, male 6, female 13). Altogether, the factory's workforce hails from seventeen different provinces. Three employees are from Taiwan, and two of them occupy high-ranking managerial positions. The third is an engineer. The official language in the factory is Mandarin. When greeting a newcomer, it is usual to ask, "Where are you from?" and "Who introduced you to this factory?" (implying "Who is your patron?") rather than asking after names (cf. Lee 1998: 117–118).

Unlike KS1, THS is not dominated by "local" workers with permanent contracts who communicate in an exclusive dialect. In this factory, the power relations among migrant groups from different provinces are more dynamic. Although the factory is located in Shenzhen, Guangdong province, workers from this province do not form a privileged stratum. On the contrary, the strongly accented Mandarin of Guangdong workers sometimes impedes their communication with the owner of factory, who does not speak Cantonese. For the owner, all workers, irrespective of province, are more local than he is. Therefore, workers from every province stand an equal chance of being favored. The dominant imagined division among workers is "mainlanders" versus "Taiwanese." The latter have the relevant "localistic relatedness" (as distinct from localistic "otherness") to the owner, and they do in fact get special treatment in Taiwanese-run factories generally.

Whereas local managers in KS1 distinguish between local and migrant workers and avoid mingling with the latter, the Taiwanese owner in THS does the opposite, going out of his way to mix with migrant workers who are cadres or potential cadres: playing mah-jongg, eating in the restaurant, drinking beer while eating BBQ, and playing billiards. He is keen to earn their loyalty by making workers feel he is one of them. Several times he mentions to me that he wants to "localize" the managerial labor force. Given the wage difference between a Taiwanese manager and a mainlander manager, he expects to replace all Taiwanese managers in his factory with mainlanders.

The average age of the workers at THS is twenty, and three-quarters of them are unmarried. Their average educational background is a junior high school certificate (only those in high-ranking managerial positions have university degrees). Compared to the middle-aged workers at KS1, they seem happier and full of hope. When they calculate the costs and benefits of their migrant journey, income and expenses are seldom the priority they are for the workers of KS1. They imagine a good future at the end of their journey and seem to truly believe it will arrive one day. The hope and imagination of a bright future help mitigate their complaints about life in the factory. But at the same time, they change jobs quickly. Once they feel they have been treated unfairly or wrongly, they just quit and return home, hoping that the next job will be better. Being a worker does not seem to be their main identification; it is merely the ladder they have to climb to achieve their dreams (normally, to be a boss, i.e., an independent entrepreneur). Most consider it unlikely that THS will be their last job.

This factory provides male and female dormitories and meals for workers. Originally, the dormitory arrangement in the factory separated basic workers from high-ranking managers by locating them on different floors. Since moving to the current location, a new arrangement places Taiwanese cadres in a separate building. The floors of cadres are well-equipped and have better furniture. The Taiwanese owner tells me that he deliberately made the ranking "materially visible" because he believes it is the best incentive to motivate his workers to work harder. Wages are paid once a month. The accountant brings the cash to the shop floor and invites the workers to line up according to their employee numbers. The most money they can hope to receive is about 1,900 renminbi per month (currently about 180 pounds sterling). They might earn less than 1,000 renminbi if business is bad.

Due to the special relationship between Taiwan and China, specific relations with the party-state have been set in place to encourage Taiwan businessmen to set up factories on the mainland, where the main attraction is the cheapness of labor.[5] Investors are received by the Taiwan Affairs Office (*guotaiban*) and given various privileges. Taiwanese managers view workers stereotypically as "mainlanders" (*daluren*) or "Chinese" (*zhongguoren*).[6] Because the Taiwanese leader and managers in THS grew up in Taiwan and feel unfamiliar with China's social context, they are keen to get local information from the workers, like where to buy medicine, or which brand of shampoo to choose. On the other hand, Taiwanese managers and engineers do not feel they need to "localize," which is reflected in the fact that the largest component of the labor force is not from Guangdong, but from distant Henan.

Because TSH workers are generally young, they did not experience the Maoist period. China has been drawn into the market economy and globalization during their lifetimes, but the collapse of the old social order does not mean disaster to them. Most tell me they feel that conditions in China are becoming better and better, though anyone who stays in the village will be excluded from these positive changes. It goes without saying that these peasant workers are victims who are obliged to bear the main burden of China's rapid economic development. In this respect my research (Fang 2012) confirms the findings of earlier studies (Anagnost 2004; Pun 2005; Pun and Lu 2010). Young migrant workers, however, do not seem to care that the organization of the economy places them in a disadvantageous position. Rather, they harbor desires that motivate them to work. They spend a lot of time thinking about the "next" stage: leaving the factory with some accumulation of money and social capital, and exploring new possibilities. Their situation reminds me of Sangren's Marxist formulation of a "mode of production of desire":

> It is important to extend traditional Marxist notions of production because production does not just take place; people's activities are motivated, goal directed—in other words, desire-driven. To fail to include desire in social analysis focusing on productive processes risks excluding individual agency or assuming that individual desire lies somehow outside or beyond the realm of culture. (Sangren 2003: 57)

Young migrant factory workers will say, for example, "I cannot spend my whole lifetime working in the factory being a worker" (*wo buneng da yibeizi de gong*). Statements like "I can't be a worker working for others all my life" do not imply a consciousness of the precarity of their employment so much as a sense that a brighter future outside the factory is open to them. They are able to sustain the hope of "being a boss" (*ziji danglaoban*, literally "harboring entrepreneurships") because the factory is a place where they can establish *guanxi* and learn how to deploy their connections.

Marxists view the worker as an atomized person. Once they enter the labor process, workers have a relationship to capital, but they are not related to each other. Most social relations in these Chinese factories have been incorporated into economic relations. But in factories such as THS the workers are still trying their best to use every opportunity to establish new social relations and maintain old ones. While maintaining networks in their hometowns that can serve as a safety net if they fail in the city, they also search for someone to act as their patron in the factory. Even if this hankering after vertical *guanxi* is often in vain, they continue their pursuit of the goal of establishing wide and firm reciprocal relationships—in short, horizontal *guanxi*.

Guanxi refers exclusively to relationships with non-kin. Migration separates young people from their kinship ties in their villages and gives them a certain freedom to negotiate their identity. They have temporarily left their position in the social structure. At the point where they enter the factory, they exchange their rural identity for a state of liminality (cf. Turner 1967: 106). Their motives for migration are similar to those analyzed by Alpa Shah (2006) in India: mobility offers a sense of freedom in that it allows individuals to leave their original social order, even if it leads them into harsh exploitation. Although young migrants declare themselves "separated" from their parents and "independent," kinship ties do not, in fact, disappear in the factory. Migrant workers continue to receive support from home and make efforts to maintain kinship ties. Within the factory, young workers confide their problems to older relatives, and some even hand over their wages for safekeeping and remittance home, after deciding how much they can legitimately "withdraw" for personal use.

However, kinship ties function in a low-profile way compared to *guanxi*, which very often occurs between people from the same hometown or province. Ties of *laoxiang* and kinship are viewed as two distinct types of social relationships. Although "cousins" (of various kinds) are important, workers tend to "hang around with" friends of the same age rather than with their older or younger relatives. Without giving up their kin-based relationships, they prioritize going beyond the given world of kin and build up friendships with strangers. The factory offers them opportunities to do so that they cannot find in villages, and establishing *guanxi* affords them a sense of empowerment, however limited it might seem to the observer (e.g., it could potentially allow a worker to put in a word for a *laoxiang* friend when the labor force is being expanded or restructured).

To establish such *guanxi* is itself a significant achievement in the eyes of relatives and co-villagers. Silk, a female migrant worker with whom I share a room, uses her network to finance her family's new house, which gains her a very high status in her natal family. She manages to establish a relatively wide network of friends in the city. Although her parents take some of the responsibility for the debt, it falls mostly on Silk's shoulders. She assumes this burden entirely of her own free will, she tells me, because she "has more (rich) friends than them." Thus the newly established social relationships that allowed Silk to raise money in the urban setting have changed her reputation and bargaining power within her family. Silk is a cousin of Ling, the wife of the director of THS. Ling has many relatives whom she is expected to care for in one way or another, including Silk, but this network is easily extended to Silk's classmates and neighbors, who all seek help from Ling. More and more acquaintances bring gifts to Ling's natal family and ask her and her husband to *guanzhao tiba* (promote them as a special consideration).

One *laoxiang* of Silk grew up in a neighboring village and was less educated than most *dagongzai* (young male wage workers). He left home when he was eighteen and within a few years managed, according to Silk, to become a "boss." I later learn that his company has no employee other than himself, and that his "business" consists of brokerage in precision instruments. His "expertise" is based in his social networks, and his success is evident in the fact that he drives a Toyota. Every young migrant can tell such stories of successful social upward mobility, typically concluding that "if you are bold enough (*jiaruni danzi gouda*), you can earn money."

I argue that this population of young migrant factory workers is a precariat (in an objective sense) without precarity (as subjectivity). Let me give a final example. Xiaoqian is a peasant worker from Hubei province. She worked in Shanghai for several years before transferring to Shenzhen, but she is reluctant to talk about her previous working experience. Instead, she describes her friends in Shanghai, how she got to know them, how they shared good times together, and how they saw her off when she left for Shenzhen by train:

> On 4 March 2006, I left Shanghai. I remember the date very clearly. In the morning of March 4, four friends saw me off at the train station. I was there too early, almost half an hour ahead of time. Once I got on the train, I asked my friend to leave because I didn't want the others to wait too long. She said it didn't matter, and insisted on waiting with me until the train left. I was sitting on the train and she was standing on the platform. It wasn't easy to talk. She then called me on my cell phone. We talked by phone, face to face, until the train departure. After I hung up the phone, I lay down and fell asleep. The day before, I hadn't slept. I kept thinking how I would leave my friends. This is the first time I left home for work and also the first time I made so many friends. They told me I don't need to rush to find a job in Shenzhen. Even if I can't find any job in Shenzhen, I can always come back to Shanghai to stay with them. If I come back to Shanghai, as long as they are still in Shanghai, I don't need to worry about accommodations and meals. When I woke up, not yet opening my eyes, tears were streaming down my face. I couldn't help crying. Now when I think of it, I feel calm, and do not want to cry. But my heart is still touched.

Xiaoqian's statement is full of emotions. Social relationships, especially friendship, are what she values the most. She stresses that even if she is one of the precariat, and might suddenly lose her job and have to leave Shanghai for Shenzhen with no clear prospect for the future, she nonetheless does not need to experience precarity because of the care of those friends, and their commitment to taking care of her while she looks for work.

A cynic might suppose that such relationships would be likely to wither fairly fast after Xiaoqian winds up in a completely different city and has not been able to meet with her *guanxi* friends for a couple of years. *Guanxi* ties are a mix of affection and calculation. Young migrant workers view the accumulation of *guanxi* positively: the more, the better, because of the sense of security they are supposed to entail. *Guanxi* ties are flexible and free, sometimes arbitrary, allowing everyone to fantasize about fulfilling their aspirations regardless of their family background, ethnicity, class, or gender. Certainly there is the risk of disappointment—the anticipated hedge against precarity may not work out—but there is also the potential for support, opportunity, and help or shelter when needed. *Guanxi* networks thus offer a degree of autonomy and agency to young migrant workers in the face of precarity.

Wang Lang was the only real rebel I came across in the factory records. One day, the manager asked if I knew that Wang Lang had been sacked from his former factory because he had participated in protests demanding higher wages. I had not known this, although I had interviewed Wang Lang. I knew he was an orphan who had been raised by state cadres after his parents were murdered in Xinjiang. He drifted from one cadre's family to another throughout his childhood and was eventually sent to the army, even though he did not want to become a soldier. Wang Lang had told me he needed freedom and was too short-tempered to fit in to that environment. He then became a worker, hopping from job to job around the coastal cities. He had no home to return to, no final destination. I realized that Wang Lang was the only true member of the precariat among all the peasant workers I encountered, for the simple reason that he lacked any social networks tying him to kin and to place.

For the great majority, *guanxi* enables peasant workers to earn money by mixing farming with factory work and petty business initiatives. They are a precariat without precarity, motivated to work in the coastal cities not by poverty but by entrepreneurship. Connections and networking in the factory open doors to an informal economy outside the factories. If this should fail, they can always go back home or to other places where they have friends they can rely on. Thus peasant workers have nothing to lose by making the initial move to the factory and then hopping from one to the next.

In the absence of unions or other associations, some other mechanism is needed to function as infrastructure to support transactions and interactions and promote trust. Traditional customs, like the rules for gift exchange, moral economy, or moral standards of reciprocal relationships, meet this need and serve as a kind of parallel resource distribution mechanism. In order to gain membership in such informal resource distribution systems, all young migrant workers need to do is to build up their *guanxi*. They are thus interconnected rather than individualistic. In a context in which both state and enterprise hierarchies are considered untrustworthy, building up interpersonal reciprocal ethics through their own activities is the most rational way to counter uncertainty (see Brandtstädter 2003).

Conclusion

In this chapter I have argued that when discussing precarity in China, we should not ignore the significance of subjective perceptions, which are largely determined by generational differences and life course. The elder generation considers precarity a threat, while the younger generation tends to celebrate it as liberating. At different stages of the life course, and with different historical memories of social order, people view work with different expectations and meanings. Precarious workers are dispossessed, but they nonetheless create their own value systems through reproduction. I have argued that their principal means of doing so is the deployment of *guanxi* in the informal sphere. While still attentive to whether they are hired or not, these workers care more about how regular or precarious employment impacts on their long-term plans and arrangements in the informal sphere or in reproduction.

Standing (2011) argues that precariat has a low degree of mastery of time and space. The cases I have examined show that peasant workers are less able to control time and space than permanent workers are. The degree of rupture (between life and work, production and reproduction) correlates with the degree of exploitation, so peasant workers suffer more than local workers. But among peasant workers, only those who lack networks and the skills to build them are in a truly bad situation. If casualization does not always lead to resistance in China (Friedman and Lee 2010), I suggest this is because precarity is effectively countered by *guanxi*.

Acknowledgments

This chapter is based on twelve months of fieldwork in China (October 2007–October 2008), primarily in an electronics factory (THS) in the Shenzhen Special Economic Zone. I also collected material in another factory (KS1) in Kunshan, near Shanghai. I thank James Carrier, Jan Breman, and Ching Kwan Lee for their constructive comments.

I-Chieh Fang is Assistant Professor at the Institute of Anthropology, National Tsing Hua University, Taiwan. She obtained her Ph.D. from the London School of Economics and Political Science in 2012 with a study of young migrant workers in south China. In her postdoctoral research she has focused on economic learning processes in two different migration trajectories: urbanization and counter-urbanization. Fang was an Associate Member of the Max Planck Institute for Social Anthropology from 2012 to 2015. She specializes in the anthropology of economy, migration, gender, morality, learning/education, and youth, and her work has been published in numerous professional journals.

Notes

1. Leaving home for city to labour in the factory was generally believed to be a great opportunity for peasants to establish *guanxi* and expand their *renmai* ['network of human resources'].
2. According to Yang, "*Guanxiwang* (*guanxi* network) refers to a person's web or network of social contacts and connects. Some people's network can be 'big' or 'wide', which means that they have established *guanxi* with a large number of people, who may vary in social and occupational position as well as geographical locations" (1994: 64).
3. Migrant workers also obtain jobs through *guanxi*. Subei Mama told me she was introduced by a co-villager and then hired as a *yuangong* after completing a test in the personnel department. The *guanxi* the migrant workers can use strategically is of the "horizontal" sort, rather than the vertical sort noted above, which affords locals privileged links to the local state.
4. For many of the female migrant workers I met, the most attractive aspect of migration was the opportunity to meet young men and subsequently marry a person of their own choice. They are "forced to" implement the "freedom" to choose a spouse, which has undermined the institutions of arranged marriages and parental power (Fang 2013).
5. In terms of China's propaganda and official ideology, Taiwanese are family and eventually will reunite with China: "Blood is thicker than water" (*xuenongyushui, liangan yijiaqin*).
6. The Taiwanese at THS consider themselves to be Taiwanese, not Chinese.

References

Anagnost, Ann. 2004. "The Corporeal Politics of Quality (suzhi)." *Public Culture* 16(2): 189–208.

———. 2006. "Strange Circulations: The Blood Economy in Rural China." *Economy and Society* 35(4): 509–529.

Bernstein, Thomas P. 1993 [1977]. *Up to the Mountains and Down to the Villages: The Transfer of Youth from Urban to Rural China*. New Haven, CT: Yale University Press.

Brandtstädter, Susanne. 2003. "The Moral Economy of Kinship and Property in Southern China." In *The Postsocialist Agrarian Question: Property Relations and the Rural Condition*, ed. Chris Hann, 419–440. Münster: Lit Verlag.

Bruun, Ole. 1995. "Fengshui and the Chinese Perception of Nature." In *Asian Perceptions of Nature: A Critical Approach*, ed. Ole Bruun and Arne Kalland, 173–188. Surrey: Curzon Press.

Cohen, Myron L. 1993. "Cultural and Political Inventions in Modern China: The Case of the Chinese 'Peasant.'" *Daedalus* 122(2): 151–170.

De Neve, Geert. 2003. "Expectations and Rewards of Modernity: Commitment and Mobility among Rural Migrants in Tirupur, Tamil Nadu." *Contributions to Indian Sociology* 37(1–2): 251–280.

Fang, I-chieh. 2012. "Growing Up and Becoming Independent: An Ethnographic Study of New Generation Migrant Workers in China." Ph.D. dissertation. London: London School of Economics and Political Science.

———. 2013. "The Girls Who Are Keen to Get Married." In *Ordinary Ethics in China*, ed. C. Stafford, 66–79. London: Berg.

Friedman, Eli, and Ching Kwan Lee. 2010. "Remaking the World of Chinese Labour: A 30-Year Retrospective." *British Journal of Industrial Relations* 48(3): 507–533.

Harrell, Steven. 2001. "The Anthropology of Reform and the Reform of Anthropology: Anthropological Narratives of Recovery and Progress in China." *Annual Review of Anthropology* 30(1): 139–161.

Honig, Emily. 1986. *Sisters and Strangers: Women in the Shanghai Cotton Mills, 1919–1949*, Stanford, CA: Stanford University Press.

Huang, Philip C.C. 2013. "Misleading Chinese Legal and Statistical Categories: Labor, Individual Entities, and Private Enterprises." *Modern China* 39(4): 347–379.

Lee, Ching-Kwan. 1998. *Gender and the South China Miracle: Two Worlds of Factory Women*. Berkeley, CA: University of California Press.

Lu, Tu. 2013. *Zhongguo xingongren: mishi yu jueqi* [The Chinese new worker: Lost and arisen]. Beijing: Beijing Falu.

Murphy, Rachel. 2002. *How Migrant Labor Is Changing Rural China*. Cambridge: Cambridge University Press.

Parry, Jonathan. 2013. "Company and Contract Labour in a Central Indian Steel Plant." *Economy and Society* 42(3): 348–374.

Perry, Elizabeth J. 1993. *Shanghai on Strike: The Politics of Chinese Labor*. Stanford, CA: Stanford University Press.

Pun, Ngai. 2005. *Made in China: Women Factory Workers in a Global Workplace*. Durham, NC: Duke University Press.

Pun, Ngai, and Lu Huilin. 2010. "Unfinished Proletarianization: Self, Anger, and Class Action among the Second Generation of Peasant-Workers in Present-Day China." *Modern China* 36(5): 493–519.

Rofel, Lisa. 1999. *Other Modernities: Gendered Yearnings in China after Socialism*. Berkeley, CA: University of California Press.

———. 1992. "Rethinking Modernity: Space and Factory Discipline in China." *Cultural Anthropology* 7(1): 93–144.

Sangren, P. Steven. 2003. "Separations, Autonomy and Recognition in the Production of Gender Differences: Reflections from Considerations of Myths and Laments." In *Living with Separation in China: Anthropological Accounts*, ed. C. Stafford, 53–84. New York, NY: Routledge Curzon.

Shah, Alpa. 2006. "The Labour of Love: Seasonal Migration from Jharkhand to the Brick Kilns of Other States in India." *Contributions to Indian Sociology* 40(1): 91–118.

Shue, Vivienne. 1980. *Peasant China in Transition: The Dynamics of Development toward Socialism, 1949–1956*. Berkeley, CA: University of California Press.

Standing, Guy. 2011. *The Precariat: The New Dangerous Class*. London: Bloomsbury.

Wang, Hui. 2014. "Liangzhong xinqiongren jiqi weilai —jieji zhengzhi de shuailuo, zaixingcheng yu xinqiongren de zunyanzhengzhi [Two kinds of new poor and their future: The decline and reshaping of class politics and the politics of dignity of the new poor]." *Kaifang Shidai* 6: 49–70.

Wolf, Margery. 1985. *Revolution Postponed: Women in Contemporary China*. Stanford, CA: Stanford University Press.

Yan, Hairong. 2003. "Spectralization of the Rural: Reinterpreting the Labor Mobility of Rural Young Women in Post-Mao China." *American Ethnologist* 30(4): 578–596.

Yan, Xiaoqing. 2015. "Xingongren jiating de mengy: gongyehua shiqi nongmin jieceng bianqian yu gongren jieji xingcheng [The sprout of the new-working family: A case study of peasants' change and working-class formation during industrialization]." *Contemporary Youth Research* 335(2): 74–80.

Yan, Yunxiang. 2005. "The Gift and Gift Economy." In *A Handbook of Economic Anthropology*, ed. J.G. Carrier, 246–274. Cheltenham: Edward Elgar.

Yang, Mayfair Mei-hui. 1994. *Gifts, Favors, and Banquets: The Art of Social Relationships in China*. Ithaca, NY: Cornell University Press.

12

From Dispossessed Factory Workers to "Micro-entrepreneurs"

The Precariousness of Employment in Trinidad's Garment Sector

Rebecca Prentice

Introduction

Global economic restructuring and post-Fordist regimes of production and consumption have generated new conditions of job insecurity now commonly referred to as "precarious employment" (Benach et al. 2014; Standing 2011). As a worldwide phenomenon, precarious employment captures two convergent sets of circumstances. For workers who benefited from legal protections and social entitlements in the latter half of the twentieth century, particularly but not exclusively in the social democracies of the Global North, precarious employment is characterized by the erosion of hard-won labor rights (Kalleberg 2011; Molé 2010). Among workers who never secured such rights—undocumented, marginalized, and informal workers, or those living in countries where civil protections were not extended—the concept of "precarious employment" indicates less a transformation in the objective conditions of work and more a growing realization that job insecurity is here to stay (Lee and Kofman 2010; Lewis et al. 2015; Muehlebach 2013). In this respect, debates about the nature and future of precarious employment resonate with earlier discussions about the informal sector (Hart 1985; Waldinger and Lapp 1993), once considered an impediment to industrial development but now described as a permanent feature of late capitalism and a special source of entrepreneurial dynamism and economic growth.

Ethnographic accounts of precarious employment move beyond the objective facts of pay, workplace standards, and labor voice to explore the subjective experience of precarity as well. This chapter draws on more than ten years of anthropological engagement with Trinidad's garment industry to explore labor precariousness under the competitive pressures of globalization. Ever since recession and trade liberalization led to the demise of Caribbean garment production in the 1990s, Trinidadian garment workers have seen job opportunities shrink and increasingly enter a casualized, informal sector. I describe how the devolution of market-oriented garment production from factories to workshops and workers' homes has taken place in tandem with a set of state-led policies to combat unemployment and poverty by promoting microenterprise. I make three key arguments. First, I contend that state and NGO-led promotion of microenterprise in Trinidad has had a depoliticizing effect on labor struggle, meaning that a deterioration of working conditions and labor rights has advanced under the protective "cover" of seemingly laudable policies to promote economic empowerment via self-employment. My second argument is that a felicitous discourse of enterprise culture elevates the rewards of microenterprise and self-employment above wage employment. Although this discourse can be seductive, it rarely accords with the actual experiences of workers. Third, with analytical attention to gender, I argue that the transformation of formal employees into home-based micro-entrepreneurs succeeds by concealing women's uncompensated domestic labor, capitalizing upon their historical failure to attain the purportedly universal and ungendered public status of "workers." I emphasize the importance of culture, subjectivity, and gender ideologies to understand the proliferation and lived experience of precarious employment. By drawing attention to the neglected relationship between global post-Fordism and state promotion of microenterprise, I show how they are mutually reinforcing in ways that obscure labor politics.

Dislocating Trinidadian Garment Production

The story of how the neoliberal restructuring of the garment industry over the past twenty-five years has transformed the geographic distribution of production and trade is a familiar one. Global trade liberalization in the form of reduced import restrictions, tariffs, and duties, as well as the 2004 phaseout of the international quota system known as the Multi-Fiber Arrangement, increasingly puts garment-producing countries in direct and ruthless competition with one another. As large Asian producers are newly freed from many export restrictions, Caribbean manufacturers, with their higher local wages and fewer economies of scale, have struggled to compete (Kowalski and Molnar 2009; Lopez-Acevedo and Robertson 2012). On the

Caribbean island of Trinidad, the impact of these global trade shifts is visible in the empty, shuttered factories that used to employ women in formal-sector, sometimes unionized jobs.

Jennifer Bair and Marion Werner (2011: 989) describe the recent demise of garment and textile production in the Caribbean and Latin America as a form of "disarticulation": the periodic severing of some locations from global circuits of trade through disinvestment and capital flight. Pointing out that scholarship on garment and textile production exhibits a bias toward sites where business is booming, they advocate that we instead train our ethnographic focus on single places to unearth their histories of inclusion *and* exclusion from the international circulation of capital. Such an approach provides insight into how and why places become integrated into or expelled from global production networks, allowing us to understand how these articulations and disarticulations impact the lives and livelihoods of people working within them.

My ethnographic and historical research in Trinidad charts the transformation of its garment industry from the early 1990s, when an IMF-imposed trade liberalization program opened the market to cheaper imported goods. During the industry's expansion under state protectionism and investment in the 1960s and 1970s, Trinidadian garment factories were major employers of women and important sites of labor struggle (Reddock 1994). But the lifting of trade barriers has led to a collapse of the formal garment industry, including a 42 percent decline in garment manufacturing jobs between 1990 and 2000 (Central Statistics Office 2003: 27).[1] However, these official statistics do not capture the extent to which garment workers' livelihoods have moved into an informal sector of irregular employment and homework where their labor is not measured. My own research on the garment industry has tracked this movement. Over fifteen months of fieldwork in 2003/04, I focused on how garment factories and workers were navigating the competitive pressures of trade liberalization (Prentice 2015). More recently, I have investigated the relationship between the growing field of microenterprise development and home-based garment production. Trinidad's garment industry has not been wholly expelled from international circuits of trade. Rather, garment manufacturing has survived by taking up residence in the informal sector.

A common narrative about the industry having been destroyed by trade liberalization appeared to take material form in ghostlike factories where a handful of employees fill production orders alongside hundreds of idle sewing machines shrouded in dusty plastic. As Mr. Gonsalves, a factory owner who pioneered large-scale garment manufacturing in Trinidad in the 1950s, said to me in 2004, the loss of protectionism was devastating, and the policy should be reversed:

The government must go back where it was 10 years ago to protect the industry. If I pay one dollar for a worker and China can pay that much less, if their products can come in, then we can't compete! We need [import] duties.

Although this is the standard explanation for the industry's collapse among an older generation of garment factory owners now in their seventies and eighties, members of a younger generation now in their forties and early fifties present narratives reflecting a different stance toward the challenges of liberalization. This younger cohort, who have owned and managed garment-producing firms since the late 1980s, see the "old heads" as relics of a former era whose massive but empty factories stand as testimony to unadaptable business practices. This characterization epitomizes a post-Fordist critique of the rigidities of mass production (cf. Holmström 1998). The younger cohort was also irritated by the old heads' seeming contentment with a regime of low-value, low-wage enterprises that relegated Trinidad to the economic and cultural periphery. Younger owners and managers contrasted this complacency with their own ambition to transcend territorial marginalization.

Born in the 1960s, the younger capitalists came of age at a time when the energy sector accelerated the country's development and raised expectations that the nation would become an active participant in global flows of technology, culture, and consumption (Miller 1994). Even though the oil boom was followed by a recession, Trinidadians with access to capital were able to create new businesses that reflected the boom-time sensibility. As the children of Mr. Gonsalves and the other industry titans of his generation mostly left the garment trade to enter more lucrative fields such as real estate development, a new generation of garment manufacturers whose own parents were petty entrepreneurs have ascended within the industry.[2] Their alignment of an entrepreneurial vision with first-world confidence, creativity, and the ability to make things happen was often contrasted with the passive nature of the old heads.

Rather than harking back to the protectionist regime as a golden era, the younger capitalists saw trade liberalization as an exciting opportunity to engage regional and global markets on new terms, and shared an obsession with orienting their firms to its challenges. To be profitable, they insisted, a firm had to become "flexible," run by managers who were innovative, enterprising, and opportunistic. While some firms pursued this flexibility by adopting high-tech innovations to mechanize production, or organizing multiply skilled work groups to adapt to changing market demands, I focus in this article on the growing practice of outsourcing production to local home-based workers. Sending factory workers home with industrial-grade sewing machines and stitching to complete for piece-rate payment is a means of increasing the flexibility of labor itself.

For garment workers—excepting the very few with coveted jobs in "high-tech" automated firms—the collapse of the formal-sector garment industry and its devolution into smaller workshops and workers' homes has been experienced as increasing casualization, informalization, and instability. After a period of plentiful job opportunities in the 1970s and early 1980s, they experienced unemployment as the nation entered recession, and then the collapse of the industry following global trade liberalization in the 1990s. Over this same period, workers describe not only the state's withdrawal from factory inspection, but also a decline in the trade unions. During the oil boom, vigorous efforts to organize garment workers resulted in the establishment of a number of collective bargaining agreements, but trade unions now focus their energies on more profitable industries and public-sector workers.[3]

The Rise of Homework

Bernard (born in 1967) runs a small garment factory that I will call "Universal Uniforms" above a fabric shop on the Eastern Main Road, outside Trinidad's capital city.[4] Founded in the 1990s, Universal Uniforms obtains contracts for uniforms from governments and businesses throughout the Caribbean. Despite the pressures of price competition, the company has stayed afloat because in the early 2000s, Bernard began an experiment of sending workers home with industrial-grade machines and stitching to complete on a piece-rate basis. By 2014, in addition to twenty workers on the shop floor, Bernard employed more than twenty-five stitchers who worked on his garments off-site. These stitchers worked for the same piece rate as factory employees, sometimes hiring other stitchers from their communities to sew for them.

The quality of home-sewn garments must be equal to what is produced on the shop floor, so the cutting of the fabric and the finishing of the garments are conducted in the factory. Stitchers must provide, and be open to spot inspection of, a secure location to accommodate sewing machines on loan from the factory, or already be in possession of their own industrial-grade machines.

By employing fewer workers on the shop floor but maintaining a reserve of labor power provided by many more stitchers at home, factory owners like Bernard lower costs by externalizing their workforce and dispensing with obligations such as guaranteed hours or base pay, National Insurance contributions, and the minimum wage. Home-based stitchers bear the expense of work space and electricity, and absorb the costs of market fluctuations by being permanently at the ready. These workers experience diminished entitlements, not only to National Insurance and paid maternity leave, but also to the national worker's compensation system in case of injury. Although Bernard's stitchers are usually former employees who contract for his factory alone, stitchers as a category of home-based workers also obtain work from independent contractors operating as intermediaries. Remuneration varies widely. While Bernard insists that the price paid for garments sewn is the same as the factory piece rate, stitchers report payment "negotiated" between firms and individual stitchers or via contractors.

Trinidad's garment sector is dualistic: modern, large-scale plants and small, informal businesses produce the same goods. Up until at least the 1920s, Trinidadian stitchers were part of a putting-out system whereby cloth merchants cut and bundled fabric, which they parceled out to stitchers to complete for piece-rate payment at home. This practice changed (although it never entirely disappeared) when merchants decided to bring production in-house to exercise tighter control over stitching quality and labor discipline. Merchants provided space and sewing machines, but workers were expected to carry with them ancillary tools such as scissors, nippers, pins, and protective garments like kerchiefs and smocks, which is still the case today in every factory.

In the mid-century, as small workshops gave way to larger firms that replicated a Fordist model of vertical integration (due in part to government initiatives like the 1950 Aid to Pioneer Industries Ordinance, which supported industrial expansion), Trinidad's garment industry still remained diverse, due to the persistence of independent seamstresses and tailors working from the their own homes and shops, who might occasionally take up bundles of stitching to make ends meet, and to the seasonal requirements of Carnival costumes and school uniforms made locally. Trinidad's garment industry has never fulfilled the grand modernist narrative that predicts home-based production will disappear as manufacturing became increasingly centered in factories. With a move toward flexible accumulation and smaller batch production under global post-Fordism, the industry's failure to centralize was recast as a strength (cf. Collins 2002).

To describe the post-Fordist revival of the putting-out system, Trinidadian factory owners speak in terms of "cottage industry" or simply "cottage," a phrase that evokes a romantic image of skilled endeavor accomplished within the home as a productive unit. The use of the term "cottage" allies homework with self-directed craft production, rather than sweated outwork reminiscent of the nineteenth- and early twentieth-century garment industry. Whereas my questions to factory owners about outsourcing always led them to believe I was asking about subcontracting from China, and questions about homeworkers often generated little response, questions about "cottage" invariably led to excited talk about the capacities of women in the Trinidadian countryside to accomplish factory-grade production in the comfort of their own homes and under their own control.

This idiom of craft production presents an ahistorical interpretation of garment work divorced from the history of labor movement. As a rhetorical device, the language of craft aligns home-based garment production with community uplift and self-reliance rather than with the bloody industrial struggles of the 1930s in which garment workers were the most visible category of female labor (Reddock 1994). The "freedom" of self-determination evoked in the language of "cottage industry" is not the freedom defined through stable and predictable, well-compensated labor that took center stage in industrial struggle.

For Lena, a 28-year-old Afro-Trinidadian woman in the rural northeast, working at home on contract is only one part of the complex of livelihood arrangements with which she sustains her life. She has three children and prefers to be at home, not only so she can "throw an eye" on them when they come home from school, and not simply as a stop-gap after the Tru-Fit garment factory where she had been employed closed down. The main reason to stitch on a piece rate at home, Lena says, is that transportation costs are so high that "traveling" to work would take too large a portion of her earnings. Commuting via public transportation to the cluster of factories along the Eastern Main Road would cost her almost two hours' pay—a quarter of her entire earnings. Lena takes in work brought to her by a contractor known to one of her sisters. She is paid 300 Trinidad and Tobago dollars for a bundle of work. It it takes her a week to complete the bundle, she will be earning less than the minimum wage of 12.50 TT dollars (1.75 euros) per hour.[5] But Lena says it does not take her a week to complete the work, and in fact she wanted more bundles than she was receiving. The benefit to her of stitching for a contractor is access to the two machines on loan to her at home (one is a straight-stitch machine; the other, a serger, which sews inner seams), which allow her to put a professional finish on the school uniforms she makes for members of her community, for cash-in-hand payment.

Like many garment workers in Trinidad, Lena is a skilled seamstress and can create entire outfits from scratch without a pattern (Prentice 2012). Seamstresses are ideal homeworkers because they can solve dressmaking dilemmas on the fly: if the fabric has not been cut precisely they can make it work, anticipating problems with the stitching and correcting accordingly. Factory owners like Bernard insist that this skill makes home-based stitchers not simply low-wage workers but "micro-entrepreneurs," free to use the machines to develop their own small businesses when not busy completing garments for their employer. A seamstress who does so can also employ stitchers (who may not know how to draft or cut a pattern but can sew proficiently on the machine) for routine needlework, turning her home into a place of employment for not only herself but other members of the community as well.

Sewing machines are expensive, with second-hand industrial models selling at prices from 3,000 TT dollars (490 US dollars) to many times that amount. They are treasured gifts from family members who have migrated overseas. Some women use rotating savings groups to raise money for them, while others use hire-purchase (although those machines are only domestic-grade and liable to break down under the strain of constant production). Lena has ambitions to sew for high-paying private clients—to do "whole weddings," making garments for everyone in a wedding party—and to produce custom-made fashion clothing. But either her skill or her access to clients beyond her own impoverished community is limited, so Lena makes school uniforms. As Elisabeth Prügl and Irene Tinker (1997) have argued, home-based work is a "descriptive" rather than "analytical" category because in the reality of everyday lives, home-based work continually—and often seamlessly—shifts between different registers of employment and income generation. It is the plural nature of home-based garment production that raises questions about the extent to which Lena is engaged in disguised wage employment, or is an aspiring micro-entrepreneur in need of support, training, and resources. Her possession and "free use" of the sewing machines on loan to her obscure the capital-labor relationship, as does the fact that Lena sews at home for kin and for cash-in-hand payment from neighbors.

Homeworking provides Lena with the ability to engage in income-generating activities while "throwing an eye" on her children and therefore satisfying the reproductive needs of her household. For this reason Prügl and Tinker (ibid.: 1475) remind us that although legal categories such as "employee" or "self-employed" imply the "autonomous and self-contained individuals" of Western liberalism, women's persistent gender subordination and uncompensated and unrecognized reproductive labor mean that their own labor power is never fully in their possession to begin with. As Silvia Federici (2012) has argued, women absorb the costs of social reproduction through their unpaid domestic labor, which is naturalized—and thereby rendered invisible—in the private space of the home. David Staples (2006: 4) explains how this burden of social reproduction can be made heavier by the introduction of home-based paid work, because a woman's continuing presence renders her available for childcare and domestic upkeep for a larger portion of the day than would be possible were she away from home. Whether in a "matrifocal" family like Lena's, in which she is the head of her own household as a single mother, or in the traditionally more "respectable" patriarchal marriage, Trinidadian women—mothers and their female kin—are expected to be the primary caretakers of children and keepers of the home.[6]

If Lena could work faster and take in more bundles of garments, she would make more money. Having the two machines means that she could do so with the help of her sister, or anyone she could hire or get to help her. Lena describes her sister as unreliable, however, and usually completes all the work on her own.

The Rise of Microenterprise

Trinidad's oil boom (1972–1983) rapidly expanded the post-colonial state with investment in social programs, education, employment, and national industries. Although Trinidad made loans to the International Monetary Fund (IMF) until 1984, the country was thrust into a balance-of-payments deficit when the price of oil on the world market began dropping in 1982 and then fell steeply in 1986 (Karides 2002: 160; Vertovec 1990: 104). At the end of the decade, in the midst of recession, the country would sign three structural adjustment agreements with the IMF and World Bank, whose conditions included the privatization of state-owned enterprises, the dismantling of trade barriers, and a reduction of the civil service (Bissessar and Hosein 2001; Moonilal 2001: 6; Sergeant and Forde 1992: 186). Structural adjustment in Trinidad meant relinquishing strong state intervention in the economy and reprivatizating national enterprises (Sergeant and Forde 1992). Through a period of economic recovery beginning in 1993, and a second oil boom in the 2000s, Trinidad remained primarily an energy-producing economy, despite the state's declared commitment to economic diversification. With the Caribbean's highest GDP, Trinidad and Tobago was reclassified by the World Bank in 2008 as a "high-income country" (Esnard-Flavius and Aziz 2011: 96). The oil and natural gas industries now account for 80 percent of exports and 45 percent of GDP, but provide only 5 percent of employment (Moya, Mohammed, and Sookram 2010: 8, cf. Katwaroo-Ragbir 2013:190). Because oil and natural gas exploitation generates revenue but few jobs—even in the so-called "downstream" industries of natural resource processing—under- and unemployment have remained chronically high over time, as have income inequalities and severe poverty (Bissessar and Hosein 2001:15).

Given its economic dependence on low-employment natural resource extraction, the government's policy is unsurprising. By training its citizens in business skills (cf. Carswell and De Neve this volume) and providing them with technical assistance, administrative support, and microfinancing, the state aims to stoke the creative capacities of its populace, harness them for economic growth, and thereby absorb the nation's "surplus labor" (Lewis 1954). This move coincides with an emerging "neoliberal" insistence that the state's role is to support and facilitate the economy by making its population and resources "available" to global capital while also stimulating entrepreneurialism within the population (cf. Bateman 2010; Freeman 2007: 257).

State-driven microenterprise development in Trinidad is a purposeful attempt to manage under- and unemployment. Sociologist Marina Karides (2010) describes it as a form of social assistance that fuses informal self-employment and government transfers together. In 2006, the Ministry of Labour was renamed the Ministry of Labour and Small and Microenterprise Development (Katwaroo-Ragbir 2013: 190; Moya et al. 2010: 27). To understand why the logics of microenterprise are so seductive in Trinidad, its arrival must not only be situated on the heels of a debt crisis and structural adjustment, but also linked to a narrative about government mismanagement of the country's immense oil wealth. Discussions about the merits of microenterprise in Trinidad have always been couched within the widespread condemnation of the excesses of the 1970s oil boom. In this telling, free enterprise and the entrepreneurial spirit were smothered by governmental largesse, which in turn created a "dependency syndrome" from which the populace had finally to be freed (Katwaroo-Ragbir 2013: 190–191; Karides 2010: 207).

In a garment sector decimated by the reduction of trade barriers in the 1990s, the state's new agenda to promote microenterprise and self-employment was the answer to unemployment. To understand how new forms of dispossession and labor precariousness could be so readily produced in this crucible, we must recognize that microenterprise valorizes the very coping techniques that already existed within poor Caribbean communities (Heron 2011). In their approach to livelihoods, working classes in Trinidad have prized flexibility, improvisation, and the kinds of bold risk-taking summed up in the phrase "thiefing a chance" (Prentice 2015). These values are expressed in the widespread practice of pursuing several income-generating activities at once, such as having a full-time job and "thiefing a chance" to generate a side income in the workplace, or cultivating a garden at home while also sewing for neighbors. As Carla Freeman (2007, 2014) has argued for Barbados, long-standing practices of occupational multiplicity and flexibility in livelihood strategies are now interpreted as an expression of an intrinsic entrepreneurial ethos that makes Caribbean people particularly well equipped for the competitive and hyper-individualistic requirements of a neoliberal economy.

The Seductions of Precarity

Trinidad's embrace of microenterprise in the 1990s is part of an international shift in development thinking and practice that redirects the state's responsibility from the centralizing impulse of state-led modernization to a decentralizing promotion of enterprise culture. Although several NGOs—including private charities, banks, and religious institutions—promote microenterprise, microenterprise development in Trinidad is largely state-driven, supported by government resources as well as the assistance of the World Bank, International Labour Organization, and United Nations Development Programme (Karides 2010: 194). These initiatives intertwine with government programs to promote youth training and apprenticeship, women's empowerment, and sustainable livelihoods. The diversity of initiatives reflects a range of different aims, from the alleviation of poverty and unemployment to the development of women's economic autonomy, with some initiatives aimed at expanding microenterprises into bigger firms with links to the international market.

Largest among the state programs is the National Enterprise Development Company (NEDCO), established in 2002 to provide training, funding, advice, and marketing support for entrepreneurs looking to start or develop a small business or microenterprise (defined as having up to five employees, with no more than 250,000 TT dollars in assets or sales). With nine branches scattered throughout Trinidad and Tobago, NEDCO is headquartered in Port of Spain. It targets petty producers and service workers (including street vendors, unregistered taxi drivers, producers of handicrafts, and independent seamstresses and tailors) engaged in informal economic activities, with the aim of assisting them in becoming successful entrepreneurs.

Geared to this purpose, the NEDCO office in Barataria offers a library, advisers for one-on-one consultations in budgeting and writing a business plan, and day-long training workshops on topics such as "Record Keeping and Cash Management," "Know Your Taxes," and "Managing Staff." Loan recipients must fulfill minimum attendance requirements at training sessions, for which they pay a reduced rate of 350 TT dollars (48 euros) per day. As a flagship state program, NEDCO sets the tone of microenterprise policy and practice in Trinidad. In addition to supporting its own loan recipients, NEDCO also conducts training for the general public and holds publicized competitions to help spread "enterprise culture" throughout Trinidad. The inclusion of entrepreneurialism as a topic in the primary school curriculum is one recent achievement.

The variegated local garment industry and microenterprise initiatives intersect with one another at various nodes. When I first met Victoria in 2003, she described herself as a "dressmaker and business woman," but today is more apt to call herself an "entrepreneur." Victoria rents a studio apartment in Port of Spain, where she meets with and measures the private clients for whom she sews. She has four sewing machines: three straight-stitchers and one serger. An ideal target for the Inter-American Development Bank– and World Bank–funded aid to small and microenterprises that became available in the late 1990s, Victoria learned her seamstressing skills from her mother and in a dressmaking course at a technical college. She worked as a receptionist in a doctor's office while stitching clothing for friends and neighbors, slowly widening her circle of clients over time. Having managed to recruit several clients from among the pharmaceutical representatives she met at work, she eventually was able to quit her job and begin sewing full-time.

In 2002, when Victoria wanted to move from her own home to a rented studio apartment in an upscale Port of Spain neighborhood in order to serve higher-paying clients who would prefer not to visit her working-class community, she completed a World-Bank–funded training course for "micro-entrepreneurs" where, she says, she learned how to set up her own business: how to choose an area of the city to set up shop in, how to calculate her starting costs, and how much rent she could shoulder. Reflecting on the course, she said,

> The business course I did was geared for entrepreneurs: accounting, insurance, where to register your business, banking. Different people come in to talk to you, and the things you need to consider. Some of the people in the course were already in business! And the things they asked about were very helpful. They were already experiencing it, and could see ahead of you, a heads up.

The path to success, then, is laid out in a progressive sequence, with fellow entrepreneurs already steps ahead. With her sewing skills, Victoria's desire for instruction on how to transform self-employment into a business made her an ideal candidate for the technical training that the program provided. For some microenterprise initiatives, this act of scaling up is the primary goal. The aim is not for Victoria to sustain herself through private endeavor, but instead to enable her to expand her business and create employment by hiring others.

Victoria insists that her three employees must be former factory workers. She complained that when she experimented with training workers herself, they took their precious new skills to jobs elsewhere. She said to me,

> So then I started putting an ad in the paper, and employing people who know the work already, just like how those people were getting my girls that I train! So, go somewhere, learn to sew, and I'll take you after, if you've been working in a factory or

something. So I would just show them my method, how I want the finishings done. It's easier, 'cause they know how to do it, and I don't have to be over them.

One way of interpreting this absorption of factory workers into microenterprises is simply to see it as an outlet for excess labor. One of the expressed objectives of NEDCO is to regularize these businesses and bring them into the formal sector. Formalization, however, is a selective and limited encompassment that involves taxing self-employed people and registering businesses, but *not* registering them as industrial sites, which would bring OSHA inspections, National Insurance requirements, and the possibility that workers would establish a collective bargaining unit.[7]

While Victoria exemplifies the benefits of entrepreneurial training, stitchers in the Trinidadian countryside who take home bundles of work from local factories are addressed by microenterprise programs of a different kind, part of rural development initiatives to promote "cottage industry" or home-based craft production. Local NGOs working to promote Trinidadian cuisine by helping local cooks bring their jams and pickles to market also offer assessments of self-employed workers that can facilitate the process of applying for microfinance through an institution like NEDCO. The application for a micro-loan includes questions about assets, in which an industrial-grade sewing machine is an item of interest: the kind of equipment one would borrow money to buy. Yet as Lena's story shows, simply having access to machinery does not make paid work appear. Although her dream is to scale up her business in much the same way as Victoria, her immediate desire is to get more work from the factories—more bundles of stitching to complete, to keep her sewing machines from standing idle.

Hebe Verrest (2013: 60) explains that microenterprise programs too often address micro-entrepreneurs as "classic" entrepreneurs, "whose objectives are innovation, growth, and profit." Her research shows that many micro-entrepreneurs in Trinidad are modest in their aims and the *most* vulnerable seek funds for consumption at the lowest risk to their household. So there is a discrepancy between how the self-employed are imagined, the qualities of their presumed latent "entrepreneurialism," and their own economic needs and goals. These findings resonate with Marina Karides' (2005) study of Trinidadian street vendors, who prioritized safe places to work, child care, and affordable health care over the kinds of microfinancing they might be offered to develop and expand their small-scale businesses. Like Faye Harrison's (1988) study of women in Jamaica's informal economy, Karides' research shows how a sexual division of reproductive labor that allocates domestic and childrearing activities to women deeply shapes Trinidadian women's livelihood activities because reproductive and productive duties are persistent and interlinked.

Victoria is a single woman without children. With the encouragement of her parents she was able to pursue her dream of creating her own business, she says, but her possession of credentials from a local technical college and a circle of professional clients met through her job as a receptionist created the social conditions in which she could establish and grow her business. Lena's lack of resources and ongoing need to look after her children are perhaps secondary to the fact that having spent many years in garment factories, she has no social network through which to cultivate a high-paying client base. Lena therefore has more in common with the former factory workers Victoria now employs than with Victoria herself.

The Labor Politics of Microenterprise

The past thirty years have seen the establishment of a worldwide neoliberal orthodoxy that sees private-sector activities as "the main engine for economic growth" (Verrest 2013: 60), with the role of the state increasingly confined to facilitating and supporting such growth. Within this vision, the poor are either lifted out of poverty through the employment opportunities provided by a growing economy, or they *climb* out of poverty using their own creative capacities, entrepreneurial energy, and ability to expand and capitalize upon their social networks. Microenterprise development's role in this new orthodoxy lies not simply in providing training, credit, and technical support for petty entrepreneurs looking to develop their own businesses, but also in creating capillary networks for the practice of individualistic self-responsibilization (Bateman 2010; Jurik 2005; Rankin 2001).

Ananya Roy (2010) discusses microfinance advocates' curious silence on issues of labor. The sudden absence of workers from development discourse coincides with a vigorous promotion of the figure of the "heroic entrepreneur" (ibid.: 73). This shift is captured by Catherine Dolan and Dinah Rajak's recent research in Nairobi (Dolan and Rajak 2016). In their analysis of a social enterprise that trains young people in Nairobi to sell household goods door-to-door, they describe how entrepreneurship has emerged as a "solution" to urban unemployment in Eastern and Southern Africa. For the young people trained in new marketing disciplines,

Prospects of formal employment in Africa's shrinking blue collar sector have receded, leaving the growing population of urban youth at the margins of formal markets, reliant on the "second economy," a vast reservoir of energy to be simultaneously contained and converted into appropriate human capital. (Dolan and Rajak 2016: 514–15)

Urban youth, long perceived as either victims of development's failure to integrate them into formal economic relationships or a lawless underclass, are now perceived as a potential solution to sluggish, jobless economic growth if their creative capacities can be appropriately stimulated and channeled. The role of microenterprise in such development efforts can be interpreted as "offering up entrepreneurship in the place of employment": turning youth away from the fading possibilities of blue-collar jobs by turning them into traders instead (ibid.: 514).

But here the Trinidadian case is instructive, pointing to a rarely acknowledged element of microenterprise development: its appropriation by manufacturing. While micro-entrepreneurship of various kinds has been presented as remedying the problem of unemployment by transforming blue-collar aspirants into bourgeoning entrepreneurs, global post-Fordism has executed a different kind of conjuring act: the disappearance of formal wage employment and its reappearance as home-based work. Garment workers who swap minimum-wage employment for microenterprise find themselves engaged in identical forms of work with significantly diminished rights, entitlements, pay, working conditions, stability, and visibility.

The pluralism of home-based economic activities that garment workers undertake, including their practice of sewing for kin and neighbors, has made it easy for these new capital-labor relations to masquerade as relations of another kind: self-authored "economic empowerment," with entrepreneurship forming part of an autonomous set of livelihood activities independently chosen by the worker herself. Elisabeth Prügl and Irene Tinker (1997) argue that the "convergent categories" of homeworker and micro-entrepreneur create conditions in which traditional development or trade union interventions are not only difficult to sustain but also can be counter-productive to the interests of women workers. From the point of view of trade unionists, workers who stitch at home for factories are disguised wage employees divested of their rights. For a microenterprise agency—like NEDCO—the concern is with a woman's livelihood as an integrated complex deserving state support as long as she devotes herself to the pursuit of economic independence. Trinidadian homeworkers usually aspire to hire stitchers from within their communities to sew for them. In such instances, the homeworker becomes an employer, with responsibilities for maintaining working conditions and wage rates. Though celebrated by development agencies, this sort of entrepreneurial "success" attracts the ire of trade unionists, who decry this informalization of labor relations as producing new home-based sweatshops.

Not every worker wants to become a micro-entrepreneur. Amidst a fragmented and informalized garment industry, several factories in Trinidad still employ full-time workers paid by the hour, and among these workers

I heard a strong counternarrative. Sitting in 2014 with a group of garment workers I had known for many years, a factory worker named Veena commented while the others nodded approvingly:

> I prefer working at a place where, when I come home, I relax, I'm not working. And you see if you sew for other people, it might have sometimes when you have to work over the weekend, in the evenings to get that work out. And it's not all year, you know! Sometimes it doesn't have work. And don't forget where I'm working they have work for me every week of the year.

Workers like Veena describe microenterprise as a "constant hustle." What some of them object to about the re-emergence of homeworking is the uneven pace of work—requiring fast-paced frenzy when stitching is available—and an inability to guard the home as a protected sphere into which market relations would not follow them. A separation between work and home is here presented as vital for their sense of control and equilibrium. Rather than become a micro-entrepreneur, workers like Veena instead prefer being an employee, with all its imperfections. That these factory workers sometimes sew clothes at home for kin or friends for cash-in-hand payment indicates that they feel a sense of ownership and control over those activities, which they worry would be lost if such self-employment became their entire means of livelihood.

Conclusion

As the Trinidadian garment industry has fragmented and informalized in the face of global competitive pressures, state strategies for managing employment and capitalist strategies for managing the labor process have converged. The effect of this convergence is an increasing precariousness of labor whereby the responsibility for generating income, along with the management of risk, has been devolved onto workers no longer employed in factories but instead now based at home. Development discourses around homework, cottage industry, and micro-entrepreneurship in Trinidad legitimize and indeed elevate precariousness over stable employment. Insecurity becomes recast as freedom; self-exploitation is reframed as "being your own boss."

It is no accident that this transition from factory to homework in Trinidad involves women workers, who make up the overwhelming majority of the nation's garment workforce. In the history of labor struggle in the Caribbean, a racist image of the worker as recalcitrant and hard to control has necessarily been countered with a collective narrative of labor as possessing dignity, rights, and obligations. The role of women workers within these histories is complicated by their gender subordination, in that women have never fully embodied the purportedly universal category "worker" but have instead maintained highly gendered ties to the home as a domain of both productive and reproductive activities. With the convergence of industrial homeworking and microenterprise development, we see a reordering of history that places women workers within a development model concerned with "livelihoods" rather than industrial labor. Thus, development practitioners and state-led microenterprise initiatives represent processes of precarization and dispossession as a form of "empowerment" whereby women are "free" to author their own destinies while negating the histories of struggle that have made this framing possible.

The intersection of the garment industry and microenterprise development in Trinidad reveals not only the subtle labor politics of microenterprise, but also its pernicious effects: its elevation of entrepreneurialism over employment and fetishization of precarity as freedom, the effects of which are usually hidden by the fact that microenterprise focuses on integrating the poor into market relations (thus identifying the mechanism of impoverishment as their incidental exclusion from the capitalist economy, rather than their purposeful dispossession). In the case of Trinidad's self-employed garment workers, microenterprise initiatives reinforce an exploitative relationship between labor and capital.

Rebecca Prentice is Senior Lecturer in Anthropology at the University of Sussex in Brighton, UK. She is author of *Thiefing a Chance: Factory Work, Illicit Labor, and Neoliberal Subjectivities in Trinidad* (University Press of Colorado, 2015), which won the Society for the Anthropology of Work (SAW) Book Prize. She is co-editor with Geert De Neve of *Unmaking the Global Sweatshop: Health and Safety of the World's Garment Workers* (University of Pennsylvania Press, 2017).

Notes

1. Tracking garment jobs in Trinidad has become more difficult since 2000, when the occupational category "needleworker" was dropped from the national census.
2. This generational shift has also been an ethnic shift, with the white and Syrian-Lebanese founders of the industry giving way to younger Indo-Trinidadian (and increasingly, Afro-Trinidadian) entrepreneurs.
3. The one exception is the National Union of Domestic Employees, a small and poorly resourced yet vocal union that campaigns for domestic workers and seeks to

represent home-based garment workers in disputes with contractors and employers (cf. Jayasinghe 2001: 78; Karides 2002).

4. All names of people and factories are pseudonyms, with the exceptions of Mr. Gonsalves, who as a public figure agreed to be named in my research.

5. This was the minimum wage rate in the summer of 2014.

6. Although Carla Freeman's (2014) recent research on middle class entrepreneurs in Barbados suggests a move toward companionate marriage with a more equal role for men and women in the domestic sphere, my research among working-class garment workers in Trinidad highlights the persistence of gender ideologies that render housekeeping and childcare a foremost responsibility of women.

7. Workers in small production units like Victoria's studio are at the mercy of their boss's good graces. The minimum wage, which is enforced in most factories, is less evenly implemented in micro-firms of this kind; not to mention National Insurance, OSHA regulations, and maternity leave. Victoria describes a personalization of the relationship between boss and employee.

References

Bair, Jennifer, and Marion Werner. 2011. "Commodity Chains and the Uneven Geographies of Global Capitalism: A Disarticulations Perspective." *Environment and Planning A* 43(5): 988–997.

Bateman, Milford. 2010. *Why Doesn't Microfinance Work? The Destructive Rise of Local Neoliberalism*. London: Zed Books.

Benach, Joan, Alejandra Vives, Marcelo Amable, Christophe Vanroelen, Gemma Tarafa, and Carles Muntaner. 2014. "Precarious Employment: Understanding an Emerging Social Determinant of Health." *Annual Review of Public Health* 35: 229–253.

Bissessar, Ann Marie, and Roger Hosein. 2001. "The Role of the State in the Economic Development of Trinidad and Tobago with Special Reference to the Petrochemical Sector." Presentation to Caribbean Centre for Money and Finance 33rd Annual Monetary Studies Conference, Belize City, 19–23 November.

Central Statistics Office. 2003. *Labour Force Statistics*. Port of Spain: CSO.

Collins, Jane L. 2002. "Mapping a Global Labor Market: Gender and Skill in the Globalizing Garment Industry." *Gender and Society* 16(6): 921–940.

Dolan, Catherine, and Dinah Rajak. 2016. "Remaking Africa's Informal Economies: Youth, Entrepreneurship and the Promise of Inclusion at the Bottom of the Pyramid." *Journal of Development Studies* 52(4): 514–529.

Esnard-Flavius, Talia, and Zainab Aziz. 2011. "Microcredit, Microenterprises and Social Welfare of the Rural Poor in North-Eastern Trinidad: An Evaluation of 'Hope.'" *Asian Academy of Management Journal* 16(1): 95–118.

Federici, Silvia. 2012. *Revolution at Point Zero: Housework, Reproduction, and Feminist Struggle*. Oakland, CA: PM Press.

Freeman, Carla. 2007. "The 'Reputation' of Neoliberalism." *American Ethnologist* 34(2): 252–267.

———. 2014. *Entrepreneurial Selves: Neoliberal Respectability and the Making of a Caribbean Middle Class*. Durham, NC: Duke University Press.

Harrison, Faye V. 1988. "Women in Jamaica's Urban Informal Economy: Insights from a Kingston Slum." *Nieuwe West-Indische Gids/New West Indian Guide* 62(3–4): 103–128.

Hart, Keith. 1985. "The Informal Economy." *Cambridge Anthropology* 10(2): 54–58.

Heron, Adom Philogene. 2011. "Taming the Spider Man: From Anticolonial Hero to Neoliberal Icon." Presentation to Société Internationale d'Ethnologie et de Folklore (SIEF) Conference, 17–21 April, Lisbon, Portugal.

Holmström, Mark. 1998. "Introduction: Industrial Districts and Flexible Specialization: The Outlook for Smaller Firms in India." In *Decentralized Production in India: Industrial Districts, Flexible Specialization, and Employment*, ed. Philippe Cadène and Mark Holmström, 7–41. London: Sage.

Jayasinghe, Daphne. 2001. "'More and More Technology, Women Have to Go Home': Changing Skills Demands in Manufacturing and Caribbean Women's Access to Training." *Gender & Development* 9(1): 70–81.

Jurik, Nancy C. 2005. *Bootstrap Dreams: U.S. Microenterprise Development in an Era of Welfare Reform*. Ithaca, NY: Cornell University Press.

Kalleberg, Arne L. 2011. *Good Jobs, Bad Jobs: The Rise of Polarized and Precarious Employment Systems in the United States, 1970s to 2000s*. New York: Russell Sage Foundation.

Karides, Marina. 2002. "Linking Local Efforts with Global Struggle: Trinidad's National Union of Domestic Employees." In *Women's Activism and Globalization: Linking Local Struggles and Transnational Politics*, ed. Nancy A. Naples and Manisha Desai, 156–171. New York: Routledge.

———. 2005. "Whose Solution is It? Development Ideology and the Work of Micro-Entrepreneurs in Caribbean Context." *International Journal of Sociology and Social Policy* 25(1–2): 30–62.

———. 2010. "Theorizing the Rise of Microenterprise Development in Caribbean Context." *Journal of World System Research* 17(2): 192–216.

Katwaroo-Ragbir, Sherry. 2013. "The Role of Regulation in the Development of the Trinidad and Tobago Microfinance Sector." *Journal of Emerging Trends in Economics and Management Sciences* 4(2): 189–195.

Kowalski, Przemyslaw, and Margit Molnar. 2009. "Economic Impacts of the Phase-Out in 2005 of Quantitative Restrictions under the Agreement on Textile and Clothing." *OECD Trade Policy Working Papers*, No. 90. Paris: OECD.

Lee, Chin Kwan, and Yelizavetta Kofman. 2012. "The Politics of Precarity: Views Beyond the United States." *Work and Occupations* 39(4): 388–408.

Lewis, Hannah, Peter Dwyer, Stuart Hodkinson, and Louise Waite. 2015. "Hyper-Precarious Lives? Migrants, Work and Forced Labour in the Global North." *Progress in Human Geography* 39(5): 580–600.

Lewis, W. Arthur. 1954. "Economic Development with Unlimited Supplies of Labour." *The Manchester School* 22(2): 139–191.

Lopez-Acevedo, Gladys, and Raymond Robertson, eds. 2012. *Sewing Success? Employment, Wages, and Poverty Following the End of the Multi-Fibre Arrangement*. Washington, DC: World Bank.

Miller, Daniel. 1994. *Modernity, an Ethnographic Approach: Dualism and Mass Consumption in Trinidad.* Oxford: Berg.

Molé, Noelle J. 2010. "Precarious Subjects: Anticipating Neoliberalism in Northern Italy's Workplace." *American Anthropologist* 112(1): 38–53.

Moonilal, Roodal. 2001. "Workers' Protection: The Case of Trinidad and Tobago." International Labour Organization working paper no. 7. Port of Spain: ILO Caribbean Office.

Moya, Ramiro, Anne-Marie Mohammed, and Sandra Sookram. 2010. "Productive Development Policies in Trinidad and Tobago: A Critical Review." In Inter-American Development Bank Working Paper Series, no. IDB-WP-115. Washington, DC: IDB.

Muehlebach, Andrea. 2013. "On Precariousness and the Ethical Imagination: The Year 2012 in Sociocultural Anthropology." *American Anthropologist* 115(2): 297–311.

Prentice, Rebecca. 2012. "'No One Ever Showed Me Nothing': Skill and Self-Making among Trinidadian Garment Workers." *Anthropology & Education Quarterly* 43(4):400–414.

———. 2015. *Thiefing a Chance: Factory Work, Illicit Labor, and Neoliberal Subjectivities in Trinidad.* Boulder, CO: University Press of Colorado.

Prügl, Elisabeth, and Irene Tinker. 1997. "Microentrepreneurs and Homeworkers: Convergent Categories." *World Development* 25(9):1471–1482.

Rankin, Katharine N. 2001. "Governing Development: Neoliberalism, Microcredit, and Rational Economic Woman." *Economy and Society* 30(1):18–37.

Reddock, Rhoda E. 1994. *Women, Labour and Politics in Trinidad and Tobago: A History.* London: Zed Books.

Roy, Ananya. 2010. *Poverty Capital: Microfinance and the Making of Development.* London: Routledge.

Sergeant, Kelvin, and Penelope Forde. 1992. "The State Sector and Divestment in Trinidad and Tobago: Some Preliminary Findings." *Social and Economic Studies* 41(4): 173–204.

Standing, Guy. 2011. *The Precariat: A New Dangerous Class.* London: Bloomsbury Academic.

Staples, David E. 2006. *No Place Like Home: Organizing Home-Based Labor in the Era of Structural Adjustment.* New York: Routledge.

Verrest, Hebe. 2013. "Rethinking Microentrepreneurship and Business Development Programs: Vulnerability and Ambition in Low-Income Urban Caribbean Households." *World Development* 47: 58–70.

Vertovec, Steven. 1990. "Oil Boom and Recession in Trinidad Indian Villages." In *South Asians Overseas: Migration and Ethnicity,* ed. Colin G. Clarke, Ceri Peach and Steven Vertovec, 89–111. Cambridge: Cambridge University Press.

Waldinger, Roger, and Michael Lapp. 1993. "Back to the Sweatshop or Ahead to the Informal Sector?" *International Journal of Urban and Regional Research* 17(1): 6–29.

13

Towards a Political Economy of Skill and Garment Work

The Case of the Tiruppur Industrial Cluster in South India

GRACE CARSWELL AND GEERT DE NEVE

Introduction: Skills, Trade Liberalization, and Precarious Employment

Across the Indian subcontinent, industrial employment has long been precarious for the majority of its workers. Deeply rooted as it is in the informal sector and in casual and unprotected labor markets, industrial work has largely thrived on informality and on the abundant supply of cheap, casual, flexibly deployed labor (Harriss-White 2002). From garments to brickmaking to construction, few industrial workers have had access to regular or permanent employment, let alone to any sort of social security within their jobs (Breman 2012; Cross 2010). Many of those lucky enough to have made it into the few citadels of formal industrial employment—widely referred to as the "aristocracy of labor"—have been rapidly sliding back into the seas of informality and precarity as formal and state-owned industries are restructured, privatized, and outsourced in the post-liberalization era (Breman 2004; Mezzadri 2008; Parry 2013; Sanchez 2012a, 2012b; Strümpell 2014, 2014b). As ever more sectors fall prey to liberalization policies, whatever formal industrial employment existed in the post-Independence period has rapidly shrunk, and whatever labor protection and labor rights were won have been gradually eroded, even for those who remain regularly employed. Various types of casual and temporary contracts dominate the majority of industrial labor markets.

However, the trade liberalization and global economic restructuring since the 1980s have had other effects too. While in some parts of the world, as described in Prentice's contribution to this volume, restructuring led to the loss of previously protected industrial jobs and a rise in precarious employment, in other regions it produced an unprecedented rise in industrial employment. South Asia's thriving garment and textile sectors are perhaps the most telling example of such novel forms of global integration. Rather than undergoing what Bair and Werner have called a "disarticulation" or expulsion from global trade circuits (2011: 989; Prentice in this volume), India's garment and textile industries have become deeply embedded in global outsourcing networks, resulting in a proliferation of employment opportunities at the bottom of the global industrial chain. This chapter focuses on one such industrial cluster, the Tiruppur garment region in western Tamil Nadu, South India, where the garment industry has boomed almost uninterruptedly—the 2009–2012 slump aside—since the 1970s.

Following economic reforms and trade liberalization in the 1980s and 1990s (Corbridge, Harriss, and Jeffrey 2013) and the gradual removal of garment export quotas between 1995 and 2005, garment production grew exponentially in Tiruppur, obtaining ever more export orders, creating hundreds of thousands of jobs, and attracting local commuters and migrants from across the country. Unfortunately, this global integration has not been accompanied by a steady improvement in employment conditions or livelihood outcomes for garment workers. A degree of "adverse incorporation" certainly marks the experiences of many, given that most employment in garments is precarious: informal, irregular, and for most, lacking any form of social security provisioning (Phillips 2011; Mezzadri 2012). Though workers in larger firms may well be regularly employed and registered on a payroll, high levels of labor turnover mean most workers are not employed at the same company for more than two or three years. In the vast sprawl of smaller and medium-sized factories in and around Tiruppur, almost all workers are casually employed through labor contractors who lead teams of workers. In the past only one particular type of tailor was recruited through contractors, but since the late 2000s this has become the main way of employing a whole range of workers across the industry. Internal subcontracting, now endemic in the industry, has added to the casualization and precarization of garment labor (De Neve 2014b).

Against this background, in 2009 the Government of India began to promote skill development with the launch of its National Skill Development Policy (NSDP) and its renewed commitment to skills training under the 2015 National Policy on Skill Development and Entrepreneurship (NPSDE). Skills training received unprecedented policy attention, and training initiatives were launched across the country with the aim of upgrading skills, enhancing the quality of employment, and improving human capital. Skills training, the 2009 policy argued, would lead not only to enhanced productivity, but also to more inclusive growth, more regular forms of employment, and more "decent work" (NSDP 2009: 1). The 2015 policy renewed its commitment to these aims and stated that to reap the "demographic dividend, which is expected to last for the next 25 years, India needs to equip its workforce with employable skills and knowledge so that they can contribute substantively to the economic growth of the country" (Ministry of Skill Development and Entrepreneurship 2015: 2). The generic belief is that improving the skills base of the labor force will enable countries like India to take advantage of new economic opportunities and to access more high-tech, value-added segments of the global production market. This would offer India's contemporary youth access to secure livelihood opportunities and ultimately lift many out of poverty. Since around 2010, India has been investing in an unprecedented way in skills training by launching skill development programs across sectors and through public and public-private initiatives, in both urban and rural areas (Comyn 2014; Nambiar 2013; Palmer et al. 2012; Vijayabaskar and Jeyaranjan 2011). Such growth strategies are intimately connected to poverty-alleviation agendas that bank on thriving industrial regions' spillover effects on the wider economy and society. Skill and technology upgrading, enhanced labor productivity, and movement up the value chain will ultimately, it is hoped, translate into social upgrading too (Vijayabaskar and Jeyaranjan 2011; see also Ashton et al. 1999). Policy approaches thus tend to focus pragmatically on skill formation through formal training institutions and vocational courses, assuming that the labor force's improved skills base will then enable a wider, more even, distribution of the gains of participation in the global economy.

But what do we know about this skill acquisition drive so far? How does skill acquisition "work" in practice? And what potential does skills training have to alleviate precarious employment and insecure working lives? We introduce ethnographic material from the garment industry of Tiruppur to explore how the acquisition and valuing of skills are shaped by the political economy of the shop floor, the household, and the village. Skills, we argue, cannot be considered in isolation. Rather, attention needs to be paid to the social processes and inequalities—of power, gender, caste, and age—that enable or constrain people's access to suitable skills and determine the economic and sociocultural values attached to skills. Policy and scholarly perspectives on skill all too often remain socially and politically disembedded, in that skills are conceptualized as a fixed entity that can be taught, passed on, and used by individual actors independent of social context. Skills are thought of as objective things that can be improved, extended, put into training sessions, applied, and measured. Moreover, skills are expected to automatically attract higher rewards; hence, it is assumed that people's investments in skills and entrepreneurship will be driven by the differential rewards those skills fetch in the market.

Such a conceptualization, much like the understanding of poverty as critiqued by Harriss (2009: 205), "is doomed to disappointment, because the focus is on measurement and on the characteristics of individuals and households with very little attention to the structural processes that move people in and out of poverty." What remains similarly obscured in much policy and social science writing on skill formation are the social relations through which skills are accessed and mobilized, as well as the social and political processes through which skill is valued (or undervalued) and therefore can translate (or fails to translate) into more secure livelihoods and upward mobility. The way in which skills are conceptualized separates them from the social processes of caste dependency, gender ideology, masculine norms, and age discrimination that shape people's engagement with skill, skill acquisition, and labor markets. Like poverty, conceptualizations of skill often "depoliticize" (Harriss 2009) by hiding the relations of power and inequality that constrain people's ability to access and deploy skills, and suppress the value of skilled jobs in the market. They also ignore the politics of employment—including the post-liberalization labor regimes— that exclude some groups of actors from employment while keeping others at levels that receive the least reward and require the most flexibility, often despite the fact that their skills warrant mobility into more secure, higher-status, better-paid jobs (Carswell and De Neve 2013).

Informative insights can be gleaned from ethnographic work, much of which has focused on the multiple, informal, and often embodied forms of skill acquisition across different crafts and trades. Multiple studies have described on-the-job kinds of learning, which often take the form of "trial and error" or "observation and imitation" and usually proceed outside formal teaching environments (Cross 2011; De Neve 2005; Prentice 2008, 2012; Venkatesan 2010; Wilkinson-Weber 1999). Much learning and skill acquisition tends to emerge from nonverbal ways of interaction between apprentice and teacher, in which tasks are demonstrated and replicated (Roman 2008; Mohsini 2010; Venkatesan 2010). This often involves a great deal of practical knowledge, transmitted through ways of learning in which bodies absorb skills through hands-on practice. As Cross puts it, "a growing body of anthropological literature on apprenticeship reminds us that … skills or techniques for using tools and machines are transmitted through physical display and demonstration, observation, imitation and mimesis as much as direct experience" (2011: 124; cf. Prentice 2008). A good deal of ethnography has therefore focused on the nature of apprenticeship and the place of learning within processes of socialization (Roman 2008).

This literature reminds us that the acquisition of practical knowledge and technique never takes place in a social vacuum. Values, ideologies, gendered subjectivities, and power relations are also produced and transmitted along with practical know-how. In the process of acquiring skills, as bodies are disciplined and imbued with techniques, minds are simultaneously inculcated with social values, norms, and ideologies (Prentice 2008; Gooptu 2009; McGuire 2013). Prentice, for example, refers to the "inculcated" body to capture the ways in which values, norms, and subjectivities are inscribed onto the body in the process of learning and mastering skills (2008: 55). Some of the values that have recently been most strongly inculcated into industrial workforces are those of neoliberal subjectivity: flexibility, self-reliance, and independence. In Trinidad, Prentice argues, learning to sew is not only about acquiring practical skills, but as much about gaining the "capacities to forge livelihoods in an instable and demanding industry" (2012: 401), and thus to learn to fend for oneself. Or, as Gooptu (2009: 46) puts it with reference to India's organized retail employment, the contemporary worker, "faced with the compulsions of an unprotected labor market and new forms of socialization at the workplace, comes to be constituted as a neoliberal subject—individualized and responsible for his/her own self-presentation, self-government, self-management and self-advancement."

We therefore suggest that particular attention needs to be paid to the social life of skills, that is, the social processes, relationships, and ideologies that enable (or constrain) people's access to skills, and subsequently to employment, wages, satisfaction, and dignity. Roman (2008: 4), in her excellent work on innovation in silk-weaving clusters in India, emphasizes the role of social relations and institutions in knowledge dynamics, arguing that although such social relations and institutions facilitate much learning and skill acquisition, "being arbitrary and incomplete, [they] can also act as divisive and exclusionary forces." Here, we examine precisely such divisive and exclusionary forces by exploring the caste, gender, and age dynamics that enable some men and women to access novel skills and earn livelihoods, while preventing others from doing so. For this we turn to the village and the household, rather than the urban shop-floor or training center (although we comment on these too), to explore some of the gender, caste, and power dynamics that shape men's and women's opportunities for skill upgrading. Then we look at the "demand" for skill acquisition among workers in order to move beyond conceptualizations of skill as merely a matter of "supply," that is, provision of training, education, and practical knowledge.

We thereby aim to disrupt linear conceptualizations that assume a direct and causal link between *supply* of skill enhancement opportunities and the *uptake* thereof; and between *uptake* of skills training and *outcomes* in terms of type, quality, and remuneration of subsequent employment. Given the socially mediated nature of skills acquisition processes, the outcome of skills training is likely to be much less uniform and predictable than policy makers might have us believe. As we shall show, they may well entrench rather than alleviate the vulnerabilities and inequalities that produce the precarious working lives of the laboring poor in the first place.

Skills Training in the Tiruppur Garment Cluster

Unlike other industries on the subcontinent, such as those described by Parry (2013), Sanchez (2012a, 2012b), and Strümpell (2014a) amongst others, the Tiruppur garment industry has never been divided along the lines of a permanent/regular versus temporary/contract labor force, for two main reasons. First, all garment employment in Tiruppur is marked by high levels of labor turnover, with workers shifting companies on an annual, if not monthly, basis. Although the largest export firms enroll a number of workers on their regular payroll, this means very little in terms of either pay or job security. Not only are jobs dependent on the flow of export orders, but workers themselves are constantly in search of better pay, more flexible conditions, less work pressure, or more suitable locations. In the smaller firms and subcontracting units, employment is highly irregular; most workers are recruited through labor contractors whom they follow from contract to contract and firm to firm. Second, aspirations to progress or develop within the garment sector are rarely informed by a desire for permanent employment in a particular company. Permanency—like job security—carries little meaning. Women tend to aspire to regular workflows in conveniently located firms that offer flexible working hours. Men, by contrast, are driven by their desire first to obtain better piece rates as tailors or cutting masters, and second to pursue upward mobility as a labor contractor and ultimately achieve entrepreneurial success through self-employment as a garment producer running their own unit (De Neve 2014a). Few, however, make it to these higher rungs.

Nevertheless, skills matter a great deal in the Tiruppur garment sector. They are predominantly acquired in informal ways and through on-the-job practice. In the cutting-making-trimming (CMT) factories where cloth is turned into garments, experienced tailors take immense pride in the skills they master, the stitches they can produce, and the speed at which they work. Skill involves not just technical mastery of tools and machines of different types, but also knowledge of different stitches, types of cloth, and designs. Skill is also about the ability to make more complex garments and produce work of a consistent quality. A key aspect of skill is the ability to deal with high levels of work intensity (Vijayabaskar and Jeyaranjan 2011: 144), at which speed needs to be combined with great concentration to maintain the necessary quality throughout the production process. High work intensity is combined with long working days (often twelve hours), regular overtime, and a six- or seven-day working week.

Garment workers in Tiruppur acquire skills in different ways. In the CMT sector, cutting cloth and sewing garments are the two core skilled jobs. By far the majority of tailors and cutting masters—and all the helpers and checkers—learn their skills on the job. Only a few tailors learn their trade through formal training, either in specialized training centers or through firm-based apprenticeships. In Tiruppur, the supply of formal training for tailoring is limited. Drawing on a language of professionalism, careers, entrepreneurship, and scientific approaches, a few new institutes and colleges serve the industry's need for better qualified professionals, catering for young men and women pursuing management-level careers within the industry by recruiting youngsters from middle-class families who are often already running their own textile businesses.[1]

Since 2010, however, the Government of India has taken an unprecedented interest in skills training across the textile industry as part of its nationwide skill development drive. With the Ministry of Textiles' introduction of the Integrated Skill Development Scheme, the pan-Indian Apparel Training and Design Centre (ATDC) has come to play a key role in the provision of skills training for the apparel sector and currently runs over two hundred training centers across India, of which eighteen are in Tamil Nadu. Following the introduction of this scheme, the ATDC developed a flagship training brand called SMART (Skills for Manufacturing of Apparels through Research and Training) aimed at enhancing the provision of skills training on the lower rungs of industrial employment in order to supply a thriving apparel sector with a skilled labor force. Under SMART, fast-track vocational training courses of one to four months were introduced to teach basic shop-floor skills to newcomers to the apparel industry. SMART also uses skill camps to reach out to rural populations in an attempt to enhance the (industrial) employability of the rural poor, women, and low-caste people in particular. In Tiruppur too, the ADTC center introduced SMART training, which includes industry placements. However, the number of people enrolled in such training courses remains remarkably low, at a few hundred trainees per year—negligible, in the context of an overall garment labor force of well over half a million.

In addition to industry-wide and government initiatives, some larger companies also offer firm-based skills training, mainly in the form of apprenticeships. New recruits typically get two or three months' training in basic sewing or cutting before going to work on a regular production line. They are paid a reduced wage until they qualify as skilled tailors and start receiving the basic starting salary. Women and migrants are the principal beneficiaries of such apprenticeships. As they often come from distant places, the company provides most of them with accommodation. However, as Vijayabaskar and Jeyaranjan (2011: 148) rightly point out, "due to the high interfirm mobility of labor, there is little incentive for the firms to offer in-plant training." Indeed, very high attrition rates across garment firms are an indication of workers' constant movement between firms in search of more skilled jobs, better pay, and more suitable working conditions (Carswell and De Neve 2013). In a survey of three hundred workers in Tiruppur in 2008/09, we found that 35 percent of the workforce had been employed for less than a year in their current company, while another 39 percent had been employed for between one to three years.[2] Only 24 percent of the sampled workers had been working for more than three years in the same company. Skilled workers often move on within months, usually following the labor contractor who employs them. Once workers have acquired the basic skills of tailoring or cutting, they shift companies in order to be promoted to tailor or cutting master. In a context where employers seek to suppress wages as much as possible, it makes little economic sense for companies to invest in worker training, given the limited chances of capturing its benefits in the long term.

Transferring and Acquiring Skill

If institutionalized training through formally taught courses and firm-based apprenticeships has little impact in the Tiruppur region, how do novice textile workers acquire the training needed to enter the garment industry and become skilled tailors or cutting masters? By far the most common route into garment work is through on-the-job learning—either in or outside of factories—in which young men and women, usually in their late teens, acquire the basic skills through observation, imitation, and hands-on practice alongside the tailor or cutting master whom they assist.

Many companies in Tiruppur consist of small and medium-sized workshops with workforces that can be either directly employed by the company or recruited by a labor contractor, who may work for one or several companies at the same time or move between companies according to the availability of work (De Neve 2014b). While there is considerable variation in the composition of garment units, as a rule a workshop is divided into four main sections: cutting, stitching, checking, and ironing and packing. Cutting is a skilled job for which only men are employed.

Skilled tailors might take a personal interest in cutting work and observe some of the cutting masters during their breaks or when work is slow. The cutting master may then allow them to cut a few basic patterns and, if they do well, take them on as cutters on their team. At first they will be given basic patterns, but gradually more complex cutting work will be passed to them, and they will learn a variety of patterns and tools. When paid piece rates, cutters can earn up to 500 rupees per day and more. Piece rates ensure that the work is done with great care, as cutting mistakes can waste meters of cloth and usually cannot be rectified. If a cutter wastes a piece of cloth, he will not be paid for it. Piece rate payment, one manufacturer explained, ensures that cutters are very careful and do not rush the work.

After cutting, the cloth moves to the second section, where the cut pieces are sewn into garments. In the tailoring section, labor is often recruited through labor contractors. The manufacturer gives the contractor a full payment for the order or "contract," and the contractor in turn recruits tailors, supervises their output, and pays them at the end of the week. The contractor is responsible for finishing the contract on time and meeting the required quality standards. He is normally paid on a piece-rate basis, while the workers on his team are usually paid either a shift-based wage or piece rates. Most manufacturers seldom interact directly with their tailors and concentrate instead on selecting trustworthy, efficient contractors. The use of labor contractors, a relatively new phenomenon in the industry, spread during the export boom of the 1990s. As orders increased in size and product specifications changed ever more frequently, management of labor became increasingly time-consuming, and the use of labor contractors proved an efficient alternative to direct employment by the company (De Neve 2014b).

Labor contractors recruit two sorts of tailors: *singer* tailors and *power table* tailors. (The latter are further divided into *flat lock* and *over lock* tailors.) The modifier *singer* refers to the old-style Singer sewing machines operated by foot, which are commonly found in tailoring shops across India. Power table machines are found only in garment factories. Singer and power table tailors differ significantly from each other in terms of how they acquire their skills and are recruited, paid, and supervised. Kumar, a singer labor contractor, explained the process of becoming a singer tailor:

> One has to learn tailoring from the age of 15 or 16 onwards. Singer machine work can only be learned outside the Tiruppur industry, from a friend or neighbor in a small tailoring shop. I myself started at the age of 15 and worked for 5 years in a shop, where I learned all sorts of tailoring, including cutting. Only experienced tailors can come to Tiruppur and be employed in the garment industry. Given that only men are trained in tailoring shops, few women can operate a singer machine.

As singer tailoring is learned in contexts where skill is informally passed on among men, it is hardly surprising that the singer sections are dominated by men. Singer tailors come to Tiruppur from all over Tamil Nadu, attracted by the prospects of higher wages and regular employment in the export sector. The constant transfer of skill from small tailoring workshops into the garment industry represents a crucial link between the garment sector and the tailoring shops outside of it that function informally as training sites for the industry. This training pattern also goes some way toward explaining the considerable gender bias in this section of the garment industry, which is not only an almost exclusively male domain but also the best paid section of the industry.

Singer tailors are always paid piece rates. Workers refuse fixed daily wages, knowing they can earn more on piece rates. An experienced singer tailor can easily earn up to 500–700 rupees per day, depending on the speed of his work and the number of hours he works. Hourly rates are not very high, but speedy work can substantially increase singer tailors' incomes. Contractors too are keen to pay piece rates, for reasons to do with the production process and quality maintenance:

> Normally, the quality goes down when we pay piece rates because the tailors will try to work faster and with less care in order to finish more pieces in a day. However, this is not the case with *singer* tailors, because the pieces are numbered and if they make a mistake, the piece will be returned to them and they will have to repair the mistakes or they will receive no payment for it. That's why we can guarantee the quality even if we pay piece rates [to singer tailors]. Also, the mistakes of a singer tailor can be repaired, but a mistake made on a power table cannot be undone. (Ganeshan, power table contractor)

Piece rates for singer tailoring work thus allow quality standards to be maintained and labor to be used more flexibly and paid according to output. At the same time, though, contractors also expect flexibility from singer tailors, who will be asked to work long hours whenever an urgent shipping deadline needs to be met. This, more than anything else, is what keeps women from joining teams of singer tailors, as gendered norms about acceptable working hours and domestic responsibilities reduce their flexibility in the labor market. Moreover, as skilled tailors, singer operators often job-hop, looking for the best contracts according to the rates, regularity of work, and treatment they receive. Such mobility requires not only physical movement between factories across the city, but also the ability to develop wide networks of social contacts with a range of tailors and contractors. This by and large excludes women, who are unable to move freely across male-dominated spaces or invest in the social networks needed to access jobs, even if they possess the relevant tailoring skills.

Acquisition of power table skills is a very different story. First of all, power table training takes place in the factory itself, though this does not mean that it happens in a formalized manner. Young adults, who typically enter the factory at the age of fifteen or sixteen, start as "helpers." Each power table tailor is assisted by a helper who hands over the required cloth, trims the completed stitches, and folds the garments into piles. The position of helper is an unskilled job requiring no prior knowledge, and helpers are paid the minimum salary. Yet the role is crucial in that it allows men and women new to garment work to get a foothold in the industry. Theoretically, a starting helper can be a man or woman at any stage of life, but in practice helpers are mostly older teens. Adult men are reluctant to take this work, as being a helper is considered a low-status job with meager wages. While most women who enter the industry do so at a young age, the role of helper enables older women to join the industry, often after having raised children or done other work, such as agricultural or home-based work. Many of them, however, never move beyond the role of helper or trimmer/checker.

It is as helpers that young men and women are informally trained by the tailor whom they assist. Tailors demonstrate how to operate the sewing machines, how to do different stitches, and how to improve the quality and speed of one's sewing. During lunch breaks and after shifts, helpers slip into the tailors' seats and practice on small pieces of cloth, trying out different stitches and gradually improving their skills. At some point the tailor may allow a helper to sew a few basic stitches on garments and work on the production line. Though some need a year or more, it usually takes helpers just a few months to reach a level of skill that allows them to move on to tailoring. However, only very rarely do garment workers move from helper to tailor within the same company. Once they feel confident that they can do the job, helpers shift factories or contractors in order to be recruited as tailors. Though men may benefit more from male networks of tailors and contractors, for women too this is the most common route into tailoring work.

Unlike singer tailors, power table tailors used to be paid shift rates. Men and women were paid the same rates, but they earned less than singer tailors. Employers usually justified their lower wages with reference to a relative notion of skill: the skill of power table tailors was limited to a few types of stitches, and they usually had no knowledge of pattern making or cloth cutting. In fact, their lower wages were just as much due to an ideological construction of singer tailors as more skilled, to the greater supply of power table tailors, and to the lack of alternative job opportunities for them outside the industry. Moreover, shift rates were paid to maintain quality standards. Mistakes made by singer tailors were returned to the tailor and could usually be rectified by them. Mistakes made by power table tailors, however, could not be undone, so the piece would be wasted. It was therefore important to keep power table tailors from speeding up just to get more pieces finished within a shift.

Around 2007/08, however, this changed significantly. Ever more (male) power table tailors began to demand piece-rate payment. Experienced power table tailors, who had seen what singer tailors could earn at piece rates and were aware of the industry's demand for their skill, started asking for piece rates and increasingly received them. This shift took place primarily in smaller companies, where contractors are constantly in search of reliable tailors and keen to hang on to experienced, skilled workers. In order to attract experienced power table tailors to their teams and retain them, contractors began to pay them piece rates. Piece rate–paid (male) tailors constitute the elite of garment workers. They have a considerable degree of leverage over their hours and working conditions, and do not hesitate to change contractors and factories when they are unhappy with their current deal (De Neve 2014a; Carswell and De Neve 2013). Meanwhile, at larger firms where women form the majority of the power table labor force, shift rates remain the norm.

Although access to skills is relatively easy and opportunities for power table tailoring abound, women often remain helpers for years and may not move on to tailoring at all. There are many reasons for this, but few have to do with a lack of skill or employer strategies (Carswell 2016). Gendered experiences of temporal flexibilities are the key issue. Women employed as tailors find it harder to take time off or do just half a shift, and they cannot refuse overtime work when an urgent order has to be finished. Moreover, as their domestic duties may require them to take regular time off to look after children or relatives, women are unable to offer employers and contractors the flexibility usually demanded of tailors. As a result, many of them, especially those with smaller children, move sideways into "checking" work.

Checking work consists of trimming loose threads and checking the finished garments for mistakes. In Tiruppur, this is the exclusive domain of women. It requires little training; women can take it up like helper work. An added advantage of checking work is that it need not follow the rhythm of sewing, in which the tailors' output is set by the speed of the assembly line. An unfinished pile can be picked up again the next day or shared among checkers. This is probably the job that gives women most flexibility, requires least overtime, and in smaller workshops allows women to take breaks and go home in the middle of the day. Often, women who used to be employed as tailors give up tailoring work upon marrying or when they have small children, and then pick up garment work again later in life. At that point, they often slot back into the factory as helper or checker rather than tailor, given that such work fits better with their ongoing domestic responsibilities and temporal routines.

The Demand for Skills Training: Gender and Age, Caste and Dependency

Having outlined the ways in which skills are acquired and jobs are divided on the shop floor, we now consider the "demand" for skill among workers striving to join the garment labor force, and reflect on the life histories that lead people in and out of garment work. Focusing on men and women interviewed in Tiruppur as well as in two villages in the city's hinterland, we turn to the relations of gender, age, and caste that shape access to skills, employment opportunities, and job mobility.

Priya is a 28-year-old woman who lives 18 km south of Tiruppur in Allapuram, a village that sends significant numbers of commuters (across castes) to work in the urban garment industry. Priya, who belongs to a Dalit caste, is married and has a seven-year-old son. She and her husband, Senthil, currently both work in a small garment factory that a local Gounder started up in the village in 2012.[3] Senthil works as a power table tailor and Priya as a checker, but this division of labor, in which he occupies the more rewarding and higher-status job, has little to do with a lack of skill on Priya's part. At the age of fourteen, Priya started her working life in a spinning mill, where she worked for some four or five years. Soon after she married she started working in Tiruppur, where she quickly became a tailor, following the informal, on-the-job training route described above. She had worked there for about a year when her first son was born, whereupon she found it difficult to sustain her job in Tiruppur. "It got too difficult to go early and come back late". She quit and worked for a while on NREGA while her son was young.[4] As soon as a garment factory opened in the village, Priya started working there—but as a checker, not a tailor, despite having tailoring skills. Her start in that job coincided with her son's starting school, but she was able to return to work because her mother-in-law was around to pick the little boy up from school. Still, Priya explains, her son is very little, so she can only work one shift per day (8:30 a.m.–5:30 p.m.), which allows her to look after him in the evenings. Importantly, Priya returned to checking work, which is more flexible than tailoring: it allows her to go home in the middle of the day and does not require her to do regular overtime.

When garment work was very irregular in Tiruppur following the economic downturn of 2008/09, Senthil left the industry too and worked for some time in woodcutting. But once the factory opened in the village in 2012, he immediately joined as a tailor. Comparing work in the village to

Tiruppur, Senthil and Priya agreed: "Here we can be more free and work is less strict. In the larger companies, where we used to work and where they have 500 machines, they had cameras watching us, and no music was allowed ... Here the music is always on!" This smaller unit only produces garments for the domestic market, so the wages are somewhat lower than what one can earn in a Tiruppur export firm. Priya pondered the advantages and disadvantages of employment at the village-based company:

> We don't have ESI [insurance] or PF [Provident Fund] here, but we can go home to eat lunch, and cook and do any other household chores. Here we don't do export quality, so they are a little more forgiving. In Tiruppur, we all worked in export companies, where the work has to be done very carefully. The salary is a bit less here than in Tiruppur ... [but] we've got certain benefits. If I urgently need some money our employer will lend it. That is also an advantage. And the company owner trusts us to work well.

Clearly, although Priya has the skills to do better paid work, skill hardly shapes her employment history or current options. Flexibility in working hours, proximity to home, a less alienating work environment, and the ability to borrow made her opt for a checking job in the village rather than a tailoring job in the city. This downward job mobility is quite common among women garment workers, especially when they have taken time off work—often over several years—to fulfill child rearing and other caring duties, and when social expectations of domesticity and respectability prevent them from taking up the most rewarding employment in the city.

But not all women's employment histories follow the same pathway. Gayathri, a 43-year-old woman belonging to a middle-ranking caste who also lives in Allapuram, commutes to Tiruppur to work as a tailor in a large export company. She has two children, both in their early twenties. When we first met her in 2008 she was living in an unhappy marriage with her second husband. An often violent alcoholic, he could not be relied on to support the family. His departure sometime in 2013 brought peace to the household. As his support for the family decreased over the years, so Gayathri's efforts to earn increased: in 2008 she did checking and trimming work in a Tiruppur company, in 2011 she worked as a helper in a large export firm, and by 2014 she was working as a skilled tailor. Gayathri has always worked for fixed shift rates, and uses the company van to travel back and forth to the factory.

At times like the period following the global economic downturn, business was slow, which meant company workers were only asked to work a single shift per day. In many ways this suited Gayathri, as she used to worry a great deal about her children being home alone—or with her drunken husband. But they got older, and once her husband left, childcare became less of a concern for her. By 2014 Gayathri was working as a tailor, regularly doing a shift and a half per day and returning home by 9 p.m. Gayathri is hardworking and often supplements her factory wages with other jobs, such as the sale of saris in the village. Having had the primary responsibility for her household, she has made huge efforts over the years to educate her children: her daughter has a bachelor's degree in education and now works in the HR department of a Tiruppur company; her son completed a BSc in computer applications and is currently studying for a master's degree. Not only did Gayathri manage to secure higher education for her children, she also invested in improving and expanding her house, which is in her own name. Gayathri's job trajectory was not determined by her skills or lack thereof, but by the vagaries of her domestic life and the requirements of her household. Unlike other women, Gayathri was able to continue work throughout most of her married life and to keep developing her skill set. Having managed to separate from a troublesome husband and reached a stage in her life where she had a degree of independence and freedom, she was finally able to take up the more time-intensive but financially more rewarding job of tailor.

As these life stories reveal for men and women alike, gender and stage in life course are key to the ability to acquire skills, access jobs, and enjoy more rewarding, better paid employment over time. For women, much is determined by domestic responsibilities, intra-household gender inequalities, and the flexibility demanded by employers. But flexibility usually comes at a cost. Very often, women's need for flexible employment also entails a shift from export to domestic garment work, from factory work to home-based work, or from larger companies to smaller and more local workshops. The women make these choices, but their agency clearly cannot simply be read as empowerment: for men, flexibility is associated with higher pay, longer working days, and higher status jobs, whereas for women it often entails low pay, part-time work, and a slide down the skill and job hierarchy (see also Prentice in this volume; Carswell and De Neve 2013).

Let us now turn to our second village, Mannapalayam, located 18 km southwest of Tiruppur, where we found that many low-caste men and women, and especially Dalits, were largely excluded from the Tiruppur garment sector. Here, relations of caste and dependency shape men and women's engagement with skills and paid employment in a particular way. In Mannapalayam, a rural power loom industry has mushroomed since the 1970s. Power loom owners rely heavily on the labor of local villagers (many of whom are Dalit) and long-distance migrants, so a central recruitment strategy is the payment of cash advances, through which they "tie" workers to their looms. Because of these cash advances, many power loom workers are now heavily indebted to their employers and unable to leave the village for work in Tiruppur, a process described in detail elsewhere (Carswell and De Neve 2013; Carswell 2013). Such debts, rather than a lack of skill, keep the men and women of this village from taking up urban garment work. On top of that, Dalit power loom workers suffer from continued caste discrimination, manifested in, for example, continued refusal to share water and allow temple access (Carswell and De Neve 2014).

Whereas Dalit men and women in their thirties and older tend to be stuck in power loom work, tied as they are to the industry through a form of bonded labor, unmarried Dalit men in their late teens and early twenties actively avoid entering power loom work. A growing number of them have started commuting to Tiruppur to take up garment work. Even though most young Dalit men start as helpers, they are strongly attracted by the promise of higher wages, long-term career options, and above all the absence of caste discrimination and the lure of freedom. As unmarried men, they can afford to spend long days away from the village and catch buses to travel back and forth. Several of them have studied beyond primary school. Seventeen-year-old Prabhu, for example, left for Tiruppur on completing tenth class (aged around 16 years) to start as a helper in a garment factory. "I was very interested in learning it," he explains: "I was never interested in power loom work, so I never did it." Working in Tiruppur, he managed to learn tailoring in four months. Once he felt confident, he left for nearby Palladam, where he started as a tailor in a domestic firm. When we interviewed him in January 2009, he had been working there for only a month but was already planning to move on to an export company in Tiruppur. "There I will be able to earn more and get a larger bonus, but I first have to improve my speed and learn how to repair the machines." Although Prabhu admitted that his current earnings were not much higher than what his friends earned at the power looms, he was confident that as a tailor in an export company, he would make double the daily wage of a power loom worker. For Prabhu, acquiring the necessary skills was only a matter of time, and he was confident that he would do well. Unfortunately, Prabhu's story remains the exception rather than the rule: the majority of his fellow villagers are power loom workers who have debts they cannot repay that keep them tied to the village power loom employers.

Two happenings in 2008 facilitated some young men's entry into the urban garment industry. For most men these events did not enable a permanent shift out of power loom work, but they nevertheless gave them a taste of garment work and of possibilities beyond the village. First, an industry-wide strike among cloth manufacturers brought all power looms in the region to a halt in August 2008. For several weeks no looms ran in the village, and power loom operators were free to try their luck in the city. A few garment companies took the opportunity to recruit new workers from the region. At the time of the strike, about eighty men from the Dalit colony started going to Tiruppur to work in garments. Second, around the same time a government textile training institute began to recruit the village's young men and women for a one-month training course. More than ten men participated in the free training scheme and subsequently got placements in garment companies. Unfortunately, this was only a temporary shift for most of them; the majority were back at the power looms when the strike folded a few weeks later.

While Gounder employers could not keep their Dalit workforce from going to Tiruppur at the time of the strike, once it was over they immediately summoned them back to the looms. Men with debts exceeding 20,000 rupees had no choice other than to return to the power looms. However, some workers with smaller debts managed to repay their village employer and continue garment work in the city. Murthy, aged nineteen, is one. After completing 8th standard, he worked for two years in the power looms; then, at the time of the strike, he joined a garment company. After four months working as a helper, he shifted to another company where he was promoted to tailor. Murthy realizes that he was lucky to be able to buy himself out of debt. He had managed to settle the debt, totaling only 5,000 rupees, with a loan obtained through a newly started self-help group set up by young Dalit men.

The second factor pulling many men back to the village was the low pay that workers in the garment sector received initially. Although the training provided them with basic tailoring skills, most men were insufficiently skilled to be employed as tailors, so most of them remained helpers. Men in their late teens could accept this as a temporary step down before becoming tailors later on, but men in their twenties and thirties could neither afford to live on the pay of a helper nor, more importantly, tolerate the humiliation of having to assist tailors half their age. This was nonetheless the track followed in 2008 by Shiva, a 26-year old Dalit who had worked at power looms since 1996. When power loom owners went on strike in August 2008 and let their workers find employment elsewhere, he was able to leave for Tiruppur, where he worked as a helper for nearly four months. His parents encouraged him, as they considered garment work to be of higher status: "garment work is cleaner, there is no oil and dirt and dust, and one can wear trousers [rather than *lungis*]." They allowed him to use his sister's jewels as collateral for a 20,000-rupee loan and use the money to repay his outstanding advance. This enabled him to continue in Tiruppur after the strike ended. By Diwali in autumn 2008, he had taken the free government training course in tailoring and subsequently been hired as a company tailor. But being inexperienced and slow, he made too many mistakes and lost his job, which left him no choice but to start again, as a helper. He found this difficult, as not only was his pay cut, but he also felt too old to assist younger tailors. When we met Shiva in early 2009, he was back in Mannapalayam's power looms. Despite wanting to avoid accepting a new advance, he feared he would have to ask his power loom employer for money again, as he still had to repay the bank to get his sister's jewels back.

Young Dalit men—and women—aspire to a working life outside the village and away from the much dreaded power looms. To date, though, few have managed to materialize their dreams and free themselves from the clutches of their Gounder employers. Nevertheless, the recent success of some young Dalit men in Tiruppur is significant. Their confidence that success in the urban economy is possible inspires others to steer away from power loom work and from accepting ever larger cash advances. It creates awareness that urban employment can be a source of livelihood and independence. By 2014, we were surprised to see an increasing number of young Dalit women too among the urban commuters. On completing the tenth or twelfth class (aged 16 or 18), ever more young women started commuting to work as helpers in Tiruppur garment companies. Compared to their male counterparts, they appear less bothered by starting at low wages and as helpers, and likelier to enjoy their time away from the village. Whether they will be able to translate their newly gained access to new skills and jobs into lasting and rewarding employment trajectories remains to be seen.

Considering the Value of Skill

Are skilled workers better paid, likely to earn more, and thus able to fulfill aspirations for mobility? A first observation is that skills yield remarkably little value in the market. As of April 2015, the official minimum daily wage rate for cutters, the most skilled garment workers, was 305 rupees per day in Tamil Nadu. For the unskilled helper or the factory sweeper at the bottom of the pay hierarchy, it was 285 rupees per day—a paltry difference. For the skilled tailor, ranking in-between, the daily minimum wage amounted to 299 rupees per day. The actual rates tailors and helpers earned in 2014 closely matched these rates, though tailors often made more on a monthly basis due to overtime or piece rates. At least as revealing is the fact that the minimum daily wage rate for management stood at 312 rupees per day or 8,101 rupees per month, again only a few rupees up from what a cutter or skilled tailor could make in a day. Even so, management entry levels in Tiruppur require at least some post-secondary education, if not a college degree. Clearly, skill and education are relatively poorly rewarded in Tamil Nadu's private-sector textile industry.

So what value do garment skills hold, then, for those involved in the industry—employers as well as workers? Put differently, why does anyone seek to acquire new or better skills, given the relatively limited reward they fetch in the market? Part of the answer lies in the labor supply. The market value of skill is easily suppressed because of the considerable influx of migrant labor from across the subcontinent and the relative ease of acquiring skills, something employers are obviously very aware of. The employment of large female and migrant workforces is part of this strategy of keeping production costs down. But the story of labor supply is itself highly mixed and explicitly gendered. As discussed, male garment workers can avail themselves of the flexibility, social networks, and transport needed to move around, work for different contractors and companies, and demand attractive piece rates, and hence can earn well above what a similarly skilled woman tailor on a regular company payroll can make.

But there is more to it than supply and demand. Gender, caste, and age shape not only access to skills but also the *price* that particular skills command in the market and the *value* people attach to them. For Dalits, for example, escape from the domination of oppressive rural elites is worth a great deal, so they are keen to acquire skills that facilitate urban employment and new identities away from the village. Given the persistence of bonded labor relations in the power loom workshops of the village, young Dalit men and women are particularly keen to acquire the skills necessary to escape debt bondage, even if this may mean initially earning less than they would in the village looms. To them, more than representing a mere salary, garment skills epitomize a much longed-for world of autonomy and dignity away from oppression by the dominant village caste. The value they place on skill can only be grasped through their struggles to escape the ties that bind them to the village and to higher caste employers, as illustrated in the story of Shiva above.

But the value of skill and individuals' keenness to acquire skills must also be understood as part of appropriate masculine identities and occupations that are in turn informed by the life course. As long as they are young, men are happy to assist skilled tailors as helpers, but as they age they hesitate to keep working as a helper. Assisting tailors younger than themselves inverts sensitive age-and work-related hierarchies on the shop floor. Tailors boss their helpers around, ordering them to fetch piles of cloth, get better scissors, or clean the tables. Helpers, for their part, struggle to take such orders from tailors younger than themselves when work-related status hierarchies defy age-related expectations of exchange and respect. Moreover, given that helpers, trimmers, and checkers are very much perceived as female roles or as roles that a man should take on only as part of his training, young men feel a considerable degree of pressure to move on to tailoring or other skilled jobs as soon as they can. Long-term association with female tasks should be avoided, not least because it can quickly tarnish masculine identities and reputations. From another angle, as Cross (2011: 128) put it with reference to male workers' engagement with technology and skill on a diamond-cutting shop floor, "relationships with technology on the factory floor also created new arenas in which men could achieve alternative forms of masculine success, recognition and personal authentication." The pursuit of appropriate age-related and masculine identities, together with a good deal of peer pressure and ridicule, incentivizes men to acquire skills and engage with technology as soon as they can, irrespective of what monetary value such skills or technical knowledge might yield on the shop floor. For women, as we have seen, movements through the life course and societal preoccupations with appropriate female employment affect their relationship with skills in different ways. Like men, many women may seek to gain new skills, yet this does not necessarily translate into access to better job opportunities or higher rewards in the job market, let alone more valued feminine identities.

Work-based hierarchies also shape masculine identities *outside* the factory. Men in their mid-twenties and older quickly lose the respect of peers and family, and risk serious damage to their marital prospects, if they do not demonstrate an ability to "move up" in the local labor hierarchy and display entrepreneurial qualities—especially in an economic environment where individual enterprise and success are much valued. General aspirations to masculine status and upward mobility in the job market interact with the prospect of the material gains to be made from climbing up the labor hierarchy. Skills are known to be necessary—even if never sufficient—to upward social and economic mobility. Male garment workers are well aware that an aspiration to become a labor contractor or start up one's own production unit cannot be fulfilled without the necessary skills and know-how. To start as a labor contractor, one has to be well versed in all aspects of tailoring and cutting, and setting up one's own production unit requires knowledge of the entire production process. But even at a lower level, ordinary tailors or cutters' ability to command attractive wages or piece rates and to guarantee fairly steady workflows depends on their capacity to combine quality and speed, and master skills and technology. Skills, therefore, play a vital role in imaginings of entrepreneurial futures and upward mobility, and the acquisition of skills acts as a motivating force in young men's pursuits of a better future. In these pursuits, masculine identity, age-related expectations, and social aspirations inform the value of skill well beyond what the going market rates reflect.

To appreciate the limited value of education, consider the relatively small pay gap between management and skilled tailors. Supervisors are the lowest rung of management but earn well below what tailors make in a month. With good piece rates and a continuous flow of work, tailors can easily make 15,000 rupees per month, whereas a supervisor with a college degree might be paid a mere 8,000–10,000 rupees. On one level, a supervisor is much less central to the production process than a tailor, whose work can result in the rejection of an order or a successful repeat order. Granted, supervisors are central to a smooth production process, but it is nevertheless clear who rules the production line. Tailors and their contractors are well aware of their sway on the shop floor and do not hide the limited value they—like the company owners—attach to supervisors. Supervisors know their limitations too and realize that any *faux pas* can turn them into an instant topic of ridicule and humiliation on the shop floor. Though the supervisor is supposed to be the one keeping the production speed going and checking on quality, in fact he is often hurrying about at tailors and contractors' behest to get cut cloth ready for stitching, buy more thread, or get a machine repaired. Supervisors swiftly follow the contractors' instructions and rush around to meet their demands. Regardless of their greater education and regular monthly salary, their in-between position on the shop floor is hardly to be envied, and their lack of career mobility leads many of them to move from factory to factory, and often out of the industry altogether. The market value of education thus appears even more restricted than the value of skill. For those unable to enter at a much higher managerial level, the lower rungs of management are anything but privileged.

Conclusion: From Precarious Employment to Tropes of Entrepreneurship

Precarious employment in the Tiruppur labor market is not simply a matter of lack of skills, nor is it likely to be alleviated merely by enhancing skills training. Men and women's engagement with garment skills, their access to industrial employment, and their ability to build secure livelihoods in the Tiruppur region are outcomes of a complex political economy of caste, gender, and power inequalities. This political economy cannot be reduced to a technical matter of skills shortage or skills mismatch resolvable through practical training.

By examining the ways in which people in the Tiruppur region acquire garment skills and engage with garment work, we sought to critique depoliticized understandings of skill that assume a linear causality between skills training and access to rewarding, dignified, secure employment. Instead we make three points. First, in the Tiruppur region as in many other parts of

India, trade liberalization and global integration have brought an impressive rise in industrial job opportunities, but not parallel growth in secure, regular, or formal employment. The rapidly spreading use of labor contractors and piece-rate payments is key to the continued reproduction of informality, precarity, and self-exploitation on the shop floor. Nevertheless, for many men and women—and not least for Dalits—in Tiruppur's hinterland, garment work is highly attractive. It offers an exit route from physically taxing agricultural labor, from bonded relationships at rural power looms, and from dependency on high-caste landlords and employers. Tiruppur's strong appeal is due less to its offer of regular and secure employment than to the promise it holds for freedom and potentially higher rewards, driven by a widespread male aspiration to independent enterprise. Many a tailor aspires to establish his own production unit, anticipating upward mobility through independent enterprise.

Second, such localized aspirations to self-employment or micro-enterprise are further kindled by a public discourse that emphasizes the importance of skills to entrepreneurial success. The 2015 government policy on skill differs from the previous policy in its pronounced emphasis on entrepreneurship. The main vision, as the policy now reads, is

> To create an ecosystem of empowerment by Skilling on a large Scale at Speed with high Standards and to promote a culture of innovation based entrepreneurship which can generate wealth and employment so as to ensure Sustainable livelihoods for all citizens in the country. (NPSDE 2015: 11)

And one of its main mission goals is to

> Catalyze an ecosystem wherein productive and innovative entrepreneurship germinates, sustains and grows leading to creation of a more dynamic entrepreneurial economy and more formal wage employment. (Ibid.)

Such a skills discourse dovetails with neoliberal discourses that promote entrepreneurship and micro-enterprise as the basis of individual success and mobility (Prentice in this volume). By kindling aspirations of upward mobility through individual enterprise, be it as contractors or small-time producers, the contemporary state-led promotion of skill development *intensifies* a discursive emphasis on individual initiative and achievement by putting ever greater pressures on men (and women) to "make it" in the new economy by investing in new skills and the development of enterprising selves (Gooptu 2013; McGuire 2013).

However, and this is our third point, such discourses of skill and entrepreneurial success obscure a complex, localized political economy of inequality that shapes not only individuals' engagements with skills but also the extent to which different groups of workers are able to benefit from skills training and translate skills into secure employment or successful entrepreneurship. We have shown how gendered domestic responsibilities, notions of respectability, and requirements for flexibility routinely limit women's industrial work opportunities whether they have the skills or not, and often even lead to downward rather than upward mobility. Similarly, bonded labor relations keep substantial sections of the rural population disconnected from the urban garment industry as indebtedness continues to tie men and women to village employers. Meanwhile, age-related concerns about status and masculinity drive men to endlessly pursue often risky and unpredictable entrepreneurial ventures (De Neve 2014b). To succeed in any such venture, however, working women have to navigate the needs and demands of husbands and family members, whereas enterprising men can rely extensively on caste, kin, and friendship networks to succeed as labor contractors or keep afloat as small-scale manufacturers. Against the widespread neoliberal rhetoric of individuality, self-reliance, and independent enterprise, our informants reveal themselves as quintessentially non-neoliberal subjects whose lives continue to be shaped by family relations and domestic responsibilities, and whose entrepreneurial success is as likely to rely on the support of kin, caste, and friendship networks as on individual skill, ability, or drive.

All of this is not to say that skills are irrelevant to the futures of millions of young Indians today. Young women in Allapuram, like Gayathri, praise garment jobs and work hard to acquire the skills needed to obtain job mobility. Young Dalit men in Mannapalayam are similarly desperate to gain the skills needed to escape bonded labor relations at rural power looms and access caste-independent employment in the city. And successful tailors aspiring to become contractors or start up on their own make every effort to master the overall production process. But all these endeavors and their outcomes remain highly mediated by social relationships and inequalities, as well as by the vagaries of a post-liberalization private industrial sector. The current concern with skills conceals these processes and ideologies, even though they continue to dictate the limits of what skills enhancement can achieve in twenty-first–century India.

Acknowledgments

Most of the research for this chapter was funded by an ESRC-DFID Research Award (RES 167 25 0296). The chapter is based on twelve months of field research in Tamil Nadu conducted between August 2008 and July 2009, as well as further research conducted in 2011 and 2014. The research would not have been possible without the support of our research assistants—most especially Gayathri, Adele, and Ponnarasu. We thank Chris Hann, Jens Lerche, Jonathan Parry, and Rebecca Prentice for valuable feedback on earlier drafts.

Grace Carswell is Reader in Geography at the University of Sussex. She has carried out extensive field research in Tamil Nadu, India, and published on Dalits, inequality, and labour markets. Her work has appeared in many professional journals, including *Transactions of the Institute of British Geographers, Antipode, Development and Change, Geoforum,* and *Journal of Agrarian Change.* Carswell has also undertaken research on agrarian change in eastern Africa and is the author of *Cultivating Success in Uganda: Kigezi Farmers and Colonial Policies* (2007).

Geert De Neve is Professor of Social Anthropology and South Asian Studies at the University of Sussex. He is author of *The Everyday Politics of Labour: Working Lives in India's Informal Economy* (2005), as well as numerous articles on labor and ethical governance in India's garment sector in journals such as *Economy and Society, Modern Asian Studies,* and *Ethnography.* De Neve is also co-editor of *Hidden Hands in the Market: Ethnographies of Fair Trade, Ethical Consumption, and Corporate Social Responsibility* (2008) and *Unmaking the Global Sweatshop: Health and Safety of the World's Garment Workers* (2017).

Notes

1. It was not until the late 1990s that a number of training institutions were set up in the region. In collaboration with the Tiruppur Exporters Association (TEA), the NIFT-TEA College of Knitwear Fashion was established in the late 1990s just outside the city. The college expanded its courses in the early 2000s and now offers a series of three-year BSc courses in fashion design, merchandising, and production management. The college primarily seeks to train post–secondary-school students who aim to either enter management-level jobs or set up their own production units. It does not offer entry-level vocational training for students with limited levels of schooling who need practical skills to enter the lower ranks of tailors and cutters in the industry. Similarly, in 2007, the Indian Institute of Textile Training was set up in Tiruppur "to impart professional training to students and potential employment seekers for the fashion and apparel industry as well as create a core group of people who are adequately trained to set up their own enterprises thus creating not only job seekers but also job providers" (Indian Institute of Textile Training 2015). Offering one-year diploma courses that primarily focus on merchandising, this institute too is aimed

at students who seek to enter the sector at the professional/managerial level, set up their own enterprises or expand their expertise to feed into already existing family businesses (Vijayabaskar and Jeyaranjan 2011: 147).
2. In a purposive sample, 300 workers were surveyed from across a variety of factories and workshops, including CMT units as well as ancillary units such as knitting and dyeing factories. The survey, conducted in 2008–9, collected basic household and demographic data on the garment workforce as well specific work-related information.
3. Gounders are erstwhile farmers and landowners, many of whom have moved into garment production since the 1960s and 1970s (Chari 2004).
4. NREGA refers to the National Rural Employment Guarantee Scheme, launched in 2006, under which each rural household is annually entitled to one hundred days of paid work on local public works.

References

Ashton, David, Francis Green, Donna James, and Johnny Sung. 1999. *Education and Training for Development in East Asia: The Political Economy of Skill Formation in East Asian Newly Industrializing Economies.* New York: Routledge.

Bair, Jennifer, and Marion Werner. 2011. "Commodity Chains and the Uneven Geographies of Global Capitalism: A Disarticulations Perspective." *Environment and Planning A* 43(5): 988–997.

Breman, Jan. 2004. *The Making and Unmaking of an Industrial Working Class: Sliding Down the Labour Hierarchy in Ahmedabad, India.* New Delhi: Oxford University Press.

———. 2012. *Outcast Labour in Asia: Circulation and Informalization of the Workforce at the Bottom of the Economy.* New Delhi: Oxford University Press.

Carswell, Grace. 2013. "Dalits and Local Labour Markets in Rural India: Experiences from the Tiruppur Textile Region in Tamil Nadu." *Transactions of the Institute of British Geographers* 38(2): 325–338.

———. 2016 "Struggles over Work Take Place at Home: Women's Decisions, Choices and Constraints in the Tiruppur Textile Industry." *Geoforum*, 77: 134–145.

Carswell, Grace, and Geert De Neve. 2013. "From Field to Factory: Tracing Bonded Labour in the Coimbatore Powerloom Industry, Tamil Nadu." *Economy and Society* 42(3): 430–453.

———. 2014. "T-shirts and Tumblers: Caste, Dependency and Work Under Neoliberalisation in South India." *Contributions to Indian Sociology* 48(1): 103–131.

Chari, Sharad. 2004. *Fraternal Capital: Peasant-Workers, Self-Made Men, and Globalization in Provincial India.* New Delhi: Orient Blackswan.

Comyn, Peter. 2014. "Linking Employment Services, Skills Development & Labor Market Needs: Issues for India." *Indian Journal of Industrial Relations* 49(3): 378–388.

Corbridge, Stuart, John Harriss, and Craig Jeffrey. 2013. *India Today: Economy, Politics and Society.* Cambridge: Polity Press.

Cross, Jamie. 2010. Neoliberalism as Unexceptional: Economic Zones and the Everyday Precariousness of Working Life in South India. *Critique of Anthropology* 30(4): 355–373.

———. 2011. "Technological Intimacy: Re-Engaging with Gender and Technology in the Global Factory." *Ethnography* 13(2): 119–143.

De Neve, Geert. 2005. *The Everyday Politics of Labour: Working Lives in India's Informal Economy*. New Delhi: Social Science Press and New York: Berghahn Books.

———. 2014a. "Fordism, Flexible Specialization and CSR: How Indian Garment Workers Critique Neoliberal Labour Regimes." *Ethnography* 15(2): 184–207.

———. 2014b. "Entrapped Entrepreneurship: Labour Contractors in the South Indian Garment Industry." *Modern Asian Studies* 48(5): 1302–1333.

Gooptu, Nandini. 2009. "Neoliberal Subjectivity, Enterprise Culture and New Workplaces: Organised Retail and Shopping Malls in India." *Economic and Political Weekly* 44(22): 45–54.

———. 2013. "Servile Sentinels of the City: Private Security Guards, Organised Informality, and Labour in Interactive Services in Globalized India." *International Review of Social History* 58: 9–38.

Harriss, John. 2009. "Bringing Politics Back into Poverty Analysis: Why Understanding of Social Relations Matters More for Policy on Chronic Poverty than Measurement." In *Poverty Dynamics: Interdisciplinary Perspective*, ed. Tony Addison, David Hulme, and Ravi Kanbur, 205–224. Oxford and New York: Oxford University Press.

Harriss-White, Barbara. 2002 *India Working: Essays on Society and Economy*. Cambridge: Cambridge University Press.

Indian Institute of Textile Training. 2015. Retrieved 14 December 2015 from http://www.iittindia.in/.

McGuire, Meredith Lindsay. 2013. "The Embodiment of Professionalism: Personality-Development Programmes in New Delhi." In *Enterprise Culture in Neoliberal India: Studies in Youth, Class, Work and Media*, ed. Nandini Gooptu, 109–123. Abingdon: Routledge.

Mezzadri, Alessandra. 2008. "The Rise of Neo-liberal Globalisation and the 'New Old' Social Regulation of Labour: The Case of Delhi Garment Sector." *The Indian Journal of Labour Economics* 51(4): 603–618.

———. 2012. "Reflections on Globalisation and Labour Standards in the Indian Garment Industry: Codes of Conduct Versus 'Codes of Practice' Imposed by the Firm." *Global Labour Journal* 3(1): 40–62.

Ministry of Skill Development and Entrepreneurship. 2015. *National Policy on Skills Development and Entrepreneurship* (NPSDE). Retrieved 14 December 2015 from http://skilldevelopment.gov.in/assets/images/Skill%20India/policy%20booklet-%20Final.pdf.

Mohsini, Mira. 2010. "Becoming an 'Asli Karigar': The Production of Authenticity Among Old Delhi's Muslim Artisans." Ph.D. dissertation. London: University of London, School of Oriental and African Studies.

Nambiar, Divya. 2013. "Creating Enterprising Subjects through Skill Development: The Network State, Network Enterprises, and Youth Aspirations in India." In *Enterprise Culture in Neoliberal India: Studies in Youth, Class, Work and Media*, ed. Nandini Gooptu, 57–72. Abingdon: Routledge.

National Skills Development Policy (NSPD). 2009. Retrieved 14 December 2015 from http://skilldevelopment.gov.in/assets/images/NationalSkillDevelopment PolicyMar09.pdf.

Palmer, Robert, Roland Akabzaa, Shehryar Janjua, Kenneth King, and Claire Noronha. 2012. "Skills, Lives and Livelihoods." In *Education Outcomes and Poverty in the South: A Reassessment*, ed. Chris Colclough, 74–93. Abingdon: Routledge.

Parry, Jonathan P. 2013. "Company and Contract Labour in a Central Indian Steel Town." *Economy and Society* 42(3): 348–374.

Phillips, Nicola. 2011. "Informality, Global Production Networks and the Dynamics of 'Adverse Incorporation.'" *Global Networks* 11(3): 380–397.

Prentice, Rebecca. 2008. "Knowledge, Skill, and the Inculcation of the Anthropologist: Reflections on Learning to Sew in the Field." *Anthropology of Work Review* 29(3): 54–61.

———. 2012. "'No One Ever Showed Me Nothing': Skill and Self-Making among Trinidadian Garment Workers." *Anthropology & Education Quarterly* 43(4): 400–414.

Roman, Camilla. 2008. "Learning and Innovation in Clusters: Case Studies from the Indian Silk Industry." Unpublished D.Phil. thesis. Department of International Development, University of Oxford.

Sanchez, Andrew. 2012a. "Deadwood and Paternalism: Rationalising Casual Labour in an Indian Company Town." *Journal of the Royal Anthropological Institute* 18(4): 808–827.

———. 2012b. "Questioning Success: Dispossession and the Criminal Entrepreneur in Urban India." *Critique of Anthropology* 32(4): 435–457.

Strümpell, Christian. 2014a. "The Politics of Dispossession in an Odishan Steel Town." *Contributions to Indian Sociology* (n.s.) 48(1): 45–72.

———. 2014b. "The Making and Unmaking of an Adivasi Working Class in Western Orissa." In *Savage Attack: Adivasi Insurgency in India*, ed. Alpa Shah and Cripsin Bates, 200–227. New Delhi: Social Science Press.

Venkatesan, Soumhya. 2010. "Learning to Weave; Weaving to Learn…What?" *Journal of the Royal Anthropological Institute* 16: 158–175.

Vijayabaskar, Manimegalai, and J. Jeyaranjan. 2011. "The Institutional Milieu of Skill Formation: A Comparative Study of Two Textile Regions in India and China." In *Industrial Dynamics in China and India: Firms, Clusters, and Different Growth Paths*, ed. Mokiri Ohara, Manimegalai Vijayabaskar, and Lin Hong, 135–154. New York: Palgrave McMillan.

Wilkinson-Weber, Clare. 1999. *Embroidering Lives: Women's Work and Skill in the Lucknow Embroidery Industry*. New York: State University of New York Press.

14

▼ From Casual to Permanent Work

Maoist Unionists and the Regularization of Contract Labor in the Industries of Western Nepal

MICHAEL PETER HOFFMANN

Introduction

In its 2012 report "From Precarious Work to Decent Work," the International Labour Organization (ILO) described the spread of precarious, insecure, and temporary work around the globe as the outcome of "a worldwide corporate attack on the right to organize and bargain collectively" (ILO 2012: 3). According to its estimate, the number of workers employed in precarious conditions in OECD countries rose from 9.4 to 12 percent of the total workforce between 1985 and 2007 (ibid.: 30). For the organized (formal) manufacturing sector in India, the same report estimates a jump from 13 to 30 percent between 1993/94 and 2005/06 due to industrial employers' increasing reliance on contract labor. Yet there has been little examination of how the dynamics between permanent and temporary labor play out in industries in the manufacturing sector of Nepal, a country that witnessed a Maoist insurgency between 1996 and 2006, followed by a highly volatile post-conflict period.

My research in the western lowland region of Nepal (see also Hoffmann 2014a, 2015, 2017) focused on the relationship between permanent and contract labor in the post-conflict context. I concentrated on industries in and around the urban municipality Nepalgunj in Banke district. While the town is famous for its large Muslim population, almost all workers in the nearby factories are Hindus who largely constitute three different groups: Indians predominantly from the Indian states of Bihar and Uttar Pradesh, flatland dwellers (*Madheshis*) from Banke district, and indigenous workers from the Tharu ethnic group in the mid and far western lowland regions of Nepal. In this context I encountered a story slightly different from the common narrative of the global precariatization of labor (Ferguson 1999; Joshi 2003; Breman 2004, Mollona 2009) in an era of "accumulation by dispossession" (Harvey 2003): in this Nepalese context over the past few years, labor in the food-processing industry has become more rather than less secure for the *Madheshi* segment of the workforce. For this ethnic group, moreover, a minimum wage has been implemented, and in contrast with the situation common elsewhere in the region, workers are now represented by leaders from their own social stratum. I argue that these changes in the situation of labor are an outcome of the Maoist revolution and the pressure that the company's Maoist union has been able to put on management—in short, a consequence of the wider political context. But, as I further argue, these results of Maoist activism have also protected workers from the intensification of labor that neoliberal conditions have promoted elsewhere (Millar 2015).

I do not claim that the Maoists have by any means solved all the problems in the factory. In fact, their union is entrenching new ethnic cleavages in the workplace. Nor do I claim that the greater labor security that I describe extends to all of western lowland of Nepal, far less to Nepal as a whole. At other factories near my field site, labor has been casualized rather than regularized, and minimum wages are still not paid. This was, for example, the case in some of the nearby factories where the Unified Communist Party of Nepal Maoist (UCPN) Union has not yet been able to organize. Where it has been able to organize, however, the situation resembles the one I describe.

The local categories that distinguish between permanent and precarious labor are important. The Nepali word *isthai* (permanent) signifies a long-term contract with a fixed, regular income. It is more or less synonymous with the Indian concept of *naukri*, and some of the Indian workers employed in the factory use this term to refer to their permanent jobs. As in India (Parry 2014: 349), *sarkari isthai* (a government job) is considered best. It is well paid, provides opportunities for additional earnings from *ghus* (bribes), and is also thought to be fairly relaxed in terms of the labor process. According to a common popular Nepalese saying, "when the king's work finishes there's still sun" (*raja ko kam kahile jaala ghaam*)—that is, you can always get off early. According to another, at such a job "hurry never comes" (*kahile haatar na hune*).

But *sarkari isthai* is hard to get if one does not have "one's own people" (*aafno manche*) in the government, even though the Nepali government, in the interim constitution of 2006, introduced quotas for "backward communities and castes" that are still in effect today. They might be implemented in modern towns like Kathmandu and Pokhara, but in western Nepal the 45 percent quota for "backward" communities and castes has little effect: the situation is more like "80 percent reservation" for the upper castes. In this light, especially considering that Nepal's political economy depends heavily on "donor countries" such as Germany, the United States, and the United Kingdom, it is unsurprising that many consider working in a large international organization, or even for one of the bodies of the United Nations, the most desirable alternative. Such jobs are extremely well paid and sometimes involve foreign postings.

In contrast to *isthai* (permanent) work, "contract" work comprises a variety of categories. At the district level, the Nepalese state distinguishes between three types of contract work. *Asthai kam* and *karaar kam* are both forms of temporary work: *asthai* refers to temporary work for more than one year of employment; *karaar*, to work contracts of up to twelve months. *Dainik jaladari kam* is daily wage work.

I open my discussion with a brief description of the broad political context and an introduction to the factory I studied most intensively, and then go on to explain the role of labor law and the way the labor unions in the factory have pressed for its implementation. To get a better understanding of the type of labor relations that emerged from the conflict period, I then look at the broader structural effects of this emerging unionism. Next I examine everyday labor relations at the shop-floor level and the way in which the Maoist Revolution affected them. The concluding section draws out potential implications of these broader changes for labor in the region.

The Revolutionary Context: Maoist Insurgency and Post-conflict Politics in Banke

Nepal's Maoist insurgency began in 1996 after the Nepali Congress–led government of Nepal ignored a forty-point demand letter composed by the Communist Party of Nepal (Maoist). The insurgency's main aim was to eradicate the semi-feudal, semi-colonial character of the Nepali state and society. From their bases in the hilly districts of Rolpa and Rukkum, Maoist guerrilla fighters spread their insurgency throughout the entire country. As Shakya (2015) recently commented, "the Nepali Maoists targeted ethnic exploitation during their People's War between 1996 and 2006 and were the first to demand a new constitution." In the initial stages of the insurgency, this exploitation of ethnic grievances meant above all that members of the Kham Magar ethnic group in the hills entered the revolutionary movement as rank-and-file fighters (De Sales 2000). However, once the revolutionaries began to mobilize support in Banke district, their strategy became more complex: in Nepalgunj the Maoists targeted their propaganda efforts predominantly against activists aligned with Shiv Shena, a Hindu chauvinist party, in order to win support among the town's large Muslim community; meanwhile, Maoist guerrillas resorted to anti-Indian rhetoric to exploit sentiments of distrust toward the neighboring country. This anti-Indian rhetoric, as Kantha (2010: 161) has stressed, "had little resonance among Madheshis."

In November 2006 the government of Nepal and the Communist Party of Nepal (Maoist) signed a peace treaty. Thereafter, violence erupted anew in the Tarai region of southern Nepal as militant groups targeted both the state and the Maoists. This event, popularly referred to as the Madheshi Uprising, involved groups that polarized the citizenry by stirring up ethnic issues largely unaddressed during the insurgency period. These violent encounters had serious consequences for Nepalgunj, where intercommunal clashes broke out in December 2006. In 2007, three Madheshi groups created an alliance called the United Democratic Madheshi Front with the aim of transforming the lowland region of Nepal into a single, autonomous province of Madhesh (Miklian 2009: 2).

These developments led to radical changes in the political topography of the Tarai lowlands. After the Constituent Assembly elections in April 2008, the newly elected Maoist Movement found itself confronted by various political actors in the Madheshi movement that tried to exploit perceived anti-Madheshi sentiments for their own gain. In this expanding political matrix, Maoist-Madheshi relationships became complex, shifting over time at the central level (Kantha 2010). Yet in the lowland region of Banke, this altered political configuration also meant that Maoist cadres had to try to win the Madheshi electorate into their fold in anticipation of the much awaited second round of elections. These broader dynamics, as the following sections will demonstrate, had profound effects on the process of regularization of labor in the local industries.

The Factory and Its Workforce

Located in Banke district in the western lowlands of Nepal, the Agrawal Food Company is one of seventeen industrial food-processing industries managed by the L.K. Agrawal Group, one of Nepal's largest industrial families.[1] This factory was built in 1995 with the help of Indian technology and skilled labor on a greenfield site next to the highway that leads from Nepalgunj to Kohalpur. Owned by a Marwari[2] industrialist, the relatively modern, clean, orderly factory compound presents a contrast to the disorderly squalor outside it. The high-walled compound, covering around twenty acres, has five distinct factory units: a flour mill, a rice mill, a mill that produces and bottles edible oils, a new unit that extracts essential ingredients for the pharmaceutical industry from herbs, and a more general food-processing unit.[3] The combined workforce comprises around five hundred persons. Within the compound there are two large accommodation blocks—one for staff and one for workers—but some local staff and workers live in the town or in surrounding villages. In the workers' block, the men (nearly all the employees are male) live in dormitory-type accommodations, packed in like sardines with up to twenty workers per room.

Next to the factory compound, various other industries including a turpentine factory, a steel recycling unit, a cement factory, and a pharmaceutical factory together form a small "industrial corridor" stretching along the main road. Compared to Nepal's largest industrial area, located at Biratnagar in the Eastern Terai, it is small, but in the context of the Western Terai these factories represent the vanguard of the industrial revolution in the area. Economically, however, cross-border smuggling and labor migration to the Gulf States remain more significant than industrial development.

In the pioneer days, the company's vision was guided by paternalist values. It promised that local people would make up 50 per cent of its workforce, though that promise remained unfulfilled. At that time its workforce was overwhelmingly Indian. "Seventy-five percent Indian workers from Bihar, twenty-five percent workers from Nepal" is how one local villager estimated the proportions. Today these ratios have changed: Indian workers now work as supervisors and machine operators in the factory, while Nepalis have simpler jobs as machine helpers, packers, and cleaners. There are two principal sorts of Nepali workers: local Madheshis and Tharus, the latter overwhelmingly employed as *paledar*s (loaders) in the factory.

Two crucial cleavages divide the workforce. The first is that between the privileged Indian supervisors and machine operators (mostly from Bihar, Uttar Pradesh, and Rajasthan) and the less affluent local "sons of the soil" often employed solely as simple laborers, mainly machine helpers and packers.[4] Nationality matters, but so too does the distinction between Madheshi and Tharu. The salience of ethnicity is hardly surprising, given the current political climate outside the factory gates and the wider politics of ethnicity in the area. The Madheshi Uprising of 2006/07 changed the way local people think about themselves: whereas Madheshis were previously looked down on, the term has now become an assertive political identity (Miklian 2009).

Both skilled and unskilled laborers have *isthai* (permanent) work. However, the differences in pay, even amongst workers with comparable levels of skill, are huge. While an Indian machine operator often earns a middle-class income and sends his children to private schools back in Uttar Pradesh or Bihar, a Madheshi machine operator doing the same job might have difficulty making ends meet on barely the minimum wage. Also, skilled and unskilled workers eat separately. The supervisors and machine operators have a canteen that charges them for lunch (about 100 Nepalese rupees 0.87 euros), while ordinary workers (like packers) and daily-wage workers eat and drink under the bicycle stand.

Company workers receive a regular monthly salary and various extras such as holiday pay, access to a provident fund, and a uniform, raincoat, and sweater; they can also participate in the yearly company excursion (which in 2013 consisted of a two-day trip to Pokhara). But the contract labor that is also necessary is mostly undertaken by Tharus who work for piece rates on an irregular basis, carrying sacks of food weighing up to 100 kg on their heads from storage rooms to the transport trucks.

Determining the exact numbers of permanent, temporary, and daily-wage workers proved difficult. At different times, and depending on whom I asked, I got different answers. For example, data provided by factory management suggested a constant trend of regularization over the past five years, as a result of which nearly 80 percent of all workers had permanent jobs. This data, however, did not take into account the number of daily wage workers in the different factory units. Trade unionists judged the number of permanent workers to be much lower. The Department of Labour indicated that 47 out of 125 registered workers are permanent. My own data from a random survey suggest that this proportion is realistic and confirm the trend toward regularization.[5] This trend contradicts the grand narrative of greater global precarity (Standing 2011). In the next section, I highlight the role of the company's unions in bringing this situation about.

The Labor Law, the Unions, and Armed Police

The Nepali Labor Act of 1992 (as amended in 1997) states that the worker "shall be kept on probation period unless he/she completes the continuous service period of one year and, based on his/her efficiency, sincerity, discipline, diligence toward works, punctuality, etc. in this period he/she shall be appointed *permanently*" (my emphasis) (Nepali Labor Act 1997). But labor law is subject to different interpretations. It has "*do side*" (two sides), as "one hand gives, the other one takes." When Agrawal first opened its gates the law was not observed, and most workers had little idea of its provisions. All were working in the factory as *dainik jaladaris* (daily-wage workers) for risible wages—roughly 33 Nepali rupees (0.29 euros) per day. But things have changed over the past two decades, and the law is now interpreted in a more worker-friendly way. Wages have gone up, and workers have obtained permanent jobs and are represented by leaders who come from their own social strata. The company's union played a crucial role in this transformation.

The two unions that historically played a role in the factory were Nepali Trade Union Congress (NTUC) and Akhil Nepal.[6] NTUC is affiliated to Nepali Congress—Nepal's "democrats"—and Akhil Nepal to the UCPN (Maoist). Representatives of the General Federation of Nepalese Trade Unions (GEFONT), which is affiliated to Nepal's United Marxist Leninists, and of the Revolutionary Akhil Nepal, a unit formed by the more militant CPN Maoists, have never entered the company compound. Nepali Congress was historically the first union in the factory compound, while the Maoist union is regarded as the more radical union of the two.

Alarmed by the increasing conflict between the state and the Maoists, the Nepali Congress appeared on the shop floors of Agrawal around 1999/2000. According to some of the older workers, the formation of the Congress union within the factory followed a minor issue over the number of machine operators.

> Before, a machine operator had to look after just one machine, but later, according to the decision of the manager, a machine operator had to look after two. That was very difficult for a single operator. At that time the union leaders were visiting the area. We had a meeting with them and they said that they would raise their voices against management to get our demands heard. Then, we started to agitate against them in 2000. Our demand was to make one machine operator run just one machine. (Mohammed, Muslim machine operator)

The owner fulfilled their demands and pressured them to resume work. But the group of friends insisted that a union be formed, and began working again only after management accepted this condition. Management evidently viewed a Nepali Congress–led union not as a threat to the status quo but as a nonmilitant body of civil society body that was manageable at a time of armed conflict between state and Maoist guerrillas.

However, only two months later the newly established union agitated more radically, submitting to the factory a letter that demanded further changes: permanent positions for those who had worked in the factory for more than 240 days; services and facilities according to the law, such as a uniform, a bicycle parking area, a sleeping place, and a dining room, as well as a sweater for the cold season. These demands were by and large fulfilled, but the workers' appointment certificates were valid for only six months, and only 40 percent of workers got them.

The second wave of agitation followed soon afterward, as Mohammed remembered:

Later, in 2003 we again submitted a demand letter for the increase of salaries and overtime. Previously, the factory used to pay us overtime at the same rate as our normal hourly rate. But according to the labor law we should be paid 1.5 times our usual rate. Then we bought a book of labor law and we stopped being dependent on the leaders. We learnt many things from that book about labor law. Thus, later our demands were fulfilled and we started working according to the rules of the government and also started to get 1.5 times our usual rate for overtime work. We also started getting sweaters and raincoats after that. We also got the provision of a provident fund. The company opened a bank account for provident fund. It also gave us a sleeping room, and an arrangement for food as well. There was the problem of water and toilet. It was bad for our health because the workers of the factory used to defecate outside the company compound. There were toilets only for staff. We raised our voices and we got toilets constructed, which were beneficial for us as well as for the factory.

The Nepali Congress union lost its grip on the factory in 2010 after its leadership organized a strike demanding an increase in the annual bonus and protesting management's decision to remove a small pocket from their uniforms—the latter, a rather trivial issue, being used by the union leaders to demonstrate their power to management. The strike went on for days until, on the sixth day, management persuaded the union leader to give up the strike. Feeling betrayed, the other unionists telephoned the Maoist party, whose local members convinced the Congress unionists to collectively change sides and join the Maoist union. There followed a meeting between the members of the local Chambers of Commerce, the Maoist party, and management, after which the general manager agreed to fulfill the union's demands and the factory resumed its operations.

Since the union affiliated itself with the UCPN (Maoist), it has had to deal with two principal agents of the state security apparatus. First, throughout their demonstrations and protests, the Maoists had to fend off the local police, whom they regarded as a highly *bhrast* (corrupt) ally of the region's captains of industrial capital. In fact, several unionists claimed that the local industrialists used the local police as a protection racket. From 2012 onward, however, the police were basically quiescent in confronting the Maoist unionists. This was because parts of the nationwide armed police had been transformed into so-called "industrial flying squads" to protect industrial properties after armed groups carried out a series of kidnappings and murders of industrialists ("Agreement with Maoist Fighters" 2011). These new industrial flying squads replaced the local police in dealings with the unionists. From the Maoist union's perspective, the armed police were much less of a problem. They were held to be less corrupt, and although they had formerly fought the Maoists on behalf of the state, now they were transformed into worker-friendly agents that allowed the Maoist union to become an effective voice for the company's workforce.

Improvements in Labor Conditions

Three themes were crucial to the impact of Maoist activism on the factory: secure employment, guaranteed minimum wages, and a new form of union organization. The Agrawal workers frequently told me that working for the company was secure employment once you had a permanent position, and that Agrawal was a factory in which a temporary contract might realistically turn into a permanent one. Consider the following cases.

> K. Yadav is a Madheshi from a small village close to the factory. When he first started work at Agrawal in 2006, he was a daily-wage worker in the rice mill. In 2011, after the Maoist union pressured the company, he became permanent. He is now a member of the Maoist union.

> S. Magar, a local from a neighboring village, started in the Agrawal flour mill in December 2007. He worked only twenty days as a dailywage laborer before being assigned to the packing department, where he put stickers on bags for two years. In 2010 he obtained a temporary contract as a machine helper in the flour mill. After the Maoist union pressured the company in 2012, he was given a permanent contract . He is now also the unit head of the Maoist trade union for the flour mill.

> L. Magar, another local and an ethnic Magar from a neighboring village who is in his mid thirties, started working at Agrawal in 1999. He spent nine years as a daily-wage laborer, working as a cleaner in the rice mill unit. The management then decided to give him a temporary contract for two years, whereupon he was promoted to assistant machine operator and helped run five different machines in the factory unit. Two years later he became an *isthai* (permanent) worker doing the same job. He too is a member of the Maoist trade union and works for the union as a "unit head" representing the workers of his factory unit.

Common to all three employment histories is the Maoist union's involvement in the regularization of contract work: 62 of the most recent 77 cases of regularization occurred with the help of the Maoist union. The majority of these were of Madheshis. To get a permanent job, a temporary worker needs to cultivate his Maoist unionist contacts, and Madheshi ethnicity seems to be a key factor.[7]

Permanent workers can count on receiving their pay on time and are, as management complains, very difficult to fire. That is true even when a worker is caught up in serious misdemeanors, as one manager illustrated with the following story:

> There was one of our permanent oil mill workers who had tried to steal. He had put down a deposit for 10kg *dal* [pulses], but then went to the *dal* mill and took 20kg. He tried to take it through the gate but the security guard caught him and he was reported to management. He then was suspended for 7 days, but was then taken back.

The Maoist union did not organize the *paledars* (loaders), who were nearly all Tharus, and their jobs were notoriously insecure. For them, redundancy was a very real threat. A manager confirmed this, telling me that "in the past there were a few cases when loaders tried to demonstrate their strength. In each case we fired them, and in one case we even fired 70 loaders at once." In their world of chronic precarity, no one gets a second chance—not even the son of one of the contractors, who was working as loader in the factory when a security guard caught him bringing a flick-knife into the compound. He was immediately fired.

Meanwhile, wages in the factory have gone up, as shown by the example of L. Yadav, a foreman in the Saurabh Oil Mill who is from a village in the Indian state of Uttar Pradesh. He has a permanent contract (*isthai*) and earns 12,000 Indian rupees per month—three times what he earned when he began work twenty years back. This has allowed him to send his three children, who live back home in Uttar Pradesh, to private school. One of them now has a BSc in computer science. He rejected my claim that children of laborers will inevitably become laborers. His would have middle-class careers.

All company workers[8] in the factory are paid the current minimum wage of 8,000 Nepali rupees (70 euros) per month. Wages in the flour mill are shown in Table 14.1.

Table 14.1 Wage ranges for different groups of workers in the flour mill

Group	Nepali rupees	Euros
Supervisors	12,000-18,000 NR	€104–157
Machine Operators	12,000-18,000 NR	€104–157
Machine Helpers	9,200 NR	€80
Packers	9,200 NR	€80
Loaders	5,000-15,000 NR	€44–131

Apart from the loaders, the range is from 8,000 Nepali rupees (70 euros) to 18,000 rupees (157 euros), and the differences are largely dependent on skill. All are above the legal minimum, in marked contrast to what is commonly reported from other parts of South Asia (e.g., Breman 2004; Parry 2014). Remarkably, they were paid regardless of frequent power cuts that at times brought production to a halt. Workers had little to do during such enforced breaks, and management often complained about paying them for "just hanging around." But pay their wages it did, along with the fringe benefits to which permanent workers are entitled—largely because of the pressure exerted by the Maoist union. Since 2010, the principle that the union leaders should themselves be members of the workforce has been firmly established. Workers adamantly rejected the possibility that someone not employed at Agrawal could lead their union. The Maoist "in-charge" (leader) of the whole company, himself a skilled machine operator in one of its units, explained that:

> ...the laborers here are now very aware. They know about laws. They know that only a person who works in industry can understand the workers' problems. That's why only workers themselves can become union leaders. Bringing in an outsider is not possible now.

In the past, things were different—as they are in many Indian factories (Ramaswamy 1977, 1981; Parry 2009). Under the Nepali Congress Party, the Agrawal labor leader had been a Nepalganj banker without any experience of industrial work. Workers explained that in those days they themselves had been entirely ignorant of the labor laws and depended on an "educated" and literate outsider. Since the coming of the Maoist union, however, each factory unit is represented by a Maoist "union head." The entire workforce of the company was represented by the Maoist in-charge, a man with a Muslim religious background who was also the district's labor in-charge of the UCPN (Maoist).

The new Maoist leadership was not exempt from criticism. An Indian contractor told me that the Maobadi are actually "Khaobadi" (a local idiom used to express the idea that Maoists have become corrupt) or "Paisa Khane Manche" (another slang expression for corrupt people). K. Yadav, a machine operator in the oil mill who had recently joined the Maoists, complained that the Maoist in-charge did not hold enough meetings and, Yadav claimed, siphoned money out of the annual excursion fund. Others were dissatisfied that the Maoists had agreed that workers should pay income tax. Although such payments remained relatively marginal and usually added up to no more than 80 Nepali rupees per month, many viewed the tax as an unfair burden that the working classes should not have to shoulder.

The Maoized Workplace

So far I have argued that sweeping structural changes in the factory have been largely an outcome of Maoist union activism. I now consider changes in everyday working relations, with a focus on different types of work in the company's mills. I begin with a brief digression on issues of access to the factories. After an initial period in which the manager introduced me to the shop floors, I was able to move freely around the factory, observe the daily working routines, and interview workers and supervisors when they were free. Much of my time was spent on a survey that helped me introduce myself and get to know workers better. I became particularly familiar with the work routines in the flour and oil mills.

One of my most striking initial impressions on the shopfloors was that despite the Maoist unionists' everyday presence in the factories, and unlike the brick-kiln workers I studied in Kailali in the aftermath of the Maoist people's war (see Hoffmann 2014), none of the workers I engaged with used the well-known Maoist greeting *lal salam* (red salute). It became obvious that at this particular historical juncture of the post-conflict period (the brief period around the nation-wide Constitution Assembly elections in November 2013), political affiliations were less clear-cut and visible. Understanding the subtler changes in the industrial labor regimes required long-term anthropological fieldwork. I began to frequently visit different workplaces inside Agrawal's company compound.

It was soon apparent that perceptions of work varied considerably between units and according to the type of work done. Workers from different shops spoke about "poisonous" (*jahar*) and "dangerous" (khataranāka) types of work. Nobody liked the idea of standing long hours beside the big tank in the oil mill that filtered and purified the mustard oil and gave off pungent fumes that stung the eyes—like peeling onions all day. The job of the machine operator in that unit involves changing large filter bags through which the mustard oil was pumped. The operator worked eight-hour shifts without eye protection and often put in another four hours of overtime. Similarly, work in the company's herbal factory was considered extremely dangerous as it involved handling lethal chemicals. So too was working as a *paledar*: loaders had to be careful not to get hit by falling rice sacks when stacking them them in the company storage rooms.

While spending more time in the oil and flour mills, however, I also discovered that much of the work in them was fairly easy, relaxed, and boring. It was spoken of as *sajilo kam* (easy work), *aram kam* (relaxed work), or boring *kam* (workers used the English word). Take, for example, the flour mill, located in a building consisting of several sections. Entering

348 ◆ Michael Peter Hoffmann

through the northern gate, one found oneself in the huge hall of the packing department, where sacks of rice were stacked. At a table by the entrance, a supervisor from Bihar monitored the work process from 6:00 a.m. to 6:00 p.m.; another, from the Nepal hills, was the monitor from 6:00 p.m. to 6:00 a.m. There was no computer; instead everything was recorded in large red registers—one for workers' attendance, one for stock, and so forth. About twenty meters behind the supervisors' table, on a large metal construction, were two "vibro tanks" where the finished and processed flour was stored. Under the vibro tanks sat two groups of workers who worked in shifts from 8:00 a.m. to 4:00 p.m., 4:00 p.m. to 12:00 p.m., or 12:00 p.m. to 8:00 a.m. Usually I counted three workers in the left-hand packing group (one permanent, one temporary, and one daily-wage worker), and four packers on the right-hand side (one daily-wage worker and three temporary workers). As with the supervisors at the entrance gate, their work was barely mechanized at all. The left packing group needed three workers: one to fill the sack of flour, one to put the sack on a modern electronic scale and use a scoop to bring it to the correct weight of exactly 50 kg, and one to take the sack off the scale and place it with the other sacks across the hall. The working group on the right consisted of one filler, one worker using archaic scales to measure the weight, and two sealers (one with a small sealing machine, one with a hot-sealing machine that seals the plastic sacks).

These workers regarded their work as *sajilo* (easy), though also monotonous and boring. The working group on the left filled, sealed, and stacked about three hundred bags per hour. Filling, sealing, and stacking one bag every twelve seconds left little time between bags to sit and chat. The same was true for the other working group, though at times a jam in the pipes leading down from the vibro tank meant that workers had to move fast to remove enough flour from the tank to clear the jam.

By comparison with the work of the packers, the work of machine operators in the same mill was regarded as more *aram* (relaxed). This became apparent on several visits to the mill. For example, when I first visited the machine operators in the "rolling room" on the second floor of the mill, which was usually full of dust, I was brought there by the Indian foreman, Yogendra Yadav, who then left me with a Madheshi Yadav machine helper who gave me a tour of the different floors. His job was to clean the machines on the second floor, but he had ample time to show me around. I then conducted a two-hour group interview with four of the workers—all good mutual friends who hailed from Bihar. No one bothered about the time, and only occasionally did one or another machine operator leave to look after his machine. A power cut occurred, and all left to do maintenance work. It was easily done within two hours, after which there were another three hours off. Things were not much different on my next visit to the mill. I interviewed three helpers, with the three machine operators eagerly listening. They soon tired of my enquiries, however, and left, leaving only one Bihari helper to answer my questions. In fact, they all disappeared for the lunch break shortly before midday. When I came back around 1:00 p.m., the foreman on the first floor was nearly asleep, and the others were hanging around. I found the machine operators and helpers sitting together on sacks in the corner of the second floor. When asked how they would describe their work, they responded, "*aram kam.*" The rule, of course, was that no one could disappear from his work post, but the foreman rarely checked on tasks and often only shouted at the helpers to clean one of the machines, which got dusty quickly. He usually came past about once per hour to check how the work was going; otherwise, he left the workers alone.

Were these "relaxed" working environments simply related to the types of work that labor engaged with? No, according to both workers and management. Madheshi workers praised the Maoist union for pressuring management to continue to pay the factory's permanent workforce at times of frequent electricity cuts, when they could roam around the factory after the machines were cleaned. And management often complained to me in interviews that the Maoists' presence on the shop floors meant management had to keep paying salaries and had trouble imposing tighter work discipline on the workforce.

By hanging out at workplaces in the factory and at the Maoist union office in a nearby village, I further learned why management was challenged to adopt the intensification of labor that neoliberal conditions have promoted elsewhere. According to my informants, every month the Maoist union took up three or four cases of excessive admonishment with management. I was told of a packer whose Indian supervisor had berated him for for falling asleep in the packing room on the night shift. The next day, the packer complained to his unit's Maoist in-charge and the latter complained to management, who then advised the supervisor to refrain from verbal attacks on the workers. The fact that complaints are now possible empowers workers and inhibits supervisors from overstepping the mark. In short, the Maoist union also protects its members from speedups in production.

In any event, though, such Maoist support was extended to only a certain ethnic segment of the workforce. Undoubtedly, far greater time discipline was required of the Tharu *paledars* (loaders), whose work was widely regarded as *mushkil* (hard). *Paledars* carried heavy sacks on their heads from the storage rooms or the factory units to trucks waiting outside. To load them, they had to walk up a long wooden plank laid on an old rusty oil barrel to form a small bridge, which occasionally led to accidents. The work was heavy and exhausting, and they sweated profusely. To endure it, many of them drank highly concentrated alcohol on their breaks at the tea stall outside the factory gates.

Also revealing is that the everyday presence of the Maoist union in the factory had caused practices associated with untouchability (*chuwa-choot*) to disappear entirely from its shop floors. Hindu workers were no longer able to discriminate against the minority of Muslim company employees. Several Muslim workers told me that formerly they had not able to sit at the same bench with Hindu co-workers or eat with them. The story was told of an engineer called Mohammed, who some twenty years back had come to the factory to repair a machine in the flour Mill. After not being allowed to sit in the canteen with his Indian colleagues, he had angrily left the company after only three days. That kind of discrimination had vanished upon the arrival of the Maoists. This applied also to spaces outside of the factory. For example, in 2001 Agrawal had rented a house to use as an office near a Shiva-Parvati temple in a nearby village. On the day it opened, the senior managers went to worship in the temple, but the *pujari* (priest) prevented the ordinary workers from witnessing the worship. They angrily challenged their exclusion, which the priest justified by saying he did not know who they were or which castes they belonged to. When the Maoist unionists heard about the priest's *rudhiwadi* (conservative) ways, they went to the temple and threatened him, with the result that he reopened the temple and let the workers in.

As a qualifying footnote to this, however, it needs to be said that not all workers in the permanent workforce appreciated the Maoist support on the shopfloors. Those most in sympathy with the Maoist union were of Nepali origin and largely Madheshis. Indian workers were more guarded and would often privately accuse the Maoists of being self-interested *khao-badi* (corrupt people), a predictable reaction to one of the Maoist union's central demands—the appointment of "locals" to skilled jobs.[9]

Conclusion

According to the argument of Guy Standing (2011), the pressures of globalization have produced a new social class comprising all those engaged in insecure forms of labor, including temporary and part-time workers, subcontracted laborers, poor immigrants, and unemployed educated knowledge workers. This new global "precariat" is further marked not only by insecurity of employment and income, but also by the lack of a clearly defined worker identity. It is a dangerous, angry, potentially violent social class that is prone to support right-wing political parties when public policy makes no effort to reintegrate it into society.

Jan Breman (2013) has recently critiqued Standing's picture by pointing out that in most parts of the world, precarity has been the condition of most workers throughout the history of urban industrial employment. I find that little of Standing's argument rings true in western Nepal, where the labor situation has become more rather than less secure over the last two decades, though not for all categories of worker. Today legal minimum wages are implemented, and workers organize themselves according to their own principles. I attribute these changes to union activism over the past decade and have highlighted the specific role that the Maoists played in the transition to a post-conflict society. I further suggest that Maoist activism has also protected workers from the intensification of labor that neoliberal conditions have promoted elsewhere.

But in drawing attention to Maoist unionists' efforts to regularize contract labor, I do not wish to swell the chorus that praises radical left-wing parties as the saviors of the working classes. The Maoist union has been complicit in the entrenchment of new ethnic cleavages in the workplace, as the benefits of its activism are not felt among the Tharu *paledars* (loaders) from outsider communities. This echoes what Ismail and Shah (2015) have recently noted about indigenous politics more generally: Nepal's Maoists, they argue on the basis of writings by senior Maoist leaders (Yami and Bhattarai 1996, Bhattarai 2004) as well as critical ethnographic work (Ogura 2007), have devoted "special emphasis to the case of Nepal's *janajatis* [its ethnic minorities] (Ismail and Shah 2015: 118). I suggest that the ethnographic material presented in this chapter confirms that Maoist union politics in Nepal appears to mirror this shift from the politics of class to the politics of indigeneity.

Two themes emerge from the findings of this chapter. The first is that Maoist union policies may in some measure be contributing to intra-ethnic tension at workplaces. This raises the question of why the Maoist unionists remain seemingly uninterested in organizing casual labor to promote an ethnic cause. Is it because of the laborers' ethnicity (in that Tharus are not their support base)? Or is it because Tharus are casual labor and as such difficult to organize? I can only speculate that the Maoist union leaders now may well have moved into new systems of local patronage that entrench ethnic grievances. Second, though regularization at Agrawal may not necessarily be representative of wider national trends, my data from factories nearby suggest at least a wider regional trend of regularizing contract workers. The latest statistical data indicate that in those factories where Maoist unions have been established (5 out of 18 factories), the proportion of regular workers (averaging 45 percent) is higher than that found in non-unionized factories (33 percent). It remains to be seen whether Nepal's Maoists will have a similar impact on the regularization of labor within industries elsewhere in the country.

Acknowledgments

This chapter is based on field research on industrial labor in the western Tarai that extended over 10 months in the periods September 2013–April 2014 and September–October 2014. I am particularly indebted to Kuchhat Chaudhary, Chris Hann, Jonathan Parry, and the Industry and Inequality research group at the Max Planck Institute for Social Anthropology for comments on drafts of this article.

Michael Peter Hoffmann is a Research Fellow at the Rework Research Group at Humboldt University in Berlin. After obtaining his doctorate in anthropology from the London School of Economics and Political Science in 2012, he was Research Fellow at the Max Planck Institute for Social Anthropology from 2012 to 2015 and a research fellow at the Global South Studies Centre and the Department of Anthropology at the University of Cologne from 2015 to 2017. Hoffmann is a specialist on the anthropology of revolutions, labor, and transnational migration. His work has appeared in journals such as *Contributions to Indian Sociology, Critique of Anthropology*, and *Focaal*.

Notes

1. The names of both the company and informants have been changed for reasons of confidentiality.
2. In the Nepali context, the term Marwari refers to one of India's preeminent merchant castes, which originated in Rajasthan but has long-established and extremely important commercial interests in a great many Indian and Nepali towns.
3. The productive capacities of the factories on the company "campus" are as follows: flour mill, 100 metric tons per 24-hour day; oil mill, 10 tons per day; rice mill, 100 tons per day; pulses mill, 50 tons per day.
4. The legal status of the Indian workers was questionable. Under the India-Nepal Friendship Treaty of 1950, Indian and Nepali laborers were allowed to work in both countries, but the Labour Act of 1992 stipulates that foreigners (including Indians) are allowed to work in Nepal only with special permission granted by the local Chief District Officer. The Labour Act of 1992 furthermore states that any Indian worker who works for five years in Nepal must be replaced by a Nepali citizen after that period.
5. I conducted a survey with a sample of fifty of the company's workers.
6. For a more general account of the history of unionism in Nepal, see Hoffmann 2014b.
7. Like the permanent workers, the factory's temporary workers have jobs that are fairly secure due to Maoist patronage.

8. Loaders are not counted as company workers in the management's scheme of payment.
9. Such demands fit in with the UCPN Maoists' broader distaste for Indian workers. Though the language against Indians softened in the post-insurgency period, senior Maoist leaders such as Baburam Bhatterai had previously railed strongly against Indian influence in Nepal (Bhatterai 2003).

References

"Agreement with Maoist Fighters Offers New Hope for Nepali Government." 2011. *The National*, 3 November. Retrieved on 27 September 2017 from https://www.thenational.ae/world/asia/agreement-with-maoist-fighters-offers-new-hope-for-nepali-government-1.452061.

Bhatterai, Baburam. 2003. *The Nature of Underdevelopment and Regional Structure in Nepal: A Marxist Analysis.* Delhi: Adroit.

———. 2004. "The Question of Building a New Type of State." *The Worker* 9: 1–26.

Breman, Jan. 2004. *The Making and Unmaking of an Industrial Working Class: Sliding Down the Labour Hierarchy in Ahmedabad, India.* New Delhi: Oxford University Press.

———. 2013. "A Bogus Concept?" *New Left Review* 84: 130–138.

De Sales, Anne. 2000. "The Kham-Magar Country, Nepal: Between Ethnic Claims and Maoism." *European Bulletin of Himalayan Research* 19: 41–71.

Ferguson, James. 1999. *Expectations of Modernity: Myths and Meanings of Urban Life on the Zambian Copperbelt.* Berkeley, CA: University of California Press.

Harvey, David. 2003. *The New Imperialism.* Oxford: Oxford University Press.

Hoffmann, Michael. 2014a. "Red Salute at Work: Brick Factory Work in Postconflict Kailali, Western Nepal." *Focaal—Journal of Global and Historical Anthropology* 70: 67–80.

———. 2014b. "A Symbiotic Coexistence: Nepal's Maoist Movement and Labour Unions in an Urban Municipality in Post-conflict Far-western Tarai". *Journal of South Asian Development* 9(3): 213–234.

———. 2015. "In the Shadows of the Maoist Revolution: On the Role of the 'People's War' in Facilitating the Occupation of Symbolic Space in Western Nepal." *Critique of Anthropology* 35(4): 389–406.

———. 2017. "Unfree Labor after the Maoist Revolution in western Nepal." In *Contributions to Indian Sociology* 51(2): 139–162.

ILO (International Labour Organization). 2012. "From Precarious Work to Decent Work: Outcome Document to the Worker's Symposium on Policies and Regulations to Combat Precarious Employment." Retrieved 27 September 2017 from: http://www.ilo.org/wcmsp5/groups/public/-ed_dialogue/-actrav/documents/ meeting-document/wcms_179787.pdf.

Ismail, Feyzi, and Shah, Alpa 2015. "Class Struggle, the Maoists and the Indigenous Question in Nepal." *Economic and Political Weekly* 50(35): 112–123.

Joshi, Chitra. 2003. *Lost Worlds: Indian Labour and Its Forgotten Histories.* New Delhi: Permanent Black.

Kantha, Pramod 2010. "Maoist-Madheshi Dynamics and Nepal's Peace Process." In *The Maoist Insurgency in Nepal: Revolution in the Twenty-First Century*, ed. Mahendra Lawoti, 156–171. Contemporary South Asia Series 20. New York: Routledge.

Mollona, Massimiliano. 2009. *Made in Sheffield: An Ethnography of Industrial Work and Politics*. New York: Berghahn Books.

Miklian, Jason 2009. "Nepal's Terai: Constructing an Ethnic Conflict." South Asia Briefing Paper No. 1, PRIO paper. Oslo: PRIO.

Millar, Kathleen. 2015 "The Tempo of Wageless Work: E.P. Thompson's Time-Sense at the Edges of Rio de Janeiro." *Focaal* 73(13): 28–40.

Nepali Labour Act 1997. *Government of Nepal: Ministry of Labour and Employment*, 3. Retrieved 27 September 2017 from http://dol.gov.np/.

Ogura, Kiyoko. 2007. "Maoists, People, and the State as Seen from Rolpa and Rukum." In *Political and Social Transformations in North India and Nepal: Social Dynamics in Northern South Asia*, ed. H. Ishii, D. Gellner, and K. Nawa, 435–475. New Delhi: Manohar.

Parry, Jonathan. 2009. "Sociological Marxism in Central India: Polanyi, Gramsci, and the Case of the Unions. In *Market and Society: The Great Transformation Today*, ed. C. Hann and K. Hart, 175–202. Cambridge: Cambridge University Press.

———. 2014. "Company and Contract Labour in a Central Indian Steel Plant." *Economy and Society* 42(3): 348–374.

Ramaswamy, E.A. 1977. *The Worker and His Union: A Study in South India*. Bombay: Allied Publishers.

———. 1981. *Industry and Labour: An Introduction*. Delhi: Oxford University Press.

Shakya, Mallika 2015. "Ethnicity in Nepal's New Constitution." *Focaalblog*, 28 September. Retrieved 16 September 2017 from http://www.focaalblog.com/2015/09/28/mallika-shakya-ethnicity-in-nepals-new-constitution/.

Standing, Guy. 2011. *The Precariat: The New Dangerous Class*. New York: Bloomsbury.

Yami, Hisila, and Bhattarai, Baburam. 1996. "Problems and Prospects of Revolution in Nepal" [Online]. Retrieved 27 September from http://www.bannedthought.net/Nepal/Problems-Prospects/bb_nationalq.html.

Afterword

Third Wave Marketization

MICHAEL BURAWOY

Wherein lies the significance of these wonderful ethnographies of industrial life? How to situate what Jonathan Parry has already so well described—the erosion of proud labor aristocracies through their bifurcation into an upper tier that is being eaten away by a lower tier, which is itself being eaten away by the ever threatening, ever expanding, ever more desperate population of dispossessed? They have fallen victim to a wave of marketization that has swept across the planet during the last forty years—not the first such wave to overtake capitalism, but at least the third. The ethnographies all hark back to a now lost world before the onset of the tsunami that began in the 1970s. I will recover that world through my own ethnographies of industry in Zambia, the United States, Hungary, and Russia.

The story begins in 1968 with an ethnography of the Zambian Copperbelt (Burawoy 1972). Four years after Zambian independence, the copper price was flying high, two multinational mining corporations were making a handsome profit, copper accounted for 95 percent of foreign revenue, African miners had a certain security of employment, and the Mineworkers Union of Zambia had just won a 22 percent increase in wages. After I left in 1972, the mines were nationalized, the price of copper plummeted, profits became losses, and the government went into debt and was ultimately subject to IMF loans conditional on privatization. Eventually the government was forced to sell the precious mines at bargain-basement price to transnational capital, which set about dismantling all the protections that had been won over the previous 70 years. When the price of copper unexpectedly began to soar, at least temporarily, the mining companies made a killing at the expense of the Zambian government, Zambian miners, and

Zambian people. Ching Kwan Lee arrived on the Copperbelt along with Chinese investment. Of all the international mining capitals, the Chinese have the longest time horizons because they are interested in copper as much as profits. Yet they too seek to subcontract labor and reimpose a form of colonial despotism, albeit with Chinese characteristics. But all this happened after I left. I did not see the tsunami arriving.

After Zambia, my next industrial sojourn was as a machine operator in South Chicago, working at the engine plant of Allis Chalmers, a large multinational manufacturer of agricultural and construction equipment (Burawoy 1979). At the time in 1973/74, Allis was weathering the storm of a recession—the steelworkers union was strong, collective bargaining delivered a class compromise that suited each side, a grievance machinery was operational, and an internal labor market gave more senior workers a chance to move around the plant. I called it a hegemonic regime. I thought it would be there for good, or at least as long as capitalism lasted. There was security of employment—even those who were laid off received a supplementary unemployment benefit, and they were the first to be rehired. And wages were high—with my overtime I was earning more than assistant professors at the University of Chicago. And then, all of a sudden, it collapsed—again, after I left. The aggressive anti-labor policy of the new Reagan administration, combined with global competition, led to the closure of the plant and the decline of the union. It was happening all over South Chicago, which was rapidly becoming an industrial wasteland and a warehouse for African-Americans displaced by the tearing down of public housing. Jan Breman (2013) notwithstanding, this rapid decimation does not seem to have visited the steel plants of India, Indonesia, or Egypt, respectively described by Christian Strümpell, Daromir Rudnyckyj, and Dina Makram-Ebeid; nor the Tata Motors factory described by Andrew Sanchez. Rather, there is a reconfiguration of the relations among tiers of employment, but not the wholesale dissolution of labor found in Britain or the United States. For that reason the ethnographers of the Global South are able to continue the traditions of industrial studies, arriving at new variants and new intersections with cultural forms and ethnic and race relations.

I did not stick around to observe the dismantling of the hegemonic regime in the United States but took another voyage, this time to Hungary. Why Hungary? I had argued that the hegemonic regime I observed at Allis Chalmers was a product of capitalism, but my critics said it was a product of a more general process of industrialization. To justify my capitalist imputation I would have to compare regimes in a capitalist economy with regimes in some non-capitalist economy, which logically would be somewhere in the Soviet orbit. And then, on 19 August 1980, the Solidarity movement broke out in Poland. How was it that the first nationwide working-class revolution took place in a so-called socialist society? That question drew my and many other people's attention, but before I could learn a bit of Polish, pack my bags, and get my sabbatical lined up, General Jarulzelski had declared martial law. Even so, this self-limiting revolution, this reconstitution of civil society, lasted sixteen months. Why did this revolution take place in state socialism, and why in Poland and not in a place like Hungary, which had already had its own revolution in 1956? Could this have something to do with the politics of production, in terms of the character of the labor process and its regulation? I took these questions to Hungary, where by hook or by crook, and with the help of well-connected friends, I managed to secure industrial jobs—first in a manufacturing plant akin to Allis Chalmers, making gear boxes for the famous Ikarus buses; and then in Hungary's biggest steel plant, the Lenin Steel Works in Miskolc, where I became a furnaceman—a 50 percent furnaceman, as my comrades in the October Revolution Socialist Brigade called me, as I clearly had neither their skills nor their strength (Burawoy and Lukács 1992).

While I was busy figuring out the peculiarities of state socialist work organization—flexible specialization on the shop floor and class-conscious critique of the party-state for failing to deliver the promised socialism—the edifice of state socialism was crumbling behind our backs. Soon we were talking about capitalism, not socialism. Well-placed managers conspired to buy up the lucrative parts of the enterprise, making sure the state continued to assume all the infrastructure obligations. Then the state set up a privatization commission, and the whole Lenin Steel Works was put up for sale. There were no buyers for this museum of an enterprise until a Slovakian company eventually took the gamble, but it was more about asset stripping than rebuilding a steel enterprise that had no business being in Miskolc. For the next decade, long after I had exited, the proud Lenin Steel Works saw itself degraded as its workforce dwindled from some fourteen thousand to just a couple of thousand. Salaries plummeted; working conditions deteriorated. Dimitra Kofti tells the same tragic story about the community around the Lenin Steel Works in Bulgaria—but it differs from the story Trevisani tells of Kazakhstan, where Mittal seems to have struck a deal with President Nazarbayev to keep the plant going, although with rising numbers of contract laborers and shrinking numbers of company workers.

I continued to visit my friends in Miskolc, but after 1989 my attention turned to the bastion of state socialism—the Soviet Union. Fortuitously, I was invited to give lectures to some 150 industrial sociologists—actually personnel officers in factories across the Soviet Union—on a boat traveling down the Volga in 1990, which gave me the contacts I needed to continue my researches into industrial labor in the very belly of the beast. At this time of late *perestroika*—the twilight of communism—anything was possible. Most Soviet sociologists thought industrial ethnography was so unscientific as to be absurd, but I did find one young sociologist devoted to the idea. He happened to live in Syktyvkar, the capital of the Republic of Komi, so that was where I spent the next decade.

Entering the Soviet Union in 1991, I knew I had to strike while the iron was hot, so to speak. Effectively bribing the trade union at a historic rubber plant in Moscow with a couple of the latest desktop computers, Kathy Hendley and I plunged into the sort of ethnography that had never been possible in the Soviet Union. This was in January–March 1991, when the Soviet Union was in turmoil. A struggle between Russia and the market on the one side, and the Soviet Union and the planned economy on the other, had left the party in tatters and thrown the plant into civil war. Meanwhile managers were quietly creating in-plant cooperatives to funnel resources out of the enterprise and into their pockets (Burawoy and Hendley 1992).

In April I moved up to Syktyvkar near the Arctic Circle where, with support from the head of the local trade union federation, I landed a job in a model furniture factory, making the wall systems of cabinets and shelving that adorned every Soviet apartment (Burawoy and Krotov 1992). After the collapse of the command economy, Northern Furniture was doing just fine. Capitalizing on the availability of nearby timber supplies, the factory was able to barter wall systems for all manner of consumer goods and even spots for children in southern summer camps. But that did not last long: the Soviet Union's death warrant was signed in December, just five months after I had left Syktyvkar. Northern Furniture sputtered along in the succeeding years, paying its dwindling number of workers in flour or sugar or vodka, or more likely not paying them at all. It tried to diversify its products but could not compete with cheap imports in a context of declining consumer demand. The lights went off at Northern Furniture in 1996, leaving its workers to grope around in the post-Soviet darkness.

In those days I also made regular trips to Komi's northern extremity—the arctic city of Vorkuta. A rich coal vein had made Vorkuta the site of notorious labor camps that had imprisoned not only petty criminals but also great political dissidents such as Alexander Solzhenitsyn. In 1989 and then again in 1991, Vorkuta's miners, together with miners across the Soviet Union, struck in unison with radical demands: dissolution of the primacy of the party, worker ownership of the mines, and the establishment of a market economy. They proved to be the dynamite that detonated the Soviet Union.

When I visited the mines in 1992, hopes were still high for untold wealth, but over the years production slowly declined and mines closed as demand for coal fell with the collapse of the metallurgical plants (Burawoy and Krotov 1995). Sealing Vorkuta's fate, transportation monopolies charged such tariffs as to price all but the richest mines out of the market. The strike committee that had once been so popular dissipated, succumbing to economic and political enticements. When I asked one holdout from the strike committee what had happened to their optimistic future, he simply replied: "That just shows the disastrous effects of seventy years of communism." There was no lack of faith in the market per se. Today Vorkuta is a shadow of its former self, reminiscent of the desultory life Eeva Keskküla describes for the Kazakh coal mines now owned by Mittal. Workers have managed to hold on to their jobs, but it is not clear how long they will do so.

The lag between my ethnography and the disaster and destruction that followed in its wake shrank with every project—Zambia's Copperbelt, South Chicago, Miskolc, and Syktyvkar. Syktyvkar had no major greenfield sites like Jeremy Morris and Sarah Hinz's car plant in Kaluga. Northern Furniture was in darkness, but the local garment factory, Komsomolskaya, was still limping along; however, many of its more skilled workers had had the reserves to purchase a sewing machine and left to set up shop at home, much as Rebecca Prentice describes for Trinidad. Nor does Syktyvkar have a garment district or anything like the Goundar caste of entrepreneurs that Grace Carswell and Geert De Neve describe for Tiruppur. Instead, a tribe of women would become shuttle traders between Syktyvkar and Moscow or even farther afield to places such as Turkey.

Across the board, the rapid decline of the Russian economy and the asset stripping that came with privatization led to an intensification of exchange at the expense of production. This was a retreat to a form of merchant capitalism based on the commodification of everything and the retreat of production into the domestic sphere. As men lost their jobs, women took up the slack as they always had, superintending the domestic economy by all sorts of ingenious methods, including petty commodity production, cultivation of small plots of land around their dachas, and negotiation for state benefits (Burawoy, Krotov, and Lytkina 2000).

Following Clifford Geertz (1963), I called this process, in which the nascent market ate away at production, "economic involution." The transition to capitalism was neither the revolutionary one called for by the devotees of shock therapy nor the evolutionary one favored by institutionalists. While economists debated which road Russia should take—revolution or evolution—the actual economy was undergoing involution. At this point I suspended my Marxist concentration on production and its regulation, if only because there was so little production—all the action was in the realm of exchange. So I took up the study of Karl Polanyi, and *The Great Transformation* (1944) became my bible.

Drawing on Polanyi's ideas and inspired by the economic growth of China, the evolutionists insisted, against the neoliberal utopians, that there was no market road to market capitalism, and that destroying everything Soviet would not miraculously spawn market capitalism. In other words, there was no need for a second (or third) Russian Revolution, as there could be no Bolshevik road to capitalism. Evolutionists would draw on a popular reading of Polanyi that saw market society as requiring a political and social infrastructure. Yet their prescriptions fell on deaf ears. Plans for rapid entry into capitalism moved ahead and the post-Soviet economy took an unprecedented dive into an abyss.

I chose, therefore, to emphasize an alternative reading of Polanyi that, rather than focusing on the prerequisites of markets, turned to their destructive consequences. Markets detached from their moorings threaten society, which then reacts by defending itself—what Polanyi called a double movement or countermovement. He simply assumed there would be a concerted reaction to any full-blown marketization, but I could see no evidence of one. What I witnessed was a wholesale retreat before the market, what I called the *Great Involution* (Burawoy 2001).

For Polanyi, the destructiveness lies in the unregulated commodification of three factors of production—land, labor, and money. There is some dispute as to why these commodities should be called "fictitious"—whether it is because they were never intended to be commodified or because they lose their use value through commodification. The latter is the more useful approach, showing how the unregulated commodification of labor power leads to such destitution as to exhaust the capacity to labor, the unregulated commodification of land leads to the destruction of the very basis of human livelihood, and the commodification of money in pursuit of speculative gain undermines money's essential role as measure of value and medium of exchange. In post-Soviet Russia, the ascent of the market and the commodification of these factors of production, far from leading to a countermovement, led labor to retreat into subsistence agriculture or petty commodity production, the reappearance of peasant landholdings, and the rise of barter. In other words, the expansion of the market led to an expulsion of factors of production from commodification, what we might call *ex-commodification* and the rise of a non-market redistributive economy. The move was temporary but nonetheless significant, showing with Weber (1930 [1905]) just how difficult the transition to capitalism is.

What we see, therefore, is that in this era of "neoliberalism" there is nothing inevitable about a countermovement to marketization. In many parts of the world the response is as likely to be exclusion as much as inclusion, and it is the relation between the two that determines the condition of precarity. What our studies of (de)industrialization in the Global South and the post-Soviet world demonstrate is that the conditions of production are increasingly shaped by the haunting presence of those who have been dispossessed, often violently, of access to the means of existence and locked out of the market. As Joan Robinson (2006 [1962]: 45) once said of exploitation, there's one thing worse than commodification, and that is ex-commodification.

Polanyi did not anticipate another round of marketization. He could not imagine that humanity would indulge in another such catastrophic experiment with the market, but that is because he had an idealistic conception of where the market came from—the heads of political economists. While the economists may flatter themselves that they originated market despotism—and here too their opponents often give them too much credit—in reality they merely give it justification. The driving force is capitalist accumulation itself, which generates crises that can only be overcome through ruthless marketization. "Neoliberalism," then, is not so new but only the latest iteration of marketization.

Reexamining Polanyi's treatise, we can see that where he saw one long arc of commodification ending in diverse forms of state regulation, two waves of marketization can be discerned (Burawoy 2013). The first began at the end of the eighteenth century and reached its peak in the mid-nineteenth century, culminating in a countermovement that sprang from working-class struggles only to end in defeat and World War I. Political economy was discovered in this period, above all in Marx and Engels' theory of capitalism, and is exemplified for Polanyi in such utopian experiments as Owenism. The second wave of marketization began at the end of the nineteenth century, picked up steam after World War I, and was eventually arrested by state regulation in the 1930s. This is the period of Stalinism, the New Deal, and Fascism. Since the 1970s we have been facing a third wave of marketization, and the scale is no longer national but global. This latest wave is marked by the rule of finance capital, in which money becomes a commodity that is bought and sold for profit. Its underside is debt. Increasingly, land is subject to expropriation—whether in cities or in the countryside—for the purposes of commodification, leaving behind destitute populations living in wastelands. The biggest challenge of our era—the plundering of nature of water and air as well as land—has led to a commodification that only intensifies the destruction. The creation of markets in carbon pollution does not restrain climate change. The labor victories achieved through state regulation against second-wave marketization have been reversed, turning de-commodification into re-commodification intensified by great swaths of ex-commodification. Third-wave marketization provides the global historical context within which to understand the industrial ethnographies of this book.

Polanyi viewed commodification as a threat to society, which reacts by pursuing an agenda of ex-commodification that is even more destructive.

Waste is the big story of our era—surplus populations, degradation of nature, indebtedness. It leads to populist mobilization, whether left or right, as liberal democracy becomes a handmaiden of destructive impulses. The radical social movements of 2011 have turned into the reactionary movements of 2016. As Polanyi warned, capitalism and democracy are uneasy bedfellows. The real choice, he claimed, was between socialism and fascism.

Michael Burawoy teaches sociology at the University of California, Berkeley. He has conducted industrial ethnographies in Africa, the United States, Hungary, and Russia. His books include *The Colour of Class on the Copper Mines* (1972), *Manufacturing Consent* (1979), *Politics of Production* (1985), *The Radiant Past* (1992), and *The Extended Case Method* (2009).

References

Breman, Jan. 2013. "A Bogus Concept?" *New Left Review* 84: 130–138.

Burawoy, Michael. 1972. *The Colour of Class on the Copper Mines: From African Advancement to Zambianization.* Manchester: Manchester University Press.

———. 1979. *Manufacturing Consent.* Chicago, IL: University of Chicago Press.

———. 2001. "Transition without Transformation: Russia's Involutionary Road to Capitalism." *East European Politics and Societies* 15(2): 269–290.

———. 2013. "Marxism after Polanyi." In *Approaches to Marxism in the Twenty-first Century: Crisis, Critique, and Struggle,* ed. Michelle Williams and Vishwas Satgar, 34–52. Johannesburg: University of Witwatersrand Press.

Burawoy, Michael, and Kathryn Hendley. 1992. "Between Perestroika and Privatization: Divided Strategies and Political Crisis in a Soviet Enterprise." *Soviet Studies* 44(3): 371–402.

Burawoy, Michael, and Pavel Krotov. 1992. "The Soviet Transition from Socialism to Capitalism: Worker Control and Economic Bargaining in the Wood Industry." *American Sociological Review* 57(1): 16–38.

———. 1995. "Russian Miners Bow to the Angel of History." *Antipode* 27(2): 115–136.

Burawoy, Michael, Pavel Krotov, and Tatyana Lytkina. 2000. "Involution and Destitution in Capitalist Russia." *Ethnography* 1(1): 43–65.

Burawoy, Michael, and János Lukács. 1992. *The Radiant Past: Ideology and Reality in Hungary's Road to Capitalism.* Chicago, IL: University of Chicago Press.

Geertz, Clifford. 1963. *Agricultural Involution: The Processes of Ecological Change in Indonesia.* Berkeley, CA: University of California Press.

Polanyi, Karl. 1944. *The Great Transformation: The Political and Economic Origins of Our Time.* Boston, MA: Beacon Press.

Robinson, Joan. 2006 [1962]. *Economic Philosophy.* New York: Aldine.

Weber, Max. 1930 [1905]. *The Protestant Ethic and the Spirit of Capitalism.* London: Unwin Hyman.

Index

CPSIA information can be obtained
at www.ICGtesting.com
Printed in the USA
LVHW052146130222
710946LV00005B/22

9 781800 731998